THE ANNOTATED®
Gulliver's Travels

Jonathan Swift. Engraving by Fourdrinier after C. Jervas. Courtesy, Prints Division, The New York Public Library.

THE ANNOTATED®
Gulliver's Travels

Gulliver's Travels by Jonathan Swift

Edited, with a biographical introduction and notes, by
ISAAC ASIMOV

Clarkson N. Potter, Inc./Publishers New York
Distributed by Crown Publishers, Inc.

Publisher's Note

The text for this edition of *Gulliver's Travels* is based on the edition printed in 1734 by George Faulkner in Dublin. It contains Swift's own corrections and emendations to the first edition text published in 1726 by Benjamin Motte in London, with the exception of five paragraphs at the end of Part III, Chapter 3, which were censored even by Faulkner and did not appear in print until 1896. For the reader's interest, these missing paragraphs have been added to the present text.

Inquiries should be addressed to Clarkson N. Potter, Inc., One Park Avenue, New York, New York 10016

Printed in the United States of America

Published simultaneously in Canada by General Publishing Company Limited

Title page and maps from the first edition of *Gulliver's Travels,* London, 1726, are reproduced courtesy Rare Book Division, The New York Public Library.
Part title and cover illustrations are by Le Febure, 1797.

Library of Congress Cataloging in Publication Data
Swift, Jonathan, 1667–1745.
      The annotated Gulliver's travels.

      I.   Asimov, Isaac, 1920–   II.   Title.
III.   Title: Gulliver's travels.
PR3724.G7 1980b   823'5   80-15032

ISBN: 0-517-539497

10 9 8 7 6 5 4 3 2 1
First Edition

To
JANE WEST,
who suggested it

CONTENTS

Biographical Introduction   *xi*

GULLIVER'S TRAVELS   *1*

PART ONE: A Voyage to Lilliput   *3*

PART TWO: A Voyage to Brobdingnag   *71*

PART THREE: A Voyage to Laputa, Balnibarbi,
Luggnagg, Glubbdubdrib, and Japan   *139*

PART FOUR: A Voyage to the Country of the Houyhnhnms   *209*

A Letter from Capt. Gulliver, to his Cousin Sympson   *287*

The Publisher to the Reader   *291*

Bibliography   *293*

Index   *297*

Engraving by J. J. Grandville, 1835. Courtesy, Library of Congress.

BIOGRAPHICAL
INTRODUCTION

The greatest of the English satirists, by common consent, is Jonathan Swift. In fact, when it comes to pillorying the vices and follies of human beings, the only three people in our Western tradition who can be mentioned in the same breath with Swift are the Frenchman Voltaire, the Englishman Charles Dickens, and the American Mark Twain.

Of the three, Swift is the oldest and the only one who was, in any sense, a paid propagandist. Of the three, he is the one who was most nearly backward-looking. Whereas Voltaire, Dickens, and Twain excoriated the establishment and took up what we would today call a "leftist" position; Swift was a "rightist" and supported a point of view that was passing. It is for this reason, perhaps, that Swift was the least effective of the four in his own time and the one who suffered the most disappointment in life.

And yet we cannot suppose that Swift, because of his conservative position, was immune to the needs of those who suffered under the conventional thought of the time. Emphatically not so. He was a humanitarian who defended the Irish, for instance, when scarcely an Englishman of social standing would have dreamed of doing so, and there, at least, he was effective.

The house in which Swift was born. Courtesy, Library of Congress.

Swift came by this conservatism honestly, for he was descended from staunch supporters of King and Church. His grandfather was Thomas Swift, a vicar who never veered from his allegiance to King Charles I in the course of the English Civil War. Charles was beheaded in 1649, and for eleven years the Dissenters (those Protestants who found the Church of England too Catholic in doctrine to be supported) ruled England. This was the period of the Commonwealth, the only time in which England was a republic.

The Commonwealth came to an end in 1660 when Charles II, the son of the executed king, assumed the throne (the Restoration), and thereafter the sons of Thomas settled in Ireland. The oldest of these was Jonathan, a lawyer, and he became steward of the King's Inns in Dublin (the equivalent of law students' dormitories). In 1664 Jonathan married the daughter of a clergyman of the Church of England and had a daughter in May 1666. Jonathan died in the spring of 1667, at which time his wife was pregnant a second time.

Her son, born after his death on November 30, 1667, was named Jonathan after his dead father, and it is he who was the satirist.

His widowed mother had no means to support her children. She returned to Leicestershire, the home of her childhood, while Jonathan remained in Dublin and was placed in the charge of his uncle Godwin.

Jonathan's uncle was sufficiently alive to his responsibilities to see that young Jonathan received a good education. He was sent to Kilkenny School, the best in Ireland, and in 1682 he entered Trinity College. Apparently, Jonathan felt his fatherless status keenly and did not find his uncle sufficiently loving, to the extent that his state of depression led to his neglecting his studies. He obtained a bachelor of arts degree in February 1686 as an act of kindness, without any pretense that he had earned it. Nevertheless, he went on to get his master of arts degree in February 1689.

In 1688, however, James II, the brother and successor of Charles II, was forced from the throne. James II was a Catholic, and the revolution that brought Protestant William III (and his wife, James II's Protestant daughter, Mary II) to the throne created considerable turmoil in Catholic Ireland.

It seemed best to Swift to leave Dublin. He visited his mother in Leicestershire and, through family connections, became secretary to the essayist and retired politician and diplomat Sir William Temple. Temple was writing his memoirs and was preparing his essays for publication, and he found Swift most useful.

Temple was a Whig, one of the party who supported William III, as opposed to the Tories who supported the exiled James II and the "legitimate" succession. Through Temple, Swift met many other Whigs and, in addition, had at his disposal Temple's library. It was through this library, far more than through his college career, that Swift obtained his education.

Also at Temple's household was a widowed housekeeper who had a daughter named Esther Johnson. Esther was eight years old when Swift first took over this secretaryship, and Swift helped with her education. As she ripened, so did their friendship—possibly into love.

During his stay with Temple, Swift returned to Ireland for two visits. During the second of these, from May 1694 to May 1696, he entered the Anglican church as a priest and was appointed vicar of Kilroot, near Belfast.

Increasingly, thereafter, his chief interest lay in the Church of England. For instance, his first important work of satire was *A Tale of a Tub*, written in the late 1690s but not published until 1704 (and then anonymously). It defended the Church of England from the attacks of the Catholic Church on the right and the Protestant Dissenters on the left.

In *A Tale of a Tub*, Swift tells the tale of three brothers: Peter (who, as St. Peter, represents the Pope and the Catholic Church), Martin (who, as Martin Luther, represents moderate Protestantism and the Church of England), and John (who, as John Calvin, represents extreme Protestantism and the Dissenters). They inherit a coat from their father (Jesus) and a will (the New Testament), and there follows then a brilliantly satirical description of what each of the brothers does, with Martin getting much the best of it. Swift developed the line of attack that was to stand him in good stead thereafter—that of using cool reason to present his views, and pointing up the irrationalities of the opposition.

It was at this period, too, that Swift developed his worship of the past and his scorn of innovation in *The Battle of the Books*. This work, written in 1697, was also published in 1704. It dealt with a mock-epic battle of modern books versus ancient books for the possession of Mount Parnassus, which the ancient books had held for many centuries.

Here, Swift was defending his patron, Temple, who, in 1690 had written an essay "Of Ancient and Modern Learning," supporting the works of the Greeks and Romans. Another scholar, William Wotton, had severely criticized him, with considerable justification, in 1694, in *Reflections Upon Ancient and Modern Learning*.

Swift, with a power that transcended both Temple and Wotton, supported the former and denounced the latter. Yet, however much we might admire Swift for the force of his writing and the strength of his reasoning, the fact remains that Swift gazed back on the past and glorified it beyond its deserts while remaining willfully blind to the merits of a changing world, which, in the end, continued to change without his permission and against his will.

Sir William Temple (1628–1699). Courtesy, Library of Congress.

Esther Johnson (Stella).
Courtesy, Library of Congress.

Hester Vanhomrigh (Vanessa).
Courtesy, Library of Congress.

In January 1699 Temple died, and with that Swift's life grew more insecure. He became chaplain and secretary to the Earl of Berkeley, who was going to Ireland as a chief justice. While living in Ireland, however, Swift visited England frequently and became increasingly famous as a powerful pamphleteer in the Whig cause. When *A Tale of a Tub* and *The Battle of the Books* were published, his own authorship was quickly recognized and his reputation was accordingly enhanced.

One of his minor victories was the cruel, but amusing, way in which he dealt with John Partridge, a popular astrologer whose works were nothing but a farrago of nonsense from beginning to end. Swift, that supreme rationalist, had nothing but contempt for astrology. Therefore, as a joke, he put out astrological pamphlets of his own under the pseudonym of Isaac Bickerstaff in 1708. In them, he predicted the death of Partridge and then, in 1709, described that death in copious detail. He did it so well that most of his readers believed that Partridge was dead, and all of Partridge's protestations to the contrary roused only disbelief in some and uproarious amusement in others. Partridge's career came to an ignominious end.

Meanwhile, Swift had risen to more important posts in the Church, the most important being a vicarage at Laracor, near Dublin. Esther Johnson lived there with him, but Swift took precautions against the association giving rise to scandal. Nevertheless, he wrote poetry and published letters to her under the name of Stella, and there is some argument as to whether he married her or not. He had a friendship with another woman, Rebecca Dingley, a companion of Esther's, who may also have been included under the name of "Stella."

Then, in 1708, while in London, he met Esther Vanhomrigh, who seems to be the Vanessa of some of his poetry. There are all sorts of theories about Stella and Vanessa and of Swift's relationships with them, of varying degrees of scandal and sensation, but there is no real knowledge concerning it all, and to those who are interested primarily in Swift's career as a writer and satirist, such matters are of little real interest.

During this period, both Queen Mary II and King William III had died, and Queen Anne, a younger daughter of James II, succeeded to the throne on March 8, 1702. Almost immediately thereafter, the War of the Spanish Succession began against the France of Louis XIV.

Louis XIV had supported the exiled James II as King of England and, after that monarch's death in 1701, had supported his son as "James III" (or "the Old Pretender"). The Whigs, who feared the succession of another Catholic monarch, were ardently prowar.

Fighting in the war was the English general John Churchill, Duke of Marlborough, who proved to be the greatest military leader the English had had since Henry V. He won spectacular victories against the French and naturally was the darling of the Whigs.

The Tories, who wanted a legitimate succession and were rather in favor of the Pretender, were antiwar and favored a negotiated peace. The battleground for the two parties were drawn about the person of Queen Anne, a woman of no great intellect, who was influenced by her female favorites. During the first part of her reign, she was much under the influence of Sarah Churchill, the wife of Marlborough, and the Whigs were therefore supreme.

Swift, who was a Whig since the beginning of his association with Temple, found himself more and more troubled by his Whig doctrines, however. He tried to negotiate some tax concessions for the Church, which the Whigs were unwilling to make. Furthermore, the Whigs, in their anti-Catholic bias, moved closer to the Dissenters and were willing, it seemed, to grant them political privileges, something Swift viewed with great alarm. Putting Church above party, Swift began to shift toward the Tory view.

It was about this time that Sarah Churchill, a brilliant and domineering woman, became too brilliant and domineering for Queen Anne, who found herself shifting to Sarah's first cousin, Abigail Hill Masham—and with that, from Whig to Tory.

Robert Harley, a smooth Tory politician was, in 1710, in the process of taking over the government. He had gained the support of the powerful political pamphleteer Daniel Defoe. By promising Swift that there would be Tory concessions to the Church of England, he also won over Swift. For the rest of his life, Swift was to be a Tory pamphleteer.

The Tory party, taking over the government, forced the retirement of Marlborough and managed to maneuver a separate peace with France, abandoning their allies and allowing Louis XIV to survive. In all of this, Swift was the most powerful propagandist on the Tory side and more than anyone else prepared the public for what the Whigs considered a cowardly and disgraceful peace.

This was the happiest period of Swift's life. He met other literary lights of the age, and in 1713 formed, with Alexander Pope, Thomas Parnell, John Gay, and John Arbuthnot the Martinus Scriblerus Club. All of the members were writers of satire, dedicated to the puncture of pretentious pseudoscholarship. Swift was the moving figure of the club.

Swift, however, was not rewarded for his labors as one might have expected he would be or as he himself expected. He was given the title of Dean of St. Patrick's Cathedral in Dublin. He was not given any English post, nor did he ever move higher. Partly, that was because he was born in Dublin, and partly, it was thought, it was because Queen Anne was offended by some of his rather scurrilous language in *A Tale of a Tub*, which she thought was irreligious.

Engraving of Swift and Pope. Courtesy, Prints Division, The New York Public Library.

John Gay (1685–1732), by an anonymous painter. Courtesy, Library of Congress.

Alexander Pope (1688–1744), by Geoffrey Kneller. Courtesy, Library of Congress.

Jonathan Swift (1667–1745), by C. Jervas, 1718. Courtesy, National Portrait Gallery, London.

There was worse to come. Queen Anne died on August 1, 1714. The successor was not the Pretender, who was favored by many of the Tories, but George of Hanover, a Protestant descendant of James I (Charles I's father). He ruled as George I and, naturally, with him the Whigs moved into power.

The Tory party passed out of favor and its leaders were retired, exiled, or, to varying degrees, persecuted. Swift now lost whatever power he had and didn't regain it.

Swift was no longer welcome in England and once again retired to Dublin, this time permanently. Only twice did he visit England and that briefly, in 1726 and again in 1727.

He went through a period of bitterness and depression, but eventually he came to champion the cause of the Irish, partly because of his sympathy for the downtrodden and partly because of his intense desire to strike back at the Whigs and, particularly, at Robert Walpole, who led the Whig party, who was the first of Great Britain's Prime Ministers in the modern sense and who maintained his role for over a quarter of a century.

In 1724 and 1725, for instance, Swift wrote a series of anonymous *Drapier's Letters*, supposedly written by a Dublin linendraper, in which he discussed a British plan to supply Ireland with a debased coinage that would profit the British and greatly increase Irish misery. His writings were so clear,

St. Patrick's, Dublin. Courtesy, Library of Congress.

"Swift's power was at this moment as great as that of any man in the nation," by T. Morten. Courtesy, Library of Congress.

cogent, and powerful that the British offered a reward for information concerning the identity of the writer, and though Swift's authorship was no great secret to many, no one officially denounced him. Even further, *Drapier's Letters* were so successful that the plan did not go through, and Swift became a hero to the Irish who saw him as their powerful and successful defender.

The great scientist Isaac Newton was the Master of the Mint at this time, and although he was far too naïve as a politician and economist (and, indeed, as anything but a scientist) to be a villain in this respect, Swift saw him as one of the moving figures in the aborted plan. Since Newton was in any case one of the "moderns" in science as opposed to Swift's revered "ancients," Newton was marked as a victim of satire.

A still more powerful piece of writing—perhaps, indeed, the bitterest and most mordant satire ever written—was Swift's *A Modest Proposal* in which he pointed out that conditions in Ireland were so miserable under deliberate British mismanagement that the only thing the poor Irish could produce that had any value at all was their children and that these children, properly fattened, would form a perfect addition to the British diet.

In this way, the Irish not only would provide excellent nourishment for their masters but would gain a modest competence for themselves and any of their surviving children. So straight-faced was the essay that some fools thought the author meant what he said, but to most British who read it there could only be shame and anger at the treatment of the Irish.

Meanwhile, through the 1720s, Swift continued to take part in the Scriblerus Club activities and was working on his masterpiece *Gulliver's Travels*. The book began as a diatribe against the Whigs in general and against Walpole in particular. It was good-natured enough in the first part, dealing with Lilliput; grew bitterer in the second part dealing with Brobdingnag; and by the time Swift wrote the third part, his anger (perhaps at seeing that Walpole and the Whigs grew ever stronger) became overwhelming and turned against humanity as a whole.

From the technicolor animated film Gulliver's Travels *by Fleischer Studios, 1939. From the collection of Leslie Cabarga.*

The evidence of the third part, concerning the Houyhn-hnms, because of its savagery, is sometimes considered to indicate that Swift was going mad, but it is clear that this is mistaken. After the third part was written, he moved it into the fourth place and inserted a new third part concerning the Laputans (inspired by his Scriblerus connections, and perhaps the weakest part of the four), which is much less angry and which he used as a vehicle for the satire of the new as against the greatness of the old. He was particularly harsh on the new science of which Newton—the villain of the coinage scheme in Swift's view—was the chief ornament.

In 1726 Swift traveled to England with the manuscript and, helped by other members of the Scriblerus Club, saw to its (anonymous) publication on October 28 and then returned to Ireland.

From Disney Studio's Gulliver Mickey, *1934. © Walt Disney Productions.*

HISTOIRE DE GULLIVER.

Départ de Gulliver, il fait ses adieux à son épouse, mais bientôt une tempête est cause de son naufrage.

Gulliver est jeté dans le pays des Lilipuciens qui étaient 95 fois plus petits que lui.

Gulliver enchaîné est conduit dans la capitale; il faut 2,400 hommes pour le lier, et 100,000 pour le conduire.

Gulliver prend d'un coup de filet une flotte ennemie; par reconnaissance, les Lilipuciens lui construisent un canot.

Gulliver éteint un incendie qui avait éclaté dans la capitale, il est fêté partout le royaume.

Gulliver quitte les Lilipuciens, comble de présents; mais il fait la promesse de revenir.

Il fait naufrage et aborde dans le pays des géants qui étaient 95 fois plus grands que lui; il se sauve.

Des moissonneurs trouvent Guliver dans un champ de blé, il est aussitôt emporté avec précaution.

Gulliver assiste à un repas de géants, on le trouve si petit qu'on lui donne pour lit une coquille de noix.

Gulliver est présenté à la reine du pays, qui le regarde avec plaisir comme une curiosité.

On lui construit une petite maison qui est emportée par un aigle, au moment où il mettait la tête à la fenêtre.

L'aigle laisse tomber sa proie. Gulliver tombe dans la mer il est repêché par un navire anglais.

Fabrique d'images de GANGEL, à Metz.

Despite the instant and enormous popularity of *Gulliver's Travels*, it did nothing to harm the Whigs or, for that matter, the new science, and that may have served to further embitter Swift's last years.

He had periods of nausea and dizziness, apparently because of an affliction of the middle ear. This has been sensationalized into tales of insanity, which are, apparently, without foundation.

He remained popular with the Irish and was Dublin's foremost citizen in the last year of his life. There was a great celebration in his honor in the fall of 1739, when he was seventy-two years old.

He then suffered a stroke that deprived him of the power of speech and in 1742 was declared incapable of caring for himself. He died on October 19, 1745, about six weeks before his seventy-eighth birthday.

He lives on, however, in *Gulliver's Travels*, which will survive as long as the English language does, with no prose competitor of its period that can even begin to match its perennial popularity, except perhaps for Defoe's *Robinson Crusoe*.

Opposite:
French popular print adaptation of Gulliver's Travels
from mid-nineteenth century.

1 *Travels Into Several Remote Nations of the World.* *Gulliver's Travels* started out as a satire on travel books, which were very popular in the lifetime of Jonathan Swift.

2 *Lemuel Gulliver.* The author is given as Lemuel Gulliver, no mention being made of Jonathan Swift on the title page, for it was thought best that the book be published anonymously—and with good reason. Swift expected there would be trouble because the period was not one that welcomed unpleasant truths (something in which it resembled all other periods in history). A satire that drew blood might well place the author in prison.

As it happened, though, the book was an immediate success, and Swift's authorship was quickly made known. The book has been known ever since as *Gulliver's Travels* by Jonathan Swift.

Nowhere in the book proper does the narrator give his own name, nor is it used by any other character. The name occurs only on the title page and in the two letters which preceded the text in later editions of the book.

3 *MDCCXXVI.* The book was published on October 28, 1726, when Jonathan Swift was a month short of his fifty-ninth birthday.

TRAVELS

INTO SEVERAL

Remote Nations

OF THE

WORLD.

In Four PARTS.

By *LEMUEL GULLIVER*,
First a Surgeon, and then a Captain of several SHIPS.

Vol. I.

LONDON:

Printed for Benj. Motte, *at the* *Middle* Temple-Gate *in* Fleet-street.
MDCCXXVI.

1

2

3

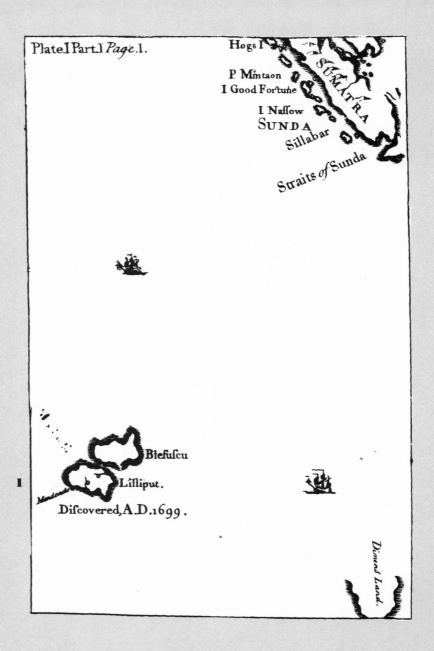

1 *Lilliput.* The name of the first land discovered by Gulliver is not given in the story itself for quite a time, but it is given in the part title and in the short summaries that pass for chapter titles (a rather tedious and infelicitous custom of the times). I will therefore use the name freely in the annotations.

Swift carefully includes a map or two in each part, to help him with his intention of describing the utter impossibilities he catalogues in as straight-faced and plausible a manner as possible. See Chapter 1 in this part, note 22 for detailed comments concerning this map.

PART ONE

A Voyage to Lilliput

CHAPTER ONE

1 *Nottinghamshire.* A county in north central England, about 4/5 the size of the state of Rhode Island. Its largest town is, not surprisingly, Nottingham, which is located 110 miles northwest of London. Nottinghamshire's greatest literary fame rests on the fact that 10 miles to the north of Nottingham is Sherwood Forest, the onetime haunt of the legendary Robin Hood.

Gulliver was thus born in a rural section of England and grew up in unsophisticated surroundings. Swift's every effort is to create a Gulliver who is solid, middle class, and endowed with an intelligent but unimaginative simplicity. Gulliver can be relied on to see and report facts accurately, but he accepts

Learning navigation. Herbert Cole, 1899.

The Author gives some account of himself and family. His first inducements to travel. He is shipwrecked, and swims for his life, gets safe on shore in the country of Lilliput, is made a prisoner, and carried up the country.

1

2,3

4

5

6

7

8

9

M Y Father had a small Estate in *Nottinghamshire*; I was the Third of five Sons. He sent me to *Emanuel-College* in *Cambridge*, at Fourteen Years old, where I resided three Years, and applied my self close to my Studies: But the Charge of maintaining me (although I had a very scanty Allowance) being too great for a narrow Fortune; I was bound Apprentice to Mr. *James Bates*, an eminent Surgeon in *London*, with whom I continued four Years; and my Father now and then sending me small Sums of Money, I laid them out in learning Navigation, and other Parts of the Mathematicks, useful to those who intend to travel, as I always believed it would be some time or other my Fortune to do. When I left Mr. *Bates*, I went down to my Father; where, by the Assistance of him and my Uncle *John*, and some other Relations, I got Forty Pounds, and a Promise of Thirty Pounds a Year to maintain me at *Leyden*: There I studied Physick two Years and seven Months, knowing it would be useful in long Voyages.

Soon after my Return from *Leyden*, I was recommended by my good Master Mr. *Bates*, to be Surgeon to the *Swallow*, Captain *Abraham Pannell* Commander; with whom I continued three Years

them at face value. (It is probably no accident that the only common English word his name resembles is "gullible.") The reader must look beyond Gulliver for an interpretation of what he reports.

2 *Cambridge.* Cambridge University was founded in 1209, when a number of discontented students from Oxford migrated there. It is located fifty miles north of London and seventy-five miles southeast of Nottingham.

Isaac Newton became a professor of mathematics at Cambridge in 1669, when he was only twenty-seven years old. In the thirty years that followed, Newton became world famous, and Cambridge University gained a preeminence in science and mathematics that it holds to this day. Newton was still alive when *Gulliver's Travels* was published (he was eighty-four years old and died the next year) and was nearly godlike in reputation, though Swift disliked him thoroughly.

Since Gulliver is represented as a science-minded person, it is only appropriate that he be described as attending Cambridge. Then, too, Cambridge did not have the enormous prestige of Oxford, so that Gulliver's presence there was another sign of his lack of social distinction. (Swift himself went to neither Oxford nor Cambridge but received his education at Trinity College in Dublin.)

3 *Fourteen Years old.* Life was shorter in those days, and one made faster beginnings. It was quite common to enter college in one's mid-teens. Swift entered Trinity College when he was fourteen. Newton entered Cambridge at eighteen, but he was rather slow in his studies as a youth.

From the data given in the first couple of pages in the book, we can deduce that Gulliver was six years older that Swift. Gulliver seems to have been born in 1661 and to have entered Cambridge in 1675. He was, in other words, born soon after Charles II was restored to the throne. His father must therefore have lived through the turbulent period of the English civil wars and the dictatorship of Oliver Cromwell. No indication of this is given, however.

In fact, all through the book, Gulliver gives no indication whatever of any event that takes place in England or the world while he is on his travels. The reader's attention is firmly fixed on the fantasy world of the lands he discovers and any intrusion of the real world would be a distraction that would weaken the satire.

4 *three Years.* Gulliver stayed in Cambridge then till 1678.

5 *Apprentice.* The notion of apprenticeship—learning a trade under a recognized experienced professional in the field—was an outgrowth of the guild system of the Middle Ages. The guilds were a kind of craft union which undertook to maintain high standards of workmanship and which did not wish anyone to practice a particular trade who was not thoroughly trained and who could not prove his ability to perform satisfactorily.

In Gulliver's time, the system of apprenticeship was still quite powerful. Even as late as 1756, James Watt, who was soon to be the inventor of the steam engine and the greatest engineer of his time, was not recognized by the guilds of Glasgow because he had not served his full term as apprentice.

The full term of apprenticeship was usually seven years, but Gulliver served only four, so that he was apprenticed from 1678 to 1682.

6 *Surgeon.* Surgery was not yet recognized as a true branch of medicine. It involved the use of the hands, which made it a branch of mechanics. It was, in early times, associated with barbers, since cutting flesh was considered to be similar to cutting hair as far as skills and social position were concerned.

It was not till 1540 that some modicum of control over the actual skill and learning of barber-surgeons was established with the formation of the "Company of Barber Surgeons of London." This guild was still in existence in Gulliver's time and it required a seven year apprenticeship.

Surgery in the eighteenth century. Courtesy, Library of Congress.

7 *Navigation.* Guiding a ship across an ocean and having it arrive at the desired destination was no easy matter in those days. To do it properly, there had to be some knowledge of descriptive astronomy and of the use of various instruments for the determination of latitude. Considerable knowledge of spherical trigonometry was required to prepare maps and to use them properly once they had been prepared. It is not surprising that Gulliver speaks of navigation as though it were a branch of mathematics. It is.

8 *Leyden.* Also called Leiden. A town in the southwestern Netherlands about two hundred miles east of London. At the time *Gulliver's Travels* was published, Leyden was the site of the most highly regarded medical school in the world.

9 *Physick.* The Greek word for nature. Used to describe the study of medicine (as used here) and as a general word for medications taken internally. To-day it is occasionally used for one specific kind of medical dose—a laxative.

10 *the Levant.* A general term for the shores of the eastern Mediterranean, from Greece to Egypt, used with particular reference to Syria and Lebanon. The word is from the French *lever,* meaning "to rise," so that the Levant is "the land in the direction of the rising sun." It was replaced by the term "Near East" in the nineteenth century, and this unaccountably became "the Middle East" in the twentieth century. The Far East, including China and Japan, for instance, was sometimes referred to in Gulliver's time as "the High Levant."

While Gulliver was surgeon on the *Swallow* (from 1684 to 1688), Charles II died and was succeeded by his younger brother, James II. Naturally, Gulliver doesn't mention this.

11 *the Old Jury.* Or, more properly, Old Jewry, so named because it had once been the ghetto area of London. The Jews were expelled from England in 1290 by Edward I, who had wrung all the money out of them to pay for his wars and saw no use in holding on to them once they were penniless. The Jews finally returned to England in Cromwell's time, three and a half centuries later, but they then found other ghettos for themselves.

The Old Jury and the other places in which Gulliver lived thereafter are lower middle-class places and fit the picture we are supposed to have of him.

12 *Mrs. Mary Burton.* "Mrs." is an abbreviation for "Mistress," which is the feminine form of "Master" (Mister). In the eighteenth century, both Mister and Mistress were quite restricted forms of address, intended only for people high enough in society to serve as employers of servants. (Servants were addressed without title, by first name only, or, in the case of women, by the truncated title of "Miss.")

Mister and Mistress were used without distinction of married state at the time. Mister still is, but Mistress has come to be restricted to married women, since Swift's time. By referring to the woman he married as Mrs. Mary Burton, Gulliver was not implying that she had been divorced or widowed, merely that she was of comfortable social station.

There is no mention of love here or later, by the way. At no time in the book does Gulliver indicate affectionate feeling for either wife or children, though he is, on occasion, homesick. He must have had sexual relations with his wife, since he begets children, but on his long voyages, Gulliver betrays no longing to resume those relations or to search for any substitutes. Nor can this be a matter of false delicacy only, since Gulliver discusses excretory matters easily enough.

Swift himself never married, and although he had some sort of relationship with two women, usually referred to as "Stella" and "Vanessa," nothing is really known of the nature of those relationships. Swift may have been, like his contemporary, Newton, and like George Bernard Shaw, simply asexual.

London in the eighteenth century. Courtesy, Prints Division, The New York Public Library.

10 and a half, making a Voyage or two into the *Levant,* and some other Parts. When I came back, I resolved to settle in *London,* to which Mr. *Bates,* my Master, encouraged me; and by him I was recommended to several Patients. I took Part of a small House in **11** the *Old Jury;* and being advised to alter my Condition, I married **12** Mrs. *Mary Burton,* second Daughter to Mr. *Edmond Burton,* Hosier, in *Newgate-street,* with whom I received four Hundred **13** Pounds for a Portion.

14 But, my good Master *Bates* dying in two Years after, and I having few Friends, my Business began to fail; for my Conscience would not suffer me to imitate the bad Practice of too many among my Brethren. Having therefore consulted with my Wife, and some of my Acquaintance, I determined to go again to Sea. I was Surgeon successively in two Ships, and made several Voyages, for **15** six Years, to the *East* and *West-Indies;* by which I got some Addition to my Fortune. My Hours of Leisure I spent in reading the best Authors, ancient and modern; being always provided with a good Number of Books; and when I was ashore, in observing the Manners and Dispositions of the People, as well as learning their Language; wherein I had a great Facility by the Strength of my Memory.

The last of these Voyages not proving very fortunate, I grew weary of the Sea, and intended to stay at home with my Wife and Family. I removed from the *Old Jury* to *Fetter Lane,* and from thence to *Wapping,* hoping to get Business among the Sailors; but it would not turn to account. After three Years Expectation that things would mend, I accepted an advantageous Offer from Captain *William Prichard,* Master of the *Antelope,* who was mak-**16,17** a Voyage to the *South-Sea.* We set sail from *Bristol, May* 4th, 1699, and our Voyage at first was very prosperous.

It would not be proper for some Reasons, to trouble the Reader with the Particulars of our Adventures in those Seas: Let it suffice to inform him, that in our Passage from thence to the *East-Indies,* **18** we were driven by a violent Storm to the North-west of *Van* **19** *Diemen's* Land. By an Observation, we found ourselves in the Latitude of 30 Degrees 2 Minutes South. Twelve of our Crew were dead by immoderate Labour, and ill Food; the rest were in a very **20** weak Condition. On the fifth of *November,* which was the begin-

13 *for a Portion.* A dowry, in other words. It is part of the male chauvinism of most societies that men had to be bribed to marry.

14 *two Years after.* Bates died in 1690. During the first two years of Gulliver's married life, James II was forced off his throne, fled to France, and was succeeded on the throne by his daughter and her husband, Mary II and William III, who ruled as joint monarchs. William had been stadtholder of the Netherlands before he succeeded to the English throne.

15 *East and West-Indies.* In ancient times, India was the farthest known land to the east. In medieval times, the term "Indies" was used vaguely to refer to all the lands beyond the eastern horizon. As trade with the Far East increased, it became known that there were large islands off the Asian continent from which spices and other commodities, much desired in Europe, could be obtained. The term "Indies" came to be applied chiefly to those islands.

When Columbus reached the American continents, he was firmly convinced he had reached Asia. Certain islands he discovered were, he was sure, the "Indies." They were not, but they retained the name just the same, just as the American natives are still called "Indians." To distinguish Columbus's Indies from the real ones, the former are called the "West Indies" and the latter the "East Indies."

Gulliver was engaged in his position as ship's surgeon from 1690 to 1696, during which time the new sovereigns established themselves firmly on the throne. Mary II died on December 28, 1694, and William III continued to rule alone.

16 *South-Sea.* The Pacific Ocean was first sighted by a European on the American continent in 1513. In that year Vasco Nuñez de Balboa moved inland from the Panamanian coast in search of gold. He had not the slightest idea that Panama was a narrow isthmus. When he got through to the other side he found himself staring at what seemed a large sea. Since the isthmus of Panama runs generally east and west and the Atlantic Ocean lies to its north, the newfound sea was to its south. Balboa therefore named the new body of water the "South Sea."

When, seven years later, the Portuguese explorer, Ferdinand Magellan, emerged into the same ocean at the western end of what is now called the Strait of Magellan, he named it the Pacific Ocean and that name stuck. Nowadays, however, the "South Seas" is a term still used for those portions of the ocean that lie in the Southern Hemisphere and, in the singular, is used in particular for the South Pacific.

17 *We set sail from Bristol.* Bristol is an English port on the southwest coast, about one hundred miles west of London. In Gulliver's time, it was second only to London as a port and had waxed prosperous in the "triangular trade" by which slaves and cocoa were picked up in West Africa, bartered for sugar and molasses in Jamaica, which were in turn bartered for tobacco in Virginia, which was in turn brought to England. Eventually, when the slave trade was banned, Liverpool gained on Bristol and overtook it, but that was after Gulliver's time.

Gulliver, leaving on the first voyage that the book treats in detail, on May 4, 1699, is thirty-eight years old, mature and experienced. It is a time of peace. England had been at war with France ("the War of the Grand Alliance") from 1689 to 1697 and that war had involved some crucial naval battles in the English Channel. However, Gulliver, in referring to his seagoing experiences in that period, makes no mention of the war or any dangers he may have run in consequence, and the war came to an end with the Treaty of Ryswick on September 20, 1697.

18 *North-west of Van Diemen's Land.* Van Diemen's Land is an island off the southeastern shore of Australia. It was discovered in 1642 by a Dutch explorer, Abel Janszoon Tasman, who had been commissioned for the task by Anton van Diemen, then governor-general of the Dutch dominions in the East Indies. Tasman named it after his superior. In 1855, it was renamed Tasmania after its discoverer, and holds that name to this day.

19 *in the Latitude of 30 Degrees 2 Minutes South.* Had Gulliver actually been driven to the northwest of Van Diemen's Land to that latitude, he would have found himself at least a hundred miles inland on the continent of Australia. But then, the southern shores of Australia had not been discovered in Gulliver's time, or at the time the book was published, either. The coasts of that island continent were not well mapped until the voyage of Captain Cook in 1770.

20 *the beginning of Summer in those Parts.* Gulliver was in the Southern Hemisphere, where the seasons are six months out of phase with those in the Northern Hemisphere. November 5 in the South Temperate Zone is the equivalent of May 5 in the North

Captain Gulliver. Gavarni, 1850s. Courtesy, Library of Congress.

Temperate Zone. This is not the beginning of summer in a strictly astronomical sense, but it is a time when warm weather can begin to be expected.

21 *three Leagues*. The "league" is an old unit of length that varied in size in different nations and at different times. In English usage, one league is generally taken to represent three miles.

ning of Summer in those Parts, the Weather being very hazy, the Seamen spyed a Rock, within half a Cable's length of the Ship; but the Wind was so strong, that we were driven directly upon it, and immediately split. Six of the Crew, of whom I was one, having let down the Boat into the Sea, made a Shift to get clear of the Ship, and the Rock. We rowed by my Computation, about three Leagues, till we were able to work no longer, being already spent with Labour while we were in the Ship. We therefore trusted ourselves to the Mercy of the Waves; and in about half an Hour the Boat was overset by a sudden Flurry from the North. What became of my Companions in the Boat, as well as of those who escaped on the Rock, or were left in the Vessel, I cannot tell; but conclude they were all lost. For my own Part, I swam as Fortune directed me, and was pushed forward by Wind and Tide. I often let my Legs drop, and could feel no Bottom: But when I was al-

"I lay all this while . . . in great uneasiness." T. Morten, 1865. Courtesy, Library of Congress.

most gone, and able to struggle no longer, I found myself within my Depth; and by this Time the Storm was much abated. The Declivity was so small, that I walked near a Mile before I got to the Shore, which I conjectured was about Eight o'Clock in the Evening. I then advanced forward near half a Mile, but could not discover any Sign of Houses or Inhabitants; at least I was in so weak a Condition, that I did not observe them. I was extremely tired, and with that, and the Heat of the Weather, and about half a Pint of Brandy that I drank as I left the Ship, I found myself much inclined to sleep. I lay down on the Grass, which was very short and soft; where I slept sounder than ever I remember to have done in my Life, and as I reckoned, above Nine Hours; for when I awaked, it was just Day-light. I attempted to rise, but was not able to stir: For as I happened to lie on my Back, I found my Arms and Legs were strongly fastened on each Side to the Ground; and

22

23

24

22 *I walked near a Mile before I got to the Shore.* The land on which Gulliver has now found himself is Lilliput, which is shown on the map (opposite the part title), that, presumably, Gulliver prepared.

Sumatra is shown at the top right and its shape is correct. Moreover, its orientation shows that north is at the top. Still further to the top right is the tip of the Malayan peninsula, also correct. The Sunda Strait is correctly placed at Sumatra's southeastern end, and beyond it is the westernmost part of the island of Java.

At the bottom right is Van Diemen's Land (Tasmania), of which the eastern and western shores are shown reasonably well. The northern shore is blank, which is correct, for it was unexplored in 1699. Van Diemen's Land is placed due south of Sumatra, which is wrong, since it is actually southeast of Sumatra.

If we ignore Van Diemen's Land, we can say that Lilliput is directly southwest of Sumatra, and is at a distance equal to ten times Sumatra's width. That means it is about twenty-seven hundred miles southwest of Sumatra, a spot in the Indian Ocean about midway between the southern tip of Sumatra and the southwestern tip of Australia. In actuality, there is no significant land near the spot.

According to Gulliver's map, Lilliput and its companion island, whose name is given on the map as Blefuscu, are each about two hundred miles wide, if they are compared to the width shown for Sumatra. Each, therefore, has an area of something like seventeen thousand square miles and the total area of the two islands is about equal to that of the state of Maine. From indications later in the story, this would seem to be a gross overestimate.

23 *the Heat of the Weather.* If the map presented by Gulliver is correct, the islands are at about thirty-five degrees south latitude, or at about the latitude of Buenos Aires. It would correspond to the northern latitude of Chattanooga, Tennessee. It seems unlikely it would have been terribly hot at 8 P.M. of an average mid-spring day, especially on the shores of an island bathed by the breezes and ocean currents of an area that might feel the distant whispers of Antarctica to the south. Again, we have to assume that Gulliver's map is wrong and that Lilliput is farther north than he shows it to be and therefore considerably more tropical.

24 *very short and soft.* This is the first indication that things are abnormally small on the island. Characteristically, Gulliver does not stop to wonder why the grass is so short and soft. He merely reports the fact.

IMPORTANT

25 *a human Creature not six Inches high.* As it turns out, everything on the island is on the scale of one to twelve; that is, the island's inches are equivalent to our feet. Since the Lilliputian whom Gulliver first sees is very nearly six inches high, we can assume that Gulliver is very nearly six feet tall. (This, in fact, is the only physical fact we ever learn about Gulliver's appearance, since he gives us nothing about himself, not so much as the color of his hair or eyes. He is deliberately colorless. We are at no time to see him, but only to see through him—what he sees. He is the unobserved observer.)

However, 1/12 is not the true measure of the size of the Lilliputians. They are 1/12 as tall as we are, but also 1/12 as wide and 1/12 as thick. The total volume of one of them, and therefore the total weight, is 1/12 × 1/12 × 1/12, or, 1/1,728 of ourselves.

If the average weight of a human being is 150 pounds or, counting 16 ounces to the pound, 2,400 ounces, the average Lilliputian would weigh 1.4 ounces. What's more, the weight of the human brain is about 3 pounds. The weight of the brain of a Lilliputian would be, in proportion, 1/36 of an ounce in weight (or less than 1 gram on the metric scale). Since cells in living creatures are much the same in size in all animals, from insects to whales, the brain of the Lilliputian should contain not more than 60 million cells, compared to our own 100 billion.

We know of no way in which intelligence on the human level can be encompassed by a brain with only 60 million cells. In fact, a Lilliputian should be no more intelligent than a mouse.

In addition, it would not be expected that the bodily proportions would be the same in a tiny creature as in a large creature, even though they were closely related biologically. If a photograph of real creatures of Lilliputian size were enlarged to make it seem as large as an ordinary human being, it would be seen that their limbs would be far more spindly than those of a human.

Then again, a small organism has a much greater surface compared to its volume than a large organism of similar shape and proportions has. The small organism loses body heat at a far faster rate. To replace it, a Lilliputian would have to be constantly eating, and would consume food in far greater proportion to its body weight than a large being would.

26 *Admiration.* Nowadays "admiration" means "a regarding with esteem and pleasure." The word is from a Latin term meaning "to wonder at" and has changed into a particular kind of wonder. In Swift's time, it still bore the general meaning of "a regarding with wonder." A frightening phenomenon, such as Gulliver was to the Lilliputians, would thus be an object of admiration (wonder) even though its contemplation gave the reverse of pleasure.

27 *cried out in a shrill, but distinct Voice.* Here Swift does bow to reality somewhat. The vocal cords of the little being would be 1/12 the length of that of ordinary human beings and the voice would be correspondingly higher pitched and therefore, shrill. I doubt that it would be distinct, however. It would

25

26,27
28

my Hair, which was long and thick, tied down in the same Manner. I likewise felt several slender Ligatures across my Body, from my Armpits to my Thighs. I could only look upwards; the Sun began to grow hot, and the Light offended my Eyes. I heard a confused Noise about me, but in the Posture I lay, could see nothing except the Sky. In a little time I felt something alive moving on my left Leg, which advancing gently forward over my Breast, came almost up to my Chin; when bending my Eyes downwards as much as I could, I perceived it to be a human Creature not six Inches high, with a Bow and Arrow in his Hands, and a Quiver at his Back. In the mean time, I felt at least Forty more of the same Kind (as I conjectured) following the first. I was in the utmost Astonishment, and roared so loud, that they all ran back in a Fright; and some of them, as I was afterwards told, were hurt with the Falls they got by leaping from my Sides upon the Ground. However, they soon returned; and one of them, who ventured so far as to get a full Sight of my Face, lifting up his Hands and Eyes by way of Admiration, cryed out in a shrill, but distinct Voice, *Hekinah Degul:* The others repeated the same Words several times, but I then knew not what they meant. I lay all this while, as the Reader may believe, in great Uneasiness: At length struggling to get loose, I had the Fortune to break the Strings, and wrench out the Pegs that fastened my left Arm to the Ground; for, by lifting it up to my Face, I discovered the Methods they had taken to bind me; and, at the same time, with a violent Pull, which gave me excessive Pain, I a little loosened the Strings that tied

"I felt above an Hundred Arrows discharged." Alfred Crawquill. 1865.

"A Person of Quality, made me a long Speech." Willy Pogány, 1919.

down my Hair on the left Side; so that I was just able to turn my Head about two Inches. But the Creatures ran off a second time, before I could seize them; whereupon there was a great Shout in a very shrill Accent; and after it ceased, I heard one of them cry aloud, *Tolgo Phonac;* when in an Instant I felt above an Hundred Arrows discharged on my left Hand, which pricked me like so many Needles; and besides, they shot another Flight into the Air, as we do Bombs in *Europe;* whereof many, I suppose, fell on my Body, (though I felt them not) and some on my Face, which I immediately covered with my left Hand. When this Shower of Arrows was over, I fell a groaning with Grief and Pain; and then striving again to get loose, they discharged another Volly larger than the first; and some of them attempted with Spears to stick me in the Sides; but, by good Luck, I had on me a Buff Jerkin, which they could not pierce. I thought it the most prudent Method to lie still; and my Design was to continue so till Night, when my left Hand being already loose, I could easily free myself: And as for the Inhabitants, I had Reason to believe I might be a Match for the greatest Armies they could bring against me, if they were all of the same Size with him that I saw. But Fortune disposed otherwise of me. When the People observed I was quiet, they discharged no more Arrows: But by the Noise increasing, I knew their Numbers were greater; and about four Yards from me, over-against my right Ear, I heard a Knocking for above an Hour, like People at work; when turning my Head that Way, as well as the Pegs and Strings would permit me, I saw a Stage erected about a Foot and a half from the Ground, capable of holding four of the Inhabitants, with two or three Ladders to mount it: From whence one of them, who seemed to be a Person of Quality, made me a long Speech, whereof I understood not one Syllable. But I should have mentioned, that before the principal Person began his Oration, he cryed out three times *Langro Dehul san:* (these Words and the former were afterwards repeated and explained to me.) Whereupon immediately about fifty of the Inhabitants came, and cut the Strings that fastened the left side of my Head, which gave me the Liberty of turning it to the right, and of observing the Person and Gesture of him who was to speak. He appeared to be of a middle

29

30

resemble the squeaking of a mouse and might well be so shrill that Gulliver wouldn't be able to hear it at all.

28 *Hekinah Degul.* Throughout the book, Swift amuses himself by making up words and phrases in the languages of the mythical lands which Gulliver visits.

In order to achieve his purposes, Swift has Gulliver prove to be a rather miraculous linguist who quickly learns each of the languages he encounters. This, however, is a much better device than having all the fantastic creatures he encounters speaking English as so many unclever satirists would have done (see any similar television program) or, worse yet, going to the desperate expedient of inventing a telepathic communication.

Some people have tried to make sense out of the words and phrases introduced by Swift but, in general, this is a waste of time. I suspect that Swift simply made up nonsense for the purpose.

29 *Bombs in Europe.* The reference is to cannonballs. An early word for a cannon was "bombard," and we still speak of "bombardment"—hence "bombs" for cannonballs.

30 *Buff Jerkin.* A leather jacket. "Buff" is short for buffalo, though the leather might be obtained from any of a variety of other large herbivorous animals and still be called buff.

31 *by the King's Orders.* Monarchy was the accepted means of government in Swift's time and everyone would have assumed, as a matter of course, that every nation would have a king. Besides, Swift's satiric intent required Lilliput to be as close to England as possible in its institutions and way of life in order to make English follies seem as contemptible as possible when portrayed in miniature.

32 *smaller than the Wings of a Lark.* Plant and animal life, and even inanimate objects, are all tiny on Lilliput, all in the same one to twelve proportion. There is no point in asking how this could have come about through any logical process of evolution. Swift's readers and, probably, Swift himself, would have been content with the statement that God had created it so, if they felt the need for logical justification of Lilliput.

33 *Hogsheads.* Large barrels that can hold anywhere from 40 to 140 gallons. Let us take a middle course and say this particular one holds 100 gallons or, counting 8 pints to a gallon, 800 pints. If a Lilliputian hogshead held 800 Lilliputian pints, we would have to divide 800 by 1,728 to get its capacity in ordinary pints. On Gulliver's scale, it would be just under half a pint, as he goes on to say. Swift is generally very careful with these conversions, although he occasionally bends them to achieve a greater effect.

34 *small Wine of Burgundy.* A small wine is a weak wine of less than normal alcoholic content. Burgundy refers to the Burgundy region of France, located southeast of Paris, that is well known for both its red and white wines.

"*The Inhabitants mounted, and walked towards my Mouth.*" *Willy Pogány, 1919.*

Age, and taller than any of the other three who attended him; whereof one was a Page, who held up his Train, and seemed to be somewhat longer than my middle Finger; the other two stood one on each side to support him. He acted every part of an Orator; and I could observe many Periods of Threatnings, and others of Promises, Pity, and Kindness. I answered in a few Words, but in the most submissive Manner, lifting up my left Hand and both my eyes to the Sun, as calling him for a Witness; and being almost famished with Hunger, having not eaten a Morsel for some Hours before I left the Ship, I found the Demands of Nature so strong upon me, that I could not forbear shewing my Impatience (perhaps against the strict Rules of Decency) by putting my Finger frequently on my Mouth, to signify that I wanted Food. The *Hurgo* (for so they call a great Lord, as I afterwards learnt) understood me very well: He descended from the Stage, and commanded that several Ladders should be applied to my Sides, on which above an hundred of the Inhabitants mounted, and walked towards my Mouth, laden with Baskets full of Meat, which had been provided,

31 and sent thither by the King's Orders upon the first Intelligence he received of me. I observed there was the Flesh of several Animals, but could not distinguish them by the Taste. There were Shoulders, Legs, and Loins shaped like those of Mutton, and very

32 well dressed, but smaller than the Wings of a Lark. I eat them by two or three at a Mouthful; and took three Loaves at a time, about the bigness of Musket Bullets. They supplied me as fast as they could, shewing a thousand Marks of Wonder and Astonishment at my Bulk and Appetite. I then made another Sign that I wanted Drink. They found by my eating that a small Quantity would not suffice me; and being a most ingenious People, they slung up with

33 great Dexterity one of their largest Hogsheads; then rolled it towards my Hand, and beat out the Top; I drank it off at a Draught, which I might well do, for it hardly held half a Pint, and tasted

34 like a small Wine of *Burgundy*, but much more delicious. They brought me a second Hogshead, which I drank in the same Manner, and made Signs for more, but they had none to give me. When I had performed these Wonders, they shouted for Joy, and danced upon my Breast, repeating several times as they did at first,

Hekinah Degul. They made me a Sign that I should throw down the two Hogsheads, but first warned the People below to stand out of the Way, crying aloud, *Borach Mivola;* and when they saw the Vessels in the Air, there was an universal Shout of *Hekinah Degul.* I confess I was often tempted, while they were passing backwards and forwards on my Body, to seize Forty or Fifty of the first that came in my Reach, and dash them against the Ground. But the Remembrance of what I had felt, which probably might not be the worst they could do; and the Promise of Honour I made them, for so I interpreted my submissive Behavior, soon drove out those Imaginations. Besides, I now considered my self as bound by the Laws of Hospitality to a People who had treated me with so much Expence and Magnificence. However, in my Thoughts I could not sufficiently wonder at the Intrepidity of these diminutive Mortals, who durst venture to mount and walk on my Body, while one of my Hands was at Liberty, without trembling at the very Sight of so prodigious a Creature as I must appear to them. After some time, when they observed that I made no more Demands for Meat, there appeared before me a Person of high Rank from his Imperial **35** Majesty. His Excellency having mounted on the Small of my Right Leg, advanced forwards up to my Face, with about a Dozen of his Retinue; And producing his Credentials under the Signet **36** Royal, which he applied close to my Eyes, spoke about ten Minutes, without any Signs of Anger, but with a kind of determinate Resolution; often pointing forwards, which, as I afterwards found, was towards the Capital City, about half a Mile distant, whither it was agreed by his Majesty in Council that I must be conveyed. I answered in few Words, but to no Purpose, and made a Sign with my Hand that was loose, putting it to the other, (but over his Excellency's Head, for Fear of hurting him or his Train) and then to my own Head and Body, to signify that I desired my Liberty. It appeared that he understood me well enough; for he shook his Head by way of Disapprobation, and held his Hand in a Posture to shew that I must be carried as a Prisoner. However, he made other Signs to let me understand that I should have Meat and Drink enough, and very good Treatment. Whereupon I once more thought of attempting to break my Bonds; but again, when I felt the Smart of their Arrows upon my Face and Hands, which were all in Blisters, and many of the Darts still sticking in them; and observing likewise that the Number of my Enemies encreased; I gave Tokens to let them know that they might do with me what **37** they pleased. Upon this, the *Hurgo* and his Train withdrew, with much Civility and chearful Countenances. Soon after I heard a general Shout, with frequent Repetitions of the Words, *Peplom Selan,* and I felt great Numbers of the People on my Left Side relaxing the Cords to such a Degree, that I was able to turn upon my Right, and to ease my self with making Water; which I very plentifully did, to the great Astonishment of the People, who conjecturing by my Motions what I was going to do, immediately opened to the right and left on that Side, to avoid the Torrent **38** which fell with such Noise and Violence from me. But before this, they had dawbed my Face and both my Hands with a sort of **39** Ointment very pleasant to the Smell, which in a few Minutes removed all the Smart of their Arrows. These Circumstances, added to the Refreshment I had received by their Victuals and Drink,

35 *Imperial Majesty.* A monarch who is not merely a king but an emperor. It is customary to think of "emperor" as the higher title, implying a sovereign who holds sway over many nations. Lilliput is therefore not only a kingdom but an empire. Gulliver, however, makes no note of the oddness or the inappropriateness of the claim. He accepts all titles, all offices at their face value, which is typical of him.

36 *Signet Royal.* Nowadays, it is the handwritten signature that authenticates a document or a contract, on the assumption that a signature is unique to its writer. In the days when literacy was rare, people in power would instead make an impression in wax with a ring on their finger or some other object to which they alone had access. The object that made the unique impression, as well as the wax or other substance that received it, was a "seal" or "signet." The king's seal (for a king, in the good old days, was no more likely to be literate than a peasant was) was the Signet Royal.

Such is the conservatism of custom, by the way, that college diplomas generally have seals on them, though it can be assumed that college presidents can write, after a fashion.

37 *I gave Tokens.* By "tokens" here is meant signs or gestures.

38 *the Torrent which fell with such Noise and Violence from me.* In most fiction, whether in books or on the screen, there seems to be no indication that people ever need to relieve themselves. Characters can undergo prolonged ordeals under conditions where they clearly have no opportunity to excrete, and yet they show no related discomfort. This is a literary convention that arises from a feeling of delicacy, but Swift does not adhere to it. It is his firm intention to ground his fantastic story in a profusion of realistic detail, and taking care of the excretory function is part of that effect.

Gulliver, incidentally, has been either sleeping or tied down for a long time and his bladder had to be just as full as it could be. Under such circumstances the bladder can hold something like a pound of urine which, on the Lilliputian scale, would be the equivalent of nearly a ton. So we can't blame them for either their astonishment or their haste in getting out of the way. One wonders, however, at the environmental impact of such a urinous flood on the Lilliputian field on which Gulliver lay.

39 *a sort of Ointment.* It is part of the stock in trade of the science fiction writer to allow strange peoples convenient advances in science when it helps smooth the progress of the plot. It would have been most inconvenient if Gulliver had developed an infection, and Swift was not the kind of writer who would simply ignore the matter. (We might wonder, though, how advanced Lilliputian medical science was. Did the ointment contain an antibiotic?)

40 *Machine*. The modern reader may involuntarily think of an automobile at this point and wonder if Swift was prophetic. In the original sense of the word, however (and it is derived from a Latin word meaning "a device"), a machine is any human-made construction, particularly one intended to serve as a means of conveyance. In that respect, a coach, a cart, or even a wheelbarrow, is a machine.

41 *Nine Foot long*. Gulliver recites the small figures that follow gravely, adjusting himself to Lilliputian standards. On the Lilliputian scale a 9-foot-long war-ship is 108 feet long, and to have them carried "three or four Hundred Yards to the Sea" is the equivalent of being conveyed two or three miles.

42 *Engines*. In Swift's time this term did not have the modern connotation of being power-driven. An engine was any device, but particularly, an ingenious one. ("Engine" and "ingenious" are derived from the same Latin word.)

Engraving from the first illustrated edition,
London, 1727. Courtesy, Rare Book Division,
The New York Public Library.

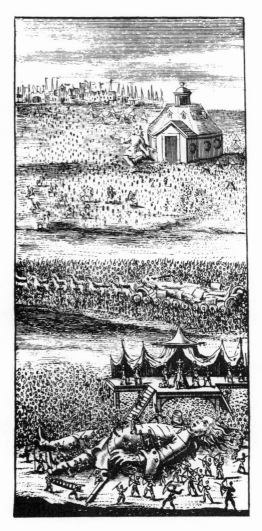

which were very nourishing, disposed me to sleep. I slept about eight Hours as I was afterwards assured; and it was no Wonder; for the Physicians, by the Emperor's Order had mingled a sleeping Potion in the Hogsheads of Wine. It seems that upon the first Moment I was discovered sleeping on the Ground after my Landing, the Emperor had early Notice of it by an Express; and determined in Council that I should be tyed in the Manner I have related, (which was done in the Night while I slept) that Plenty of **40** Meat and Drink should be sent me, and a Machine prepared to carry me to the Capital City.

This Resolution perhaps may appear very bold and dangerous, and I am confident would not be imitated by any Prince in *Europe* on the like Occasion; however, in my Opinion it was extremely Prudent as well as Generous. For supposing these People had endeavoured to kill me with their Spears and Arrows while I was asleep; I should certainly have awaked with the first Sense of Smart, which might so far have rouzed my Rage and Strength, as to enable me to break the Strings wherewith I was tyed; after which, as they were not able to make Resistance, so they could expect no Mercy.

These People are most excellent Mathematicians, and arrived to a great Perfection in Mechanicks by the Countenance and Encouragement of the Emperor, who is a renowned Patron of Learning. This Prince hath several Machines fixed on Wheels, for the Carriage of Trees and other great Weights. He often buildeth his **41** largest Men of War, whereof some are Nine Foot long, in the Woods where the Timber grows, and has them carried on these **42** Engines three or four Hundred Yards to the Sea. Five Hundred Carpenters and Engineers were immediately set at work to prepare the greatest Engine they had. It was a Frame of Wood raised three Inches from the Ground, about seven Foot long and four wide, moving upon twenty two Wheels. The Shout I heard, was upon the Arrival of this Engine, which, it seems, set out in four Hours after my Landing. It was brought parallel to me as I lay. But the principal Difficulty was to raise and place me in this Vehicle. Eighty Poles, each of one Foot high, were erected for this Purpose, and very strong Cords of the bigness of Pack-thread were fastned by Hooks to many Bandages, which the Workmen had girt round my Neck, my Hands, my Body, and my Legs. Nine Hundred of the strongest Men were employed to draw up these Cords by many Pullies fastned on the Poles; and thus in less than three Hours, I was raised and slung into the Engine, and there tyed fast. All this I was told; for while the whole Operation was performing, I lay in a profound Sleep, by the Force of that soporiferous Medicine infused into my Liquor. Fifteen hundred of the Emperor's largest Horses, each about four Inches and a half high, were employed to draw me towards the Metropolis, which, as I said, was half a Mile distant.

About four Hours after we began our Journey, I awaked by a very ridiculous Accident; for the Carriage being stopt a while to adjust something that was out of Order, two or three of the young Natives had the Curiosity to see how I looked when I was asleep; they climbed up into the Engine, and advancing very softly to my **43** Face, one of them, an Officer in the Guards, put the sharp End of **44** his Half-Pike a good way up into my left Nostril, which tickled my

Nose like a Straw, and made me sneeze violently: Whereupon they stole off unperceived; and it was three Weeks before I knew the Cause of my awaking so suddenly. We made a long March the remaining Part of the Day, and rested at Night with Five Hundred Guards on each Side of me, half with Torches, and half with Bows and Arrows, ready to shoot me if I should offer to stir. The next morning at Sunrise we continued our March, and arrived within two Hundred Yards of the City-Gates about Noon. The Emperor, and all his Court, came out to meet us; but his great Officers would by no Means suffer his Majesty to endanger his Person by mounting on my Body.

43 *an Officer in the Guards.* In England, the household troops, those with the special duty of guarding the king, were called the Guards; so, of course, Lilliput had Guards, too.

44 *Half-Pike.* A pike is a long spear used for thrusting by soldiers of Swift's time. (It was not many decades before it was superseded by the bayonet.) A half-pike is a short spear that was sometimes carried by officers for ceremonial purposes. The Lilliputian soldiers were armed with bows and arrows and pikes in European fashion, but they did not have gunpowder. If they had had gunpowder, Gulliver would have been in trouble. Even a Lilliputian cannon, fired at close range, would have done him damage.

"The Emperor, and all his Court, came out to meet us." McLoughlin Brothers, 1856.

Westminster Hall. Courtesy, Library of Congress.

45 *an ancient Temple . . . polluted some Years before by an unnatural Murder.* Since Swift did intend many hidden topical allusions in this book, commentators have always been hot on the trail of them and may well have found some allusions that Swift did not intend as such. For instance, it is usually assumed that this large building, in which "an unnatural Murder" had taken place some years before, represents Westminster Hall where, in January 1649, Charles I of England was tried, convicted, and sentenced to death.

It is my own experience, however, that commentators are far more ingenious at finding meaning than authors are at inserting it. After all, Charles I was not actually executed in Westminster Hall, nor was Westminster Hall abandoned. Swift merely may have needed a building which was at once large enough to hold Gulliver, and, for some reason, unused for any other purpose. He chose one way of accounting for such a building, and it might be hard to find another.

45 At the Place where the Carriage stopt, there stood an ancient Temple, esteemed to be the largest in the whole Kingdom; which having been polluted some Years before by an unnatural Murder, was, according to the Zeal of those People, looked upon as Prophane, and therefore had been applied to common Uses, and all the Ornaments and Furniture carried away. In this Edifice it was determined I should lodge. The great Gate fronting to the North was about four Foot high, and almost two Foot wide, through which I could easily creep. On each Side of the Gate was a small Window not above six Inches from the Ground: Into that on the Left Side, the King's Smiths conveyed fourscore and eleven Chains, like those that hang to a Lady's Watch in *Europe*, and almost as large, which were locked to my Left Leg with six and thirty Padlocks. Over against this Temple, on the other Side of the great Highway, at twenty Foot Distance, there was a Turret at least five Foot high. Here the Emperor ascended with many principal Lords of his Court, to have an Opportunity of viewing me, as I was told, for I could not see them. It was reckoned that above an hundred thousand Inhabitants came out of the Town upon the same Errand; and in spight of my Guards, I believe there could not be fewer than ten thousand, at several Times, who mounted upon my Body by the Help of Ladders. But a Proclamation was soon issued to forbid it, upon Pain of Death. When the Workmen found it was impossible for me to break loose, they cut all the Strings that bound me; whereupon I rose up with as melancholy a Disposition as ever I had in my Life. But the Noise and Astonishment of the People at seeing me rise and walk, are not to be expressed. The Chains that held my left Leg were about two Yards long, and gave me not only the Liberty of walking backwards and forwards in a Semicircle; but being fixed within four Inches of the Gate, allowed me to creep in, and lie at my full Length in the Temple.

"Whereupon I rose up." C. E. Brock, 1894.
Courtesy, Library of Congress.

The Emperor of Lilliput, attended by several of the Nobility, comes to see the Author in his confinement. The Emperor's person and habit described. Learned men appointed to teach the Author their language. He gains favour by his mild disposition. His pockets are searched, and his Sword and Pistols taken from him.

HEN I found myself on my Feet, I looked about me, and must confess I never beheld a more entertaining Prospect. The Country round appeared like a continued Garden; and the inclosed Fields, which were generally Forty Foot square, resembled so many Beds of Flowers. These Fields were intermingled with Woods of half a Stang, and the tallest Trees, as I could judge, appeared to be seven Foot high. I viewed the Town on my left Hand, which looked like the painted Scene of a City in a Theatre.

I had been for some Hours extremely pressed by the Necessities of Nature; which was no Wonder, it being almost two Days since I had last disburthened myself. I was under great Difficulties between Urgency and Shame. The best Expedient I could think on, was to creep into my House, which I accordingly did; and shutting the Gate after me, I went as far as the Length of my Chain would suffer; and discharged my Body of that uneasy Load. But this was the only Time I was ever guilty of so uncleanly an Action; for which I cannot but hope the candid Reader will give some Allowance, after he hath maturely and impartially considered my Case, and the Distress I was in. From this Time my constant Practice was, as soon as I rose, to perform that Business in open Air, at the full

1

2

1 *half a Stang.* A stang is an obsolete unit of area equal to about a quarter of an acre. Half a stang is, therefore, 1/8 of an acre, or 605 square yards. In Lilliputian terms this is equivalent to $1/8 \times 12 \times 12$, or 18 acres, which is respectable enough.

2 *appeared to be seven Foot high.* Gulliver is viewing a world in which *everything* has shrunk in equal proportions and only he himself is at a natural size. Under such circumstances, it would seem more logical to suppose that everything is as it always was and that he alone has expanded. This does not occur to Gulliver, nor should it to the reader.

3 *Princes of the Blood.* Since the prescientific notion was that hereditary characteristics were carried by the blood, the royal family could be referred to as "the Blood Royal" or simply "the Blood." The children and grandchildren of a monarch were therefore "Princes of the Blood."

4 *his Person; which I am now going to describe.* It is generally supposed from later references in the tale that the Emperor is a satiric representation of George I, who succeeded to the British throne in 1714 and was still king at the time *Gulliver's Travels* was published in 1726. (He died the year after, in 1727.) The physical description of the Emperor of Lilliput is altogether different from that of George I, however. That difference would help Swift maintain that no resemblance was intended—if the point was ever put to him by an officer of the law.

George I, before he became king, was the elector of the German state of Hanover. He was fifty-four years old when he came to the throne and was fat and ungainly. He could speak no English at all so that he had to communicate with his ministers in French (and was, in any case, interested only in Hanover and not at all in Great Britain). He brought with him two German mistresses, each as fat and as ungainly as he.

On the whole, George I was not a popular monarch, and Swift disliked him intensely because of his politics.

The two English parties of the time were the Tories, representing the landowners, who were High Church in religion and favored Catholic-like ritual and a restoration of the old Stuart line in the form of the son of James II, James Edward Stuart; and the Whigs, representing the commercial interests, who were Low Church in religion, favored Protestant-like ritual, and supported George I. The Tories were pro-French and anti-Dutch in foreign policy, and conservative and traditional in domestic policy. The Whigs were pro-Dutch and anti-French in foreign policy, and somewhat reformist in domestic policy.

In his younger days, Swift was a Whig, but he disapproved more and more of Whig religious policy, and was finally converted to the Tory party, which came to power in 1710. With all the zeal of the convert, Swift became the foremost of the Tory pamphleteers.

Extent of my Chain; and due Care was taken every Morning before Company came, that the offensive Matter should be carried off in Wheel-barrows, by two Servants appointed for that Purpose. I would not have dwelt so long upon a Circumstance, that perhaps at first Sight may appear not very momentous; if I had not thought it necessary to justify my Character in Point of Cleanliness to the World; which I am told, some of my Maligners have been pleased, upon this and other Occasions, to call in Question.

When this Adventure was at an End, I came back out of my House, having Occasion for fresh Air. The Emperor was already descended from the Tower, and advancing on Horseback towards me, which had like to have cost him dear; for the Beast, although very well trained, yet wholly unused to such a Sight, which appeared as if a Mountain moved before him, reared up on his hinder Feet: But that Prince, who is an excellent Horseman, kept his Seat, until his Attendants ran in, and held the Bridle, while his Majesty had Time to dismount. When he alighted, he surveyed me round with great Admiration, but kept beyond the Length of my Chains. He ordered his Cooks and Butlers, who were already prepared, to give me Victuals and Drink, which they pushed forward in a sort of Vehicles upon Wheels until I could reach them. I took these Vehicles, and soon emptied them all; twenty of them were filled with Meat, and ten with Liquor; each of the former afforded me two or three good Mouthfuls, and I emptied the Liquor of ten Vessels, which was contained in earthen Vials, into one Vehicle, drinking it off at a Draught; and so I did with the rest. The **3** Empress, and young Princes of the Blood, of both Sexes, attended by many Ladies, sate at some Distance in their Chairs; but upon the Accident that happened to the Emperor's Horse, they alighted, **4** and came near his Person; which I am now going to describe. He

The emperor of Lilliput. Herbert Cole. 1899.

King George I (1660–1727).
Courtesy, Library of Congress.

An audience with the emperor of Lilliput. Gavarni, 1850s. Courtesy, Library of Congress.

When George I became king, however, the Tory party was thrown over and the Whigs were restored to power for virtually all of George's reign. That was enough in itself for George to become a satiric target for Swift.

5 *taller . . . than any of his Court.* Height has always been admired by human beings, perhaps because through most of history, aristocrats, who are less likely to be half-starved during youth, were more likely to grow to something like their full potential. The upper classes tended, therefore, to be taller than the lower classes, and there was the feeling that the king should be tallest of all.

In the Greek myths, the tallness of the gods and goddesses is repeatedly emphasized, as is the tallness of the heroes, who are frequently described as a head taller than their followers.

In keeping with that custom, the Emperor of Lilliput is taller than his subjects by almost the breadth of a fingernail, which is the equivalent, in human terms, of five or six inches higher than his fellows. Gulliver, characteristically, finds that awe-inspiring.

6 *an Austrian Lip.* The Hapsburg family, which ruled Austria in Swift's time, and which had ruled Spain also until 1700, was characterized by thick underlips and jutting lower jaws. This was an inherited characteristic.

It was not beautiful and, in the case of Charles II, the last Hapsburg king of Spain, the "Austrian lip" was so pronounced and the lower jaw stuck out so far that he could not chew his food properly and it had to be cut into small pieces for him. Nevertheless, because the Hapsburgs reigned as Holy Roman Emperors, and had greater social standing than any other European monarchs, this physical distortion took on a kind of aristocratic distinction, so that the Emperor of Lilliput had it as an almost inevitable consequence of his being emperor.

is taller by almost the Breadth of my Nail, than any of his Court; **5** which alone is enough to strike an Awe into the Beholders. His Features are strong and masculine, with an *Austrian* Lip, and **6** arched Nose, his Complexion olive, his Countenance erect, his Body and Limbs well proportioned, all his Motions graceful, and his Deportment majestick. He was then past his Prime, being twenty- **7** eight Years and three Quarters old, of which he had reigned about seven, in great Felicity, and generally victorious. For the better Convenience of beholding him, I lay on my Side, so that my Face was parallel to his, and he stood but three Yards off: However, I have had him since many Times in my Hand, and therefore cannot be deceived in the Description. His Dress was very plain and simple, the Fashion of it between the *Asiatick* and the *European;* but he had on his Head a light Helmet of Gold, adorned with Jewels, and a Plume on the Crest. He held his Sword drawn in his Hand, to defend himself, if I should happen to break loose; it was almost three Inches long, the Hilt and Scabbard were Gold en-

Head of Philip II, with a Hapsburg lip.

7 *twenty-eight Years and three Quarters old.* In the real world, mammalian creatures generally have shorter lives the smaller they are. A mammal no larger than the Emperor of Lilliput would not be likely to live longer than a year and a half or so. We don't expect Swift to take such a matter into account, but later in the tale he does indicate that the Lilliputians age more rapidly than we do and says that their fifteen is equivalent to our twenty-one.

If that ratio is considered as holding rigidly (and there is no indication that Swift paid much attention to it), the Emperor was the equivalent of a little over forty years old on our scale and had ruled for the equivalent of just under ten years.

8 *by their Habits.* "Habit" is from a Latin word meaning "appearance" or "dress." It is applied to any habitual costume worn by a person because of his profession, a use that is still preserved in our phrase "nun's habit." The word can also be used to indicate some behavior that is as characteristic of you as your professional costume, and it is this meaning that is most frequently encountered these days.

The older meaning is the one used by Swift. Gulliver could tell the priests and lawyers by their costumes, not by their behavior. Notice that although Swift is realistic enough to give the Lilliputians a language of their own, he assumes the presence of priests and lawyers and even assumes that their costumes would be sufficiently English to allow Gulliver to recognize them.

9 *High and Low Dutch.* Swift uses "Dutch" here where we would say "German." High German is the language of the southern highlands of Germany, and Low German the language of the northern coast lands. Dutch is a form of Low German, which has become a language rather than a dialect since the Netherlands gained its independence of the Holy Roman Empire in 1648.

The English of Swift's time were better acquainted with the Dutch than with the Germans, and if you combine this with the fact that the Germans call themselves "*Deutsch*," you can see reason for confusing Dutch and German. In the United States, the descendants of German immigrants in south-central Pennsylvania are spoken of as Pennsylvania Dutch, a similar confusion.

10 *Lingua Franca.* In general, any jargon consisting of words (sometimes distorted) from several different languages, used between people with no common language. It springs up rather naturally as people try to make themselves understood and pick up some words from each other's language.

One modern lingua franca is "pidgin English," used in various places in the Pacific. The term "pidgin English" is itself a corruption of "business English," the language in which different peoples are forced to do their business.

The language Gulliver used was one that grew up in the Mediterranean, when Europeans and Muslims tried to trade, in a language mixture containing Italian, French, Spanish, and Arabic. (Lingua franca originally meant "Frankish language," since to the Muslims all west-Europeans were "Franks.")

riched with Diamonds. His Voice was shrill, but very clear and articulate, and I could distinctly hear it when I stood up. The Ladies and Courtiers were all most magnificently clad, so that the Spot they stood upon seemed to resemble a Petticoat spread on the Ground, embroidered with Figures of Gold and Silver. His Imperial Majesty spoke often to me, and I returned Answers, but neither of us could understand a Syllable. There were several of

8 his Priests and Lawyers present (as I conjectured by their Habits) who were commanded to address themselves to me, and I spoke to them in as many Languages as I had the least Smattering of, which

9 were *High* and *Low Dutch, Latin, French, Spanish, Italian,* and

10 *Lingua Franca;* but all to no purpose. After about two Hours the Court retired, and I was left with a strong Guard, to prevent the Impertinence, and probably the Malice of the Rabble, who were very impatient to crowd about me as near as they durst; and some of them had the Impudence to shoot their Arrows at me as I sate on the Ground by the Door of my House; whereof one very narrowly missed my left Eye. But the Colonel ordered six of the Ringleaders to be seized, and thought no Punishment so proper as to deliver them bound into my Hands, which some of his Soldiers accordingly did, pushing them forwards with the But-ends of their Pikes into my Reach: I took them all in my right Hand, put five of them into my Coat-pocket; and as to the sixth, I made a Countenance as if I would eat him alive. The poor Man squalled terribly, and the Colonel and his Officers were in much Pain, especially when they saw me take out my Penknife: But I soon put them out

"I made a Countenance as if I would eat him alive." Bouchot. 1855. Courtesy. The New York Public Library.

of Fear; for, looking mildly, and immediately cutting the Strings he was bound with, I set him gently on the Ground, and away he ran. I treated the rest in the same Manner, taking them one by one out of my Pocket; and I observed, both the Soldiers and People were highly obliged at this Mark of my Clemency, which was represented very much to my Advantage at Court.

Towards Night I got with some Difficulty into my House, where I lay on the Ground, and continued to do so about a Fortnight; during which time the Emperor gave Orders to have a Bed prepared for me. Six Hundred Beds of the common Measure were brought in Carriages, and worked up in my House; an Hundred and Fifty of their Beds sown together made up the Breadth and Length, and these were four double, which however kept me but very indifferently from the Hardness of the Floor, that was of smooth Stone. By the same Computation they provided me with Sheets, Blankets, and Coverlets, tolerable enough for one who had been so long enured to Hardships as I.

As the News of my Arrival spread through the Kingdom, it brought prodigious Numbers of rich, idle, and curious People to see me; so that the Villages were almost emptied, and great Neglect of Tillage and Household Affairs must have ensued, if his Imperial Majesty had not provided by several Proclamations and Orders of State against this Inconveniency. He directed that those, who had already beheld me, should return home, and not presume to come within fifty Yards of my House, without Licence from Court; whereby the Secretaries of State got considerable Fees.

In the mean time, the Emperor held frequent Councils to debate what Course should be taken with me; and I was afterwards assured by a particular Friend, a Person of great Quality, and who was as much in the *Secret* as any; that the Court was under many Difficulties concerning me. They apprehended my breaking loose; that my Diet would be very expensive, and might cause a Famine. Sometimes they determined to starve me, or at least to shoot me in the Face and Hands with poisoned Arrows, which would soon dispatch me: But again they considered, that the Stench of so large a Carcase might produce a Plague in the Metropolis, and probably spread through the whole Kingdom. In the midst of these Consultations, several Officers of the Army went to the Door of the great Council-Chamber; and two of them being admitted, gave an Account of my Behavior to the six Criminals above-mentioned; which made so favourable an Impression in the Breast of his Majesty, and the whole Board, in my Behalf, that an Imperial Commission was issued out, obliging all the Villages nine hundred Yards round the City, to deliver in every Morning six Beeves, forty Sheep, and other Victuals for my Sustenance; together with a proportionable Quantity of Bread and Wine, and other Liquors: For the due Payment of which his Majesty gave Assignments upon his Treasury. For this Prince lives chiefly upon his own Demesnes; seldom, except upon great Occasions raising any Subsidies upon his Subjects, who are bound to attend him in his Wars at their own Expence. An Establishment was also made of Six Hundred Persons to be my Domesticks, who had Board-Wages allowed for their Maintenance, and Tents built for them very conveniently on each side of my Door. It was likewise ordered, that three hundred Taylors should make me a Suit of Cloaths after

11 *kept me but very indifferently from the Hardness of the Floor.* Gulliver's bed should, in area, be twelve by twelve—144 times—that of a Lilliputian bed. The use of 150 beds is fine, therefore. The thickness, however, should be 12 times that of a Lilliputian bed. The use of only four thicknesses, as Gulliver complains, is far from enough.

12 *a Person of great Quality.* Gulliver means a nobleman. Gulliver is always very proud of any attention paid him by his social superiors, even when they are only six inches tall.

13 *in the Secret.* Involved in the secret conferences of state.

14 *Beeves.* Full-grown cattle, fattened for food. The flora and fauna of Lilliput, please notice, are, except for the difference in size, precisely that of England.

15 *Demesnes.* An archaic form of "domains" or "dominions." The Emperor's demesne is that portion of the kingdom over which he is the direct lord (or *dominus*, in Latin) and which he can tax directly. Other portions of the land were the estates of subject lords who alone could tax them, but who were compelled to make payments to the king in money or in services upon demand.

16 *Lumos Kelmin pesso desmar lon Emposo.* It is hard to make up a language that has no grounding whatever in one's own. Clearly *pesso* is "peace" and *Emposo* is "Empire." While there are such coincidences in entirely unrelated languages, two of them in a short sentence is rather more than is likely.

17 *searched by two of his Officers.* It is often said that this passage is a satire on the way in which the Whig government of George I investigated the actions of Henry St. John, Viscount Bolingbroke; and Robert Harley, earl of Oxford.

Bolingbroke and Oxford were Tories who, toward the end of the reign of Anne, negotiated a secret deal with France that led to the Treaty of Utrecht in 1713. This was advantageous to England, but let France off the hook rather lightly—a clear betrayal of England's allies in the Netherlands and Germany.

When the Whigs gained power on the accession of George I in 1714, Bolingbroke and Oxford found their political careers finished. Both were regarded as traitors by the Whigs and were investigated in detail.

Swift, as a loyal Tory, and as a personal friend of both Bolingbroke and Oxford, might, conceivably, have been satirizing their investigation in his descrip-

Henry St. John, Viscount Bolingbroke (1678–1751).
Courtesy, Library of Congress.

the Fashion of the Country: That, six of his Majesty's greatest Scholars should be employed to instruct me in their Language: And, lastly, that the Emperor's Horses, and those of the Nobility, and Troops of Guards, should be exercised in my Sight, to accustom themselves to me. All these Orders were duly put in Execution; and in about three Weeks I made a great Progress in Learning their Language; during which Time, the Emperor frequently honoured me with his Visits, and was pleased to assist my Masters in teaching me. We began already to converse together in some Sort; and the first Words I learnt, were to express my Desire, that he would please to give me my Liberty; which I every Day repeated on my Knees. His Answer, as I could apprehend, was, that this must be a Work of Time, not to be thought on without the Advice of his Council; and that first I must *Lumos Kelmin pesso desmar lon Emposo*; that is, *Swear a Peace with him and his Kingdom.* However, that I should be used with all Kindness; and he advised me to acquire by my Patience and discreet Behavior, the good Opinion of himself and his Subjects. He desired I would not take it ill, if he gave Orders to certain proper Officers to search me; for probably I might carry about me several Weapons, which must needs be dangerous Things, if they answered the Bulk of so prodigious a Person. I said, his Majesty should be satisfied, for I was ready to strip my self, and turn up my Pockets before him. This I delivered, part in Words, and part in Signs. He replied, that by the Laws of the Kingdom, I must be searched by two of his Officers: That he knew this could not be done without my Consent and Assistance; that he had so good an Opinion of my Generosity and Justice, as to trust their Persons in my Hands: That whatever they took from me should be returned when I left the Country, or paid for at the Rate which I would set upon them. I took up the two Officers in my Hands, put them first into my Coat-Pockets, and then into every other Pocket about me, except my two Fobs, and another secret Pocket which I had no Mind should be searched, wherein I had some little Necessaries of no Consequence to any but my self. In one of my Fobs there was a Silver Watch, and in the other a small Quantity of Gold in a Purse. These Gentlemen, having Pen, Ink, and Paper about them, made an exact Inventory of every thing they saw; and when they had done, desired I would set them down, that they might deliver it to the Emperor. This Inventory I afterwards translated into *English*, and is Word for Word as follows.

18 Imprimis, In the right Coat-Pocket of the *Great Man Mountain* (for so I interpret the Words *Quinbus Flestrin*) after the strictest

19 Search, we found only one great Piece of coarse Cloth, large enough to be a Foot-Cloth for your Majesty's chief Room of State. In the left Pocket, we saw a hugh Silver Chest, with a Cover of the same Metal, which we, the Searchers, were not able to lift. We desired it should be opened; and one of us stepping into it, found

20 himself up to the mid Leg in a sort of Dust, some part whereof flying up to our Faces, set us both a sneezing for several Times together. In his right Waistcoat-Pocket, we found a prodigious Bundle of white thin Substances, folded one over another, about the Bigness of three Men, tied with a strong Cable and marked with black Figures; which we humbly conceive to be Writings; every Letter almost half as large as the Palm of our Hands. In

*Robert Harley, earl of Oxford
(1661–1724).
Courtesy, Library of Congress.*

tion of the Lilliputian search of Gulliver, and making fun of Whig suspicions by way of his straight-faced, detailed descriptions of the harmless items discovered by the Lilliputians. But the logic of this analogy breaks down. After all, the Lilliputian desire to search Gulliver is only natural and is not activated out of malicious suspicion. What would *we* do if a comparable monster were in our power and if we were concerned about his intentions?

18 *Imprimis.* Latin for "in the first place" or "to begin with."

19 *one great Piece of coarse Cloth.* In other words, a handkerchief.

20 *a sort of Dust.* Snuff, the taking of which is a habit that, mercifully, has gone out of favor.

21 *hollow Pillar of Iron.* A pistol, as we soon find out.

"*These Gentlemen . . . made an exact Inventory of every thing they saw.*"
T. Morten, 1865. Courtesy, Library of Congress.

the left there was a sort of Engine, from the Back of which were extended twenty long Poles, resembling the Pallisado's before your Majesty's Court; wherewith we conjecture the *Man Mountain* combs his Head; for we did not always trouble him with Questions, because we found it a great Difficulty to make him understand us. In the large Pocket on the right Side of his middle Cover, (so I translate the Word *Ranfu-Lo,* by which they meant my Breeches) we saw a hollow Pillar of Iron, about the Length of a Man, fastened to a strong Piece of Timber, larger than the Pillar; and upon one side of the Pillar were huge Pieces of Iron sticking out, cut into strange Figures; which we know not what to make of. In the left Pocket, another Engine of the same kind. In the smaller Pocket on the right Side, were several round flat Pieces of white and red Metal, of different Bulk: Some of the white, which seemed to be Silver, were so large and heavy, that my Comrade and I could hardly lift them. In the left Pocket were two black Pillars

21

22 *Engines.* See Chapter 1, note 42.

23 *transparent Metal.* Not only do the Lilliputians lack gunpowder, they also have no knowledge of glass. This is plausible, for ever since the beginning of the Age of Exploration, three centuries before Swift's time, Europeans had been encountering peoples who were amazed at the products of European technology.

24 *he seldom did any Thing without consulting it.* A joke at the time-bound nature of modern civilization.

25 *Globes or Balls of a most ponderous Metal.* Bullets.

26 *black Grains.* Gunpowder.

27 *the fourth Day of the eighty ninth Moon.* The earliest calendars were lunar, and men counted the number of new moons (months) before they counted the cycle of seasons (years). The lunar month is roughly 29 1/2 days long and earlier Gulliver said the monarch had reigned "about seven years." Eighty-eight months plus four days is just 2,600 days, which is equal to 7 1/8 years. In these little things, Swift is always particularly careful to maintain consistency.

28 *Scymiter.* More usually spelled scimitar. A sword is a straight weapon, suitable for thrusting; a scimitar is curved, with the convex outer edge sharpened, suitable for slashing.

irregularly shaped: we could not, without Difficulty, reach the Top of them as we stood at the Bottom of his Pocket: One of them was covered, and seemed all of a Piece; but at the upper End of the other, there appeared a white round Substance, about twice the bigness of our Heads. Within each of these was inclosed a prodigious Plate of Steel; which, by our Orders, we obliged him to shew us, because we apprehended they might be dangerous Engines. He took them out of their Cases, and told us, that in his own Country his Practice was to shave his Beard with one of these, and to cut his Meat with the other. There were two Pockets which we could not enter: These he called his Fobs; they were two large Slits cut into the Top of his middle Cover, but squeezed close by the Pressure of his Belly. Out of the right Fob hung a great Silver Chain, with a wonderful kind of Engine at the Bottom. We directed him to draw out whatever was at the End of that Chain; which appeared to be a Globe, half Silver, and half of some transparent Metal: For on the transparent Side we saw certain strange Figures circularly drawn, and thought we could touch them, until we found our Fingers stopped with that lucid Substance. He put this Engine to our Ears, which made an incessant Noise like that of a Water-Mill. And we conjecture it is either some unknown Animal, or the God that he worships: But we are more inclined to the latter Opinion, because he assured us (if we understood him right, for he expressed himself very imperfectly) that he seldom did any Thing without consulting it. He called it his Oracle, and said it pointed out the Time for every Action of his Life. From the left Fob he took out a Net almost large enough for a Fisherman, but contrived to open and shut like a Purse, and served him for the same Use: We found therein several massy Pieces of yellow Metal, which if they be of real Gold, must be of immense Value.

Having thus, in Obedience to your Majesty's Commands, diligently searched all his Pockets; we observed a Girdle about his Waist made of the Hyde of some prodigious Animal; from which, on the left Side, hung a Sword of the Length of five Men; and on the right, a Bag or Pouch divided into two Cells; each Cell capable of holding three of your Majesty's Subjects. In one of these Cells were several Globes or Balls of a most ponderous Metal, about the Bigness of our Heads, and required a strong Hand to lift them: The other Cell contained a Heap of certain black Grains, but of no great Bulk or Weight, for we could hold about fifty of them in the Palms of our Hands.

This is an exact Inventory of what we found about the Body of the *Man Mountain;* who used us with great Civility, and due Respect to your Majesty's Commission. Signed and Sealed on the fourth Day of the eighty ninth Moon of your Majesty's auspicious Reign.

Clefren Frelock, Marsi Frelock.

When this Inventory was read over to the Emperor, he directed me to deliver up the several Particulars. He first called for my Scymiter, which I took out, Scabbard and all. In the mean time he ordered three thousand of his choicest Troops, who then attended him, to surround me at a Distance with their Bows and Arrows just ready to discharge: But I did not observe it; for my Eyes were wholly fixed upon his Majesty. He then desired me to draw my Scymiter, which, although it had got some Rust by the Sea-Water, was in most Parts exceeding bright. I did so, and immediately all the Troops gave a Shout between Terror and Surprize; for the Sun shone clear, and the Reflexion dazzled their Eyes, as I waved the Scymiter to and fro in my Hand. His Majesty, who is a most magnanimous Prince, was less daunted than I could expect; he ordered me to return it into the Scabbard, and cast it on the Ground as gently as I could, about six Foot from the End of my Chain. The next Thing he demanded was one of the hollow Iron Pillars, by which he meant my Pocket-Pistols. I drew it out, and at his Desire, as well as I could, expressed to him the Use of it, and charging it only with Powder, which by the Closeness of my Pouch, happened to escape wetting in the Sea, (an Inconvenience that all prudent Mariners take special Care to provide against) I first cautioned the Emperor not to be afraid; and then I let it off in the Air. The Astonishment here was much greater than at the Sight of my Scymiter. Hundreds fell down as if they had been struck dead; and even the Emperor, although he stood his Ground, could not recover himself in some time. I delivered up both my Pistols in the same Manner as I had done my Scymiter, and then my Pouch of Powder and Bullets; begging him that the former might be kept from Fire; for it would kindle with the smallest Spark, and blow up his Imperial Palace into the Air. I likewise delivered up my Watch, which the Emperor was very curious to see; and commanded two of his tallest Yeomen of the Guards to bear it on a Pole upon their Shoulders, as Dray-men in *England* do a Barrel of Ale. He was amazed at the continual Noise it made, and the Motion of the Minute-hand, which he could easily discern; for their Sight is much more acute than ours: He asked the Opinions of his learned Men about him, which were various and remote, as the Reader may well imagine without my repeating; although indeed I could not very perfectly understand them. I then gave up my Silver and Copper Money, my Purse with nine large Pieces of Gold, and some smaller ones; my Knife and Razor, my Comb and

29

"I let it off in the Air." J. J. Grandville, 1835. Courtesy, Library of Congress.

29 *which he could easily discern.* The motion of a minute hand would describe an arc that would be twelve times as long on the Lilliputian scale as on our own. The tip of the minute hand of a pocket watch two inches across would sweep across about 1/20 of an inch in a minute. On the Lilliputian scale this would be the equivalent of 3/5 of an inch in a minute, and would be easily noticeable.

"He asked the Opinions of his learned Men about him." T. Morten, 1865. Courtesy, Library of Congress.

30 *Pocket Perspective.* A small telescope, which would be of obvious use to a seaman.

Silver Snuff-Box, my Handkerchief and Journal Book. My Scymiter, Pistols, and Pouch, were conveyed in Carriages to his Majesty's Stores; but the rest of my Goods were returned me.

I had, as I before observed, one private Pocket which escaped their Search, wherein there was a Pair of Spectacles (which I **30** sometimes use for the Weakness of my Eyes) a Pocket Perspective, and several other little Conveniences; which being of no Consequence to the Emperor, I did not think my self bound in Honour to discover; and I apprehended they might be lost or spoiled if I ventured them out of my Possession.

Illustration by Herbert Cole, 1899.

CHAPTER THREE

The Author diverts the Emperor and his Nobility of both sexes, in a very uncommon manner. The diversions of the Court of Lilliput described. The Author hath his liberty granted him upon certain conditions.

Y Gentleness and good Behavior had gained so far on the Emperor and his Court, and indeed upon the Army and People in general, that I began to conceive Hopes of getting my Liberty in a short Time. I took all possible Methods to cultivate this favourable Disposition. The Natives came by Degrees to be less apprehensive of any Danger from me. I would sometimes lie down, and let five or six of them dance on my Hand. And at last the Boys and Girls would venture to come and play at Hide and Seek in my Hair. I had now made a good Progress in understanding and speaking their Language. The Emperor had a mind one Day to entertain me with several of the Country Shows; wherein they exceed all Nations I have known, both for Dexterity and Magnificence. I was diverted with none so much as that of the Rope-Dancers, performed upon a Slender white Thread, extended about two Foot, and twelve Inches from the Ground. Upon which, I shall desire Liberty, with the Reader's Patience, to enlarge a little.

This Diversion is only practised by those Persons, who are Candidates for great Employments, and high Favour, at Court. They are trained in this Art from their Youth, and are not always

1 *succeeds in the Office*. This is a double-barreled satire of considerable savagery. The implication is that qualifications for office are by no means related to intelligence, honor, industry, and virtue—but to the ability to please in trivial ways. (Naturally, this is meant as a comment on the England of Swift's time.)

Second, the ability to perform on the high wire is compared with the agility required to cut corners and shift sides in politics, maintaining one's footing with sure dexterity as the wind changes, and all without falling—from power, that is.

2 *Flimnap, the Treasurer*. Flimnap is generally supposed to represent Robert Walpole (1676–1745). He was a Whig, who served as secretary of War from 1708 to 1710, and then, briefly, as secretary of the Navy till the Whigs fell from power at the end of 1710.

Once the Tories were in power, they impeached Walpole for corruption, convicted him, and drove him out of power. It was Bolingbroke and Oxford who spearheaded this action, and Walpole did not forget them.

When George I became king and the Whigs returned to power, it was Walpole who headed the secret committee that investigated those two Tories and, in turn, drove them from power—permanently so, in their case, something for which Swift never forgave Walpole.

Since George I was unable to speak English and since he had no interest whatever in the internal affairs of the British kingdom, his ministers gained extraordinary independence of the royal power, something they have retained ever since. Walpole was therefore the first of the modern prime ministers of Great Britain.

Walpole was prime minister from 1715 to 1717 and then again from 1721 to 1742. He was thus prime minister at the time *Gulliver's Travels* was published.

Walpole remained in power by shrewd political maneuvering, which Swift bitterly alluded to in the statement that Flimnap could cut capers higher than any other official in the realm.

Posterity has been kinder to Walpole than Swift was. To be sure, Walpole is supposed to have stayed in power partly through the extensive use of bribery (he said of the members of Parliament: "All those men have their price"), but he used his power to keep Great Britain at peace, to improve her finance and trade, to establish a sensible colonial policy, and to form her present prime ministerial and parliamentary system.

3 *Summer-set*. Better known to us as "somersault."

4 *Trencher*. A wooden platter, of a sort once used as a crude dish. We still speak of a hearty eater as "a good trencherman."

5 *Packthread*. A thread or thin twine used to sew or bind packs or parcels.

6 *My Friend Reldresal*. Some have suggested that Reldresal is Charles, Viscount Townshend (1674–1738),

of noble Birth, or liberal Education. When a great Office is vacant, either by Death or Disgrace, (which often happens) five or six of those Candidates petition the Emperor to entertain his Majesty and the Court with a Dance on the Rope; and whoever jumps the highest without falling, **succeeds in the Office**. Very often the chief Ministers themselves are commanded to shew their Skill, and to convince the Emperor that they have not lost their Faculty. *Flimnap*, the Treasurer, is allowed to cut a Caper on the strait Rope, at least an Inch higher than any other Lord in the whole Empire. I have seen him do the **Summer-set** several times together, upon a **Trencher** fixed on the Rope, which is no thicker than a common **Packthread** in *England*. My Friend *Reldresal*, principal Secretary for private Affairs, is, in my Opinion, if I am not partial, the second after the Treasurer; the rest of the great Officers are much upon a Par.

These Diversions are often attended with fatal Accidents, whereof great Numbers are on Record. I my self have seen two or three Candidates break a Limb. But the Danger is much greater, when the Ministers themselves are commanded to shew their Dexterity: For, by contending to excel themselves and their Fellows, they strain so far, that there is hardly one of them who hath not received a Fall; and some of them two or three. I was assured, that a Year or two before my arrival, *Flimnap* would have infallibly broke his Neck, if one of the *King's Cushions*, that accidentally lay on the Ground, had not weakened the Force of his Fall.

There is likewise another Diversion, which is only shewn before the Emperor and Empress, and first Minister, upon particular Occasions. The Emperor lays on a Table three fine silken Threads of six Inches long. One is Blue, the other Red, and the third Green. These Threads are proposed as Prizes, for those Persons whom the Emperor hath a mind to distinguish by a peculiar Mark of his Favour. The Ceremony is performed in his Majesty's great Chamber of State; where the Candidates are to undergo a Tryal of Dexterity very different from the former; and such as I have not observed the least Resemblance of in any other Country of the old or the new World. The Emperor holds a Stick in his Hands, both Ends parallel to the Horizon, while the Candidates advancing one by one, sometimes leap over the Stick, sometimes creep under it backwards and forwards several times, according as the Stick is advanced or depressed. Sometimes the Emperor holds one End of the Stick, and his first Minister the other; sometimes the Minister has it entirely to himself. Whoever performs his Part with most Agility, and holds out the longest in *leaping* and *creeping*, is rewarded with the Blue-coloured Silk; the Red is given to the next, and the Green to the third, which they all wear girt twice round about the Middle; and you see few great Persons about this Court, who are not adorned with one of these Girdles.

The Horses of the Army, and those of the Royal Stables, having been daily led before me, were no longer shy, but would come up to my very Feet, without starting. The Riders would leap them over my Hand as I held it on the Ground; and one of the Emperor's Huntsmen, upon a large Courser, took my Foot, Shoe and all; which was indeed a prodigious Leap. I had the good Fortune to divert the Emperor one Day, after a very extraordinary Manner. I desired he would order several Sticks of two Foot high, and the

Diversions of the court of Lilliput. T. Morten, 1865. Courtesy, Library of Congress.

Jumping over the stick. Ad. Laluze, 1875.
Courtesy, Library of Congress.

brother-in-law of Walpole and, at the time *Gulliver's Travels* was published, second in importance in the government only to Walpole. Others have suggested James, earl of Stanhope (1673–1721), as a candidate. He was a leader of the Whig opposition in Parliament while the Tories were in power under Anne, and held high office when the Whigs came to power.

However, since Gulliver calls Reldresal "my Friend," the likeliest choice may be John Carteret, Earl Granville (1690–1763). He was secretary of state under Walpole from 1721 to 1724 and then became lord lieutenant of Ireland. He was lord lieutenant at the time *Gulliver's Travels* was published and, although a Whig official, became a friend of Swift's.

This uncertainty in the identification of Reldresal is the sort of thing that helped make *Gulliver's Travels* popular. The fictitious characters represented real people, and when it was first published, much of the fun lay in trying to guess who they were. Even the possible victims enjoyed the game.

7 *received a Fall.* Actually, although the tightrope is twelve feet high on the Lilliputian scale, any Lilliputian falling would not hurt himself. He would have only one foot of real distance in which to gain velocity and he would have a mass of but 1.4 ounces. The kinetic energy he would gain and, therefore, the damage he would sustain on striking the floor would be negligible. However, we are talking of a satirical fall.

8 *his Fall.* Walpole fell from power the first time in 1717 but is supposed to have cultivated the favor of the duchess of Kendall, one of the king's mistresses and, therefore, rather literally, "one of the King's cushions." It was with the assistance of the duchess and her influence on the king that Walpole regained the royal favor and his post as prime minister.

9 *Blue . . . Red . . . Green.* These are the colors, respectively, of the Order of the Garter, of the Bath, and of the Thistle. The Order of the Garter was founded by Edward III about 1346; the Order of the Bath was founded by Henry IV about 1410; the Order of the Thistle was founded by James II in 1687. These were all honorary societies to which people were appointed by the sovereign, presumably for their great deeds or for their services to king and country. These appointments were naturally much coveted and the king could win over politicians cheaply by promising these largely empty honors. Walpole was made a Knight of the Garter in May 1726, just half a year before *Gulliver's Travels* was published.

10 *leaping and creeping.* That is, excelling at unprincipled changes of belief and sycophantic currying of favor—in Britain. The awards are naturally given in the order of ancientness of the Orders (see previous note), and hence of the honor conferred.

11 *this Plain.* Swift is obviously eager to present the humorous spectacle of a cavalry engagement on a pocket handkerchief, but for once he lets his enthusiasm get the better of his usual mathematical preci-

Thickness of an ordinary Cane, to be brought me; whereupon his Majesty commanded the Master of his Woods to give Directions accordingly; and the next Morning six Wood-men arrived with as many Carriages, drawn by eight Horses to each. I took nine of these Sticks, and fixing them firmly in the Ground in a Quadrangular Figure, two Foot and a half square; I took four other Sticks, and tyed them parallel at each Corner, about two Foot from the Ground; and then I fastened my Handkerchief to the nine Sticks that stood erect; and extended it on all Sides, till it was as tight as the Top of a Drum; and the four parallel Sticks rising about five Inches higher than the Handkerchief, served as Ledges on each Side. When I had finished my Work, I desired the Emperor to let a Troop of his best Horse, Twenty-four in Number, **11** come and exercise upon this Plain. His Majesty approved of the Proposal, and I took them up one by one in my Hands, ready mounted and armed, with the proper Officers to exercise them. As soon as they got into Order, they divided into two Parties, performed mock Skirmishes, discharged blunt Arrows, drew their Swords, fled and pursued, attacked and retired; and in short discovered the best military Discipline I ever beheld. The parallel Sticks secured them and their Horses from falling over the Stage; and the Emperor was so much delighted, that he ordered this Entertainment to be repeated several Days; and once was pleased to be lifted up, and give the Word of Command; and, with great Difficulty, persuaded even the Empress her self to let me hold **12** her in her close Chair, within two Yards of the Stage, from whence she was able to take a full View of the whole Performance. It was my good Fortune that no ill Accident happened in these Entertainments; only once a fiery Horse that belonged to one of the Captains, pawing with his Hoof struck a Hole in my Handkerchief, and his Foot slipping, he overthrew his Rider and himself; but I immediately relieved them both: For covering the Hole with one Hand, I set down the Troop with the other, in the same Manner as I took them up. The Horse that fell was strained in the left Shoulder, but the Rider got no Hurt, and I repaired my Handkerchief as well as I could: However, I would not trust to the Strength of it any more in such dangerous Enterprizes.

About two or three Days before I was set at Liberty, as I was entertaining the Court with these Kinds of Feats, there arrived an Express to inform his Majesty, that some of his Subjects riding near the Place where I was first taken up, had seen a great black Substance lying on the Ground, very oddly shaped, extending its Edges round as wide as his Majesty's Bedchamber, and rising up in the Middle as high as a Man. That it was no living Creature, as they at first apprehended; for it lay on the Grass without Motion, and some of them had walked round it several Times: That by mounting upon each others' Shoulders, they had got to the Top, which was flat and even; and, stamping upon it, they found it was hollow within: That they humbly conceived it might be something belonging to the *Man-Mountain*; and if his Majesty pleased, they **13** would undertake to bring it with only five Horses. I presently knew what they meant; and was glad at Heart to receive this Intelligence. It seems, upon my first reaching the Shore, after our Shipwreck, I was in such Confusion, that before I came to the Place where I went to sleep, my Hat, which I had fastened with a

String to my Head while I was rowing, and had stuck on all the Time I was swimming, fell off after I came to Land; the String, as I conjecture, breaking by some Accident which I never observed, but thought my Hat had been lost at Sea. I intreated his Imperial Majesty to give Orders it might be brought to me as soon as possible, describing to him the Use and the Nature of it: And the next Day the Waggoners arrived with it, but not in a very good Condition; they had bored two Holes in the Brim, within an Inch and a half of the Edge, and fastened two Hooks in the Holes; these Hooks were tied by a long Cord to the Harness, and thus my Hat was dragged along for above half an *English* Mile: but the Ground in that country being extremely smooth and level, it received less **14** Damage than I expected.

Two Days after this Adventure, the Emperor having ordered that Part of his Army, which quarters in and about his Metropolis, to be in a Readiness, took a fancy of diverting himself in a very singular Manner. He desired I would stand like a *Colossus*, with **15** my Legs as far asunder as I conveniently could. He then com-

The Lilliputian troops march under Gulliver. Le Febure, 1797.

sion. A Lilliputian horse would have to be a foot long or so, and if there were twenty-four of them performing military evolutions, Gulliver would have to have had the grand-daddy of all handkerchiefs.

12 *close Chair.* A sedan chair, an enclosed conveyance with windows, and with two poles at either end so that it could be carried by two sturdy footmen. In it, a woman of high rank could sit enclosed, able to look out but retain her privacy.

13 *presently.* In American usage, this means "after a little while," but even Gulliver didn't have that much trouble recognizing his hat. In British usage, "presently" means "at once."

14 *smooth and level.* Inanimate nature being of Lilliputian scale on the island, the natural unevennesses of the ground would have been to a scale of only 1/12 that of the normal world.

Robert Walpole (1676–1745) as the Colossus of Rhodes.

15 *Colossus.* The Greeks used a word of unknown origin, *kolossos* (Latin, *colossus*), for any statue that was larger than life. The most famous colossus of all time was the bronze statue of the sun-god, Helios, built on the Greek island of Rhodes by the sculptor, Chares. It stood over a hundred feet tall and was supposed to have taken twelve years to build (292–280 B.C.). It stood in the harbor of the city of Rhodes for only a little over half a century, and then an earthquake in 224 B.C. tumbled it. Its fragments remained where they fell till carted away in A.D. 653.

Known as the Colossus of Rhodes, it was included by the ancients in their list of the seven wonders of the world. In the Middle Ages, the tales of its one-time existence exaggerated the fact. It came to be believed that the statue was so large that it straddled the harbor, with one leg on each shore, and that ships sailing into the harbor passed between its legs. The statue couldn't have been that large, however. The Greeks didn't have the techniques for supporting the weight of so large a statue on two legs of proportionate thinness at such a straddling angle.

16 *Skyresh Bolgolam.* Supposed to represent Daniel Finch, earl of Nottingham (1647–1730), who was first lord of the Admiralty from 1681 to 1684 under Charles II, and who held high office in subsequent reigns. Although a Tory, he frequently opposed the policies of Robert Harley, earl of Oxford, the Tory leader during Anne's reign, and this annoyed Swift. Nottingham was also so High Church as to be virtually Catholic, and that, too, bothered Swift, who wasn't *that* High Church and who was markedly anti-Catholic.

Skyresh Bolgolam. Herbert Cole, 1899.

17 *to hold my right Foot in my left Hand . . . my Thumb on the Tip of my right Ear.* This may be another poke at the Whigs. The Whigs had attacked the legality of the Treaty of Utrecht by saying it wasn't properly countersigned. Therefore, Gulliver is required to make the most difficult and ridiculous countersigning as though to say, "Well, that should satisfy the Whigs."

18 *most Mighty . . . Terror of the Universe.* The tiny Emperor goes through the usual sonority of names and titles and hyperbole just as though he were a normal-sized European monarch. The implication,

manded his General (who was an old experienced Leader, and a great Patron of mine) to draw up the Troops in close Order, and march them under me; the Foot by Twenty-four in a Breast, and the Horse by Sixteen, with Drums beating, Colours flying, and Pikes advanced. This Body consisted of three Thousand Foot, and a Thousand Horse. His Majesty gave Orders, upon Pain of Death, that every Soldier in his March should observe the strictest Decency, with regard to my Person; which, however, could not prevent some of the younger Officers from turning up their Eyes as they passed under me. And, to confess the Truth, my Breeches were at that Time in so ill a Condition, that they afforded some Opportunities for Laughter and Admiration.

I had sent so many Memorials and Petitions for my Liberty, that his Majesty at length mentioned the Matter first in the Cabinet, and then in a full Council; where it was opposed by none, except **16** *Skyresh Bolgolam,* who was pleased, without any Provocation, to be my mortal Enemy. But it was carried against him by the whole Board, and confirmed by the Emperor. That Minister was *Galbet,* or Admiral of the Realm; very much in his Master's Confidence, and a Person well versed in Affairs, but of a morose and sour Complection. However, he was at length persuaded to comply; but prevailed that the Articles and Conditions upon which I should be set free, and to which I must swear, should be drawn up by himself. These Articles were brought to me by *Skyresh Bolgolam* in Person, attended by two under Secretaries, and several Persons of Distinction. After they were read, I was demanded to swear to the Performance of them; first in the Manner of my own Country, and afterwards in the Method prescribed by their Laws; which **17** was to hold my right Foot in my left Hand, to place the middle Finger of my right Hand on the Crown of my Head, and my Thumb on the Tip of my right Ear. But, because the Reader may perhaps be curious to have some Idea of the Style and Manner of Expression peculiar to that People, as well as to know the Articles upon which I recovered my Liberty; I have made a Translation of the whole Instrument, Word for Word, as near as I was able; which I here offer to the Publick.

GOLBASTO MOMAREN EVLAME GURDILO SHEFIN MULLY ULLY GUE,

18
19 most Mighty Emperor of *Lilliput,* Delight and Terror of the Universe, whose Dominions extend five Thousand Blustrugs, (about twelve Miles in Circumference) to the Extremities of the Globe: Monarch of all Monarchs: Taller than the Sons of Men; whose Feet press down to the Center, and whose Head strikes against the Sun: At whose Nod the Princes of the Earth shake their Knees; pleasant as the Spring, comfortable as the Summer, fruitful as Autumn, dreadful as Winter. His most sublime Majesty proposeth to the *Man-Mountain,* lately arrived at our Celestial Dominions, the following Articles, which by a solemn Oath he shall be obliged to perform.

FIRST, The *Man-Mountain* shall not depart from our Dominions, without our Licence under our Great Seal.

SECONDLY, He shall not presume to come into our Metropolis, without our express Order; at which time, the Inhabitants shall have two Hours Warning, to keep within their Doors.

THIRDLY, The said *Man-Mountain* shall confine his Walks to our principal high Roads; and not offer to walk or lie down in a Meadow, or Field of Corn.

FOURTHLY, As he walks the said Roads, he shall take the utmost Care not to trample upon the Bodies of any of our loving Subjects, their Horses, or Carriages; nor take any of our said Subjects into his Hands, without their own Consent.

FIFTHLY, If an Express require extraordinary Dispatch; the *Man-Mountain* shall be obliged to carry in his Pocket the Messenger and Horse, a six Days Journey once in every Moon, and return the said Messenger back (if so required) safe to our Imperial Presence.

SIXTHLY, He shall be our Ally against our Enemies in the Island of *Blefuscu*, and do his utmost to destroy their Fleet, which is now preparing to invade Us. **20**

SEVENTHLY, That the said *Man-Mountain* shall, at his Times of Leisure, be aiding and assisting to our Workmen, in helping to raise certain great Stones, towards covering the Wall of the principal Park, and our other Royal Buildings.

EIGHTHLY, That the said *Man-Mountain* shall, in two Moons Time, deliver in an exact survey of the Circumference of our Dominions, by a Computation of his own Paces round the Coast.

LASTLY, That upon his solemn Oath to observe all the above Articles, the said *Man-Mountain* shall have a daily Allowance of Meat and Drink, sufficient for the Support of 1728 of our Subjects; with free Access to our Royal Person, and other Marks of our Favour. Given at our Palace at *Belfaborac* the Twelfth Day of the Ninety-first Moon of our Reign. **21** **22**

I swore and subscribed to these Articles with great Chearfulness and Content, although some of them were not so honourable as I could have wished; which proceeded wholly from the Malice of *Skyresh Bolgolam* the High Admiral: Whereupon my Chains were immediately unlocked, and I was at full Liberty: The Emperor himself, in Person, did me the Honour to be by at the whole Ceremony. I made my Acknowledgments, by prostrating myself at his Majesty's Feet: But he commanded me to rise; and after many gracious Expressions, which, to avoid the Censure of Vanity, I shall not repeat; he added, that he hoped I should prove a useful Servant, and well deserve all the Favours he had already conferred upon me, or might do for the future.

The Reader may please to observe, that in the last Article for the Recovery of my Liberty, the Emperor stipulates to allow me a Quantity of Meat and Drink, sufficient for the Support of 1728 *Lilliputians*. Some time after, asking a Friend at Court how they came to fix on that determinate Number; he told me, that his Majesty's Mathematicians, having taken the Height of my Body by the Help of a Quadrant, and finding it to exceed theirs in the Proportion of Twelve to One, they concluded from the Similarity of their Bodies, that mine must contain at least 1728 of theirs, and consequently would require as much Food as was necessary to support that Number of *Lilliputians*. By which, the Reader may conceive an Idea of the Ingenuity of that People, as well as the prudent and exact Oeconomy of so great a Prince. **23**

of course, is the reverse, that European monarchs were as petty and silly as the tiny Emperor.

This is the first place in the tale, proper, that Lilliput is mentioned by name. It is, of course, an invented name, but it has entered the English language. "Lilliputian" is now a perfectly respectable adjective meaning "tiny" or "minute."

I have not seen any comment on this, but it seems to me that "Lilliput" is an obvious distortion of, or perhaps baby talk for, "little bit."

19 *about twelve Miles in Circumference.* If that is the case, then the map of Lilliput, presented earlier in the chapter, is gravely distorted. If the size of Sumatra is as given, then an island with a circumference of 12 miles should be little more than a dot.

With a circumference of 12 miles, and assuming a more-or-less circular shape, the area of the island would be about 11.5 square miles, or just half the size of Manhattan. On the Lilliputian scale though, it would be the equivalent of 1,650 square miles, or twice the size of Swift's native Nottinghamshire.

20 *the Island of Blefuscu.* Although Blefuscu is shown on the same map on which Lilliput is shown, this is the first mention of the companion island in the actual tale. Whereas Lilliput represents England in the satire, Blefuscu represents France.

Lilliput and Blefuscu are, it would seem, in a state of war. This is not surprising, since England had just been at war with France. (In the course of the war, in 1707, England, Scotland, and Wales were united into the single nation of Great Britain.) This was only the latest in a series of wars that had been continuing for some six and a half centuries, since William of Normandy invaded and conquered England, and would, as far as any Englishman could tell in 1726, continue forever. The wars did, in fact, continue for another ninety years; then they came to what appears to be a final end in 1815.

21 *1728 of our Subjects.* Swift knows the volume of Gulliver is equal to $12 \times 12 \times 12$, or 1,728 times that of a Lilliputian, and he believes that the number of calories needed to sustain him would be calculated proportionately.

In this, he was wrong. Smaller mammals must eat considerably more in proportion to their mass than larger mammals do (see Chapter 1 in this part, note 25). It is very likely that the Lilliputians would eat something like twelve times as much as Gulliver would in proportion to their weight and would seem, to Gulliver, to be fearful gluttons.

22 *the Twelfth Day of the Ninety-first Moon.* Since Gulliver's pockets were searched, sixty-seven days have passed.

23 *Quadrant.* An instrument used in determining altitudes. There is a plumb line which determines the vertical, a graduated scale giving degrees and a sighting device. From the angle to the vertical, and from the distance of the object being surveyed, the height can be calculated by trigonometry.

1 *Mildendo, the Metropolis*. This is, presumably, the capital city of Lilliput. Capital is from the Latin word for "head" and metropolis is from the Greek words for "mother city." Both terms mean the most important city of a region, and usually the largest. Nowadays, though, the capital is generally the site of the government, regardless of its size, so that Washington is the capital of the United States and New York City the metropolis.

2 *five Hundred Foot long*. Mildendo, then, is a square that, in Lilliputian terms, is the equivalent of 6,000 feet long on each side and 1.3 square miles in area. This is a respectable size for an eighteenth-century town.

1

Mildendo, the Metropolis of Lilliput, described, together with the Emperor's Palace. A conversation between the Author and a principal Secretary, concerning the affairs of that Empire. The Author's offers to serve the Emperor in his Wars.

THE first Request I made after I had obtained my Liberty, was that I might have Licence to see *Mildendo*, the Metropolis; which the Emperor easily granted me, but with a special Charge to do no Hurt, either to the Inhabitants, or their Houses. The People had Notice by Proclamation of my Design to visit the Town. The Wall which encompassed it, is two Foot and an half high, and at least eleven Inches broad, so that a Coach and Horses may be driven very safely round it; and it is flanked with strong Towers at ten Foot Distance. I stept over the great *Western* Gate, and passed very gently, and sidelong through the two principal Streets, only in my short Waistcoat, for fear of damaging the Roofs and Eves of the Houses with the Skirts of my Coat. I walked with the utmost Circumspection, to avoid treading on any Stragglers, who might remain in the Streets, although the Orders were very strict, that all People should keep in their Houses, at their own Peril. The Garret Windows and Tops of Houses were so crowded with Spectators, that I thought in all my Travels I had not seen a more populous Place. The City is an exact Square, each Side of the Wall being five Hundred Foot long. The two great Streets which run cross and divide it into four Quarters, are five Foot wide. The Lanes and Alleys which I could not enter, but only viewed them as I passed, are from Twelve to Eighteen Inches. The Town is capable of holding five Hundred Thousand Souls. The Houses are from three to five Stories. The Shops and Markets well provided.

The Emperor's Palace is in the Center of the City, where the two great Streets meet. It is inclosed by a Wall of two Foot high, and Twenty Foot distant from the Buildings. I had his Majesty's Permission to step over this Wall; and the Space being so wide between that and the Palace, I could easily view it on every Side. The outward Court is a Square of Forty Foot, and includes two other Courts: In the inmost are the Royal Apartments, which I was very desirous to see, but found it extremely difficult; for the great Gates, from one Square into another, were but Eighteen Inches high, and seven Inches wide. Now the Buildings of the outer Court were at least five Foot high; and it was impossible for me to stride over them, without infinite Damage to the Pile, although the Walls were strongly built of hewn Stone, and four Inches thick. At the same time, the Emperor had a great Desire that I should see the Magnificence of his Palace: But this I was not able to do till three Days after, which I spent in cutting down with my Knife some of the largest Trees in the Royal Park, about an Hundred Yards distant from the City. Of these Trees I made two Stools, each about three Foot high, and strong enough to bear my Weight. The People having received Notice a second time, I went again through the City to the Palace, with my two Stools in my hands. When I came to the Side of the outer Court, I stood upon one Stool, and took the other in my Hand: This I lifted over the Roof, and gently set it down on the Space between the first and second Court, which was eight Foot wide. I then stept over the Buildings very conveniently from one Stool to the other, and drew up the first after me with a hooked Stick. By this Contrivance I got into the inmost Court; and lying down upon my Side, I applied my Face to the Windows of the middle Stories, which were left open on Purpose, and discovered the most splendid Apartments that can be imagined. There I saw the Empress, and the young Princes in their several Lodgings, with their chief Attendants about them. Her Imperial Majesty was pleased to smile very graciously upon me and gave me out of the Window her Hand to kiss.

But I shall not anticipate the Reader with farther Descriptions of this Kind, because I reserve them for a greater Work, which is **3** now almost ready for the Press; containing a general Description of this Empire, from its first Erection, through a long Series of Princes, with a particular Account of their Wars and Politicks, Laws, Learning, and Religion; their Plants and Animals, their peculiar Manners and Customs, with other Matters very curious and useful; my chief Design at present being only to relate such Events and Transactions as happened to the Publick, or to my self, during a Residence of about nine Months in that Empire.

One Morning, about a Fortnight after I had obtained my Liberty, *Reldresal,* Principal Secretary (as they style him) of private Affairs, came to my House, attended only by one Servant. He ordered his Coach to wait at a Distance, and desired I would give him an Hour's Audience; which I readily consented to, on Account of his Quality, and Personal Merits, as well as of the many good Offices he had done me during my Sollicitations at Court. I

"I walked with the utmost Circumspection." Willy Pogány, 1919.

3 *a greater Work . . . with other Matters very curious and useful.* It was customary for those who wrote travel books to include such information about the places they visited. Their model in this respect was the greatest of all (legitimate) travel books, the one by Marco Polo describing the Mongol Empire in the Far East. It may be that at the beginning of the writing of *Gulliver's Travels* Swift did plan a more detailed book on Lilliput, but as he went on to other places there seemed to be no point in further elaborating the first voyage.

"He . . . let me hold him in my Hand
during our Conversation." Willy
Pogány, 1919.

offered to lie down, that he might the more conveniently reach my
Ear; but he chose rather to let me hold him in my Hand during
our Conversation. He began with Compliments on my Liberty;
said, he might pretend to some Merit in it; but, however, added,
that if it had not been for the present Situation of things at Court,
perhaps I might not have obtained it so soon. For, *said he,* as
flourishing a Condition as we appear to be in to Foreigners, we
labour under two mighty Evils; a violent Faction at home, and the
Danger of an Invasion by a most potent Enemy from abroad. As
to the first, you are to understand, that for above seventy Moons
past, there have been two struggling Parties in this Empire, under
4 the names of *Tramecksan* and *Slamecksan,* from the high and low
Heels on their Shoes, by which they distinguish themselves.

5   It is alledged indeed, that the high Heels are most agreeable
to our ancient Constitution: But however this be, his Majesty hath
6 determined to make use of only low Heels in the Administration
of the Government, and all Offices in the Gift of the Crown; as you
cannot but observe; and particularly, that his Majesty's Imperial
Heels are lower at least by a *Drurr* than any of his Court; (*Drurr*
is a Measure about the fourteenth Part of an Inch.) The Animosities

Low heels in favor. Herbert Cole, 1899.

4 *high and low Heels.* The Tramecksans, or High-
Heels, are the Tories, and the Slamecksans are the
Whigs. The High and Low are in reference to the
fact that though both Tories and Whigs were Angli-
cans (Church of England), the Tories tended to be
High Church (more nearly Catholic) and the Whigs
Low Church (more nearly Protestant).

5 *high Heels are most agreeable to our ancient Constitution.* Prior to Henry VIII's break with the Papacy,
two centuries before *Gulliver's Travels* was written,
England was Catholic—very high-heel, indeed.
Without going quite that far back, the British government in the last years of Anne's reign was domi-
nated by the Tories.

6 *only low Heels in the Administration of the Government.* George I, with whom the Emperor of Lilliput
is now clearly identified, was a Whig. He had to be.
The Tories included many who favored the Old Pretender and who would have liked to see George off
the throne. You can't blame a man for siding with
his friends.

"A Hobble in his Gait." Herbert Cole, 1899.

between these two Parties run so high, that they will neither eat nor drink, nor talk with each other. We compute the *Tramecksan,* or High-Heels, to exceed us in Number; but the Power is wholly on our Side. We apprehend his Imperial Highness, the Heir to the Crown, to have some Tendency towards the High-Heels; at least we can plainly discover one of his Heels higher than the other; which gives him a Hobble in his Gait. Now, in the midst of these intestine Disquiets, we are threatened with an Invasion from the Island of *Blefuscu,* which is the other great Empire of the Universe, almost as large and powerful as this of his Majesty. For as to what we have heard you affirm, that there are other Kingdoms and States in the World, inhabited by human Creatures as large as your self, our Philosophers are in much Doubt; and would rather conjecture that you dropt from the Moon, or one of the Stars; because it is certain, that an hundred Mortals of your Bulk, would, in a short Time, destroy all the Fruits and Cattle of his Majesty's Dominions. Besides, our Histories of six Thousand Moons make no Mention of any other Regions, than the two great Empires of *Lilliput* and *Blefuscu.* Which two mighty Powers have, as I was going to tell you, been engaged in a most obstinate War for six and thirty Moons past. It began upon the following Occasion. It is allowed on all Hands, that the primitive Way of breaking Eggs before we eat them, was upon the larger End: But his present Majesty's Grand-father, while he was a Boy, going to eat an Egg, and breaking it according to the ancient Practice, happened to cut one of his Fingers. Whereupon the Emperor his Father, published an Edict, commanding all his Subjects, upon great Penalties, to break the smaller End of their Eggs.   The People so highly resented this Law, that our Histories tell us, there have been six Rebellions raised on that Account; wherein one Emperor lost his Life, and another his Crown. These civil Commotions were constantly fomented by the Monarchs of *Blefuscu;* and when they were quelled, the Exiles always fled for Refuge to that Empire. It is computed that eleven Thousand Persons have, at several

7
8
9

10

11

12

13

14

15

16
17
18
19

7 *the Power is wholly on our Side.* There was no such thing as popular elections in Great Britain in Swift's time. There were elections, but only a small fraction of the population could vote and most of them, voting with open ballots, had to vote as they were told to by those who were in control of the district. The numbers backing either party could only be guessed at, therefore, but Swift, a Tory, preferred to believe that even though the Whigs were in power, most Englishmen preferred the Tories.

8 *a Hobble in his Gait.* Once it is clear that a reigning monarch is approaching the end of his life, the heir to the throne is naturally wooed by the various parties and interests in a kingdom. George, Prince of Wales, was being so wooed at the time *Gulliver's Travels* was published, for George I was sixty-six years old, in bad health, and clearly near his end (he died the next year).

It frequently happens that the heir to the throne is in opposition to his father (there is actually a tradition to this effect in the English royal house), so that those politicians out of power are in particular favor with him. That would tend to make Prince George a Tory in his sympathies.

On the other hand, his wife, Caroline of Anspach, who was in full charge of the family brains, was a determined Whig, and that made Prince George a Whig in sympathies. The net result was that the prince wobbled between the two parties, wearing one high heel and one low one.

9 *the other great Empire of the Universe.* To the Lilliputians (and the Blefuscans), the two small islands made up the whole of the universe—a Swiftian thrust at provincialism in general.

10 *our Philosophers are in much Doubt.* The term "philosopher" in Swift's day meant much what "scientist" means in ours. The word "scientist" is actually a comparatively recent term and was not used in its present sense until more than a century after the time that *Gulliver's Travels* was published.

The Lilliputian scientists would reasonably be expected to assume that other nations were on the same scale as their own and that it was therefore impossible for many Gulliver-like beings to exist. All arguments, however rational, are no better than the assumptions on which they are based.

11 *Six Thousand Moons.* Less than five hundred years. That would mean that Lilliputian history began about 1240. This, as it happens, is a not entirely ridiculous assumption. The South Sea Islands were settled in the first millennium A.D., and Lilliput might have been settled a little later—except, of course, that there is no place from which the Lilliputians could have come.

(Swift might have argued that there was something about the air or soil of Lilliput that shrank everything that existed, grew or arrived on it; that the Lilliputians were ordinary in size when they arrived, and reached their present diminutive proportions over the course of six thousand moons, and that if Gulliver had remained there long enough he too

"He happened to cut one of his Fingers." Herbert Cole, 1899.

would have found himself beginning to shrink. However, Swift didn't do this and I must restrain the impulse to rewrite his book for him.)

Incidentally, the choice of six thousand moons (months) for the length of the Lilliputian version of history might conceivably have been deliberate. In Swift's time, Europeans accepted without question the biblical creation story and thought of it as having taken place in 4004 B.C.. This meant that the European version of history was nearly six thousand years long. This is again the twelve to one ratio.

12 *a most obstinate War for six and thirty Moons past.* Commentators generally suppose this to be a satirical reference to the War of the Spanish Succession (which the Whigs strongly supported and the Tories as strongly opposed), and it undoubtedly was. Nevertheless, at the time Gulliver left on his first voyage, in 1699, the war had not yet begun. It began in 1702. The earlier War of the Grand Alliance, between England and France, was already over. It had ended in 1697. The war between Lilliput and Blefuscu thus filled the interval between the two Anglo-French wars—but this in no way diminishes the effectiveness of the satire.

13 *the primitive Way of breaking Eggs . . . was upon the larger End.* The ritual of cracking an egg at the larger end is here allowed to represent Catholic ritual in general, which was accepted by all Englishmen virtually without question prior to the sixteenth century. Swift demonstrates his view of doctrinal disputes by substituting an argument over the least important issue he can invent.

14 *cut one of his Fingers.* The prince who cut his fingers is usually taken to be Henry VIII. Henry VIII was not, however, the grandfather of George I. He was the son of the great-great-great-great-great-

King Henry VIII (1491–1547). after Hans Holbein. National Portrait Gallery. London.

grandfather of George I. However, a satirist doesn't want to make his targets too obvious. (Some leeway must also be left for the argument that no comparison was intended.) By this reading, Henry VIII "cut his fingers" on Catholic doctrine when he sought a divorce from his queen and found that he could get one only through the Pope and that the Pope would not give him one.

15 *to break the smaller End of their Eggs.* This is generally taken to represent the Protestant view of Christianity. (The larger and smaller end of the eggs can also be taken to represent the High Church and Low Church wings of the Anglican church.) It was not Henry VIII's father but Henry VIII himself, who, to avoid further "cut fingers," rejected the Pope's authority, made himself head of the Church of England, and granted himself a divorce in 1533.

16 *one Emperor lost his Life.* There was indeed considerable Catholic unrest in England after Henry VIII established the Anglican church. There was, however, also Protestant unrest among those who thought that Henry VIII did not go far enough in disestablishing the Pope; that he ought also to root out Catholic religious practices.

Swift refers only to Catholic revolts, but it was the Protestant revolts that were the most far-reaching and the most effective. The Emperor who lost his life is a clear reference to Charles I, a High Church Anglican who was executed in 1649 by the Protestants.

17 *another his Crown.* The Emperor who lost his crown is a reference to James II, a Catholic, who was driven from the throne in 1688, mainly by the efforts of Low Church Anglicans.

18 *fomented by the Monarchs of Blefuscu.* Blefuscu, remember, represents France. During the sixteenth century, France was torn by eight religious wars between the majority Catholics and a stubborn minority of Protestants. It was the Catholics who won out in the end. In Swift's time Louis XIV, an ardent Catholic, was eager to see England turn Catholic, first of all, because that would suit his religious views, and second, because that would be a way of helping make Britain subservient to France. It was to his interest to strengthen the High Church branch of Anglicanism as much as possible and do his best to shift it ever more in the direction of Catholicism.

19 *fled for Refuge to that Empire.* Many of the defeated royalists in the civil war of the 1640s fled to France, including the wife and children of Charles I. When James II was driven off the throne, he, too, fled to France.

James II (1633–1701).
Courtesy, Library of Congress.

William III (1650–1702).
Courtesy, Library of Congress.

Mary II (1662–1694).
Courtesy, Library of Congress.

Illustration by Willy Pogány, 1919.

20 *incapable by Law of holding Employments.* In Swift's time, although Catholics weren't killed, they were forbidden to hold public office, and had many other difficulties placed in their way. (However, Protestants, who found even Low Church Anglicanism too Catholic, and who therefore eschewed Anglicanism altogether—they were called "Dissenters"—suffered under similar restrictions.)

21 *Alcoran.* The reference here is to the Koran, the Holy Book of Islam, a collection of the inspired sayings of Muhammad. It would have been more natural for Gulliver to compare the *Brundrecal* to the Bible, but this would undoubtedly have been placing the satire too close to its target for safety.

22 *left to every Man's Conscience.* This indirect suggestion that biblical injunctions are vague enough to be interpreted in opposite fashions by ingenious men, and that the interpretations are not worth fighting over, is a clear stroke for religious freedom—from which, however, Swift has Gulliver instantly back away.

23 *in the Power of the chief Magistrate to determine.* In Germany, there was, more or less, religious liberty—for the princes or heads of the many small German states. Each prince could choose his religion and would then expect all his subjects to worship accordingly. Gulliver apparently feels that, in the interest of civil peace, that degree of religious freedom may have to suffice.

24 *a bloody War . . . between the two Empires.* This sounds like a reference to the War of the Grand Alliance rather than to the War of the Spanish Succession. James II fled to France in December 1688. Louis XIV of France allowed him to set up a virtual government-in-exile and supported him in his invasion of Ireland (which came to naught). In May 1689, war between England and France broke out in consequence.

Times, suffered Death, rather than submit to break their Eggs at the smaller End. Many hundred large Volumes have been published upon this Controversy: But the Books of the *Big-Endians* have been long forbidden, and the whole Party rendred incapable by Law of holding Employments. During the Course of these Troubles, the Emperors of *Blefuscu* did frequently expostulate by their Ambassadors, accusing us of making a Schism in Religion, by offending against a fundamental Doctrine of our great Prophet *Lustrog,* in the fifty-fourth Chapter of the *Brundrecal,* (which is their *Alcoran.*) This, however, is thought to be a meer Strain upon the Text: For the Words are these; *That all true Believers shall break their Eggs at the convenient End:* and which is the convenient End, seems, in my humble Opinion, to be left to every Man's Conscience, or at least in the Power of the chief Magistrate to determine. Now the *Big-Endian* Exiles have found so much Credit in the Emperor of *Blefuscu's* Court; and so much private Assistance and Encouragement from their Party here at home, that a

20

21

22

23

24

The Big-Endian and Little-Endian controversy. Herbert Cole. 1899.

bloody War has been carried on between the two Empires for six and thirty Moons with various Success; during which Time we have lost Forty Capital Ships, and a much greater Number of smaller Vessels, together with thirty thousand of our best Seamen and Soldiers; and the Damage received by the Enemy is reckoned to be somewhat greater than ours. However, they have now equipped a numerous Fleet, and are just preparing to make a Descent upon us: And his Imperial Majesty, placing great Confidence in your Valour and Strength, hath commanded me to lay this Account of his Affairs before you.

I desired the Secretary to present my humble Duty to the Emperor, and to let him know, that I thought it would not become me, who was a Foreigner, to interfere with Parties; but I was ready, with the Hazard of my Life, to defend his Person and State against all Invaders.

25 *Forty Capital Ships . . . greater than ours.* The War of the League of Augsburg was indeed marked by important naval actions. Louis XIV had a good navy, thanks to the efforts of his capable minister, Colbert, and on June 30, 1690, the French fleet defeated the English fleet at Beachy Head. If Louis had been navy-minded he might have won control of the channel with incalculable consequences, but he thought only of land victories. He did not follow up the naval victory, gave the English and Dutch (who were then allied) a chance to rebuild their fleet, and on May 19, 1692, the Anglo-Dutch allies resoundingly defeated the French fleet at La Hogue. Louis's chance was gone.

The battle at La Hogue. Courtesy, Library of Congress.

26 *preparing to make a Descent upon us.* The Battle of La Hogue actually ended the danger of a French invasion, but England always dreaded the possibility of another enemy invasion; it was a besetting nightmare. For that matter, though no enemy had invaded and conquered England, several English monarchs were overthrown by invasions of English contenders for the throne who received French assistance: Richard II, Henry VI, Edward IV, Richard III, were overthrown (temporarily, in Edward's case) in this manner.

CHAPTER FIVE

1 *situated to the North North-East Side of Lilliput.*
France is located to the south-southeast of England.
Swift is careful to make the analogy between Ble-
fuscu and France deviate in unimportant ways.

2 *eight Hundred Yards wide.* On the Lilliputian scale
this is the equivalent of five and a half miles wide.
The English Channel, separating England and
France, is at its narrowest about twenty miles wide.
  Although it is nowhere specifically stated, one must
assume that the channel between Lilliput and Blefuscu shares in the general diminution of everything.
It is not only unusually narrow and unusually shallow, but we must assume that it is unusually calm,
with waves of only 1/12 the height of ordinary waves
and winds of only 1/12 the velocity of ordinary
winds. The cockleshells of the Blefuscan navy could
scarcely have navigated ordinary wind and waves of
the sea.

*The Author by an extraordinary strata-
gem prevents an invasion. A high Title
of Honour is conferred upon him. Ambassadors arrive from the Emperor of
Blefuscu, and sue for Peace. The Empress's Apartment on fire by an accident; the Author instrumental in saving the rest of the Palace.*

HE Empire of *Blefuscu,* is an Island situated to the North North-
East Side of *Lilliput,* from whence
it is parted only by a Channel of
eight Hundred Yards wide. I had
not yet seen it, and upon this
Notice of an intended Invasion, I avoided appearing on that Side
of the Coast, for fear of being discovered by some of the Enemies
Ships, who had received no Intelligence of me; all intercourse between the two Empires having been strictly forbidden during the
War, upon Pain of Death; and an Embargo laid by our Emperor
upon all Vessels whatsoever. I communicated to his Majesty a
Project I had formed of seizing the Enemies whole Fleet; which
as our Scouts assured us, lay at Anchor in the Harbour ready to
sail with the first fair Wind. I consulted the most experienced Seamen, upon the Depth of the Channel, which they had often
plummed; who told me, that in the Middle at high Water it was
seventy *Glumgluffs* deep, which is about six Foot of *European*
Measure; and the rest of it fifty *Glumgluffs* at most. I walked to
the North-East Coast over against *Blefuscu;* where, lying down behind a Hillock, I took out my small Pocket Perspective Glass, and

viewed the Enemy's Fleet at Anchor, consisting of about fifty Men
of War, and a great Number of Transports: I then came back to
my House, and gave Order (for which I had a Warrant) for a
great Quantity of the strongest Cable and Bars of Iron. The Cable
was about as thick as Packthread, and the Bars of the Length and
Size of a Knitting-Needle. I trebled the Cable to make it stronger;
and for the same Reason I twisted three of the Iron Bars together,
binding the Extremities into a Hook. Having thus fixed fifty Hooks
to as many Cables, I went back to the North-East Coast, and putting
off my Coat, Shoes, and Stockings, walked into the Sea in my
Leathern Jerken, about half an Hour before high Water. I waded
with what Haste I could, and swam in the Middle about thirty
Yards until I felt the Ground; I arrived at the Fleet in less than
half an Hour. The Enemy was so frighted when they saw me, that
they leaped out of their Ships, and swam to Shore; where there
could not be fewer than thirty thousand Souls. I then took my
Tackling, and fastning a Hook to the Hole at the Prow of each, I
tyed all the Cords together at the End. While I was thus employed,

"I waded with what Haste I could." Bofa, 1929.

3 *Imagination.* Today the word implies a fictional or fanciful idea, but Swift uses it simply as a synonym for "idea."

Illustration by Rex Whistler, 1930.

"I took up the knotted End of the Cables." T. Morten, 1865. Courtesy, Library of Congress.

the Enemy discharged several Thousand Arrows, many of which stuck in my Hands and Face; and besides the excessive Smart, gave me much Disturbance in my Work. My greatest Apprehension was for my Eyes, which I should have infallibly lost, if I had not suddenly thought of an Expedient. I kept, among other little Necessaries, a Pair of Spectacles in a private Pocket, which, as I observed before, had escaped the Emperor's Searchers. These I took out, and fastened as strongly as I could upon my Nose; and thus armed went on boldly with my Work in spight of the Enemy's Arrows; many of which struck against the Glasses of my Spectacles, but without any other Effect, further than a little to discompose them. I had now fastened all the Hooks, and taking the Knot in my Hand, began to pull; but not a Ship would stir, for they were all too fast held by their Anchors; so that the boldest Part of my Enterprize remained. I therefore let go the Cord, and leaving the Hooks fixed to the Ships, I resolutely cut with my Knife the Cables that fastened the Anchors; receiving above two hundred Shots in my Face and Hands: Then I took up the knotted End of the Cables to which my Hooks were tyed; and with great Ease drew fifty of the Enemy's largest Men of War after me.

3 The *Blefuscudians*, who had not the least Imagination of what I intended, were at first confounded with Astonishment. They had seen me cut the Cables, and thought my Design was only to let the Ships run a-drift, or fall foul on each other: But when they perceived the whole Fleet moving in Order, and saw me pulling at the End; they set up such a Scream of Grief and Dispair, that it is almost impossible to describe or conceive. When I had got out of Danger, I stopt a while to pick out the Arrows that stuck in my Hands and Face, and rubbed on some of the same Ointment that was given me at my first Arrival, as I have formerly mentioned. I then took off my Spectacles, and waiting about an Hour until the Tyde was a little fallen, I waded through the Middle with my Cargo, and arrived safe at the Royal Port of *Lilliput.*

The Emperor and his whole Court stood on the Shore, expecting the Issue of this great Adventure. They saw the Ships move forward in a large Half-Moon, but could not discern me, who was up to my Breast in Water. When I advanced to the Middle of the Channel, they were yet more in Pain because I was under Water to my Neck. The Emperor concluded me to be drowned, and that the Enemy's Fleet was approaching in a hostile Manner: But he was soon eased of his Fears; for the Channel growing shallower every Step I made, I came in a short Time within Hearing; and holding up the End of the Cable by which the Fleet was fastened, I cryed in a loud Voice, *Long live the most puissant Emperor of Lilliput!* This great Prince received me at my Landing with all possible Encomiums, and created me a *Nardac* upon the Spot, which is the highest Title of Honour among them. **4** **5**

His Majesty desired I would take some other Opportunity of bringing all the rest of his Enemy's Ships into his Ports. And so unmeasurable is the Ambition of Princes, that he seemed to think

4 *Long live the most puissant Emperor of Lilliput!* Gulliver's victory was by means of a naval maneuver, and this reflects the Tory attitude during the War of the Spanish Succession. The Tories had supported naval action by Great Britain as being less expensive and less dangerous than land action. What's more, during the war, the British navy had won a number of engagements in the Mediterranean, had captured Gibraltar (which Great Britain was to continue to hold down to the present day), and had reduced the Spanish and French navies to helplessness. It was the Tories' view that this was the decisive blow that had won the war and that nothing more was needed to insure British domination over Europe and the world.

5 *created me a Nardac.* Gulliver is terribly impressed with being created a "Nardac" and is rather endearingly vain over it, something which suits his character and his ability to accept the Lilliputians at their own evaluation. There may, however, be a hidden sarcastic thrust here.

In addition to the naval victories Great Britain had won in the War of the Spanish Succession, there were land victories as well. These were the result of the feats of John Churchill, who had been made earl of Marlborough by a grateful William III, since Churchill had helped him to the throne in the place of the exiled James II.

John Churchill, duke of Marlborough.
Courtesy, Library of Congress.

"The Emperor and his whole Court stood on the Shore." Ad. Laluze, 1875.
Courtesy, Library of Congress.

In the first ten years of the eighteenth century, Marlborough fought ten campaigns against Louis XIV and, despite the foot-dragging of the Dutch and the uncertainties of the British government, he won four great victories at Blenheim (1704), Ramillies (1706), Oudenarde (1708), and Malplaquet (1709) without once being defeated.

After the very first of his campaigns, he was made the first duke of Marlborough, "duke" being the highest title any Englishman not of the royal family could receive.

The Tories, however, were not impressed by these victories. The victories were bloody and, however spectacular, not decisive, since Louis XIV was not driven to surrender by them. To the Tories, Marlborough was just seeking personal glory, along with a great deal of political power and private profit, which he accrued as a result of his position.

While "Nardac" is simply a made-up word, and Swift may have just pulled it out of the air, "-dac" is very much like "duke" and "Nar-" is very much like the German word *Narr* for "fool." Was Swift trying to imply that the British were fools for thinking Marlborough was worth a dukedom?

6 *reducing the whole Empire of Blefuscu into a Province.* In the last years of the War of the Spanish Succession, the Whigs were the "war party" intent on trying to inflict still more military defeats on Louis XIV, and forcing utter capitulation upon him. The more ardent dreamers among them might well have had visions of a Protestant France in the role of British puppet (much as Louis XIV had almost converted England into a French puppet under Charles II and James II.)

The Emperor (who represents the Whigs, generally, as well as George I particularly) is thus anxious for a total victory.

The Tories, on the other hand were the "peace party," and wanted a compromise peace with France, feeling that British naval victories were sufficient. They carried this through in the Treaty of Utrecht, signed on April 11, 1713. Gulliver, with his statement later in the paragraph that "I would never be an Instrument of bringing a free and brave People into Slavery," represents the Tories.

7 *Of so little Weight are the greatest Services to Princes.* Gulliver's falling into disfavor with the Emperor of Lilliput because of his desire for a compromise peace that would preserve Blefuscan independence, is a clear analogy to the manner in which Oxford and Bolingbroke, the architects of the Treaty of Utrecht, fell into disfavor with the new monarch, George I, and were driven from public life.

However, such things cut two ways. Swift was probably concentrating on the ingratitude to which his Tory friends were subjected in 1714. Three years earlier, when the Tories were in power, they had displayed a similar degree of ingratitude toward Marlborough who, after all, was the most successful British general in the four centuries between Henry V and the duke of Wellington. He was not only relieved of his command in 1711, but he was tried and convicted on the charge of having misused public funds.

6 of nothing less than reducing the whole Empire of *Blefuscu* into a Province, and governing it by a Viceroy; of destroying the *Big-Endian* Exiles, and compelling that People to break the smaller End of their Eggs; by which he would remain sole Monarch of the whole World. But I endeavored to divert him from this Design, by many Arguments drawn from the Topicks of Policy as well as Justice: And I plainly protested, that I would never be an Instrument of bringing a free and brave People into Slavery: And when the Matter was debated in Council, the wisest Part of the Ministry were of my Opinion.

This open bold Declaration of mine was so opposite to the Schemes and Politicks of his Imperial Majesty, that he could never forgive me: He mentioned it in a very artful Manner at Council, where I was told, that some of the wisest appeared, at least by their Silence, to be of my Opinion; but others, who were my secret Enemies, could not forbear some Expressions, which by a Side-wind reflected on me. And from this Time began an Intrigue between his Majesty, and a Junta of Ministers maliciously bent against me, which broke out in less than two Months, and had like **7** to have ended in my utter Destruction. Of so little Weight are the greatest Services to Princes, when put into the Balance with a Refusal to gratify their Passions.

About three Weeks after this Exploit, there arrived a solemn Embassy from *Blefuscu*, with humble Offers of a Peace; which was

"There arrived a solemn Embassy from Blefuscu." T. Morten. 1865. Courtesy, Library of Congress.

soon concluded upon Conditions very advantageous to our Emperor; wherewith I shall not trouble the Reader. There were six Ambassadors, with a Train of about five Hundred Persons; and their Entry was very magnificent, suitable to the Grandeur of their Master, and the Importance of their Business. When their Treaty was finished, wherein I did them several good Offices by the Credit I now had, or at least appeared to have at Court; their Excellencies, who were privately told how much I had been their Friend, made me a Visit in Form. They began with many Compliments upon my Valour and Generosity; invited me to that Kingdom in the Emperor their Master's Name; and desired me to shew them some Proofs of my prodigious Strength, of which they had heard so many Wonders; wherein I readily obliged them, but shall not interrupt the Reader with the Particulars.

When I had for some time entertained their Excellencies to their infinite Satisfaction and Surprize, I desired they would do me the Honour to present my most humble Respects to the Emperor their Master, the Renown of whose Virtues had so justly filled the whole World with Admiration, and whose Royal Person I resolved to attend before I returned to my own Country. Accordingly, the next time I had the Honour to see our Emperor, I desired his general Licence to wait on the *Blefuscudian* Monarch, which he was pleased to grant me, as I could plainly perceive, in a very cold Manner; but could not guess the Reason, till I had a Whisper from a certain Person, that *Flimnap* and *Bolgolam* had represented my Intercourse with those Ambassadors, as a Mark of Disaffection, from which I am sure my Heart was wholly free. And this was the first time I began to conceive some imperfect Idea of Courts and Ministers.

It is to be observed, that these Ambassadors spoke to me by an Interpreter; the Languages of both Empires differing as much from each other as any two in *Europe*, and each Nation priding itself upon the Antiquity, Beauty, and Energy of their own Tongues, with an avowed Contempt for that of their Neighbour: Yet our Emperor standing upon the Advantage he had got by the Seizure of their Fleet, obliged them to deliver their Credentials, and make their Speech in the *Lilliputian* Tongue. And it must be confessed, that from the great Intercourse of Trade and Commerce between both Realms; from the continual Reception of Exiles, which is mutual among them; and from the Custom in each Empire to send their young Nobility and richer Gentry to the other, in order to polish themselves, by seeing the World, and understanding Men and Manners; there are few Persons of Distinction, or Merchants, or Seamen, who dwell in the Maritime Parts, but what can hold Conversation in both Tongues; as I found some Weeks after, when I went to pay my Respects to the Emperor of *Blefuscu,* which in the Midst of great Misfortunes, through the Malice of my Enemies, proved a very happy Adventure to me, as I shall relate in its proper Place.

The Reader may remember, that when I signed those Articles upon which I recovered my Liberty, there were some which I disliked upon Account of their being too servile, neither could any thing but an extreme Necessity have forced me to submit. But being now a *Nardac,* of the highest Rank in that Empire, such Offices were looked upon as below my Dignity; and the Emperor (to do him Justice) never once mentioned them to me. How-

8 *Conditions very advantageous to our Emperor.* The Tory view was, of course, that the Treaty of Utrecht was a very advantageous one. Louis XIV was forced to recognize George I as king of Great Britain and to end his support of the son of James II. He had to cede Newfoundland to Great Britain, as well as Nova Scotia, and the land about Hudson Bay. Spain also had to cede Gibraltar to Great Britain. And both France and Spain were forced to accept naval inferiority to Great Britain. All this made Great Britain the clear victor of the War of the Spanish Succession.

The Whigs were dissatisfied, however, because a French prince remained on the Spanish throne. (He was Philip V, grandson of Louis XIV.) While Louis was forced to agree that France and Spain would never be ruled by the same person, it was clear there would always be a community of interests between the two nations if both were ruled by the same family.

Then, too, France itself was left intact, and it was clear that it would quickly recover its military strength.

9 *the Custom in each Empire to send their young Nobility and richer Gentry to the other.* In Swift's time, it was the custom for English families of rank and wealth to send their sons on a "grand tour" through France, Switzerland, Italy, and Germany, as a kind of practical postgraduate course after they had finished college. In this way, they learned the customs of the nations of western Europe, their languages, and histories, becoming more cosmopolitan and less provincial. Apparently, the Lilliputians and Blefuscans do the same, although their world is limited to two small islands.

10 *reading a Romance.* Swift may be amusing himself by comparing the dullness of romances with the interest of the supposedly true tale of Gulliver.

11 *a Moon-shine Night.* A night on which the moon was shining.

12 *the Flame was so violent.* Again, natural phenomena are Lilliputianized. Since the Lilliputian palace had 1/1,728 the volume of an analogous European palace, a fire would have consumed it in 1/1,728 the time it would have taken to consume Buckingham Palace, for instance. Gulliver could not possibly have saved it. We must, however, envisage miniature flames progressing with miniature speed.

ever, it was not long before I had an Opportunity of doing his Majesty, at least, as I then thought, a most signal Service. I was alarmed at Midnight with the Cries of many Hundred People at my Door; by which being suddenly awaked, I was in some Kind of Terror. I heard the Word *Burglum* repeated incessantly; several of the Emperor's Court making their Way through the Croud, intreated me to come immediately to the Palace, where her Imperial Majesty's Apartment was on fire, by the Carelessness of a Maid **10** of Honour, who fell asleep while she was reading a Romance. I got up in an Instant; and Orders being given to clear the Way be- **11** fore me; and it being likewise a Moon-shine Night, I made a shift to get to the Palace without trampling on any of the People. I found they had already applied Ladders to the Walls of the Apartment, and were well provided with Buckets, but the Water was at some Distance. These Buckets were about the Size of a large Thimble, and the poor People supplied me with them as fast as **12** they could; but the Flame was so violent, that they did little Good. I might easily have stifled it with my Coat, which I unfortunately left behind me for haste, and came away only in my Leathern Jerkin. The Case seemed wholly desperate and deplorable; and this magnificent Palace would have infallibly been burnt down to

"In three Minutes the Fire was wholly extinguished." J. J. Grandville, 1835. Suppressed in later editions.

the Ground, if, by a Presence of Mind, unusual to me, I had not suddenly thought of an Expedient. I had the Evening before drank plentifully of a most delicious Wine, called *Glimigrim*, (the *Blefuscudians* call it *Flunec*, but ours is esteemed the better Sort) which is very diuretick. By the luckiest Chance in the World, I had not discharged myself of any Part of it. The Heat I had contracted by coming very near the Flames, and by my labouring to quench them, made the Wine begin to operate by Urine; which I voided in such a Quantity, and applied so well to the proper Places, that in three Minutes the Fire was wholly extinguished; and the rest of that noble Pile, which had cost so many Ages in erecting, preserved from Destruction.

It was now Day-light, and I returned to my House, without waiting to congratulate with the Emperor; because although I had done a very eminent Piece of Service, yet I could not tell how his Majesty might resent the Manner by which I had performed it: For, by the fundamental Laws of the Realm, it is Capital in any Person, of what Quality soever, to make water within the Precincts of the Palace. But I was a little comforted by a Message from his Majesty, that he would give Orders to the Grand Justiciary for passing my Pardon in Form; which, however, I could not obtain. And I was privately assured, that the Empress conceiving the greatest Abhorrence of what I had done, removed to the most distant Side of the Court, firmly resolved that those Buildings should never be repaired for her Use; and, in the Presence of her chief Confidents, could not forbear vowing Revenge. **13**

Illustration by Le Febure, 1797. Suppressed in later editions.

13 *the Empress . . . could not forbear vowing Revenge.* Some commentators think that the incident of Gulliver's putting out the fire symbolizes the Treaty of Utrecht, by which means the Tories put out the fire of war. In that case, the fact that Gulliver fell into disfavor as a result mirrors the fall of the Tories after the death of Queen Anne. In the Tory view, the treaty, necessary to avert total disaster, brought shame and political destruction to those who brought it about because of their opponents' trivial objections to the details of the treaty.

Queen Anne (1665–1714). Courtesy, Library of Congress.

The mention of the queen as the specific enemy, however, seems to many commentators to be a reference to Queen Anne. In 1704, Swift had published *A Tale of a Tub* in which, under the guise of clever symbolism and biting satire, Swift firmly upheld the Church of England against attack by the Catholics on the right and the Dissenters on the left.

Queen Anne, however, misunderstanding the satire (her mind was not of the keenest), viewed it as irreligious and was furthermore repelled by the coarseness of its language (as the Lilliputian queen was offended by the urine). Anne was thereafter ill-disposed to Swift and would not consent to his advance in the religious hierarchy past his deanship.

It is quite possible that Swift thought of Gulliver's urine as representing his own satire, spattered abroad for a worthy purpose but unpleasant in itself.

1 *an invisible Needle with invisible Silk.* This is very plausible and an excellent touch, since what would be visible to Lilliputian eyes might well be invisible to Gulliver's grosser vision.

Of the Inhabitants of Lilliput; their Learning, Laws, and Customs. The Manner of Educating their Children. The Author's way of Living in that Country. His Vindication of a Great Lady.

LTHOUGH I intend to leave the Description of this Empire to a particular Treatise, yet in the mean time I am content to gratify the curious Reader with some general Ideas. As the common Size of the Natives is somewhat under six Inches, so there is an exact Proportion in all other Animals, as well as Plants and Trees: For Instance, the tallest Horses and Oxen are between four and five Inches in Height, the Sheep an Inch and a half, more or less; their Geese about the Bigness of a Sparrow; and so the several Gradations downwards, till you come to the smallest, which, to my Sight, were almost invisible; but Nature hath adapted the Eyes of the *Lilliputians* to all Objects proper for their View: They see with great Exactness, but at no great Distance. And to show the Sharpness of their Sight towards Objects that are near, I have been much pleased with observing a Cook pulling a Lark, which was not so large as a **1** common Fly; and a young Girl threading an invisible Needle with invisible Silk. Their tallest Trees are about seven Foot high; I mean some of those in the great Royal Park, the Tops whereof I could but just reach with my Fist clinched. The other Vegetables are in the same Proportion: But this I leave to the Reader's Imagination.

I shall say but little at present of their Learning, which for many Ages hath flourished in all its Branches among them: But their Manner of Writing is very peculiar; being neither from the Left to the Right, like the *Europeans*; nor from the Right to the Left, like the *Arabians*; nor from up to down like the *Chinese*; nor from down to up, like the *Cascagians*; but aslant from one Corner of the Paper to the other, like Ladies in *England*.

2
3

They bury their Dead with their Heads directly downwards; because they hold an Opinion, that in eleven Thousand Moons they are all to rise again; in which Period, the Earth (which they conceive to be flat) will turn upside down, and by this Means they shall, at their Resurrection, be found ready standing on their Feet. The Learned among them confess the Absurdity of this Doctrine; but the Practice still continues, in Compliance to the Vulgar.

4

There are some Laws and Customs in this Empire very peculiar; and if they were not so directly contrary to those of my own dear Country, I should be tempted to say a little in their Justification. It is only to be wished, that they were as well executed. The first I shall mention, relateth to Informers. All Crimes against the State, are punished here with the utmost Severity; but if the Person accused make his Innocence plainly to appear upon his Tryal, the Accuser is immediately put to an ignominious Death; and out of his Goods or Lands, the innocent Person is quadruply recompensed for the Loss of his Time, for the Danger he underwent, for the Hardship of his Imprisonment, and for all the Charges he hath been at in making his Defence. Or, if that Fund be deficient, it is largely supplied by the Crown. The Emperor doth also confer on him some publick Mark of his Favour; and Proclamation is made of his Innocence through the wholly City.

5

6

They look upon Fraud as a greater Crime than Theft, and therefore seldom fail to punish it with Death: For they alledge, that Care and Vigilance, with a very common Understanding, may preserve a Man's Goods from Thieves; but Honesty hath no Fence against superior Cunning: And since it is necessary that there should be a perpetual Intercourse of·buying and selling, and dealing upon Credit; where Fraud is permitted or connived at, or hath no Law to punish it, the honest Dealer is always undone, and the Knave gets the Advantage. I remember when I was once interceeding with the King for a Criminal who had wronged his Master of a great Sum of Money, which he had received by Order, and ran away with; and happening to tell his Majesty, by way of Extenuation, that it was only a Breach of Trust; the Emperor thought it monstrous in me to offer, as a Defence, the greatest Aggravation of the Crime: And truly, I had little to say in Return, farther than the common Answer, that different Nations had different Customs; for, I confess, I was heartily ashamed.

Although we usually call Reward and Punishment, the two Hinges upon which all Government turns; yet I could never observe this Maxim to be put in Practice by any Nation except that of *Lilliput*. Whoever can there bring sufficient Proof that he hath strictly observed the Laws of his Country for Seventy-three Moons, hath a Claim to certain Privileges, according to his Quality and Condition of Life, with a proportionable Sum of Money out of a Fund appropriated for that Use: He likewise acquires the Title of *Snilpall*, or *Legal*, which is added to his Name, but doth not descend to his Posterity. And these People thought it a prodigious Defect of Policy among us, when I told them that our Laws were

7

2 *the Cascagians.* A mythical tribe introduced by Swift to complete the horizontal and vertical possibilities. He might have mentioned, though, the possibility of writing left to right, then right to left, then left to right, and so on, alternating in successive lines. This is called *boustrophedon* (from the Greek for "ox-turning" because it resembles the manner in which oxen are used to plow successive furrows in opposite directions), and was actually used by the ancient Greeks in their early period.

3 *like Ladies in England.* Swift was not, *for his time*, a male chauvinist, but like most men, he could not resist a cheap shot at the expense of the "gentler sex."

In most places and in most times and, to be specific, in Swift's England, education was not usually "wasted" on women, who were felt to be of limited intelligence and, in any case, to have a very limited role to play in life. That women could not write as well as the men of their social circle was the natural consequence of lack of education and practice, but was put down to lack of intelligence and was used as further excuse to skimp on their education. This sort of circular reasoning has been used by oppressors to justify oppression since human reasoning began.

4 *Vulgar.* Our modern use of this word implies "unrefined" or "boorish." In Swift's time, it simply referred to the common people without necessarily implying anything derogatory. (The Latin word for the common people is *vulgus*.) However, since (in the eyes of the gentry) the common people were unrefined and boorish, due to their lack of education, the change in meaning was inevitable.

Swift, in this paragraph, must be commenting wryly on any number of religious beliefs that are purely superstitious and silly, but which, nevertheless, could not be touched because they had been sanctified and made holy by custom. He deliberately chose a Lilliputian example, no doubt, that was as far removed as possible from any specific religious custom in Great Britain, in order to avoid trouble.

5 *my own dear Country.* There are two ways of satirizing the way of life of your society. You can invent a mythical society which is similar to your own in many ways, but appears to the reader under a particularly contemptible guise. Or you can invent a mythical society that possesses a supernatural virtue, the very nobility of which casts a shade on the practices of your own society. A society worse than our own is, these days, referred to as a "dystopia" (from Greek words meaning "bad place"), while a society better than our own is a "utopia" (usually thought of as from Greek words meaning "good place," though that should more properly be "eutopia"; "utopia" actually means "no place").

There are both dystopic and utopic aspects to Lilliputian society and Swift uses both to satirize his England. Whenever Swift has Gulliver refer to "my own dear Country," by the way, you can count on a particularly hard satiric thrust against it.

6 *an ignominious Death*. In all nations, there are paranoid periods when the public, or the ruler, or both, are ready to believe in the existence of crimes on very little evidence. It then becomes possible for a false informer to implicate many people who find it very difficult to clear themselves since all their supporters fall away for fear of being denounced as accomplices. Because this sort of thing happened in those periods when people searched feverishly for witches, it has been called "witch-hunting."

Swift may have been thinking of the accusations against Oxford and Bolingbroke, but England had a more notable example of it a generation earlier when Titus Oates (1649–1705) in 1678 fabricated a "Popish plot" that ended in the execution of thirty-five innocent Catholics. (In the United States, we had a much more recent example in the person of Joseph R. McCarthy who, in the early 1950s, became a temporary hero because of his fabricated accusations.)

7 *Whoever . . . hath a Claim to certain Privileges*. I find this notion attractive, and it would cost so little. Of course, proving a person to have strictly observed all the laws for six years would be nearly impossible— but suppose that everyone whose income tax returns had been audited for six years running and who had not been penalized by, say, more than one percent of his tax payment could receive permission to put "Taxpayer" after his name and get to sit in the reviewing stands at parades. It could set up a certain healthful spirit of emulation.

8 *the common Size of human Understandings is fitted to some Station or other*. This is egalitarianism carried to an uncomfortable degree, and is one of Swift's favorite views, for he frequently expressed it in his writings.

The Athenians believed the same, for at the height of their democracy they chose citizens for many offices by lot. Andrew Jackson believed it and when he became president in 1829, he turned out previous officeholders in wholesale lots, feeling that any loyal Democrat could fill the office. I would like to believe this Swiftian view, too, but the results of using political loyalty as the only criterion for office have made the civil service examination seem to be a useful advance. (The Chinese have had such examinations for many centuries, by the way.)

Swift does, of course, state that there should be moral qualifications, but they may be even more susceptible to abuse than intellectual qualifications. As Swift points out earlier, it is much more difficult to defend one's self against fraud than against theft, so that fraud is the greater crime. Well, it is a lot easier to pretend to be moral than to pretend to be intelligent so that one runs a much greater risk assuming a man to be moral than assuming him to be intelligent.

9 *a Man, whose Inclinations led him to be corrupt . . . and defend his Corruptions*. This form of anti-intellectualism is often popular in democracies, and in 1952 and 1956 Adlai Stevenson lost large numbers of votes because he was suspected (with justice) of being more intelligent than Dwight Eisenhower.

enforced only by Penalties, without any Mention of Reward. It is upon this account that the Image of Justice, in their Courts of Judicature, is formed with six Eyes, two before, as many behind, and on each Side one, to signify Circumspection; with a Bag of Gold open in her right Hand, and a Sword sheathed in her left, to shew she is more disposed to reward than to punish.

8 In chusing Persons for all Employment, they have more Regard to good Morals than to great Abilities: For, since Government is necessary to Mankind, they believe that the common Size of human Understandings, is fitted to some Station or other; and that Providence never intended to make the Management of publick Affairs a Mystery, to be comprehended only by a few Persons of sublime Genius, of which there seldom are three born in an Age: But, they suppose Truth, Justice, Temperance, and the like, to be in every Man's Power; the Practice of which Virtues, assisted by Experience and a good Intention, would qualify any Man for the Service of his Country, except where a Course of Study is required. But they thought the Want of Moral Virtues was so far from being supplied by superior Endowments of the Mind, that Employments could never be put into such dangerous Hands as those of Persons so qualified; and at least, that the Mistakes committed by Ignorance in a virtuous Disposition, would never be of such fatal Consequence **9** to the Publick Weal, as the Practices of a Man, whose Inclinations led him to be corrupt, and had great Abilities to manage, to multiply, and defend his Corruptions.

10 In like Manner, the Disbelief of a Divine Providence renders a Man uncapable of holding any publick Station: For, since Kings avow themselves to be the Deputies of Providence, the *Lilliputians* think nothing can be more absurd than for a Prince to employ such Men as disown the Authority under which he acteth.

11 In relating these and the following Laws, I would only be understood to mean the original Institutions, and not the most scandalous Corruptions into which these People are fallen by the degenerate Nature of Man. For as to that infamous Practice of acquiring great Employments by dancing on the Ropes, or Badges of Favour and Distinction by leaping over Sticks, and creeping under them; the Reader is to observe, that they were first introduced by the Grandfather of the Emperor now reigning; and grew to the present Height, by the gradual Increase of Party and Faction.

Ingratitude is among them a capital Crime, as we read it to have been in some other Countries: For they reason thus; that whoever makes ill Returns to his Benefactor, must needs be a common Enemy to the rest of Mankind, from whom they have received no Obligation; and therefore such a Man is not fit to live.

Their Notions relating to the Duties of Parents and Children differ extremely from ours. For, since the Conjunction of Male and Female is founded upon the great Law of Nature, in order to propagate and continue the Species; the *Lilliputians* will needs have it, that Men and Women are joined together like other Animals, by the Motives of Concupiscence; and that their Tenderness towards their Young, proceedeth from the like natural Principle: For which Reason they will never allow, that a Child is under any Obligation to his Father for begetting him, or to his Mother for bringing him into the World; which, considering the Miseries of human Life, was neither a Benefit in itself, nor intended so by his

Parents, whose Thoughts in their Love-encounters were otherwise employed. Upon these, and the like Reasonings, their Opinion is, that Parents are the last of all others to be trusted with the Education of their own Children: And therefore they have in every Town publick Nurseries, where all Parents, except Cottagers and Labourers, are obliged to send their Infants of both Sexes to be reared and educated when they come to the Age of twenty Moons; at which Time they are supposed to have some Rudiments of Docility. These Schools are of several Kinds, suited to different Qualities, and to both Sexes. They have certain Professors skilled in preparing Children for such a Condition of Life as befits the Rank of their Parents, and their own Capacities as well as Inclinations.   I shall first say something of the Male Nurseries, and then of the Female.

The Nurseries for Males of Noble or Eminent Birth, are provided with grave and learned Professors, and their several Deputies. The Clothes and Food of the Children are plain and simple. They are bred up in the Principles of Honour, Justice, Courage, Modesty, Clemency, Religion, and Love of their Country: They are always employed in some Business, except in the Times of eating and sleeping, which are very short, and two Hours for Diversions, consisting of bodily Exercises. They are dressed by Men until four Years of Age, and then are obliged to dress themselves, although their Quality be ever so great; and the Women Attendants, who are aged proportionally to ours at fifty, perform only the most menial Offices.   They are never suffered to converse with Servants, but go together in small or greater Numbers to take their Diversions, and always in the Presence of a Professor, or one of his Deputies; whereby they avoid those early bad Impressions of Folly and Vice to which our Children are subject. Their Parents are suffered to see them only twice a Year; the Visit is not to last above an Hour; they are allowed to kiss the Child at Meeting and Parting; but a Professor, who always standeth by on those Occasions, will not suffer them to whisper, or use any fondling Expressions, or bring any Presents of Toys, Sweetmeats, and the like.

The Pension from each Family for the Education and Entertainment of a Child, upon Failure of due Payment, is levied by the Emperor's Officers.

The Nurseries for Children of ordinary Gentlemen, Merchants, Traders, and Handicrafts, are managed proportionably after the same Manner; only those designed for Trades, are put out Apprentices at seven Years old; whereas those of Persons of Quality continue in their Exercises until Fifteen, which answers to One and Twenty with us: But the Confinement is gradually lessened for the last three Years.

In the Female Nurseries, the young Girls of Quality are educated much like the Males, only they are dressed by orderly Servants of their own Sex, but always in the Presence of a Professor or Deputy, until they come to dress themselves, which is at five Years old. And if it be found that these Nurses ever presume to entertain the Girls with frightful or foolish Stories, or the common Follies practised by Chamber-Maids among us; they are publickly whipped thrice about the City, imprisoned for a Year, and banished for Life to the most desolate Parts of the Country. Thus the young Ladies there are as much ashamed of being

10 *the Disbelief of a Divine Providence . . . under which he acteth.* Swift is defending a .kind of religious intolerance here in that he considers atheism a bar to public office. He is undoubtedly sincere in his argument. It would have occurred to virtually no one in Swift's time that the assumption that a ruler is the Lord's Anointed was, indeed, only an assumption and need not be held.

Nor need *we* feel particularly virtuous in this respect. In secular democracies, the rulers of the state are, in theory, deputies of the people, so that their religious views are, again in theory, irrelevant to their qualifications for office. Nevertheless, in the United States today, I doubt that an atheist could be elected to high office unless he compounded his sin by assuming a hypocritical religiosity.

11 *the original Institutions.* Swift's view, expressed over and over again in *Gulliver's Travels* and in his other writings, is that human society was more virtuous in the past and that it had degenerated since. This "good old days" notion is very common; almost everyone longs for a lost time when all men were honest and frugal and unselfish, and all women were modest and virtuous and loyal.

No such time ever existed, however, for if we go back, we invariably find writers bemoaning the degeneration of their society and longing for a set of good old days of their own.

12 *in every Town publick Nurseries.* This was a very daring notion for Swift's time.

13 *except Cottagers and Labourers.* Swift's egalitarianism had its sharp limits. It was difficult for him to recognize the lower classes as human.

14 *twenty Moons.* A Lilliputian child of twenty moons (1 2/3 years) is old enough to go to school. This is the first indication that Lilliputians age more rapidly than do Europeans.

15 *Clothes and Food . . . are plain and simple.* Many of Swift's utopian notions are obtained from Plato's *Republic*, and much of the *Republic* is modeled on the Spartan way of life (or, at least, on the Spartan way of life as it was ideally supposed to be). The Spartan way of life, and particularly of bringing up children, was incredibly austere, and is often praised by those who have never been subjected to it.

16 *Fifteen, which answers to One and Twenty with us.* Apparently Lilliputians age 1.4 times as fast as we do, so that the Emperor, whose age was given as 28 3/4 years, was 40 1/4 years old in the European sense.

17 *to entertain the Girls with . . . Stories.* The clarity and directness of Swift's style, together with the exciting imaginativeness of the incidents he described, has made *Gulliver's Travels* an ideal children's classic (with some judicious pruning). It is rather ironic that Swift's book has in its turn been considered by some to contain "frightful or foolish stories" that ought not to be told to "young girls of quality."

18 *neither did I perceive any Difference in their Education, made by their Difference of Sex.* Swift is unusually feminist for his period. There were very few who believed in educating women.

19 *Rules were given them relating to domestic Life.* Of course, Swift didn't go all the way. It was considered unthinkable then that men and women should share domestic chores as a matter of course.

20 *twelve Years old, which among them is the marriageable Age.* The Lilliputian twelve is nearly seventeen by European standards on the basis of the 1.4 to 1 ratio.

21 *the meaner Sort.* The adjective "mean" is now usually taken to signify "nasty" or "spiteful" or "irritating"—in fact, quite a variety of unpleasant characteristics. Before this degradation of the word, it simply meant "common," or pertaining to the lower classes. (It is derived from the same root as the German word *gemeine*, meaning "common" or "ordinary.") Of course, all the unpleasant qualities now suggested by the word "mean" were supposed (by people of the upper classes) to be very common among the lower classes.

22 *nothing can be more unjust, than that people . . . bring Children into the World and leave the Burthen of supporting them on the Publick.* This sounds like a good, modern planned population position. Today, though, limiting the birthrate involves methods that need not seriously interfere with sexual activities (the use of pills, condoms, diaphragms, intrauterine devices, vasectomies, and so on).

In Swift's time, however, the only birth control method countenanced, or even recognized, was abstinence. What Swift is saying, therefore, is that it was unjust for poor people to show "subservience to their own appetites," that is, to have sex. It takes a rather unfeeling heart to suggest that the poor be deprived of the one pleasure in which they could indulge as freely as the rich.

23 *their Education is of little Consequence to the Publick.* Here, even the relatively enlightened Swift adopts the common belief of the time that the peasant is not far removed from an animal. Furthermore, he seems to believe that education is had only to serve some material use, rather than for the inner good it may bring about. Nor does it occur to him that through education there may be culled out of the peasants many who could usefully serve in other kinds of occupation.

24 *begging is a Trade unknown in this Empire.* Lilliput is clearly a welfare state. The absence of beggars is of interest, as we shall see, in connection with the next voyage.

25 *Domestick.* I.e., domestics—Gulliver's household arrangements or day-to-day way of life.

26 *twice round the Thumb is once round the Wrist.* It sounds good, but there is a clear fallacy in this. Even

Cowards and Fools, as the Men; and despise all personal Ornaments beyond Decency and Cleanliness; **18** neither did I perceive any Difference in their Education, made by their Difference **19** of Sex, only that the Exercises of the Females were not altogether so robust; and that some Rules were given them relating to domestick Life, and a smaller Compass of Learning was enjoyed them: For, their Maxim is, that among People of Quality, a Wife should be always a reasonable and agreeable Companion, **20** because she cannot always be young. When the Girls are twelve Years old, which among them is the marriageable Age, their Parents or Guardians take them home, with great Expressions of Gratitude to the Professors, and seldom without Tears of the young Lady and her Companions.

21 In the Nurseries of Females of the meaner Sort, the Children are instructed in all Kinds of Works proper for their Sex, and their several Degrees: Those intended for Apprentices are dismissed at seven Years old, the rest are kept to eleven.

The meaner Families who have Children at these Nurseries, are obliged, besides their annual Pension, which is as low as possible, to return to the Steward of the Nursery a small Monthly Share of their Gettings, to be a Portion for the Child; and therefore all Parents are limited in their Expences by the Law. For the *Lilli-* **22** *putians* think nothing can be more unjust, than that people, in Subservience to their own Appetites, should bring Children into the World, and leave the Burthen of supporting them on the Publick. As to Persons of Quality, they give Security to appropriate a certain Sum for each Child, suitable to their Condition; and these Funds are always managed with good Husbandry, and the most exact Justice.

The Cottagers and Labourers keep their Children at home, their Business being only to till and cultivate the Earth; and therefore **23** their Education is of little Consequence to the Publick; but the Old **24** and Diseased among them are supported by Hospitals: For begging is a Trade unknown in this Empire.

25 And here it may perhaps divert the curious Reader, to give some Account of my Domestick, and my Manner of living in this Country, during a Residence of nine Months and thirteen Days. Having a Head mechanically turned, and being likewise forced by Necessity, I had made for myself a Table and Chair convenient enough, out of the largest Trees in the Royal Park. Two hundred Sempstresses were employed to make me Shirts, and Linnen for my Bed and Table, all of the strongest and coarsest kind they could get; which, however, they were forced to quilt together in several Folds; for the thickest was some Degrees finer than Lawn. Their Linnen is usually three Inches wide, and three Foot make a Piece. The Sempstresses took my Measure as I lay on the Ground, one standing at my Neck, and another at my Mid-Leg, with a strong Cord extended, that each held by the End, while the third measured the Length of the Cord with a Rule of an Inch long. Then they measured my right Thumb, and desired no more; for by a **26** mathematical Computation, that twice round the Thumb is once round the Wrist, and so on to the Neck and the Waist; and by the Help of my old Shirt, which I displayed on the Ground before them for a Pattern, they fitted me exactly. Three hundred Taylors were employed in the same Manner to make me Clothes; but they

Gulliver is measured by the tailors. E. J. Wheeler. 1895.

if there were simple relations between bodily measurements that held without variation for all persons, the circumference of the thumb is the smallest of the measurements mentioned and will, therefore, experience the largest percentage error of measurement. If you can measure the circumference of the thumb to, say, 1/10 of an inch and make no other measurements, then the circumference of the wrist will be correct to 1/5 of an inch, that of the neck to perhaps 1/2 of an inch, and that of the waist to perhaps 2 inches. Anyone who wears clothes designed after measurements based on the circumference of the thumb alone, will look very odd. Not to mention the fact that the circumference of the average person's wrist is considerably more than twice that of the thumb.

had another Contrivance for taking my Measure. I kneeled down, and they raised a Ladder from the Ground to my Neck; upon this Ladder one of them mounted, and let fall a Plum-Line from my Collar to the Floor, which just answered the Length of my Coat; but my Waist and Arms I measured myself. When my Cloaths were finished, which was done in my House, (for the largest of theirs would not have been able to hold them) they looked like the Patch-work made by the Ladies in *England,* only that mine were all of a Colour.

I had three hundred Cooks to dress my Victuals, in little convenient Huts built about my House, where they and their Families lived, and prepared me two Dishes a-piece. I took up twenty Waiters in my Hand, and placed them on the Table; an hundred more attended below on the Ground, some with Dishes of Meat, and some with Barrels of Wine, and other Liquors, slung on their Shoulders; all which the Waiters above drew up as I wanted, in a very ingenious Manner, by certain Cords, as we draw the Bucket up a Well in *Europe.* A Dish of their Meat was a good Mouthful, and a Barrel of their Liquor a reasonable Draught. Their Mutton yields to ours, but their Beef is excellent. I have had a Sirloin so

27 *as he was pleased to call it.* Gulliver is very proud of the Imperial condescension toward him and makes a modest disclaimer of deserving it.

28 *white Staff.* The badge of office of the lord high treasurer.

29 *eat more than usual, in Honour to my dear Country.* Gulliver proudly displays the gluttony which was considered characteristic of Englishmen at that time.

30 *Admiration.* See Chapter 1 of this part, note 26.

Dining with his Imperial Majesty and the Royal Consort of Lilliput. T. Morten, 1865. Courtesy, Library of Congress.

large, that I have been forced to make three Bits of it; but this is rare. My Servants were astonished to see me eat it Bones and all, as in our Country we do the Leg of a Lark. Their Geese and Turkeys I usually eat at a Mouthful, and I must confess they far exceed ours. Of their smaller Fowl I could take up Twenty or thirty at the End of my Knife.

One Day his Imperial Majesty being informed of my Way of living, desired that himself, and his Royal Consort, with the young **27** Princes of the Blood of both Sexes, might have the Happiness (as he was pleased to call it) of dining with me. They came accordingly, and I placed them upon Chairs of State on my Table, just over against me, with their Guards about them. *Flimnap* the Lord High **28** Treasurer attended there likewise, with his white Staff; and I ob-served he often looked on me with a sour Countenance, which I **29** would not seem to regard, but eat more than usual, in Honour to **30** my dear Country, as well as to fill the Court with Admiration. I have some private Reasons to believe, that this Visit from his Majesty gave *Flimnap* an Opportunity of doing me ill Offices to his Master. That Minister had always been my secret Enemy, although he outwardly caressed me more than was usual to the Moroseness of his Nature. He represented to the Emperor the low Condition of his Treasury; that he was forced to take up Money at great Discount; that Exchequer Bills would not circulate under nine *per Cent.* below Par; that I had cost his Majesty about a Million and a half of *Sprugs,* (their greatest Gold Coin, about the Bigness of a Spangle;) and upon the whole, that it would be adviseable in the Emperor to take the first fair Occasion of dismissing me.

I am here obliged to vindicate the Reputation of an excellent Lady, who was an innocent Sufferer upon my Account. The Treasurer took a Fancy to be jealous of his Wife, from the Malice of some evil Tongues, who informed him that her Grace had taken a violent Affection for my Person; and the Court-Scandal ran for some Time that she once came privately to my Lodging. This I solemnly declare to be a most infamous Falshood, without any Grounds, farther than that her Grace was pleased to treat me with all innocent Marks of Freedom and Friendship. I own she came often to my House, but always publickly, nor ever without three more in the Coach, who were usually her Sister, and young Daughter, and some particular Acquaintance; but this was common to many other Ladies of the Court. And I still appeal to my Servants round, whether they at any Time saw a Coach at my Door without knowing what Persons were in it. On those Occasions, when a Servant had given me Notice, my Custom was to go immediately to the Door; and after paying my Respects, to take up the Coach and two Horses very carefully in my Hands, (for if there were six Horses, the Postillion always unharnessed four) and place them on a Table, where I had fixed a moveable Rim quite round, of five Inches high, to prevent Accidents. And I have often had four Coaches and Horses at once on my Table full of Company, while I sat in my Chair leaning my Face towards them; and when I was engaged with one Sett, the Coachmen would gently drive the others round my Table. I have passed many an Afternoon very agreeably in these Conversations: But I defy the Treasurer, or his two Informers, (I will name them, and let them make their best of it) *Clustril* and *Drunlo,* to prove that any Person ever came to me *incognito,* except the Secretary *Reldresal,* who was sent by express Command of his Imperial Majesty, as I have before related. I should not have dwelt so long upon this Particular, if it had not been a Point wherein the Reputation of a great Lady is so nearly concerned; to say nothing of my own; although I had the Honour to be a *Nardac,* which the Treasurer himself is not; for all the World knows he is only a *Clumglum,* a Title inferior by one Degree, as that of a Marquess is to a Duke in *England;* yet I allow he preceded me in right of his Post. These false Informations, which I afterwards came to the Knowledge of, by an Accident not proper to mention, made the Treasurer shew his Lady for some Time an ill Countenance, and me a worse: For although he were at last undeceived and reconciled to her, yet I lost all Credit with him; and found my Interest decline very fast with the Emperor himself, who was indeed too much governed by that Favourite.

31

32

33

"I own she came often to my House." Willy Pogány, 1919.

31 *my secret Enemy.* Flimnap (Walpole) is roused by Gulliver's foolish display of gluttony to inveigh against the cost of feeding him and the danger to the Emperor's finances. Some commentators find in Flimnap's accusations against Gulliver a parallel to Whig accusations against Bishop Francis Atterbury (1662–1732), a close friend of Swift. He was a prominent Tory and High Churchman; a great orator who held considerable power under Anne and who openly favored the succession of her half brother, James III, rather than George of Hanover. As soon as George I came to power, Atterbury was out of favor. In 1723, he was arrested for complicity in a Jacobite plot to replace George I with the Pretender James, convicted, and forced into exile.

32 *a violent Affection for my Person.* There is satire in several respects here. First, it is a humorous dig at court gossips, whose impossible stories sometimes ruined reputations. (After all there is clearly no possibility of misconduct between Gulliver and any Lilliputian lady, considering the difference in physical dimensions, yet the Lilliputians seem to take the gossip seriously and Gulliver, as always, accepting the Lilliputians at their own evaluation, labors desperately to defend himself.) The satire may also be pointed at Walpole, whose first wife, Catherine Shorter, was supposed to have been unfaithful—although Walpole (unlike Flimnap) never seems to have displayed any concern over the matter.

33 *Clumglum.* The word invented by Swift to express Flimnap's rank, seems humorously appropriate since Gulliver speaks earlier of "the moroseness of his [Flimnap's] nature." Again we are shown Gulliver's absurd pride in his Lilliputian rank. It is clear that Gulliver's besetting sin is pride, and we will see later in the book how this comes into play.

1 *the Meanness of my Condition*. It was a literary convention to contrast the viciousness, intrigue, backbiting, and general insincerity and dishonesty of the courts with the virtues of the simple life of the lower middle class.

2 *a considerable Person at Court*. Probably Reldresal, who represents the earl of Granville (See Chapter 3 of this part, note 6).

The Author being informed of a design to accuse him of High Treason, makes his escape to Blefuscu. His reception there.

BEFORE I proceed to give an Account of my leaving this Kingdom, it may be proper to inform the Reader of a private Intrigue which had been for two Months forming against me. I had been hitherto all my Life a Stranger to Courts, from which I was unqualified by

1 the Meanness of my Condition. I had indeed heard and read enough of the Dispositions of great Princes and Ministers; but never expected to have found such terrible Effects of them in so remote a Country, governed, as I thought, by very different Maxims from those in *Europe*.

When I was just preparing to pay my Attendance on the Emperor

2 *Blefuscu*; a considerable Person at Court (to whom I had been very serviceable at a time when he lay under the highest Displeasure of his Imperial Majesty) came to my House very privately at Night in a close Chair, and without sending his Name, desired Admittance: The Chair-men were dismissed; I put the Chair, with his Lordship in it, into my Coat-Pocket; and giving Orders to a trusty Servant to say I was indisposed and gone to sleep, I fastened the Door of my House, placed the Chair on the Table, according to

Gulliver is visited by a court official. Anonymous artist, 1895.

3 *Articles of Impeachment against you.* Here again the satire is thought to apply to the investigation of Oxford and Bolingbroke by the Whigs after the accession of George I (see Chapter 2 of this part, note 17).

4 *Article I.* The first article, which involves the putting out of the fire by Gulliver, would seem to parallel the conclusion of the Treaty of Utrecht by the Tories (see Chapter 5 in this part, note 13).

my usual Custom, and sat down by it. After the common Salutations were over, observing his Lordship's Countenance full of Concern; and enquiring into the Reason, he desired I would hear him with Patience, in a Matter that highly concerned my Honour and my Life. His Speech was to the following Effect, for I took Notes of it as soon as he left me.

You are to know, said he, that several Committees of Council have been lately called in the most private Manner on your Account: And it is but two Days since his Majesty came to a full Resolution.

You are very sensible that *Skyris Bolgolam* (*Galbet,* or High Admiral) hath been your mortal Enemy almost ever since your Arrival. His original Reasons I know not; but his Hatred is much increased since your great Success against *Blefuscu,* by which his Glory, as Admiral, is obscured. This Lord, in Conjunction with *Flimnap* the High Treasurer, whose Enmity against you is notorious on Account of his Lady; *Limtoc* the General, *Lalcon* the Chamberlain, and *Balmuff* the grand Justiciary, have prepared Articles of Impeachment against you, for Treason, and other capital Crimes. **3**

This Preface made me so impatient, being conscious of my own Merits and Innocence, that I was going to interrupt; when he intreated me to be silent; and thus proceeded.

Out of Gratitude for the Favours you have done me, I procured Information of the whole Proceedings, and a Copy of the Articles, wherein I venture my Head for your Service.

Articles of Impeachment against Quinbus Flestrin,
(*the* Man-Mountain.)

ARTICLE I **4**

Whereas, by a Statute made in the Reign of his Imperial Majesty *Calin Deffar Plune,* it is enacted, That whoever shall make water within the Precincts of the Royal Palace, shall be liable to the Pains and Penalties of High Treason: Notwithstanding, the said *Quinbus Flestrin,* in open Breach of the said Law, under Colour of extinguishing the Fire kindled in the Apartment of his Majesty's most dear Imperial Consort, did maliciously, traitorously, and devilishly, by discharge of his Urine, put out the said Fire kindled in the said Apartment, lying and being within the Precincts of the said Royal Palace; against the Statute in that Case provided, *&c.* against the Duty, *&c.*

5 *Article II.* This article seems to parallel charges against Oxford and Bolingbroke, who were accused of having been unwilling, out of pro-French and Jacobite sympathies, to carry on the war to a complete French defeat.

6 *Article III.* A further parallel to Oxford and Bolingbroke, who were also accused of carrying on secret correspondence with the French negotiators.

7 *Article IV.* Oxford and Bolingbroke were accused of planning to flee to France if things grew too hot for them at home and, in France, to raise a French and Jacobite army against King George.

8 *die in the utmost Torture.* This is precisely the manner in which the mythical Greek hero, Herakles (or Hercules) met his death. A shirt soaked in the poisoned blood of the centaur, Nessus, was sent to him. It stuck to him, the poison entered his blood, and he tore off his own flesh in his efforts to remove the shirt, dying in agony.

Hercules and the Pygmies. Dosso Dossi, early sixteenth century.

5
ARTICLE II
THAT the said *Quinbus Flestrin* having brought the Imperial Fleet of *Blefuscu* into the Royal Port, and being afterwards commanded by his Imperial Majesty to seize all the other Ships of the said Empire of *Blefuscu*, and reduce that Empire to a Province, to be governed by a Vice-Roy from hence; and to destroy and put to death not only all the *Big-Endian Exiles,* but likewise all the People of that Empire, who would not immediately forsake the *Big-Endian* Heresy: He the said *Flestrin*, like a false Traitor against his most Auspicious, Serene, Imperial Majesty, did petition to be excused from the said Service, upon Pretence of Unwillingness to force the Consciences, or destroy the Liberties and Lives of an innocent People.

6
ARTICLE III
THAT, whereas certain Embassadors arrived from the Court of *Blefuscu* to sue for Peace in his Majesty's Court: He the said *Flestrin* did, like a false Traitor, aid, abet, comfort, and divert the said Embassadors; although he knew them to be Servants to a Prince who was lately an open Enemy to his Imperial Majesty, and in open War against his said Majesty.

7
ARTICLE IV
THAT the said *Quinbus Flestrin*, contrary to the Duty of a faithful Subject, is now preparing to make a Voyage to the Court and Empire of *Blefuscu*, for which he hath received only verbal Licence from his Imperial Majesty; and under Colour of the said Licence, doth falsly and traitorously intend to take the said Voyage, and thereby to aid, comfort, and abet the Emperor of *Blefuscu*, so late an Enemy, and in open War with his Imperial Majesty aforesaid.

There are some other Articles, but these are the most important, of which I have read you an Abstract.

In the several Debates upon this Impeachment, it must be confessed that his Majesty gave many Marks of his great *Lenity;* often urging the Services you had done him, and endeavouring to extenuate your Crimes. The Treasurer and Admiral insisted that you should be put to the most painful and ignominious Death, by setting Fire on your House at Night; and the General was to attend with Twenty Thousand Men armed with poisoned Arrows, to shoot you on the Face and Hands. Some of your Servants were to have private Orders to strew a poisonous Juice on your Shirts and Sheets, which would soon make you tear your own Flesh, and
8 die in the utmost Torture. The General came into the same Opinion; so that for a long time there was a Majority against you. But his Majesty resolving, if possible, to spare your Life, at last brought off the Chamberlain.

Upon this Incident, *Reldresal,* principal Secretary for private Affairs, who always approved himself your true Friend, was commanded by the Emperor to deliver his Opinion, which he accordingly did; and therein justified the good Thoughts you have of him. He allowed your Crimes to be great; but that still there was room for Mercy, the most commendable Virtue in a Prince, and for which his Majesty was so justly celebrated. He said, the Friendship between you and him was so well known to the World, that perhaps the most honourable Board might think him partial: However, in Obedience to the Command he had received, he would freely offer his Sentiments. That if his Majesty, in Consideration of your Services, and pursuant to his own merciful Disposition, would please to spare your Life, and only give order to put out **9** both your Eyes; he humbly conceived, that by this Expedient, Justice might in some measure be satisfied, and all the World would applaud the *Lenity* of the Emperor, as well as the fair and generous Proceedings of those who have the Honour to be his Counsellors. That the Loss of your Eyes would be no Impediment to your bodily Strength, by which you might still be useful to his Majesty. That Blindness is an addition to Courage, by concealing Dangers from us; that the Fear you had for your Eyes, was the greatest Difficulty in bringing over the Enemy's Fleet; and it would be sufficient for you to see by the Eyes of the Ministers, since the greatest Princes do no more.

This Proposal was received with the utmost Disapprobation by the whole Board. *Bolgolam,* the Admiral, could not preserve his Temper; but rising up in Fury, said, he wondered how the Secretary durst presume to give his Opinion for preserving the Life of a Traytor: That the Services you had performed, were, by all true Reasons of State, the great Aggravation of your Crimes; that you, who were able to extinguish the Fire, by discharge of Urine in her Majesty's Apartment (which he mentioned with Horror) might, at another time, raise an Inundation by the same Means, to drown the whole Palace; and the same Strength which enabled you to bring over the Enemy's Fleet, might serve, upon the first Discontent, to carry it back: That he had good Reasons to think you were a *Big-Endian* in your Heart; and as Treason begins in the Heart before it appears in Overt-Acts; so he accused you as a Traytor on that Account, and therefore insisted you should be put to death.

The Treasurer was of the same Opinion; he shewed to what Streights his Majesty's Revenue was reduced by the Charge of maintaining you, which would soon grow insupportable: That the Secretary's Expedient of putting out your Eyes, was so far from being a Remedy against this Evil, that it would probably increase it; as it is manifest from the common Practice of blinding some Kind of Fowl, after which they fed the faster, and grew sooner fat: That his sacred Majesty, and the Council, who are your Judges, were in their own Consciences fully convinced of your Guilt; which was a sufficient Argument to condemn you to death without **10** the *formal Proofs required by the strict Letter of the Law.*

But his Imperial Majesty fully determined against capital Punishment, was graciously pleased to say, that since the Council thought the Loss of your Eyes too easy a Censure, some other may be inflicted hereafter. And your Friend the Secretary humbly desiring to be heard again, in Answer to what the Treasurer had objected concerning the great Charge his Majesty was at in maintaining you; said, that his Excellency, who had the sole Disposal of the Emperor's Revenue, might easily provide against this Evil, by gradually lessening your Establishment; by which, for want of sufficient Food, you would grow weak and faint, and lose your Appetite, and consequently decay and consume in a few Months; neither would the Stench of your Carcass be then so dangerous, when it should become more than half diminished; and immedi-

9 *to put out both your Eyes.* The analogy is to the suggestion that Oxford and Bolingbroke, instead of suffering the death penalty, merely forfeit their titles and estates.

10 *without the formal Proofs required by the strict Letter of the Law.* The satire is against those who would bend the full formality of law to fit their prejudices and preconceived notions of guilt. The specific reference may be again to Atterbury (see Chapter 6 in this part, note 31), who probably was conspiring on behalf of the Pretender but who was convicted on it by weak evidence and by the waiving of "the strict letter of the law."

11 *great Lenity and Tenderness, as Qualities known and confessed by all the World.* This kind of double-talk is something we are used to from contemporary figures in power, from Hitler to Nixon, but it is as old as government. The specific target seems to have been George I, who ordered the execution of Jacobites and had it accompanied by parliamentary praise for his mercy and kindness.

12 *to terminate as the Judges thought fit to direct.* An example (though perhaps not the one Swift had in mind) was George Jeffreys, baron of Wem, who, in the reign of Charles II and James II, was notorious as a cruel and bullying judge. In the time of Titus Oates (see Chapter 6 in this part, note 6), Jeffreys savagely excoriated the Catholic defendants, who were given no chance whatever. When James II, a Catholic, became king, it was Protestant rebels who were on trial, and Jeffreys saw to it that no shadow of fairness ever intruded there either. After James II lost his throne, Jeffreys was imprisoned in the Tower of London and died there.

ately upon your Death, five or six Thousand of his Majesty's Subjects might, in two or three Days, cut your Flesh from your Bones, take it away by Cart-loads, and bury it in distant Parts to prevent Infection; leaving the skeleton as a Monument of Admiration to Posterity.

Thus by the great Friendship of the Secretary, the whole Affair was compromised. It was strictly enjoined, that the Project of starving you by Degrees should be kept a Secret; but the Sentence of putting out your Eyes was entered on the Books; none dissenting except *Bolgolam* the Admiral, who being a Creature of the Empress, was perpetually instigated by her Majesty to insist upon your Death; she having born perpetual Malice against you, on Account of that infamous and illegal Method you took to extinguish the Fire in her Apartment.

In three Days your Friend the Secretary will be directed to come to your House, and read before you the Articles of Impeachment; and then to signify the great *Lenity* and Favour of his Majesty and Council; whereby you are only condemned to the Loss of your Eyes, which his Majesty doth not question you will gratefully and humbly submit to; and Twenty of his Majesty's Surgeons will attend, in order to see the Operation well performed, by discharging very sharp pointed Arrows into the Balls of your Eyes, as you lie on the Ground.

I leave to your Prudence what Measures you will take; and to avoid Suspicion, I must immediately return in as private a Manner as I came.

His Lordship did so, and I remained alone, under many Doubts and Perplexities of Mind.

It was a Custom introduced by this Prince and his Ministry, (very different, as I have been assured, from the Practices of former Times) that after the Court had decreed any cruel Execution, either to gratify the Monarch's Resentment, or the Malice of a Favourite; the Emperor always made a Speech to his whole **11** Council, expressing his *great Lenity and Tenderness, as Qualities known and confessed by all the World.* This Speech was immediately published through the Kingdom; nor did any thing terrify the People so much as those Encomiums on his Majesty's Mercy; because it was observed, that the more these Praises were enlarged and insisted on, the more *inhuman* was the Punishment, and the *Sufferer more innocent.* Yet, as to myself, I must confess, having never been designed for a Courtier, either by my Birth or Education, I was so ill a Judge of Things, that I could not discover the *Lenity* and Favour of this Sentence; but conceived it (perhaps erroneously) rather to be rigorous than gentle. I sometimes thought of standing my Tryal; for although I could not deny the Facts alledged in the several Articles, yet I hoped they would admit of some Extenuations. But having in my Life perused many State-**12** Tryals, which I ever observed to terminate as the Judges thought fit to direct; I durst not rely on so dangerous a Decision, in so critical a Juncture, and against such powerful Enemies. Once I was strongly bent upon Resistance: For while I had Liberty, the whole Strength of that Empire could hardly subdue me, and I might easily with Stones pelt the Metropolis to Pieces: But I soon rejected that Project with Horror, by remembering the Oath I had made to the Emperor, the Favours I received from him, and the high Title of *Nardac* he conferred upon me. Neither had I so soon learned the Gratitude of Courtiers, to persuade myself that his Majesty's *present Severities acquitted me of all past Obligations.*

At last I fixed upon a Resolution, for which it is probable I may incur some Censure, and not unjustly; for I confess I owe the preserving my Eyes, and consequently my Liberty, to my own great Rashness and Want of Experience: Because if I had then known the Nature of Princes and Ministers, which I have since observed in many other Courts, and their Methods of treating Criminals less obnoxious than myself; I should with great Alacrity and Readiness have submitted to so *easy* a Punishment. But hurried on by the Precipitancy of Youth; and having his Imperial Majesty's Licence to pay my Attendance upon the Emperor of *Blefuscu;* I took this Opportunity, before the three Days were elapsed, to send a Letter to my Friend the Secretary, signifying my Resolution of setting out that Morning for *Blefuscu,* pursuant to the Leave I had got; and without waiting for an Answer, I went to that Side of the Island where our Fleet lay. I seized a large Man of War, tied a Cable to the Prow, and lifting up the Anchors, I stript myself, put my Cloaths (together with my Coverlet, which I carryed under my Arm) into the Vessel; and drawing it after me, between wading and swimming, arrived at the Royal Port of *Blefuscu,* where the People had long expected me: They lent me two Guides to direct me to the Capital City, which is of the same Name; I held them in my Hands until I came within two Hundred Yards of the Gate; and desired them to signify my Arrival to one of the Secretaries, and let him know, I there waited his Majesty's Commands. I had an Answer in about an Hour, that his Majesty, attended by the Royal Family, and great Officers of the Court, was coming out to receive me. I advanced a Hundred Yards; the Emperor, and his Train, alighted from their Horses, the Empress and Ladies from their Coaches; and I did not perceive they were in any Fright or Concern. I lay on the Ground to kiss his Majesty's and the Empress's Hand. I told his Majesty, that I was come according to my Promise, and with the Licence of the Emperor my Master, to have the Honour of seeing so mighty a Monarch, and to offer him any Service in my Power, consistent with my Duty to my own Prince; not mentioning a Word of my Disgrace, because I had hitherto no regular Information of it, and might suppose myself wholly ignorant of any such Design; neither could I reasonably conceive that the Emperor would discover the Secret while I was out of his Power: Wherein, however, it soon appeared I was deceived.

I shall not trouble the Reader with the particular Account of my Reception at this Court, which was suitable to the Generosity of so great a Prince; nor of the Difficulties I was in for want of a House and Bed, being forced to lie on the Ground, wrapt up in my Coverlet.

13 *Youth.* Engaged in a particularly bitter piece of irony here, Swift seems to forget that Gulliver is no youth, but is about thirty-eight years old at the time of his Lilliputian adventure.

14 *arrived at the Royal Port of Blefuscu.* Just before the trial of Oxford and Bolingbroke, the latter escaped to France, and this is analogous to Gulliver's flight to Blefuscu. Oxford chose to remain in England and take his chances. The charges against him were dropped after two years but he never reentered public life.

15 *Discover.* Used here in the earlier sense of "*uncover*"; that is, "to make known."

1 *a real Boat*. Actually, to be realistic for a moment, there should be, on occasion, the arrival not only of boats but of other objects from the rest of the world, which would give the Lilliputians and the Blefuscans sufficient occasions to realize that a land of giants existed beyond the horizon. In particular, seabirds of ordinary size would surely arrive occasionally—with devastating effect on the native flora and fauna.

The Author, by a lucky accident, finds means to leave Blefuscu; and, after some difficulties, returns safe to his Native Country.

THREE Days after my Arrival, walking out of Curiosity to the North East Coast of the Island; I observed, about half a League off, in the Sea, somewhat that looked like a Boat overturned: I pulled off my Shoes and Stockings, and wading two or three Hundred Yards, I found the Object to approach nearer by Force of the Tide; **1** and then plainly saw it to be a real Boat, which I supposed might, by some Tempest, have been driven from a Ship. Whereupon I returned immediately towards the City, and desired his Imperial Majesty to lend me Twenty of the tallest Vessels he had left after the Loss of his Fleet, and three Thousand Seamen under the Command of his Vice-Admiral. This Fleet sailed round, while I went back the shortest Way to the Coast where I first discovered the Boat; I found the Tide had driven it still nearer; the Seamen were all provided with Cordage, which I had beforehand twisted to a sufficient Strength. When the Ships came up, I stript myself, and waded till I came within an Hundred Yards of the Boat; after which I was forced to swim till I got up to it. The Seamen threw me the End of the Cord, which I fastened to a Hole in the fore-part of the Boat, and the other End to a Man of War: But I found all my

Labour to little Purpose; for being out of my Depth, I was not able to work. In this Necessity, I was forced to swim behind, and push the Boat forwards as often as I could, with one of my Hands; and the Tide favouring me, I advanced so far, that I could just hold up my Chin and feel the Ground. I rested two or three Minutes, and then gave the Boat another Shove, and so on till the Sea was no higher than my Arm-pits. And now the most laborious Part being over, I took out my other Cables which were stowed in one of the Ships, and fastening them first to the Boat, and then to nine of the Vessels which attended me; the Wind being favourable, the Seamen towed, and I shoved till we arrived within forty Yards of the Shore; and waiting till the Tide was out, I got dry to the Boat, and by the Assistance of two Thousand Men, with Ropes and Engines, I made a shift to turn it on its Bottom, and found it was but little damaged.

I shall not trouble the Reader with the Difficulties I was under by the Help of certain Paddles, which cost me ten Days making, to get my Boat to the Royal Port of *Blefuscu;* where a mighty Concourse of People appeared upon my Arrival, full of Wonder at the Sight of so prodigious a Vessel. I told the Emperor, that my good Fortune had thrown this Boat in my Way, to carry me to some Place from whence I might return into my native Country; and begged his Majesty's Orders for getting Materials to fit it up; together with his Licence to depart; which, after some kind Expostulations, he was pleased to grant.

I did very much wonder, in all this Time, not to have heard of any Express relating to me from our Emperor to the Court of *Blefuscu.* But I was afterwards given privately to understand, that his Imperial Majesty, never imagining I had the least Notice of his Designs, believed I was only gone to *Blefuscu* in Performance of my Promise, according to the Licence he had given me, which was well known at our Court; and would return in a few Days when that Ceremony was ended. But he was at last in pain at my long absence; and, after consulting with the Treasurer, and the rest of that Cabal; a Person of Quality was dispatched with the Copy of the Articles against me. This Envoy had Instructions to represent to the Monarch of *Blefuscu,* the great *Lenity* of his Master, who was content to punish me no further than with the Loss of my Eyes: That I had fled from Justice, and if I did not return in two Hours, I should be deprived of my Title of *Nardac,* and declared a Traitor. The Envoy further added; that in order to maintain the Peace and Amity between both Empires, his Master expected, that his Brother of *Blefuscu* would give Orders to have me sent back to *Lilliput,* bound Hand and Foot, to be punished as a Traitor.

The Emperor of *Blefuscu* having taken three Days to consult, returned an Answer consisting of many Civilities and Excuses. He said, that as for sending me bound, his Brother knew it was impossible; that although I had deprived him of his Fleet, yet he owed great Obligations to me for many good Offices I had done him in making the Peace. That however, both their Majesties would soon be made easy; for I had found a prodigious Vessel on the Shore, able to carry me on the Sea, which he had given order to fit up with my own Assistance and Direction; and he hoped in a few Weeks both Empires would be freed from so insupportable an Incumbrance.

Gulliver brings his boat into the royal port of Blefuscu. Rouget, 1895.

2 *never more to put any Confidence in Princes or Ministers.* A common quotation, "Put not your trust in princes," is from Psalms 146:3. The implication in the Bible is that God is a more powerful helper than any human being could be. When quoted in an earthly context, however, it usually implies that rulers are bound to sacrifice their word and their honor whenever it is necessary to do so for "reasons of state."

Gulliver, who began as an amiable, good-natured human being who likes the Lilliputians, is impressed by them, and goes to considerable trouble to avoid harming them, even under provocation, thus begins his road to disillusionment.

3 *glad of my Resolution.* This may be another reference to Bolingbroke. Having fled to France, Bolingbroke openly entered the service of the Pretender and acted as his adviser. The Pretender, however, found Bolingbroke's estimate of the situation in England too pessimistically realistic. Bolingbroke was therefore dismissed and the Pretender had the pleasure of listening to advisers with more flattering predictions—who, however, did not manage to get him onto the British throne with their flattery.

4 *a Dozen of the Natives.* It was routine to take back natives of a newly discovered country, both as a curiosity and as evidence of having visited strange lands. Columbus, on his return from his first voyage, brought Indians with him as the best proof that he had not been merely wandering about the ocean.

5 *Twenty-fourth Day of September 1701.* This is nearly two years and five months after Gulliver left Bristol to begin this journey. While Gulliver was gone, the War of the Spanish Succession (which had been parodied and satirized in Lilliput), had actually begun. Of course, Gulliver makes no mention of it.

"I took with me six Cows and two Bulls alive." Bouchot, 1855. Courtesy, The New York Public Library.

With this Answer the Envoy returned to *Lilliput,* and the Monarch of *Blefuscu* related to me all that had past; offering me at at the same time (but under the strictest Confidence) his gracious Protection, if I would continue in his Service; wherein although **2** I believed him sincere, yet I resolved never more to put any Confidence in Princes or Ministers, where I could possibly avoid it; and therefore, with all due Acknowledgments for his favourable Intentions, I humbly begged to be excused. I told him, that since Fortune, whether good or evil, had thrown a Vessel in my Way; I was resolved to venture myself in the Ocean, rather than be an Occasion of Difference between two such mighty Monarchs. Neither did I find the Emperor at all displeased; and I discovered **3** by a certain Accident, that he was very glad of my Resolution, and so were most of his Ministers.

These Considerations moved me to hasten my Departure somewhat sooner than I intended; to which the Court, impatient to have me gone, very readily contributed. Five hundred Workmen were employed to make two Sails to my Boat, according to my Directions, by quilting thirteen fold of their strongest Linnen together. I was at the Pains of making Ropes and Cables, by twisting ten, twenty or thirty of the thickest and strongest of theirs. A great Stone that I happened to find, after a long Search by the Seashore, served me for an Anchor. I had the Tallow of three hundred Cows for greasing my Boat, and other Uses. I was at incredible Pains in cutting down some of the largest Timber Trees for Oars and Masts, wherein I was, however, much assisted by his Majesty's Ship-Carpenters, who helped me in smoothing them, after I had done the rough Work.

In about a Month, when all was prepared, I sent to receive his Majesty's Commands, and to take my leave. The Emperor and Royal Family came out of the Palace; I lay down on my Face to kiss his Hand, which he very graciously gave me; so did the Empress, and young Princes of the Blood. His Majesty presented me with fifty Purses of two hundred *Sprugs* a-piece, together with his Picture at full length, which I put immediately into one of my Gloves, to keep it from being hurt. The Ceremonies at my Departure were too many to trouble the Reader with at this time.

I stored the Boat with the Carcasses of an hund̵d Oxen, and three hundred Sheep, with Bread and Drink proportionable, and as much Meat ready dressed as four hundred Cooks could provide. I took with me six Cows and two Bulls alive, with as many Yews and Rams, intending to carry them into my own Country and propagate the Breed. And to feed them on board, I had a good Bundle of Hay, and a Bag of Corn. I would gladly have taken a **4** Dozen of the Natives; but this was a thing the Emperor would by no Means permit; and besides a diligent Search into my Pockets, his Majesty engaged my Honour not to carry away any of his Subjects, although with their own Consent and Desire.

Having thus prepared all things as well as I was able; I set sail **5** on the Twenty-fourth Day of *September* 1701, at six in the Morning; and when I had gone about four Leagues to the Northward, the Wind being at South-East; at six in the Evening, I descryed a small Island about half a League to the North West. I advanced forward, and cast Anchor on the Lee-side of the Island, which seemed to be uninhabited. I then took some Refreshment, and

His Majesty presents him with fifty purses of two-hundred Sprugs a-piece together with his picture at full length

Illustration by Rex Whistler, 1930.

6 *North-East of Van Diemen's Land.* This is an interesting example of Swift's occasional ability to make a lucky guess. There *are* islands to the northeast of Van Diemen's Land (Tasmania). These are the Furneaux Islands, discovered by the English explorer, Tobias Furneaux (1735–1781) who had not yet been born at the time *Gulliver's Travels* was published and who discovered the islands in 1773, a half century after it was published. The largest of the Furneaux Islands is Flinders Island, which is about eight hundred square miles in area. Furneaux, by the way, was the first human being in history to circumnavigate the globe both ways, east to west *and* west to east.

Of course, if the map given in the chapter is to be trusted, Lilliput and Blefuscu are perhaps three thousand miles from Van Diemen's Land. But the simplest way out of that dilemma is to suppose that the map is not to be trusted.

7 *hung out her Antient.* The first impression the modern reader gets is that the ship allowed her oldest sailor to dangle from some rope. Actually, "ancient" is, in this case, a version of "ensign," and refers to the flag which the ship now hoisted to indicate her nationality. The firing of the gun that followed was a signal rather than a sign of hostility. In the days before radio, flags and gunshots, appealing to the senses of sight and sound, were the only means of communication between ships at a considerable distance from each other.

8 *dear Pledges.* That is, Gulliver's wife and children. It is a common thought that a wife and children are the pledges given to fortune, which it may foreclose on at any time.

9 *North and South Seas.* The North Pacific and the South Pacific oceans. From Japan, the merchantman has traveled through the Pacific Ocean into the Indian Ocean, where Lilliput is located, and it will therefore return to England by way of the Cape of Good Hope.

10 *Deptford.* A town located about ten miles southeast of London.

11 *Latitude of 30 Degrees South.* Specifying the latitude is not sufficient to locate a spot on the globe; the longitude is also required. In this case, it would be particularly interesting to know, for some two thousand miles of the 30 degrees south line runs through Australia.

12 *the Downs.* Protected anchorage off the eastern shore of Kent, a county in southeasternmost England. Gulliver, arriving there on April 13, 1702, reaches England just about a month after William III had died and been succeeded by Anne, and just one month before England entered the War of the Spanish Succession. The first voyage had taken Gulliver three weeks short of three years.

went to my Rest. I slept well, and as I conjecture at least six Hours; for I found the Day broke in two Hours after I awaked. It was a clear Night; I eat my Breakfast before the Sun was up; and heaving Anchor, the Wind being favourable, I steered the same Course that I had done the Day before, wherein I was directed by my Pocket-Compass. My Intention was to reach, if possible, one of **6** those Islands, which I had reason to believe lay to the North-East of *Van Diemen's* Land. I discovered nothing all that Day; but upon the next, about three in the Afternoon, when I had by my Computation made Twenty-four Leagues from *Blefuscu,* I descryed a Sail steering to the South-East; my Course was due East. I hailed her, but could get no Answer; yet I found I gained upon her, for the Wind slackened. I made all the Sail I could, and in half an **7** Hour she spyed me, then hung out her Antient, and discharged a Gun. It is not easy to express the Joy I was in upon the unexpected **8** Hope of once more seeing my beloved Country, and the dear Pledges I had left in it. The Ship slackned her Sails, and I came up with her between five and six in the Evening, *September* 26; but my Heart leapt within me to see her *English* Colours. I put my Cows and Sheep into my Coat-Pockets, and got on board with all my little Cargo of Provisions. The Vessel was an *English* Merchant- **9** man returning from *Japan* by the *North* and *South Seas;* the Cap- **10** tain, Mr. *John Biddel* of *Deptford,* a very civil Man, and an ex- **11** cellent Sailor. We were now in the Latitude of 30 Degrees South; there were about fifty Men in the Ship; and here I met an old Comrade of mine, one *Peter Williams,* who gave me a good Character to the Captain. This Gentleman treated me with Kindness, and desired I would let him know what Place I came from last, and whither I was bound; which I did in few Words; but he thought I was raving, and that the Dangers I underwent had disturbed my Head; whereupon I took my black Cattle and Sheep out of my Pocket, which, after great Astonishment, clearly convinced him of my Veracity. I then shewed him the Gold given me by the Emperor of *Blefuscu,* together with his Majesty's Picture at full Length, and some other Rarities of that Country. I gave him two Purses of two Hundred *Sprugs* each, and promised, when we arrived in *England,* to make him a Present of a Cow and a Sheep big with Young.

I shall not trouble the Reader with a particular Account of this Voyage; which was very prosperous for the most Part. We arrived **12** in the *Downs* on the 13th of *April* 1702. I had only one Misfortune, that the Rats on board carried away one of my Sheep; I found her Bones in a Hole, picked clean from the Flesh. The rest of my Cattle I got safe on Shore, and set them a grazing in a Bowling- **13** Green at *Greenwich,* where the Fineness of the Grass made them feed very heartily, although I had always feared the contrary: Neither could I possibly have preserved them in so long a Voyage, if the Captain had not allowed me some of his best Bisket, which rubbed to Powder, and mingled with Water, was their constant Food. The short Time I continued in *England,* I made a considerable Profit by shewing my Cattle to many Persons of Quality, and others: And before I began my second Voyage, I sold them for six Hundred Pounds. Since my last Return, I find the Breed is considerably increased, especially the Sheep; which I hope will prove much to the Advantage of the Woollen Manufacture, by the Fineness of the Fleeces.

I stayed but two Months with my Wife and Family; for my **14** insatiable Desire of seeing foreign Countries would suffer me to continue no longer. I left fifteen Hundred Pounds with my Wife, and fixed her in a good House at *Redriff*. My remaining Stock I **15** carried with me, Part in Money, and Part in Goods, in Hopes to improve my Fortunes. My eldest Uncle, *John*, had left me an Estate in Land, near *Epping*, of about Thirty Pounds a Year; and I **16** had a long Lease of the *Black-Bull* in *Fetter-Lane*, which yielded me as much more: So that I was not in any Danger of leaving my Family upon the Parish. My Son *Johnny*, named so after his Uncle, was at the Grammar School, and a towardly Child. My Daughter **17** *Betty* (who is now well married, and has Children) was then at her Needle-Work. I took Leave of my Wife, and Boy and Girl, with Tears on both Sides; and went on board the *Adventure*, a Merchant-Ship of three Hundred Tons, bound for *Surat*, Captain **18** *John Nicholas* of *Liverpool*, Commander. But my Account of this Voyage must be referred to the second Part of my Travels.

The End of the First Part.

"I took Leave of my Wife." Bouchot, 1855. *Courtesy, The New York Public Library.*

13 *Greenwich.* This city is on the Thames River about five miles downstream from the center of London. It is best known as the original site of the Royal Observatory, established in 1675 under the patronage of Charles II.

14 *I stayed but two Months with my Wife and Family.* Gulliver's inability to remain with his family strikes an odd note for most settled people, but at least Swift makes it clear that his first voyage was a very profitable one and that his family does not suffer financially because of his absences. Swift, of course, was not a family man and probably could not empathize with the matter of wives and children.

15 *Redriff.* Or Rotherhithe, a parish in the Southwark borough of London, just south of London Bridge.

16 *Epping.* A town in the county of Essex, seventeen miles northeast of the center of London.

17 *towardly.* Now an archaic word, it could mean "thriving" or it could mean "dutiful and well-behaved." Possibly Swift intends both.

18 *Surat.* A city on the west coast of India, 150 miles north of Bombay. It was the first piece of Indian soil held by the English (1608); they had established a factory there in 1612. In Swift's time it was still the most considerable English possession in India.

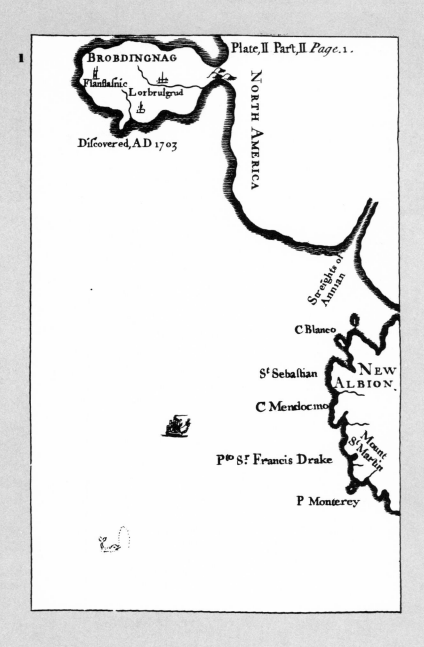

1 *Brobdingnag*. The second land visited by Gulliver. The map shows it to be a peninsula off the western coast of North America.

PART TWO

A Voyage to Brobdingnag

1 *the 20th Day of June, 1702.* Gulliver is now forty-one years old. At the time he leaves, Marlborough, based in Holland, is trying to invade the Spanish Netherlands to the south and is being hampered by the cautious Dutch.

2 *a very prosperous Gale.* A fresh wind that speeds a ship along in the direction it wants to go.

3 *the Cape of Good-hope.* Near the southern tip of Africa. The shortest sea route to India was around Africa. The Suez Canal cut the distance greatly but wasn't built until the 1860s, almost a century and a half after *Gulliver's Travels* was published.

4 *Ague.* A term no longer used in medicine. A person suffering from ague had fever and chills, probably due to malaria.

5 *the Streights of Madagascar.* The channel between the large island of Madagascar and the African continent. At its narrowest it is 250 miles wide. It is now called the Mozambique Channel.

6 *five Degrees South Latitude.* To go through the straits to 5 degrees south latitude would bring the ship somewhere near the Seychelles islands to the southeast of the shores of what are now the African nations of Tanzania and Kenya.

A great Storm described. The Long Boat sent to fetch Water, the Author goes with it to discover the Country. He is left on Shoar, is seized by one of the Natives, and carried to a Farmer's House. His Reception there, with several Accidents that happened there. A Description of the Inhabitants.

AVING been condemned by Nature and Fortune to an active and restless Life; in two Months after my Return, I again left my native Country, and took Shipping in the *Downs* on the 20*th* Day of *June*

1
1702, in the *Adventure*, Capt. *John Nicholas*, a *Cornish* Man, Com-

2 mander, bound for *Surat*. We had a very prosperous Gale till we

3 arrived at the *Cape* of *Good-hope*, where we landed for fresh

4 Water; but discovering a Leak we unshipped our Goods, and wintered there; for the Captain falling sick of an Ague, we could not leave the *Cape* till the End of *March*. We then set sail, and had

5 a good Voyage till we passed the *Streights* of *Madagascar;* but hav-

6 ing got Northward of that Island, and to about five Degrees South

7 Latitude, the Winds, which in those Seas are observed to blow a constant equal Gale between the North and West, from the Beginning of *December* to the Beginning of *May*, on the 19*th* of *April* began to blow with much greater Violence, and more Westerly than usual; continuing so for twenty Days together, during

8 which time we were driven a little to the East of the *Molucca* Is-

9 lands, and about three Degrees Northward of the *Line*, as our

Captain Lemuel Gulliver, of
Redriff Ætat. fuæ *58.*

Frontispiece to the first edition, London, 1726. Courtesy, Rare Book Division, The New York Public Library.

7 *the Winds . . . blow a constant equal Gale between the North and West.* This is the "monsoon," from an Arabic word meaning "season." It is, in other words, a seasonal wind which blows in one direction for half the year and then in the opposite direction for the other half.

8 *the Molucca Islands.* These islands are part of Indonesia and lie between Celebes, New Guinea, and Timor. During the Age of Exploration, they were called the Spice Islands. The Moluccas lie about five thousand miles nearly due east of the Seychelles, and Gulliver's ship, which covered the distance in twenty days must therefore have been driven eastward at an average rate of two hundred fifty miles per day. That's pretty good traveling, and it is made the more remarkable in that it must have ploughed right through Sumatra, Borneo, and Celebes to get to the Moluccas.

9 *three Degrees Northward of the Line.* To be at three degrees north in the Moluccas is to be just north of the island of Halmahera, the largest of the group, and about seven thousand square miles in area.

10 *to overblow.* That is, to have the wind grow to such a speed as to endanger the ship. In this paragraph, Swift has copied a description of a storm from *Mariners' Magazine* practically word for word, satirizing nautical jargon since no one but a trained mariner of the time can possibly tell what is going on. On another level, it is typical of Gulliver whose naïve pride (never far from the surface) lures him into trotting out all these wearisome details to impress the landlubbers.

11 *the Guns were all fast.* The ship was a merchantman, of course, but it would carry guns. The people of Asia and Africa still showed occasional resentment when European traders arranged the terms of trade to suit themselves. Besides, England was at war with France, and French ships sailed the seas, too.

If guns were on board then in a storm they had better be made fast. A heavy gun, coming loose, and sliding about the deck with each lurch of the ship, would do more damage than the waves would.

Captain found by an Observation he took the *2d* of *May,* at which time the Wind ceased, and it was a perfect Calm, whereat I was not a little rejoyced. But he being a Man well experienced in the Navigation of those Seas, bid us all prepare against a Storm, which accordingly happened the Day following: For a Southern Wind, called the Southern *Monsoon,* began to set in.

Finding it was like to overblow, we took in our Sprit-sail, and stood by to hand the Fore-sail; but making foul Weather, we looked the Guns were all fast, and handed the Missen. The Ship lay very broad off, so we thought it better spooning before the Sea, than trying or hulling. We reeft the Fore-sail and set him, we hawled aft the Fore-sheet; the Helm was hard a Weather. The Ship wore bravely. We belay'd th Foredown-hall; but the Sail was split, and we hawl'd down the Yard, and got the Sail into the Ship,

10

11

12 *five hundred Leagues to the East*. That is, fifteen hundred miles, which would carry the ship into the middle of the North Pacific Ocean, about where the Marshall Islands are to be found. Under these conditions the ship would indeed be completely lost. It was not until the time of Captain James Cook (1728–1779), who scoured the length and breadth of the Pacific Ocean in three voyages between 1769 and 1779 (a half century after *Gulliver's Travels* was published), that the Pacific came to be reasonably well known.

13 *great Tartary*. The name given to the lands ruled by the Tartars (more properly, Tatars) or Mongols. The interior of Asia was called "Great Tartary" to distinguish it from "Little Tartary" which was in southern Russia and the Crimea.

Actually, if the ship had headed northward from the Marshall Islands, they would have reached the northeastern corner of Great Tartary—or of Siberia, at any rate.

14 *frozen sea*. The Arctic Ocean. At the time *Gulliver's Travels* was published, there was no knowledge concerning the connection of the Pacific and the Arctic oceans. Gulliver's ship would have had difficulty blundering through the narrow Bering Strait, which was the only connection and which was first discovered by the Danish navigator, (in Russian employ), Vitus Jonassen Bering (1680–1741) in 1728, two years after *Gulliver's Travels* was published.

15 *the 16th Day of June, 1703*. Gulliver has now been on his second voyage for four days less than a year and is forty-two years old. By now Marlborough had won considerable ground in the Spanish Netherlands.

16 *whether*. Which. The land which Gulliver has now reached turns out to be Brobdingnag.

According to the map presented with this chapter, the country is a peninsula connected with the North American continent by a narrow and mountainous neck of land. "New Albion" is shown and that represents the region around San Francisco, which Francis Drake first reached about 1578 and to which he gave the name of New Albion (Albion being a poetic name for England). At that time, Drake traveled from California to the Moluccas; Gulliver has reversed that trip.

Monterey is also shown. The straight line distance from Monterey to San Francisco is about eighty miles. If the map is to scale, then the peninsula is perhaps one hundred fifty miles north of San Francisco, or about halfway between San Francisco and the northern boundary of California.

17 *I observed a huge Creature walking*. This is the first indication that Brobdingnag is a land of giants, as Lilliput was a land of pygmies. In fact, as we shall see, the proportions are precisely reversed. Whereas all linear measurements are reduced to 1/12 in Lilliput, they are all multiplied by 12 in Brobdingnag. European inches are feet to the Lilliputians; European feet are inches to the Brobdingnagians. To the

and unbound all the things clear of it. It was a very fierce Storm; the Sea broke strange and dangerous. We hawl'd off upon the Lanniard of the Wipstaff, and helped the Man at Helm. We would not get down our Top-Mast, but let all stand, because she scudded before the Sea very well, and we knew that the Top-Mast being aloft, the Ship was the wholesomer, and made better way through the Sea, seeing we had Sea room. When the Storm was over, we set Fore-sail and Main-sail, and brought the Ship too. Then we set the Missen, Maintop-Sail and the Foretop-Sail. Our Course was East North-east, the Wind was at South-west. We got the Star-board Tack aboard, we cast off our Weather-braces and Lifts; we set in the Lee-braces, and hawl'd forward by the Weather-bowlings, and hawl'd them tight, and belayed them, and hawl'd over the Missen Tack to Windward, and kept her full and by as near as she would lye.

12 During this Storm, which was followed by a strong Wind West South-west, we were carried by my Computation about five hundred Leagues to the East, so that the oldest Sailor on Board could not tell in what part of the World we were. Our Provisions held out well, our Ship was staunch, and our Crew all in good Health; but we lay in the utmost Distress for Water. We thought it best to hold on the same Course rather than turn more Northerly, which might **13** have brought us to the North-west Parts of great *Tartary*, and into **14** the frozen Sea.

15 On the 16*th* Day of *June* 1703, a Boy on the Top-mast discovered Land. On the 17*th* we came in full View of a great Island or Con- **16** tinent, (for we knew not whether) on the South-side whereof was a small Neck of Land jutting out into the Sea, and a Creek too shallow to hold a Ship of above one hundred Tuns. We cast Anchor within a League of this Creek, and our Captain sent a dozen of his Men well armed in the Long Boat, with Vessels for Water if any could be found. I desired his leave to go with them, that I might see the Country, and make what Discoveries I could. When we came to Land we saw no River or Spring, nor any Sign of Inhabitants. Our Men therefore wandered on the Shore to find out some fresh Water near the Sea, and I walked alone about a Mile on the other Side, where I observed the Country all barren and rocky. I now began to be weary, and seeing nothing to entertain my Curiosity, I returned gently down towards the Creek; and the Sea being full in my View, I saw our Men already got into the Boat, and rowing for Life to the Ship. I was going to hollow after them, al- **17** though it had been to little purpose, when I observed a huge Creature walking after them in the Sea, as fast as he could: He waded not much deeper than his Knees, and took prodigious strides: But our Men had the start of him half a League, and the Sea thereabouts being full of sharp pointed Rocks, the Monster was not able to overtake the Boat. This I was afterwards told, for I durst not stay to see the Issue of that Adventure; but run as fast as I could the Way I first went; and then climbed up a steep Hill, which gave me some Prospect of the Country. I found it fully cul- **18** tivated; but that which first surprized me was the Length of the Grass, which in those Grounds that seemed to be kept for Hay, was over twenty Foot high.

I fell into a high Road, for so I took it to be, although it served to the Inhabitants only as a foot Path through a Field of Barley.

Brobdingnagians, Gulliver is as the Lilliputians were to him.

18 *the Length of the Grass . . . was over twenty Foot high.* All Brobdingnagian linear measures must be divided by 12 to bring them to European size, so that the grass was actually 20 inches high on the Brobdingnagian scale of things. The corn referred to later was 40 inches or 3 1/2 feet tall. Swift is as careful in his measurements in this second voyage as he was in the first. All Brobdingnagian areas are 144 times the European equivalent; all volumes and masses, 1,728 times the European equivalent.

19 *Trees so lofty that I could make no Computation of their Altitude.* All things, animate and inanimate, are drawn out to the Brobdingnagian scale so that the trees must be over a thousand feet high in some cases. A giant redwood, if one existed in Brobdingnag, would be nearly a mile high.

20 *as Tall as an ordinary Spire-steeple.* Brobdingnagian adult males would range between fifty and seventy-five feet in height, and would be as tall as, let us say, a seven-story building. Naturally, if human beings (or any living thing, including trees) were extended in size in this fashion, with no change in proportions—and the story doesn't indicate any change—they would not be able to function. A Brobdingnagian adult male would weigh something like 130 tons. He would be the equivalent of the largest whale tipped up on end. His legs, if they were no larger in proportion to his body than our legs are to ours, could not possibly support that huge weight. For that matter, if an eighty-foot tree were expanded to a height of one thousand feet and if its trunk expanded proportionately, it could not stand.

"I . . . could see little on either Side." French edition, 1795. Courtesy, Library of Congress.

"He appeared as Tall as an ordinary Spire-steeple." J. J. Grandville, 1835. Courtesy, Library of Congress.

Here I walked on for sometime, but could see little on either Side, it being now near Harvest, and the Corn rising at least forty Foot. I was an Hour walking to the end of this Field; which was fenced in with a Hedge of at least one hundred and twenty Foot high, and the Trees so lofty that I could make no Computation of their Altitude. There was a Stile to pass from this Field into the next: It had four Steps, and a Stone to cross over when you came to the utmost. It was impossible for me to climb this Stile, because every Step was six Foot high, and the upper Stone above twenty. I was endeavouring to find some Gap in the Hedge; when I discovered one of the Inhabitants in the next Field advancing towards the Stile, of the same size with him whom I saw in the Sea pursuing our Boat. He appeared as Tall as an ordinary Spire-steeple; and took about ten Yards at every Stride, as near as I could guess. I was struck with the utmost Fear and Astonishment, and ran to hide my self in the Corn, from whence I saw him at the Top of the Stile, looking back

19

20

21 *Thunder.* Naturally, these large creatures with enormously long vocal cords would make noises many octaves below our own, and their voices would sound like the deep roll of distant thunder, if indeed, those voices could be heard at all.

22 *Savage and cruel in Proportion to their Bulk.* Gulliver's assumption that size lends savagery is completely wrong. A large animal may do more damage through carelessness or fright than a small animal will, simply because the large animal is more massive. However, a tiny shrew has a disposition far worse than that of an elephant or gorilla. In fact, it is much more reasonable to argue that small animals are likely to be more savage (to the extent that their size allows) than large, since small animals are more likely to be frightened than large ones are.

Gulliver's own experience in Lilliput would testify to that. The Lilliputians, frightened of the monster in their midst, could not help but plot a savage return for his services and to debate in what different ways they could put him to death. Gulliver, on the other hand, having nothing to fear from individual Lilliputians, or even from a great number, could afford to be gentle and kind.

23 *nothing is great or little otherwise than by Comparison.* The philosopher who Swift seems to have in mind was his friend, George Berkeley (1685–1753) who developed a subjective theory of knowledge, whereby one could learn only by sense perception (outside of the areas of religious faith and revelation) with such sense perception notoriously unreliable and incapable of demonstrating truth or reality. In his book, *Essay Towards a New Theory of Vision*, Berkeley stressed the relativity of judgment. The book was published in 1709, six years after Gulliver landed in Brobdingnag.

24 *some Nation, where the People were as diminutive with respect to them, as they were to me.* If we imagine the Lilliputians finding a race of infra-Lilliputians, each of whom is but half an inch high, then such a race might, in principle, find still smaller creatures, each only 1/24 of an inch high, and so on. Starting with an ordinary human being, it would take only nine steps, each involving a twelve to one shrinkage, to end up with a being only slightly larger than an atom. Five more steps and the creature would be smaller than a proton.

25 *equally over-matched in some distant Part of the World.* It would take only seven steps of a one to twelve expansion, starting with an average-sized human being, to end with an individual almost as tall as the earth's diameter; only nineteen more to make an individual almost as tall as the diameter of the universe.

21

22

23

24

25

into the next Field on the right Hand; and heard him call in a Voice many Degrees louder than a speaking Trumpet; but the Noise was so High in the Air, that at first I certainly thought it was Thunder. Whereupon seven Monsters like himself came towards him with Reaping-Hooks in their Hands, each Hook about the largeness of six Scythes. These People were not so well clad as the first, whose Servants or Labourers they seemed to be. For, upon some Words he spoke, they went to reap the Corn in the Field where I lay. I kept from them at as great a Distance as I could, but was forced to move with extreme Difficulty; for the Stalks of the Corn were sometimes not above a Foot distant, so that I could hardly squeeze my Body betwixt them. However, I made a shift to go forward till I came to a part of the Field where the Corn had been laid by the Rain and Wind: Here it was impossible for me to advance a step; for the Stalks were so interwoven that I could not creep through, and the Beards of the fallen Ears so strong and pointed, that they pierced through my Cloaths into my Flesh. At the same time I heard the Reapers not above an hundred Yards behind me. Being quite dispirited with Toil, and wholly overcome by Grief and Despair, I lay down between two Ridges, and heartily wished I might there end my Days. I bemoaned my desolate Widow, and Fatherless Children: I lamented my own Folly and Wilfulness in attempting a second Voyage against the Advice of all my Friends and Relations. In this terrible Agitation of Mind I could not forbear thinking of *Lilliput*, whose Inhabitants looked upon me as the greatest Prodigy that ever appeared in the World; where I was able to draw an Imperial Fleet in my Hand, and perform those other Actions which will be recorded for ever in the Chronicles of that Empire, while Posterity shall hardly believe them, although attested by Millions. I reflected what a Mortification it must prove to me to appear as inconsiderable in this Nation, as one single *Lilliputian* would be among us. But, this I conceived was to be the least of my Misfortunes: For, as human Creatures are observed to be more Savage and cruel in Proportion to their Bulk; what could I expect but to be a Morsel in the Mouth of the first among these enormous Barbarians who should happen to seize me? Undoubtedly Philosophers are in the Right when they tell us, that nothing is great or little otherwise than by Comparison: It might have pleased Fortune to let the *Lilliputians* find some Nation, where the People were as diminutive with respect to them, as they were to me. And who knows but that even this prodigious Race of Mortals might be equally over-matched in some distant Part of the World, whereof we have yet no Discovery?

Scared and confounded as I was, I could not forbear going on with these Reflections; when one of the Reapers approaching within ten Yards of the Ridge where I lay, made me apprehend that with the next Step I should be squashed to Death under his Foot, or cut in two with his Reaping Hook. And therefore when he was again about to move, I screamed as loud as Fear could make me. Whereupon the huge Creature trod short, and looking round about under him for some time, at last espied me as I lay on the Ground. He considered a while with the Caution of one who endeavours to lay hold on a small dangerous Animal in such a Manner that it shall not be able either to scratch or to bite him; as I myself have sometimes done with a *Weasel* in *England*. At length he ventured to take me up behind by the middle between his Fore-finger and

He screams as loud as Fear can make him, where-upon the huge Creature at last espies him

Illustration by Rex Whistler, 1930.

"They all sate down in a Circle about me." Richard
Corbould, 1816. Courtesy, The New York Public
Library.

26 *he would dash me . . . as . . . any little hateful Animal.* Commentators universally find Brobdingnagians to outstrip Europeans in morality, as they do in size, just as Lilliputians fell as far behind Europeans (or at least Gulliver) in morality as they did in size. Swift is, however, more complicated than that. Both Lilliputians and Brobdingnagians are mixtures of good and evil, and if Swift emphasizes the evil in the first case and the good in the second it is for satiric purposes. The Lilliputians may safely be described as spiteful and murderous since they cannot really harm Gulliver. The Brobdingnagians must be pictured as reasonably moral and good-natured or they would instantly wipe out Gulliver and put an end to the story.

If, however, the Brobdingnagians are looked upon as morality personified, every instance in which they fall short of the ideal must be dismissed or downplayed.

In Lilliput, for instance, Gulliver instantly recognized the Lilliputians as people and treated them as such at their own evaluation. We are amused by his doing so, but it was nevertheless an act of great humanity. The Brobdingnagians, though, from beginning to end, never recognize Gulliver as human, as a "little Brobdingnagian," so to speak. They view him as either a little animal or a little toy. It may be to their credit that they did not kill him and that they treated him well, but it was only his physical body they treated well. They took no care whatever of his feelings, his emotions, his pride; and in so far as they did not, their behavior fell far short of the ideal and far short of Gulliver's own behavior in Lilliput.

27 *Hinds.* Farm servants. If Brobdingnagians are nobler than Europeans, they nevertheless have a thoroughly European class system. Swift could conceive of nothing else.

Thumb, and brought me within three Yards of his Eyes, that he might behold my Shape more perfectly. I guessed his Meaning; and my good Fortune gave me so much Presence of Mind, that I resolved not to struggle in the least as he held me in the Air above sixty Foot from the Ground; although he grievously pinched my Sides, for fear I should slip through his Fingers. All I ventured was to raise my Eyes towards the Sun, and place my Hands together in a supplicating Posture, and to speak some Words in an humble melancholy Tone, suitable to the Condition I then was in. For, I apprehended every Moment that he would dash me against the Ground, as we usually do any little hateful Animal we have a Mind to destroy. But my good Star would have it, that he appeared pleased with my Voice and Gestures, and began to look upon me as a Curiosity; much wondering to hear me pronounce articulate Words, although he could not understand them. In the mean time I was not able to forbear Groaning and shedding Tears, and turning my Head towards my Sides; letting him know, as well as I could, how cruelly I was hurt by the Pressure of his Thumb and Finger. He seemed to apprehend my Meaning; for, lifting up the Lappet of his Coat, he put me gently into it, and immediately ran along with me to his Master, who was a substantial Farmer, and the same Person I had first seen in the Field.

The Farmer having (as I supposed by their Talk) received such an Account of me as his Servant could give him, took a piece of a small Straw, about the Size of a walking Staff, and therewith lifted up the Lappets of my Coat; which it seems he thought to be some kind of Covering that Nature had given me. He blew my Hairs aside to take a better View of my Face. He called his Hinds about him, and asked them (as I afterwards learned) whether they had ever seen in the Fields any little Creature that resembled me. He then placed me softly on the Ground upon all four; but I got immediately up, and walked slowly backwards and forwards, to let those People see I had no Intent to run away. They all sate down in a Circle about me, the better to observe my Motions. I pulled off my Hat, and made a low Bow towards the Farmer: I fell on my Knees, and lifted up my Hands and Eyes, and spoke several Words as loud as I could: I took a Purse of Gold out of my Pocket, and humbly presented it to him. He received it on the Palm of his Hand, then applied it close to his Eye, to see what it was, and afterwards turned it several times with the point of a Pin, (which he took out of his Sleeve,) but could make nothing of it. Whereupon I made a Sign that he should place his Hand on the Ground: I then took the Purse, and opening it, poured all the Gold into his Palm. There were six *Spanish*-Pieces of four Pistoles each, besides twenty or thirty smaller Coins. I saw him wet the Tip of his little Finger upon his Tongue, and take up one of my largest Pieces, and then another; but he seemed to be wholly ignorant what they were. He made me a Sign to put them again into my Purse, and the Purse again into my Pocket; which after offering to him several times, I thought it best to do.

The Farmer by this time was convinced I must be a rational Creature. He spoke often to me, but the Sound of his Voice pierced my Ears like that of a Water-Mill; yet his Words were articulate enough. I answered as loud as I could in several Languages; and he often laid his Ear within two Yards of me, but all in vain, for we were wholly unintelligible to each other. He then sent his Servants to their Work, and taking his Handkerchief out of his Pocket, he doubled and spread it on his Hand, which he placed flat on the Ground with the Palm upwards, making me a Sign to step into it, as I could easily do, for it was not above a Foot in thickness. I thought it my part to obey; and for fear of falling, laid my self at full Length upon the Handkerchief, with the Remainder of which he lapped me up to the Head for further Security; and in this Manner carried me home to his House. There he called his Wife, and shewed me to her; but she screamed and ran back as Women in *England* do at the Sight of a Toad or a Spider. However, when she had a while seen my Behavior, and how well I observed the Signs her Husband made, she was soon reconciled, and by Degrees grew extreamly tender of me.

It was about twelve at Noon, and a Servant brought in dinner. It was only one substantial Dish of Meat (fit for the plain Condition of an Husband-Man) in a Dish about four and twenty Foot Diameter. The Company were the Farmer and Wife, three Children, and an old Grandmother: When they were sat down, the Farmer placed me at some Distance from him on the Table, which

Engraving from the first illustrated edition, London, 1727. Courtesy, Rare Book Division, The New York Public Library.

"He . . . shewed me to her; but she screamed." H. K. Browne, 1865.

"I . . . drank to her Lady-ship's Health." Herbert Cole. 1899.

28 *small Cyder*. A sweet cider with a low alcoholic content.

29 *placed me within three Yards of her*. The farmer and his wife feed Gulliver and do not allow their son to torment him. The wife makes sure the cat cannot get at Gulliver—and yet the farmer places him within the equivalent of nine inches (European) of the cat. Why, if not to be amused at Gulliver's fright? Is not this a sadistic act? Clearly, Brobdingnagians have their moments.

was thirty Foot high from the Floor. I was in a terrible Fright, and kept as far as I could from the Edge, for fear of falling. The Wife minced a bit of Meat, then crumbled some Bread on a Trencher, and placed it before me. I made her a low Bow, took out my Knife and Fork, and fell to eat; which gave them exceeding Delight. The Mistress sent her Maid for a small Dram-cup, which held about two Gallons; and filled it with Drink: I took up the Vessel with much difficulty in both Hands, and in a most respectful Manner drank to her Lady-ship's Health, expressing the Words as loud as I could in *English*; which made the Company laugh so heartily, that I was almost deafened with the Noise. This Liquour tasted like a small Cyder, and was not unpleasant. Then the Master made me a Sign to come to his Trencher side; but as I walked on the Table, being in great surprize all the time, as the indulgent Reader will easily conceive and excuse, I happened to stumble against a Crust, and fell flat on my Face, but received no hurt. I got up immediately, and observing the good People to be in much Concern, I took my Hat (which I held under my Arm out of good Manners) and waving it over my Head, made three Huzza's, to shew I had got no Mischief by the Fall. But advancing forwards towards my Master (as I shall henceforth call him) his youngest Son who sate next him, an arch Boy of about ten Years old, took me up by the Legs, and held me so high in the Air, that I trembled every Limb; but his Father snatched me from him; and at the same time gave him such a Box on the left Ear, as would have felled an *European* Troop of Horse to the Earth; ordering him to be taken from the Table. But, being afraid the Boy might owe me a Spight; and well remembring how mischievous all Children among us naturally are to Sparrows, Rabbits, young Kittens, and Puppy-Dogs; I fell on my Knees, and pointing to the Boy, made my Master understand, as well as I could, that I desired his Son might be pardoned. The Father complied, and the Lad took his Seat again; whereupon I went to him and kissed his Hand, which my Master took, and made him stroak me gently with it.

In the Midst of Dinner my Mistress's favourite Cat leapt into her Lap. I heard a Noise behind me like that of a Dozen Stocking-Weavers at work; and turning my Head, I found it proceeded from the Purring of this Animal, who seemed to be three Times larger than an Ox, as I computed by the View of her Head, and one of her Paws, while her Mistress was feeding and stroaking her. The Fierceness of this Creature's Countenance altogether discomposed me; although I stood at the further End of the Table, above fifty Foot off; and although my Mistress held her fast for fear she might give a Spring, and seize me in her Talons. But it happened there was no Danger; for the Cat took not the least Notice of me when my Master placed me within three Yards of her. And as I have been always told, and found true by Experience in my Travels, that flying, or discovering Fear before a fierce Animal, is a certain Way to make it pursue or attack you; so I resolved in this dangerous Juncture to shew no Manner of Concern. I walked with Intrepidity five or six Times before the very Head of the Cat, and came within half a Yard of her; whereupon she drew her self back, as if she were more afraid of me: I had less Apprehension concerning the Dogs, whereof three or four came into the Room, as it is usual in Farmers Houses; one of which was a Mastiff equal in Bulk to four Elephants, and a Grey-hound somewhat taller than the Mastiff, but not so large.

When Dinner was almost done, the Nurse came in with a Child of a Year old in her Arms; who immediately spyed me, and began a Squall that you might have heard from *London-Bridge* to *Chelsea*; **30** after the usual Oratory of Infants, to get me for a Play-thing. The **31** Mother out of pure Indulgence took me up, and put me towards the Child, who presently seized me by the Middle, and got my Head in his Mouth, where I roared so loud that the Urchin was frighted, and let me drop; and I should infallibly have broke my Neck, if the Mother had not held her Apron under me. The Nurse to quiet her Babe made use of a Rattle, which was a Kind of hollow Vessel filled with great Stones, and fastned by a Cable to the Child's Waist: But all in vain, so that she was forced to apply the last Remedy by giving it suck. I must confess no Object ever disgusted me so much as the Sight of her monstrous Breast, which I cannot tell what to compare with, so as to give the curious Reader an Idea of its Bulk, Shape and Colour. It stood prominent six Foot, and could not be less than sixteen in Circumference. The Nipple was about half the Bigness of my Head, and the Hue both of that and the Dug so varified with Spots, Pimples and Freckles, that nothing could appear more nauseous: For I had a near Sight of her, she sitting down the more conveniently to give Suck, and I standing on the Table. This made me reflect upon the fair Skins of our *English* Ladies, who appear so beautiful to us, only because they are of our own Size, and their Defects not to be seen but through a magnifying Glass, where we find by Experiment that the smoothest and **32** whitest Skins look rough and coarse, and ill coloured.

I remember when I was at *Lilliput*, the Complexions of those diminutive People appeared to me the fairest in the World: And talking upon this Subject with a Person of Learning there, who was an intimate Friend of mine; he said, that my Face appeared much fairer and smoother when he looked on me from the Ground, than it did upon a nearer View when I took him up in my Hand, and brought him close; which he confessed was at first a very shocking **33** Sight. He said, he could discover great Holes in my Skin; that the Stumps of my Beard were ten Times stronger than the Bristles of a Boar; and my Complexion made up of several Colours altogether disagreeable: Although I must beg Leave to say for my self, that I am as fair as most of my Sex and Country, and very little Sunburnt by all my Travels. On the other Side, dis- **34** coursing of the Ladies in that Emperor's Court, he used to tell me, one had Freckles, another too wide a Mouth, a third too large a Nose; nothing of which I was able to distinguish. I confess this Reflection was obvious enough; which, however, I could not for-bear, lest the Reader might think those vast Creatures were actually deformed: For I must do them Justice to say they are a comely Race of People; and particularly the Features of my Master's Countenance, although he were but a Farmer, when I beheld him from the Height of sixty Foot, appeared very well proportioned.

When Dinner was done, my Master went out to his Labourers; and as I could discover by his Voice and Gesture, gave his Wife a strict Charge to take Care of me. I was very much tired and dis-posed to sleep, which my Mistress perceiving, she put me on her own Bed, and covered me with a clean white Handkerchief, but

30 *from London-Bridge to Chelsea.* Chelsea is about three miles southwest of London Bridge.

31 *a Play-thing.* Gulliver is forced to undergo a series of humiliations. The satiric purpose is to have us (since we cannot help but identify with Gulliver) realize our own puny helplessness in the grip of the great forces of the world. In the first voyage, we were forced to realize it by seeing it mirrored in the tiny Lilliputians, but here the realization is more direct and, therefore, harder to endure.

Gulliver in the hands of a Brobdingnagian baby.
C. E. Brock, 1894.

32 *the smoothest and whitest Skins look rough and coarse.* Naturally, if all the measurements are multiplied by twelve, all the small imperfections would be as well. Swift may be implying here that if the Brobdingnagians are later portrayed as virtuous, they have faults as well that are correspondingly enlarged.

33 *a very shocking Sight.* Gulliver's unpleasant appearance to the Lilliputians might have been referred to in the first part of the book, but Swift either chose not to, as detracting from the satiric purpose, or didn't think of it. For one thing, it makes it less likely that the wife of Flimnap was enamored of Gulliver and gave her husband cause for jealousy.

34 *very little Sunburnt by all my Travels.* The standard for beauty in any age is always the appearance characteristic of the upper classes. In Swift's time, and through most of European history, the vast majority of the population was compelled to work in the open and consequently was browned by the sun. Gentlemen and ladies of leisure could afford to remain indoors, and were therefore proud of their fair complexions as a sign of the uselessness of their lives.

The women, particularly, went to great lengths to remain out of the sun, covered themselves with clothes, carried parasols, and so on. It is for this reason that Gulliver must protest that he is fair, despite his sea duty.

Nowadays, of course, the majority of the population must work indoors and are therefore pale-faced. Those not condemned to such work have time to loll about in the sun, engage in open air games, visit sunnier climes, and expose themselves on the beach. To be tanned is now an aristocratic characteristic and all aspire to it. And, as a matter of fact, since an even tan would tend to obscure and minimize variegations in coloring and minute imperfections, Gulliver would have been better off in this respect had he been tanned.

35 *Hanger.* A dagger or short sword, so-called because its scabbard hung from the belt.

Gulliver defends himself against a rat. Willy Pogány, 1919

36 *pressed to do more than one Thing.* Poor Gulliver had to both urinate and defecate and did not wish to do it on the bed.

larger and coarser than the Main Sail of a Man of War.

I slept about two Hours, and dreamed I was at home with my Wife and Children, which aggravated my Sorrows when I awaked and found my self alone in a vast Room, between two and three Hundred Foot wide, and above two Hundred high; lying in a Bed twenty Yards wide. My Mistress was gone about her houshold Affairs, and had locked me in. The Bed was eight Yards from the Floor. Some natural Necessities required me to get down: I durst not presume to call, and if I had, it would have been in vain with such a Voice as mine at so great a Distance from the Room where I lay, to the Kitchen where the Family kept. While I was under these Circumstances, two Rats crept up the Curtains, and ran smelling backwards and forwards on the Bed: One of them came up almost to my Face; whereupon I rose in a Fright, and drew out

35

my Hanger to defend my self. These horrible Animals had the Boldness to attack me on both Sides, and one of them held his Fore-feet at my Collar; but I had the good Fortune to rip up his Belly before he could do me any Mischief. He fell down at my Feet; and the other seeing the Fate of his Comrade, made his Escape, but not without one good Wound on the Back, which I gave him as he fled, and made the Blood run trickling from him. After this Exploit I walked gently to and fro on the Bed, to recover my Breath and Loss of Spirits. These Creatures were of the Size of a large Mastiff, but infinitely more nimble and fierce; so that if I had taken off my Belt before I went to sleep, I must have infallibly been torn to Pieces and devoured. I measured the Tail of the dead Rat, and found it to be two Yards long, wanting an Inch; but it went against my Stomach to drag the Carcass off the Bed, where it lay still bleeding; I observed it had yet some Life, but with a strong Slash cross the Neck, I thoroughly dispatched it.

Soon after, my Mistress came into the Room, who seeing me all bloody, ran and took me up in her Hand. I pointed to the dead *Rat*, smiling and making other Signs to shew I was not hurt; whereat she was extremely rejoyced, calling the Maid to take up the dead *Rat* with a Pair of Tongs, and throw it out of the Window. Then she set me on a Table, where I shewed her my Hanger all bloody, and wiping it on the Lappet of my Coat, returned it to the

36

Scabbard. I was pressed to do more than one Thing, which another could not do for me; and therefore endeavored to make my Mistress understand that I desired to be set down on the Floor; which after she had done, my Bashfulness would not suffer me to express my self farther than by pointing to the Door, and bowing several Times. The good Woman with much Difficulty at last perceived what I would be at; and taking me up again in her Hand, walked into the Garden where she set me down. I went on one Side about two Hundred Yards; and beckoning to her not to look or follow me, I hid my self between two Leaves of Sorrel, and there discharged the Necessities of Nature.

I hope, the gentle Reader will excuse me for dwelling on these and the like Particulars; which however insignificant they may appear to grovelling vulgar Minds, yet will certainly help a Philosopher to enlarge his Thoughts' and Imagination, and apply them to the Benefit of publick as well as private Life; which was my sole Design in presenting this and other Accounts of my Travels to the World; wherein I have been chiefly studious of

Truth, without affecting any Ornaments of Learning, or of Style. **37**
But the whole Scene of this Voyage made so strong an Impression
on my Mind, and is so deeply fixed in my Memory, that in committing it to Paper, I did not omit one material Circumstance:
However, upon a strict Review, I blotted out several Passages of
less Moment which were in my first Copy, for fear of being censured as tedious and trifling, whereof Travellers are often, perhaps not without Justice, accused.

37 *without affecting any Ornaments of Learning, or of
Style.* It is precisely this characteristic of his writing
that Swift exercises with great and skillful delibera-
tion, and now excuses with mock humility, which
makes him the most effective satirist in the English
language, to be approached only by Mark Twain and
Charles Dickens.

*"I hid my self between two Leaves of Sorrel, and there discharged the Necessities
of Nature." Gavarni, 1850s. Courtesy, Library of Congress.*

CHAPTER TWO

1 *nine Years old.* In Lilliput, it is several times made clear that the Lilliputians age more quickly than Europeans, as would be expected from their smaller size. Ther is no indication, however, that the Brobdingnagians age more slowly, as would be expected from their larger size. A nine-year-old Brobdingnagian girl would appear to be the equivalent of a nine-year-old European girl.

2 *Baby.* Her doll. The humiliations crowd upon Gulliver, for he is to take the place of the nine-year-old girl's doll. It is characteristic of Gulliver that he is pleased at her careful attention, just as he was pleased at becoming a Lilliputian Nardac.

3 *forty Foot high.* This is the equivalent of three feet four inches on the European scale.

A Description of the Farmer's Daughter. The Author carried to a Market-Town, and then to the Metropolis. The Particulars of his Journey.

1

2

M Y Mistress had a Daughter of nine Years old, a Child of towardly Parts for her Age, very dextrous at her Needle, and skilful in dressing her Baby. Her Mother and she contrived to fit up the Baby's cradle for me against Night: The Cradle was put into a small Drawer of a Cabinet, and the Drawer placed upon a hanging Shelf for fear of the *Rats.* This was my Bed all the Time I stayed with those People, although made more convenient by Degrees, as I began to learn their Language, and make my Wants known. This young Girl was so handy, that after I had once or twice pulled off my Cloaths before her, she was able to dress and undress me, although I never gave her that Trouble when she would let me do either my self. She made me seven Shirts, and some other Linnen of as fine Cloth as could be got, which indeed was coarser than Sackcloth; and these she constantly washed for me with her own Hands. She was likewise my School-Mistress to teach me the Language: When I pointed to any thing, she told me the Name of it in her own Tongue, so that in a few Days I was able to call for whatever I had a mind to. She was very good natured, and not

3 above forty Foot high, being little for her Age. She gave me the name of *Grildrig*, which the Family took up, and afterwards the whole Kingdom. The Word imports what the *Latins* call *Nanunculus*, the *Italians Homunceletino*, and the *English Mannikin*. To her I chiefly owe my Preservation in the Country: We never parted while I was there; I called her my *Glumdalclitch*, or little Nurse: And I should be guilty of great Ingratitude if I omitted this honourable Mention of her Care and Affection towards me, which I heartily wish it lay in my Power to requite as she deserves, instead of being the innocent but unhappy Instrument of her Disgrace, as I have too much Reason to fear.

It now began to be known and talked of in the Neighbourhood, that my Master had found a strange Animal in the Fields, about the Bigness of a *Splacknuck*, but exactly shaped in every Part like a human Creature which it likewise imitated in all its Actions; seemed to speak in a little Language of its own, had already learned several Words of theirs, went erect upon two Legs, was tame and gentle, would come when it was called, do whatever it was bid, had the finest Limbs in the World, and a Complexion fairer than a Nobleman's Daughter of three Years old. Another Farmer who lived hard by, and was a particular Friend of my Master, came on a Visit on Purpose to enquire into the Truth of this Story. I was immediately produced, and placed upon a Table; where I walked as I was commanded, drew my Hanger, put it up again, made my Reverence to my Master's Guest, asked him in his own Language how he did, and told him he was welcome; just as my little Nurse had instructed me. This Man, who was old and dimsighted, put on his Spectacles to behold me better, at which I could not forbear laughing very heartily; for his Eyes appeared like the Full-Moon shining into a Chamber at two Windows. Our People, who discovered the Cause of my Mirth, bore me Company in Laughing; at which the old Fellow was Fool enough to be angry and out of Countenance. He had the Character of a great Miser; and to my Misfortune he well deserved it by the cursed Advice he gave my Master, to shew me as a Sight upon a Market-Day in the next Town, which was half an Hour's Riding, about two and twenty Miles from our House. I guessed there was some Mischief contriving, when I observed my Master and his Friend whispering long together, sometimes pointing at me; and my Fears made me fancy that I overheard and understood some of their Words. But, the next Morning *Glumdalclitch* my little Nurse told me the whole matter, which she had cunningly picked out from her Mother. The poor Girl laid me on her Bosom, and fell a weeping with Shame and Grief. She apprehended some Mischief would happen to me from rude vulgar Folks, who might squeeze me to Death, or break one of my Limbs by taking me in their Hands. She had also observed how modest I was in my Nature, how nicely I regarded my Honour; and what an Indignity I should conceive it to be exposed for Money as a publick Spectacle to the meanest of the People. She said, her *Papa* and *Mamma* had promised that *Grildrig* should be hers; but now she found they meant to serve her as they did last Year, when they pretended to give her a Lamb; and yet, as soon as it was fat, sold it to a Butcher. For my own Part, I may truly affirm that I was less concerned than my Nurse. I had a strong Hope which never left me, that I should one Day recover my Liberty; and as to the Ignominy of being carried about for a

4 *what the Latins call Nanunculus, the Italians homunceletino.* Swift allows Gulliver to indulge in mock erudition, probably as a satire on travel tales. The Latin word is *homunculus* (little man), but the Greek word for "dwarf" is *nanos* and "nanunculus" could be a Greek-Latin hybrid meaning "little dwarf." The supposed Italian word simply doesn't exist.

5 *Splacknuck.* Swift doesn't bother to give the European equivalent of the "Splacknuck." It might be a lizard or a weasel, but by leaving it untranslated, he gets across the idea that the Brobdingnagians considered Gulliver a nondescript bit of vermin. This fits in with Swift's desire to force his readers to see themselves stripped of the false dignity conferred by self-love.

Since Glumdalclitch calls Gulliver "mannikin," it might seem that she at least recognizes him as a human being. She, however, is a little girl, and she sees him only as a doll.

6 *Reverence.* Respect. In this case demonstrated by a low bow.

7 *two and twenty Miles.* To go 22 miles in half an hour is to travel at a rate of 44 miles an hour, a startling speed indeed in Swift's time. However, we must reduce distances by 12. On a European scale, the distance is 1 5/6 miles; therefore the speed involved is only 3 2/3 miles an hour, a brisk walking speed.

8 *exposed for Money as a publick Spectacle.* It was customary in Swift's England to put on display all sorts of freaks and misshapen monsters for money. It was even customary to spend money to go to a madhouse and amuse one's self by laughing at the antics of mad people. We no longer consider it decent to laugh at the mad in our present society, although the sideshow freak still draws our curiosity. It is interesting, though, that in this respect, the virtuous Brobdingnagians are no whit advanced over the Europeans.

A madhouse. From "Rake's Progress" (Plate 8) by William Hogarth, 1735. Courtesy, Library of Congress.

9 *the King of Great Britain himself . . . must have undergone the same Distress.* This is a sly dig at George I, who was of German birth and breeding, did not speak English, and *was* a perfect stranger in the country he ruled.

10 *Pillion.* A cushioned saddle used for women and children.

11 *from London to St. Albans.* St. Albans is twenty-two miles northwest of the center of London, which is the distance Gulliver mentioned earlier.

12 *aimed a Hazel-Nut directly at my Head.* This is a malicious action, worthy of the Lilliputians. Some commentators tend to excuse this. The schoolboy is only young, they say. It might be as well to excuse the malicious acts of the Lilliputians against Gulliver as being inspired by fear. Why find excuses in one case and not in the other?

13 *Pumpion.* A pumpkin.

Monster, I considered my self to be a perfect Stranger in the Country; and that such a Misfortune could never be charged upon me as a Reproach if ever I should return to *England;* since the King of *Great Britain* himself, in my Condition, must have undergone the same Distress.

My Master, pursuant to the Advice of his Friend, carried me in a Box the next Market-Day to the neighbouring Town; and took along with him his little Daughter my Nurse upon a Pillion behind me. The Box was close on every Side, with a little Door for me to go in and out, and a few Gimlet-holes to let in Air. The Girl had been so careful to put the Quilt of her Baby's Bed into it, for me to lye down on. However, I was terribly shaken and discomposed in this Journey, although it were but of half an Hour. For the Horse went about forty Foot at every Step; and trotted so high, that the agitation was equal to the rising and falling of a Ship in a great Storm, but much more frequent: Our Journey was somewhat further than from *London* to St. *Albans.* My Master alighted at an Inn which he used to frequent; and after consulting a while with the Inn-keeper, and making some necessary Preparations, he hired the *Grultrud,* or Cryer, to give Notice through the Town, of a strange Creature to be seen at the Sign of the Green *Eagle,* not so big as a *Splacknuck,* (an Animal in that Country very finely shaped, about six Foot long) and in every Part of the Body resembling an human Creature; could speak several Words, and perform an Hundred diverting Tricks.

I was placed upon a Table in the largest Room of the Inn, which might be near three Hundred Foot square. My little Nurse stood on a low Stool close to the Table, to take care of me, and direct what I should do. My Master, to avoid a Croud, would suffer only Thirty People at a Time to see me. I walked about on the Table as the Girl commanded; she asked me Questions as far as she knew my Understanding of the Language reached, and I answered them as loud as I could. I turned about several Times to the Company, paid my humble Respects, said they were welcome; and used some other Speeches I had been taught. I took up a Thimble filled with Liquor, which *Glumdalclitch* had given me for a Cup, and drank their Health. I drew out my Hanger, and flourished with it after the Manner of Fencers in *England.* My Nurse gave me Part of a Straw, which I exercised as a Pike, having learned the Art in my Youth. I was that Day shewn to twelve Sets of Company; and as often forced to go over again with the same Fopperies, till I was half dead with Weariness and Vexation. For, those who had seen me, made such wonderful Reports, that the People were ready to break down the Doors to come in. My Master for his own Interest would not suffer any one to touch me, except my Nurse; and, to prevent Danger, Benches were set round the Table at such a Distance, as put me out of every Body's Reach. However, an unlucky School-Boy aimed a Hazel-Nut directly at my Head, which very narrowly missed me; otherwise, it came with so much Violence, that it would have infallibly knocked out my Brains; for it was almost as large as a small Pumpion: But I had the Satisfaction to see the young Rogue well beaten, and turned out of the Room.

My Master gave publick Notice, that we would shew me again the next Market-Day: And in the mean time, he prepared a more

14 *I could hardly stand upon my Legs, or speak a Word.* It is clear that the farmer is so greedy for money that he is ready to work poor Gulliver to death. This is excused by some commentators as mere "thoughtlessness," contrasted with Lilliputian "malice." But thoughtlessness can kill, too, and at least the Lilliputians were not greedy. They fed Gulliver for as long as he was with them, at enormous expense to themselves. It is ridiculous oversimplification to contrast the "good" Brobdingnagians with the "bad" Lilliputians. Both were clearly intended by Swift to be amalgams of good and bad and he used each as he saw fit for his satiric purposes.

Gulliver on exhibit. E. J. Wheeler, 1895.

convenient Vehicle for me, which he had Reason enough to do; for I was so tired with my first Journey, and with entertaining Company eight Hours together, that I could hardly stand upon my **14** Legs, or speak a Word. It was at least three Days before I recovered my Strength; and that I might have no rest at home, all the neighbouring Gentlemen from an Hundred Miles round, hearing of my Fame, came to see me at my Master's own House. There could not be fewer than thirty Persons with their Wives and Children; (for the Country is very populous;) and my Master demanded the Rate of a full Room whenever he shewed me at Home, although it were only to a single Family. So that for some time I had but little Ease every Day of the Week, (except *Wednesday,* which is their Sabbath) although I were not carried to the Town.

My Master finding how profitable I was like to be, resolved to carry me to the most considerable Cities of the Kingdom. Having

The journey to the Metropolis. Ad. Laluze, 1875.
Courtesy, Library of Congress.

15 *three Thousand Miles distance from our House.* Since the farmer's house is near the shore where Gulliver was stranded, and since the metropolis is near the middle of Brobdingnag, then the peninsula would be 6,000 miles across. If it is of the shape shown in the map then, in absolute terms, it would be larger than Asia. This would be equivalent, however, in ordinary measurements, to a national width of 500 miles and an area of about 125,000 square miles, or about the size of Italy.

16 *seven or eight Score Miles a Day.* This would be about twelve miles a day in European measure.

therefore provided himself with all things necessary for a long Journey, and settled his Affairs at Home; he took Leave of his Wife, and upon the 17*th* of *August* 1703, about two Months after my Arrival, we set out for the Metropolis, situated near the Middle of that Empire, and about three Thousand Miles distance from our House: My Master made his Daughter *Glumdalclitch* ride behind him. She carried me on her Lap in a Box tied about her Waist. The Girl had lined it on all Sides with the softest Cloth she could get, well quilted underneath; furnished it with her Baby's Bed, provided me with Linnen and other Necessaries; and made every thing as convenient as she could. We had no other Company but a Boy of the House, who rode after us with the Luggage.

My Master's Design was to shew me in all the Towns by the Way, and to step out of the Road for Fifty or an Hundred Miles, to any Village or Person of Quality's House where he might expect Custom. We made easy Journies of not above seven or eight Score Miles a Day: For *Glumdalclitch*, on Purpose to spare me, complained she was tired with the trotting of the Horse. She often took me out of my Box at my own Desire, to give me Air, and shew me

*"She often took me out of my Box . . . to give me Air." Gavarni, 1850s.
Courtesy, Library of Congress.*

17 *hardly a Rivulet so small as the Thames at London-Bridge.* Clearly, the inanimate world, as in Lilliput, partakes of the size distortion of the land. One wonders to what extremes this would go. Do the rivers flow correspondingly more rapidly? Does the wind blow in Brobdingnagian gusts? Actually, Swift merely makes use of those aspects of the general expansion he finds useful or dramatic and leaves out those he would find unnecessary or troublesome.

Gulliver arrives in Lorbrulgrud. Gavarni, 1850s. Courtesy, Library of Congress.

the Country; but always held me fast by Leading-strings. We passed over five or six Rivers many Degrees broader and deeper than the *Nile* or the *Ganges*; and there was hardly a Rivulet so **17** small as the *Thames* at *London-Bridge.* We were ten Weeks in our Journey; and I was shewn in Eighteen large Towns, besides many Villages and private Families.

On the 26*th* Day of *October*, we arrived at the Metropolis, called in their Language *Lorbrulgrud,* or *Pride of the Universe.* My Master took a Lodging in the principal Street of the City, not far from the Royal Palace; and put out Bills in the usual Form, containing an exact Description of my Person and Parts. He hired a large Room between three and four Hundred Foot wide. He provided a Table sixty Foot in Diameter, upon which I was to act my Part; and pallisadoed it round three Foot from the Edge, and as many high, to prevent my falling over. I was shewn ten Times a Day to the Wonder and Satisfaction of all People. I could now speak the Language tolerably well; and perfectly understood every Word

18 *Sanson's Atlas.* The reference is to Nicolas Sanson (1600–1667), a French map maker, whose atlases were popular and much copied.

that was spoken to me. Besides, I had learned their Alphabet, and could make a shift to explain a Sentence here and there; for *Glumdalclitch* had been my Instructor while we were at home, and at leisure Hours during our Journey. She carried a little Book **18** in her Pocket, not much larger than a *Sanson's Atlas;* it was a common Treatise for the use of young Girls, giving a short Account of their Religion; out of this she taught me my Letters, and interpreted the Words.

Glumdalclitch teaches Gulliver to read. Arthur Rackham, 1900.

CHAPTER THREE

The Author sent for to Court. The Queen buys him of his Master the Farmer, and presents him to the King. He disputes with His Majesty's great Scholars. An Apartment at Court provided for the Author. He is in high favour with the Queen. He stands up for the Honour of his own Country. His quarrels with the Queen's Dwarf.

1 *Gentleman Usher*. An usher is someone who allows entrance and escorts you to the place you want to go. In an elaborate household, an usher would be in charge of allowing entrance to visitors and of introducing them to the master of the house. Where royalty is involved, the role of usher (ordinarily a rather menial job) carries high honor because of its contact with the ruler, so that men of high station are eager for the post of "Gentleman Usher."

HE frequent Labours I underwent every Day, made in a few Weeks a very considerable Change in my Health: The more my Master got by me, the more unsatiable he grew. I had quite lost my Stomach, and was almost reduced to a Skeleton. The Farmer observed it; and concluding I soon must die, resolved to make as good a Hand of me as he could. While he was thus reasoning and resolving with himself; a *Slardral*, or Gentleman Usher, came from Court, commanding my Master to bring me immediately thither for the Diversion of the Queen and her Ladies. Some of the latter had already been to see me; and reported strange Things of my Beauty, Behaviour, and good Sense. Her Majesty and those who attended her, were beyond Measure delighted with my Demeanor. I fell on my Knees, and begged the Honour of kissing her Imperial Foot; but this Gracious Princess held out her little Finger towards me (after I was set on a Table) which I embraced in both my Arms, and put the Tip of it, with the utmost Respect, to my Lip. She made me some general Questions about my Country and my Travels, which I answered as distinctly and in as few Words as I could. She asked, whether I would be content to live at Court. I bowed down to the Board of the Table, and humbly answered, that

2 *Moydores.* Or moidores, Portuguese gold coins. The word is a corruption of *moeda de ouro,* which means "coin of gold." Gulliver sounds a little hurt at being sold for so little.

3 *if my Master had not thought my Life in Danger, her Majesty perhaps would not have got so cheap a Bargain.* Not having had the advantage of reading most commentaries on the book, Gulliver clearly does not dismiss his former master as merely "thoughtless." He hates him, and considers him a monster of greed. But neither the queen, nor any other Brobdingnagian, ever expresses horror or distress at the farmer's treatment of Gulliver.

4 *the Phoenix of the Creation.* The phoenix is a legendary bird, which, according to Greek tales, lives for five hundred years, then constructs a nest of spices, sings a final song, sets fire to the nest with a flap of its wings, and burns itself to ashes. Out of the ashes a new phoenix arises. At any one time only one phoenix exists, so that to be "the Phoenix of the Creation" is to be one of a kind, a nonpareil.

The phoenix.

5 *Scrutore.* A distortion of the now obsolete French word *escritoire,* which is a writing desk.

I was my Master's Slave; but if I were at my own Disposal, I should be proud to devote my Life to her Majesty's Service. She then asked my Master whether he were willing to sell me at a good Price. He, who apprehended I could not live a month, was ready enough to part with me; and demanded a Thousand Pieces of Gold; which were ordered him on the Spot, each Piece being about **2** the Bigness of eight Hundred Moydores: But, allowing for the Proportion of all Things between that Country and *Europe,* and the high Price of Gold among them; was hardly so great a Sum as a Thousand Guineas would be in *England.* I then said to the Queen; since I was now her Majesty's most humble Creature and Vassal, I must beg the Favour, that *Glumdalclitch,* who had always tended me with so much Care and Kindness, and understood to do it so well, might be admitted into her Service, and continue to be my Nurse and Instructor. Her Majesty agreed to my Petition; and easily got the Farmer's Consent, who was glad enough to have his Daughter preferred at Court: And the poor Girl herself was not able to hide her Joy. My late Master withdrew, bidding me farewell, and saying he had left me in a good Service; to which I replyed not a Word, only making him a slight Bow.

The Queen observed my Coldness; and when the Farmer was gone out of the Apartment, asked me the Reason. I made bold to tell her Majesty, that I owed no other Obligation to my late Master, than his not dashing out the Brains of a poor harmless Creature found by Chance in his Field; which Obligation was amply recompenced by the Gain he had made in shewing me through half the Kingdom, and the Price he had now sold me for. That the Life I had since led, was laborious enough to kill an Animal of ten Times my Strength. That my Health was much impaired by the continual Drudgery of entertaining the Rabble every Hour of the Day; and **3** that if my Master had not thought my Life in Danger, her Majesty perhaps would not have got so cheap a Bargain. But as I was out of all fear of being ill treated under the Protection of so great and good an Empress, the Ornament of Nature, the Darling of the **4** World, the Delight of her Subjects, the Phoenix of the Creation; so, I hoped my late Master's Apprehensions would appear to be groundless; for I already found my Spirits to revive by the Influence of her most August Presence.

This was the Sum of my Speech delivered with great Improprieties and Hesitation; the latter Part was altogether framed in the Style peculiar to that People, whereof I learned some Phrases from *Glumdalclitch,* while she was carrying me to Court.

The Queen giving great Allowance for my Defectiveness in speaking, was however surprised at so much Wit and good Sense in so diminutive an Animal. She took me in her own Hand, and carried me to the King, who was then retired to his Cabinet. His Majesty, a Prince of much Gravity, and austere Countenance, not well observing my shape at first View, asked the Queen after a cold Manner, how long it was since she grew fond of a *Splacknuck;* for such it seems he took me to be, as I lay upon my Breast in her Majesty's right Hand. But this Princess, who hath an infinite deal of Wit and Humour, set me gently on my Feet upon the Scrutore; **5** and commanded me to give His Majesty an Account of my self,

"The Queen . . . took me in her own Hand." Herbert Cole, 1899.

which I did in a very few Words; and *Glumdalclitch*, who attended at the Cabinet Door, and could not endure I should be out of her Sight, being admitted; confirmed all that had passed from my Arrival at her Father's House.

The King, although he be as learned a Person as any in his Dominions; and had been educated in the Study of Philosophy, **6** and particularly Mathematicks; yet when he observed my Shape exactly, and saw me walk erect, before I began to speak, conceived I might be a piece of Clockwork, (which is in that Country arrived to a very great Perfection) contrived by some ingenious Artist. But, when he heard my Voice; and found what I delivered to be regular and rational, he could not conceal his Astonishment. He was by no means satisfied with the Relation I gave him of the Manner I came into his Kingdom; but thought it a Story concerted between *Glumdalclitch* and her Father, who had taught me a Sett of Words to make me sell at a higher Price. Upon this Imagination he put several other Questions to me, and still received rational Answers, no otherwise defective than by a Foreign Accent, and an

6 *Philosophy.* Swift refers to what we would now call "science." The word "science" did not come into use till the nineteenth century.

7 *weekly waiting*. Apparently, the three scholars visited the court once a week to make themselves available to the philosophic King for a discussion of science, if he desired it.

8 *the Queen's favourite Dwarf . . . was near thirty Foot high*. In medieval and early modern times, dwarfs were commonly kept in noble and royal households for diversion, and the dwarfs quickly learned that their livelihood and security depended on their being amusing. This was still a practice in Great Britain and in Spain even in Swift's time, and in Russia, right into the nineteenth century. Apparently, the Brobdingnagians also indulged in this barbarous custom. "Near thirty Foot high" would be two and a half feet on the European scale.

The three great scholars. T. Morten, 1865. Courtesy, Library of Congress.

Queen Henrietta Maria and Her Dwarf Jeffery Hudson by Van Dyke, c. 1635. National Gallery of Art, Washington, D.C.

imperfect Knowledge in the Language; with some rustick Phrases which I had learned at the Farmer's House, and did not suit the polite Style of a Court.

His Majesty sent for three great Scholars who were then in their **7** weekly waiting (according to the Custom in that Country.) These Gentlemen, after they had a while examined my Shape with much Nicety, were of different Opinions concerning me. They all agreed that I could not be produced according to the regular Laws of Nature; because I was not framed with a Capacity of preserving Life, either by Swiftness, or climbing of Trees, or digging Holes in the Earth. They observed by my Teeth, which they viewed with great Exactness, that I was a carnivorous Animal; yet most Quadrupeds being an Overmatch for me; and Field-Mice, with some others, too nimble, they could not imagine how I should be able to support my self, unless I fed upon Snails and other Insects; which they offered by many learned Arguments to evince that I could not possibly do. One of them seemed to think that I might be an Embrio, or abortive Birth. But this Opinion was rejected by the other two, who observed my Limbs to be perfect and finished; and that I had lived several Years, as it was manifested from my Beard; the Stumps whereof they plainly discovered through a Magnifying-Glass. They would not allow me to be a Dwarf, because my Littleness was beyond all Degrees of Comparison; for **8** the Queen's favourite Dwarf, the smallest ever known in that

Kingdom, was near thirty Foot high. After much Debate, they concluded unanimously that I was only *Relplum Scalcath*, which is interpreted literally *Lusus Naturæ*; a Determination exactly agreeable to the Modern Philosophy of *Europe*: whose Professors disdaining the old Evasion of *occult Causes*, whereby the Followers of *Aristotle* endeavor in vain to disguise their ignorance; have invented this wonderful Solution of all Difficulties, to the unspeakable Advancement of human Knowledge.

After this decisive Conclusion, I entreated to be heard a Word or two. I applied my self to the King, and assured His Majesty, that I came from a Country which abounded with several Millions of both Sexes, and of my own Stature; where the Animals, Trees, and Houses were all in Proportion; and where by Consequence I might be as able to defend my self, and to find Sustenance, as any of his Majesty's Subjects could do here; which I took for a full Answer to those Gentlemen's Arguments. To this they only replied with a Smile of Contempt; saying, that the Farmer had instructed me very well in my Lesson. The King, who had a much better Understanding, dismissing his learned Men, sent for the Farmer, who by good Fortune was not yet gone out of Town: Having therefore first examined him privately, and then confronted him with me and the young Girl; his Majesty began to think that what we told him might possibly be true. He desired the Queen to order, that a particular Care should be taken of me; and was of Opinion, that *Glumdalclitch* should still continue in her Office of tending me, because he observed we had a great Affection for each other. A convenient Apartment was provided for her at Court; she had a sort of Governess appointed to take care of her Education, a Maid to dress her, and two other Servants for menial Offices; but, the Care of me was wholly appropriated to her self. The Queen commanded her own Cabinet-maker to contrive a Box that might serve me for a Bed-chamber, after the Model that *Glumdalclitch* and I should agree upon. This Man was a most ingenious Artist; and according to my Directions, in three Weeks finished for me a wooden Chamber of sixteen Foot square, and twelve High; with Sash Windows, a Door, and two Closets, like a *London* Bed-chamber. The Board that made the Cieling was to be lifted up and down by two Hinges, to put in a Bed ready furnished by her Majesty's Upholsterer; which *Glumdalclitch* took out every Day to air, made it with her own Hands, and letting it down at Night, locked up the Roof over me. A Nice Workman, who was famous for little Curiosities, undertook to make me two Chairs, with Backs and Frames, of a Substance not unlike Ivory; and two Tables, with a Cabinet to put my Things in. The Room was quilted on all Sides, as well as the Floor and the Ceiling, to prevent any Accident from the Carelessness of those who carried me; and to break the Force of a Jolt when I went in a Coach. I desired a Lock for my Door to prevent Rats and Mice from coming in: The Smith after several Attempts made the smallest that was ever seen among them; for I have known a larger at the Gate of a Gentleman's House in *England*. I made a shift to keep the Key in a Pocket of my own, fearing *Glumdalclitch* might lose it. The Queen likewise ordered the thinnest Silks that could be gotten, to make me Cloaths; not much thicker than an *English* Blanket, very cumbersome till I was

9 *Lusus naturae.* Latin for "a freak of nature," something that nature, so to speak, produced idly for its amusement.

10 *occult Causes.* "Occult" means "hidden" or "concealed," so that an "occult cause" is one we don't know. "A freak of nature" is something that does not follow from the natural laws we think we know, so that we cannot predict or explain it. What Swift is saying is that modern scientists, scorning the phraseology of the ancients, have created a new term in which to clothe their ignorance.

As it happens, Swift was strongly opposed to the science of his day, and was a great admirer of the lore of the ancients, which he thought (quite wrongly) to be far the superior. There will be many places in which this prejudice of his will be plainly shown.

11 *a much better Understanding.* Swift had contempt for "experts" and it was his belief that any sensible person could fill any post and understand anything that needed understanding. The "great scholars" are incapable of expanding their imaginations to include a miniature world, as the Lilliputian philosophers could not imagine a giant one. The King, however, being a sensible man, is not afflicted with a closed mind, but investigates further.

12 *Artist.* We would say "artisan" or "workman."

13 *Nice.* Used here in its older meaning of "delicate" or "precise."

14 *to prevent Rats and Mice from coming in.* Gulliver had to fight rats in the farmer's bed chamber, and he assumes the presence of rats and mice even in the palace. Nor does Gulliver refer to the matter with surprise or disgust. It tells us something about the Britain of his time, and indicates that the Brobdingnagians are no further advanced in the battle against vermin.

15 *two Princesses Royal.* A princess royal is the eldest daughter of a reigning monarch. To have two of them seems a little odd.

16 *a very nauseous Sight.* Gulliver eating Lilliputian food before the Lilliputians, seemed to the little people just as the giant Queen now seems to him. Yet Gulliver in Lilliput was proud of how much he could eat, and on one occasion ate particularly prodigiously in order to impress them. The shoe is on the other foot now.

17 *a white Staff, near as tall as the Main-mast of the Royal Sovereign.* The white staff is an emblem of authority in England, and so it was in Lilliput, and so it is in Brobdingnag. The *Royal Sovereign* was one of the largest ships in the British navy.

18 *they contrive little Nests . . . they betray.* In Lilliput, Swift forced us to laugh at the posturings of the Lilliputians and to see in them the follies of Europe. Here he does the same but even more sharply. Taking advantage of the all-is-relative notion, he successfully converts Europeans into Lilliputians and holds his fellow men up to scorn—directly.

Gulliver dines with the queen. J. J. Grandville, 1835. Courtesy, Library of Congress.

accustomed to them. They were after the Fashion of the Kingdom, partly resembling the *Persian,* and partly the *Chinese;* and are a very grave decent Habit.

The Queen became so fond of my Company, that she could not dine without me. I had a Table placed upon the same at which her Majesty eat, just at her left Elbow; and a Chair to sit on. *Glumdalclitch* stood upon a Stool on the Floor, near my Table, to assist and take Care of me. I had an entire set of Silver Dishes and Plates, and other Necessaries, which in Proportion to those of the Queen, were not much bigger than what I have seen in a *London* Toy-shop, for the Furniture of a Baby-house: These my little Nurse kept in her Pocket, in a Silver Box, and gave me at Meals as I wanted them; always cleaning them her self. No Person dined with the Queen **15** but the two Princesses Royal; the elder sixteen Years old, and the younger at that time thirteen and a Month. Her Majesty used to put a Bit of Meat upon one of my Dishes, out of which I carved for my self; and her Diversion was to see me eat in Miniature. For the Queen (who had indeed but a weak Stomach) took up at one Mouthful, as much as a dozen *English* Farmers could eat at a **16** Meal, which to me was for some time a very nauseous Sight. She would craunch the Wing of a Lark, Bones and all, between her Teeth, although it were nine Times as large as that of a full grown Turkey; and put a Bit of Bread in her Mouth, as big as two twelve-penny Loaves. She drank out of a golden Cup, above a Hogshead at a Draught. Her Knives were twice as long as a Scythe set strait upon the Handle. The Spoons, Forks, and other Instruments were all in the same Proportion. I remember when *Glumdalclitch* carried me out of Curiosity to see some of the Tables at Court, where ten or a dozen of these enormous Knives and Forks were lifted up together; I thought I had never till then beheld so terrible a Sight.

It is the Custom, that every *Wednesday,* (which as I have before observed, was their Sabbath) the King and Queen, with the Royal Issue of both Sexes, dine together in the Apartment of his Majesty; to whom I was now become a Favourite; and at these Times my little Chair and Table were placed at his left Hand before one of the Salt-sellers. This Prince took a Pleasure in conversing with me; enquiring into the Manners, Religion, Laws, Government, and Learning of *Europe,* wherein I gave him the best Account I was able. His Apprehension was so clear, and his Judgment so exact, that he made very wise Reflections and Observations upon all I said. But, I confess, that after I had been a little too copious in talking of my own beloved Country; of our Trade, and Wars by Sea and Land, of our Schisms in Religion, and Parties in the State; the Prejudices of his Education prevailed so far, that he could not forbear taking me up in his right Hand, and stroaking me gently with the other; after an hearty Fit of laughing, asked me whether I were a *Whig* or a *Tory.* Then turning to his first Minister, who **17** waited behind him with a white Staff, near as tall as the Main-mast of the Royal *Sovereign;* he observed, how contemptible a Thing was human Grandeur, which could be mimicked by such diminutive Insects as I: And yet, said he, I dare engage, those **18** Creatures have their Titles and Distinctions of Honour; they contrive little Nests and Burrows, that they call Houses and Cities; they make a Figure in Dress and Equipage; they love, they fight, they dispute, they cheat, they betray. And thus he continued on, while

Gulliver answers the questions of the king. Gavarni, 1850s. Courtesy, Library of Congress.

19 *the Scourge of France.* The English never forgot the three great battles of Crécy, Poitiers, and Agincourt in which, during the Hundred Years War, they utterly defeated much larger French armies. The English won through the use of the longbow, which the French could not, at that time, counter, but the natural assumption (of the English) was that one Englishman was as good as ten Frenchmen.

The fact that eventually the French developed the use of artillery to the point where it supplied them with power the longbow couldn't counter and thereby drove the English from their country never changed the opinion of the English about themselves.

20 *to laugh as much at them as this King and his Grandees did at me.* Feeling naturally superior to the Lilliputians, Gulliver never identified with them, but always knew his own size was normal. In Brobdingnag, however, Gulliver's pride is trampled in the dust and he therefore begins to identify with the giants and to feel contempt for Europeans and himself. Identification with oppressors is a well-known psychological development and is also the beginning of madness, as we shall see later in the book.

my Colour came and went several Times, with Indignation to hear our noble Country, the Mistress of Arts and Arms, the Scourge of **19** *France*, the Arbitress of *Europe*, the Seat of Virtue, Piety, Honour and Truth, the Pride and Envy of the World, so contemptuously treated.

But, as I was not in a Condition to resent Injuries, so, upon mature Thoughts, I began to doubt whether I were injured or no. For, after having been accustomed several Months to the Sight and Converse of this People, and observed every Object upon which I cast my Eyes, to be of proportionable Magnitude; the Horror I had first conceived from their Bulk and Aspect was so far worn off, that if I then beheld a Company of *English* Lords and Ladies in their Finery and Birth-day Cloaths, acting their several Parts in the most courtly Manner of Strutting, and Bowing and Prating; to say the Truth, I should have been strongly tempted to laugh as **20** much at them as this King and his Grandees did at me. Neither indeed could I forbear smiling at my self, when the Queen used to place me upon her Hand towards a Looking-Glass, by which both our Persons appeared before me in full View together; and there could nothing be more ridiculous than the Comparison: So that I really began to imagine my self dwindled many Degrees below my usual Size.

Nothing angred and mortified me so much as the Queen's

21 *malicious Urchin.* Here is one Brobdingnagian who *does* act out of sheer malice, but the usual remark by commentators is that he is deformed and therefore, presumably, not a true Brobdingnagian. It might be more reasonable to argue that he saw in Gulliver an infra-dwarf who would win away the affections of his royal mistress and lose the dwarf his cushy position—which is exactly what happened. Under such pressures, any Brobdingnagian might have grown malicious. Swift shows us nothing to the contrary.

"A scurvy Trick." C. E. Brock, 1894.
Courtesy, Library of Congress.

Dwarf, who being of the lowest Stature that was ever in that Country, (for I verily think he was not full Thirty Foot high) became so insolent at seeing a Creature so much beneath him, that he would always affect to swagger and look big as he passed by me in the Queen's Antichamber, while I was standing on some Table talking with the Lords or Ladies of the Court; and he seldom failed of a smart Word or two upon my Littleness; against which I could only revenge my self by calling him *Brother,* challenging him to wrestle; and such Repartees as are usual in the Mouths of *Court Pages.* One Day at Dinner, this malicious little Cubb was so nettled with something I had said to him, that raising himself upon the Frame of her Majesty's Chair, he took me up by the Middle, as I was sitting down, not thinking any Harm, and let me drop into a large Silver Bowl of Cream; and then ran away as fast as he could. I fell over Head and Ears, and if I had not been a good Swimmer, it might have gone very hard with me; for *Glumdalclitch* in that Instant happened to be at the other End of the Room; and the Queen was in such a Fright, that she wanted Presence of Mind to assist me. But my little Nurse ran to my Relief; and took me out, after I had swallowed above a Quart of Cream. I was put to Bed; however I received no other Damage than the Loss of a Suit of Cloaths, which was utterly spoiled. The Dwarf was soundly whipped, and as a further Punishment, forced to drink up the Bowl of Cream, into which he had thrown me; neither was he ever restored to Favour: For, soon after the Queen bestowed him to a Lady of high Quality; so that I saw him no more, to my very great Satis- **21** faction; for I could not tell to what Extremitys such a malicious Urchin might have carried his Resentment.

He had before served me a scurvy Trick, which set the Queen a laughing, although at the same time she were heartily vexed, and would have immediately cashiered him, if I had not been so generous as to intercede. Her Majesty had taken a Marrow-bone upon her Plate; and after knocking out the Marrow, placed the Bone again in the Dish erect as it stood before; the Dwarf watching his Opportunity, while *Glumdalclitch* was gone to the Sideboard, mounted the Stool that she stood on to take care of me at Meals; took me up in both Hands, and squeezing my Legs together, wedged them into the Marrow-bone above my Waist; where I stuck for some time, and made a very ridiculous Figure. I believe it was near a Minute before any one knew what was become of me; **22** for I thought it below me to cry out. But, as Princes seldom get their Meat hot, my Legs were not scalded, only my Stockings and Breeches in a sad Condition. The Dwarf at my Entreaty had no other Punishment than a sound whipping.

I was frequently raillied by the Queen upon Account of my Fearfulness; and she used to ask me whether the People of my Country were as great Cowards as my self. The Occasion was this. The Kingdom is much pestered with Flies in Summer; and these **23** odious Insects, each of them as big as a *Dunstable* Lark, hardly gave me any Rest while I sat at Dinner, with their continual Humming and Buzzing about my Ears. They would sometimes alight upon my Victuals, and leave their loathsome Excrement or Spawn behind, which to me was very visible, although not to the Natives of that Country, whose large Opticks were not so acute as mine in viewing smaller Objects. Sometimes they would fix upon my Nose or Forehead, where they stung me to the Quick, smelling very offensively; and I could easily trace that viscous Matter, which our Naturalists tell us enables those Creatures to walk with their Feet upwards upon a Cieling. I had much ado to defend my self against these detestable Animals, and could not forbear starting when they came on my Face. It was the common Practice of the Dwarf to catch a Number of these Insects in his Hand, as School-boys do among us, and let them out suddenly under my Nose, on Purpose to frighten me, and divert the Queen. My Remedy was to cut them in Pieces with my Knife as they flew in the Air; wherein my Dexterity was much admired.

I remember one Morning when *Glumdalclitch* had set me in my Box upon a Window, as she usually did in fair Days to give me Air, (for I durst not venture to let the Box be hung on a Nail out of the Window, as we do with Cages in *England*) after I had lifted up one of my Sashes, and sat down at my Table to eat a Piece of Sweet-Cake for my Breakfast; above twenty Wasps, allured by the Smell, came flying into the Room, humming louder than the Drones of as many Bagpipes. Some of them seized my Cake, and carried it piecemeal away; others flew about my Head and Face, confounding me with the Noise, and putting me in the utmost Terror of their Stings. However I had the Courage to rise and draw my Hanger, and attack them in the Air. I dispatched four of them, but the rest got away; and I presently shut my Window. These Insects were as large at Partridges; I took out their Stings, found them an Inch and a half long, and as sharp as Needles. I carefully preserved them all, and having since shewn them with some other Curiosities in several Parts of *Europe*; upon my Return to *England* I gave three of them to *Gresham College*, and kept the fourth for my self.

24

Gulliver's combat with the wasps. Arthur Rackham, 1909.

22 *Princes seldom get their Meat hot.* Louis XIV of France (who reached the throne in 1643 and was still on it when Gulliver was in Brobdingnag) had greatly exaggerated the complexities of etiquette in a deliberate attempt to break the power of the nobility. He kept them about his great palace and taught them to value the small menial tasks he gave them (for which he repaid them with pensions, of course). In this way, the noblemen ceased to be brawling malcontents and became, instead, pliant and utterly useless courtiers.

All other monarchs attempted to imitate Louis XIV as far as they could. The result was that the simple task of placing a dish of food before the monarch meant such an elaborate ritual of passing from hand to hand, with such delays through flourish and ceremony, that by the time it reached the royal table, the food was cold. Apparently, the Brobdingnagian king was as ridiculously enslaved by etiquette as were his European counterparts.

Louis XIV, after a painting by L. Gérôme. Courtesy, Library of Congress.

23 *as big as a Dunstable Lark.* Dunstable is a town about thirty-five miles northwest of London and was notable, apparently, for its larks.

Insects as large as birds would of course be completely nonviable. Their flimsy wings, even expanded in proportion, would not support them. Their respiratory systems, quite workable for a tiny insect-sized body, would fail to supply a large one with oxygen. Swift, however, was not concerned with such trivialities.

24 *Gresham College.* At one time Gresham College was the meeting place of the Royal Society of London, the most prestigious scientific organization of its time.

1 *Our Geographers . . . are in a great Error, by supposing nothing but Sea between Japan and California.* The European geographers were, of course, perfectly right, but the fact of the matter was not clearly established until Captain Cook's voyages, fifty years after Gulliver's.

2 *Tartary.* Asia. See Chapter 1 of this part, note 13.

3 *Mountains thirty Miles high.* These are prodigious mountains indeed. The highest mountain on earth, Mount Everest, raises its peak five and a half miles above sea level. It is presumed, however, that the mountains of Brobdingnag are of Brobdingnagian dimensions. If their height were reduced by a factor of twelve, they would be only two and a half miles high, and thus we see that such mountains would be to the Brobdingnagians as the Alps are to the Europeans.

4 *Volcanoes upon the Tops.* Swift has to account for the fact that the giants have not spread out over the world, but there is no reason to pile the volcanoes on the mountains to explain that. A mountain range thirty miles high is, in any case, impassable to any people not equipped with rocket ships. The range lifts itself high into the stratosphere and people would require space suits before they had made their way one-third up the mountain slopes.

The country described. A proposal for correcting modern maps. The King's palace, and some account of the metropolis. The Author's way of travelling. The chief temple described.

NOW intend to give the Reader a short Description of this Country, as far as I travelled in it, which was not above two thousand Miles round *Lorbrulgrud* the Metropolis. For, the Queen, whom I always attended, never went further when she accompanied the King in his Progresses; and there staid till his Majesty returned from viewing his Frontiers. The whole Extent of this Prince's Dominions reacheth about six thousand Miles in Length, and from three

1 to five in Breadth. From whence I cannot but conclude, that our Geographers of *Europe* are in a great Error, by supposing nothing but Sea between *Japan* and *California*: For it was ever my Opinion, that there must be a Balance of Earth to counterpoise the great

2 Continent of *Tartary*; and therefore they ought to correct their Maps and Charts, by joining this vast Tract of Land to the Northwest Parts of *America*; wherein I shall be ready to lend them my Assistance.

The Kingdom is a Peninsula, terminated to the North-east by a

3 Ridge of Mountains thirty Miles high which are altogether impas-

4 sable by Reason of the Volcanoes upon the Tops. Neither do the most Learned know what sort of Mortals inhabit beyond those

Mountains, or whether they be inhabited at all. On the three other Sides it is bounded by the Ocean. There is not one Sea-port in the whole Kingdom; and those Parts of the Coasts into which the Rivers issue, are so full of pointed Rocks, and the Sea generally so rough, that there is no venturing with the smallest of their Boats; so that these People are wholly excluded from any Commerce with the rest of the World. But the large Rivers are full of Vessels, and abound with excellent Fish; for they seldom get any from the Sea, because the Sea-fish are of the same Size with those in *Europe*, and consequently not worth catching; whereby it is manifest, that Nature in the Production of Plants and Animals of so extraordinary a Bulk, is wholly confined to this Continent; of which I leave the Reasons to be determined by Philosophers. However, now and then they take a Whale that happens to be dashed against the Rocks, which the common People feed on heartily. These Whales I have known so large that a Man could hardly carry one upon his Shoulders; and sometimes for Curiosity they are brought in Hampers to *Lorbrulgrud*: I saw one of them in a Dish at the King's Table, which passed for a Rarity; but I did not observe he was fond of it; for I think indeed the Bigness disgusted him, although I have seen one somewhat larger in *Greenland*.

The Country is well inhabited, for it contains fifty one Cities, near an hundred walled Towns, and a great Number of Villages. To satisfy my curious Reader, it may be sufficient to describe *Lorbrulgrud*. This City stands upon almost two equal Parts on each Side the River that passes through. It contains above eighty thousand Houses. It is in Length three *Glonglungs* (which make about fifty four English Miles) and two and a half in Breadth, as I measured it myself in the Royal Map made by the King's Order, which was laid on the Ground on purpose for me, and extended an hundred Feet; I paced the Diameter and Circumference several times Bare-foot, and computing by the Scale, measured it pretty exactly.

The King's Palace is no regular Edifice, but an Heap of Buildings about seven Miles round: The chief Rooms are generally two hundred and forty Foot high, and broad and long in Proportion. A Coach was allowed to *Glumdalclitch* and me, wherein her Governess frequently took her out to see the Town, or go among the Shops; and I was always of the Party, carried in my Box; although the Girl at my own Desire would often take me out, and hold me in her Hand, that I might more conveniently view the Houses and the People as we passed along the Streets. I reckoned our Coach to be about a Square of *Westminster-Hall*, but not altogether so high; however, I cannot be very exact. One Day the Governess ordered our Coachman to stop at several Shops; where the Beggars watching their Opportunity, crouded to the Sides of the Coach, and gave me the most horrible Spectacles that ever an *European* Eye beheld. There was a Woman with a Cancer in her Breast, swelled to a monstrous Size, full of Holes, in two or three of which I could have easily crept, and covered my whole Body. There was a Fellow with a Wen in his Neck, larger than five Woolpacks; and another with a couple of wooden Legs, each about twenty Foot high. But, the most hateful Sight of all was the Lice crawling on their Cloaths: I could see distinctly the Limbs of these Vermin with my naked Eye, much better than those of an *European* Louse

5 *the Sea-fish are of the same Size with those in Europe.* It is necessary that the sea be normal or there would be nothing to prevent Brobdingnagian fish from filling the oceans of the world. In fact, if we stop to think of it at this point, to the Lilliputians, the ocean around the islands of Lilliput and Blefuscu must have contained life forms that were to them Brobdingnagian. But of course no mention of this is made in the first part of the book.

6 *I have seen one somewhat larger in Greenland.* Whales that were once common about Greenland, and in Arctic waters generally, were avidly hunted by the European whalers because they were slow, oily, and floated after being killed. That was what made them the "right" whales to hunt. They were large, reaching a maximum length of sixty-five feet—or as long as a Brobdingnagian was tall. The more savage and dangerous sperm whales could also reach that length.

On the Brobdingnagian scale, such whales would appear something over five feet long, or about as long as the common dolphin is to us. (Had I been Swift, in fact, I would not have been able to resist explaining, with a straight face, that some of the river dolphins of Brobdingnag had escaped to sea in ages past and constituted our great whales.)

Of course, there are still larger whales in the Antarctic, of which Swift was not cognizant. The largest of these is the blue whale, which can attain a length of nearly one hundred feet, or, on the Brobdingnagian scale, over eight feet.

A Greenland whale.

7 *fifty four English Miles.* A city which is 54 miles in length and 45 in breadth would have an area of 2,430 square miles and would be eight times as large as the five boroughs of New York City. On the Brobdingnagian scale it would be equivalent to only 17 square miles in area, however, and would be no more than a respectable European city like London or Paris in Swift's time, both in area and population.

To be sure, 600,000 Brobdingnagians would weigh as much as a *billion* human beings. The city of Lorbrulgrud would contain 78 million tons of human flesh and blood, or 32,000 tons per square mile. The island of Manhattan never contains more than 10,000 tons per square mile. The problem of feeding Lorbrulgrud with a technology no higher than that possessed by Swift's England (which was probably not surpassed by Brobdingnag) would probably have been insuperable, but . . . oh, well.

8 *Westminster-Hall.* The great hall of the English Parliament.

9 *But, the most hateful Sight of all was the Lice . . .* There are commentators who interpret this scene as implying that although the beggars (Brobdingnagians) are bad, the lice and other vermin (Europeans) are even worse. This seems to me to be an unreasonable example of forcing a passage to fit a preconceived notion. Once a commentator has gotten it into his head that the Brobdingnagian society is a virtuous one, even the plainest English has to be turned upside down to make it fit that preconception.

After all, Swift is a writer even before he is a satirist, and here he takes the opportunity to draw an enormously dramatic picture. It reinforces the nausea he has previously tried to induce in describing the results of changing ordinary objects by mere expansion: the nurse's breast, the Queen crunching on bones. And he emphasizes Gulliver's smallness by having him aspire to anatomize lice.

Most of all, it shows once more that far from being a utopia, Brobdingnag has the faults of England in the existence of beggars and the low state of medicine and hygiene.

"There was a Fellow with a Wen in his Neck." J. J. Grandville, 1835. Courtesy, Library of Congress.

through a Microscope; and their Snouts with which they rooted like Swine. They were the first I had ever beheld; and I should have been curious enough to dissect one of them, if I had proper Instruments (which I unluckily left behind me in the Ship) although indeed the Sight was so nauseous, that it perfectly turned my Stomach.

Beside the large Box in which I was usually carried, the Queen ordered a smaller one to be made for me, of about twelve Foot Square, and ten high, for the Convenience of Travelling; because the other was somewhat too large for *Glumdalclitch's* Lap, and cumbersom in the Coach; it was made by the same Artist, whom I directed in the whole Contrivance. This travelling Closet was an exact Square with a Window in the Middle of three of the Squares, and each Window was latticed with Iron Wire on the outside, to prevent Accidents in long Journeys. On the fourth Side, which had no Window, two strong Staples were fixed, through which the Person that carried me, when I had a Mind to be on Horseback, put in a Leathern Belt, and buckled it about his Waist. This was always the Office of some grave trusty Servant in whom I could confide, whether I attended the King and Queen in their Progresses, or were disposed to see the Gardens, or pay a Visit to some great Lady or Minister of State in the Court, when *Glumdalclitch* happened to be out of Order: For I soon began to be known and esteemed among the greatest Officers, I suppose more upon Account of their Majesty's Favour, than any Merit of my own. In Journeys, when I was weary of the Coach, a Servant on Horseback would buckle my Box, and place it on a Cushion before him; and there I had a full Prospect of the Country on three Sides from my three

Windows. I had in this Closet a Field-Bed and a Hammock hung from the Cieling, two Chairs and a Table, neatly screwed to the Floor, to prevent being tossed about by the Agitation of the Horse or the Coach. And having been long used to Sea-Voyages, those Motions, although sometimes very violent, did not much discompose me.

Whenever I had a Mind to see the Town, it was always in my Travelling-Closet; which *Glumdalclitch* held in her Lap in a kind of open Sedan, after the Fashion of the Country, born by four Men, and attended by two others in the Queen's Livery. The People who had often heard of me, were very curious to croud about the Sedan; and the Girl was complaisant enough to make the Bearers stop, and to take me in her Hand that I might be more conveniently seen.

I was very desirous to see the chief Temple, and particularly the Tower belonging to it, which is reckoned the highest in the Kingdom. Accordingly one Day my Nurse carried me thither, but I may truly say I came back disappointed; for, the Height is not above three thousand Foot, reckoning from the Ground to the **10** highest Pinnacle top; which allowing for the Difference between the Size of those People, and us in *Europe*, is no great matter for Admiration, nor at all equal in Proportion, (if I rightly remember) to *Salisbury* Steeple. But, not to detract from a Nation to which **11** during my Life I shall acknowledge myself extremely obliged; it must be allowed, that whatever this famous Tower wants in Height, is amply made up in Beauty and Strength. For the Walls are near an hundred Foot thick, built of hewn Stone, whereof each is about forty Foot square, and adorned on all Sides with Statues of Gods and Emperors cut in Marble larger than the Life, placed in their several Niches. I measured a little Finger which had fallen down from one of these Statues, and lay unperceived among some Rubbish; and found it exactly four Foot and an Inch in Length. **12** *Glumdalclitch* wrapped it up in a Handkerchief, and carried it home in her Pocket to keep among other Trinkets, of which the Girl was very fond, as Children at her Age usually are.

The King's Kitchen is indeed a noble Building, vaulted at Top, and about six hundred Foot high. The great Oven is not so wide by ten Paces as the Cupola at St. *Paul's*: For I measured the latter on **13**

St. Paul's. Courtesy, Prints Division, The New York Public Library.

10 *three thousand Foot.* Gulliver is identifying more and more with the Brobdingnagians, so he is naturally disappointed. Three thousand feet to the Brobdingnagians is 250 feet to a European, and that isn't much.

11 *Salisbury Steeple.* Gulliver remembers rightly. The spire of Salisbury Cathedral (in Salisbury, a town eighty miles southwest of London) is the highest in England and is 404 feet high. On the Brobdingnagian scale, that would be 4,848 feet, or better than 9/10 of a mile high. Europeans, in proportion, have outbuilt the Brobdingnagians. (As a matter of interest, the Brobdingnagians would have had to build a structure 3.3 miles high to match the Sears Tower in present-day Chicago.)

Salisbury steeple. Courtesy, Library of Congress.

12 *four Foot and an Inch in Length.* The length of the index finger of the Statue of Liberty in New York Harbor is eight feet.

13 *the Cupola at St. Paul's.* By dismissing the great oven as ten paces smaller in diameter than the cupola (or dome) of St. Paul's, Gulliver emphasizes its size. St. Paul's Cathedral, the chief church of the Church of England, has the second largest dome in the world, 145 feet in diameter. Only the dome of St. Peter's in Rome surpasses it.

14 *Brobdingnag.* This is the first time the name of the land is given in the text of the book. It, too, has entered the general language so that "brobdingnagian" has come to mean "colossal" or "gigantic."

15 *Battalia.* In battle array; lined up, presumably, and ready for a charge. Note that Brobdingnag has an army.

purpose after my Return. But if I should describe the Kitchengrate, the prodigious Pots and Kettles, the Joints of Meat turning on the Spits, with many other Particulars; perhaps I should be hardly believed; at least a severe Critick would be apt to think I enlarged a little, as Travellers are often suspected to do. To avoid which Censure, I fear I have run too much into the other Extream; and that if this Treatise should happen to be translated into the **14** Language of *Brobdingnag,* (which is the general Name of that Kingdom) and transmitted thither; the King and his People would have Reason to complain; that I had done them an Injury by a false and diminutive Representation.

His Majesty seldom keeps above six hundred Horses in his Stables: They are generally from fifty four to sixty Foot high. But, when he goes abroad on solemn Days, he is attended for State by a Militia Guard of five hundred Horse, which indeed I thought was the most splendid Sight that could be ever beheld, till I saw part **15** of his Army in Battalia; whereof I shall find another Occasion to speak.

CHAPTER FIVE

Several Adventures that happened to the Author. The Execution of a Criminal. The Author shews his skill in Navigation.

"*The malicious Rogue . . . shook it directly over my Head.*" *Thomas Stothard,* The Novelist's Magazine, *1782. Courtesy,* The New York Public Library.

SHOULD have lived happy enough in that Country, if my Littleness had not exposed me to several ridiculous and troublesome Accidents; some of which I shall venture to relate. *Glumdalclitch* often carried me into the Gardens of the Court in my smaller Box, and would sometimes take me out of it and hold me in her Hand, or set me down to walk. I remember, before the Dwarf left the Queen, he followed us one Day into those Gardens; and my Nurse having set me down, he and I being close together, near some Dwarf Apple-trees, I must need shew my Wit by a silly Allusion between him and the Trees, which happens to hold in their Language as it doth in ours. Whereupon, the malicious Rogue watching his Opportunity, when I was walking under one of them, shook it directly over my Head, by which a dozen Apples, each of them near as large as a *Bristol* Barrel, came tumbling about my Ears; one of them hit me on the Back as I chanced to stoop, and knocked me down flat on my Face, but I received no other Hurt; and the Dwarf

1 *as large as a Bristol Barrel.* Measures had not yet been standardized in Swift's England. Barrels came in different sizes in different regions, and a Bristol barrel was one of the larger ones.

2 *Hail-stones.* Hail, too, partakes of a Brobdingnagian character. This is, of course, impossible to explain in any rational way.

3 *near Eighteen Hundred Times as large.* Of course! After all 12 × 12 × 12 is 1,728, and Gulliver used the exact figure several times while in Lilliput.

"Apples . . . came tumbling about my Ears." Arthur Rackham, 1909.

was pardoned at my Desire, because I had given the Provocation.

Another Day, *Glumdalclitch* left me on a smooth Grass-plot to divert my self while she walked at some Distance with her Governess. In the mean time, there suddenly fell such a violent Shower of Hail, that I was immediately by the Force of it struck to the

2 Ground: And when I was down, the Hail-stones gave me such cruel Bangs all over the Body, as if I had been pelted with Tennis-Balls; however I made a Shift to creep on all four, and shelter my self by lying flat on my Face on the Lee-side of a Border of Lemmon Thyme; but so bruised from Head to Foot, that I could not go abroad in ten Days. Neither is this at all to be wondered at; because Nature in that Country observing the same Proportion through all her Operations, a Hailstone is near Eighteen Hundred

3 Times as large as one in *Europe;* which I can assert upon Experience, having been so curious to weigh and measure them.

But, a more dangerous Accident happened to me in the same Garden, when my little Nurse, believing she had put me in a secure Place, which I often entreated her to do, that I might enjoy my own Thoughts; and having left my Box at home to avoid the Trouble of carrying it, went to another Part of the Gardens with her Governess and some Ladies of her Acquaintance. While she was absent and out of hearing, a small white Spaniel belonging to one of the chief Gardiners, having got by Accident into the Garden, happened to range near the Place where I lay. The Dog following the Scent, came directly up, and taking me in his Mouth, ran strait to his Master, wagging his Tail, and set me gently on the Ground. By good Fortune he had been so well taught, that I was carried between his Teeth without the least Hurt, or even tearing my Cloaths. But, the poor Gardiner, who knew me well, and had a great Kindness for me, was in a terrible Fright. He gently took me up in both his Hands, and asked me how I did; but I was so amazed and out of Breath, that I could not speak a Word. In a few Minutes I came to my self, and he carried me safe to my little Nurse, who by this time had returned to the Place where she left me, and was in cruel Agonies when I did not appear, nor answer when she called; she severely reprimanded the Gardiner on Account of his Dog. But, the Thing was hushed up, and never known at Court; for the Girl was afraid of the Queen's Anger; and truly as to my self, I thought it would not be for my Reputation that such a Story should **4** go about.

This Accident absolutely determined *Glumdalclitch* never to trust me abroad for the future out of her Sight. I had been long afraid of this Resolution; and therefore concealed from her some little unlucky Adventures that happened in those Times when I was left by my self. Once a Kite hovering over the Garden, made **5** a Stoop at me, and if I had not resolutely drawn my Hanger, and run under a thick Espalier, he would have certainly carried me **6** away in his Talons. Another time, walking to the Top of a fresh Molehill, I fell to my Neck in the Hole through which that Animal had cast up the Earth; and coined some Lye not worth remembring, to excuse my self for spoiling my Cloaths. I likewise broke my **7** right Shin against the Shell of a Snail, which I happened to stumble over, as I was walking alone, and thinking on poor *England*.

I cannot tell whether I were more pleased or mortified to observe in those solitary Walks, that the smaller Birds did not appear to be at all afraid of me; but would hop about within a Yard Distance, looking for Worms, and other Food, with as much Indifference and Security as if no Creature at all were near them. I remember, a Thrush had the Confidence to snatch out of my Hand with his Bill, a Piece of Cake that *Glumdalclitch* had just given me for my Breakfast. When I attempted to catch any of these Birds, they would boldly turn against me, endeavoring to pick my Fingers, which I durst not venture within their Reach; and then they would hop back unconcerned to hunt for Worms or Snails, as they did before. But, one Day I took a thick Cudgel, and threw it with all my Strength so luckily at a Linnet, that I knocked him down, and seizing him by the Neck with both my Hands, ran with him in **8** Triumph to my Nurse. However, the Bird who had only been stunned, recovering himself, gave me so many Boxes with his Wings on both Sides of my Head and Body, although I held him at Arm's Length, and was out of the Reach of his Claws, that I was twenty Times thinking to let him go. But I was soon relieved by one of our Servants, who wrung off the Bird's Neck; and I had him

4 *my Reputation.* Gulliver is identifying more and more with the giants and growing more and more ashamed of himself for not being one. (In Lilliput, on the other hand, he was proud of being outsized.) His misadventures are, after all, a source of laughter to the Brobdingnagians and Gulliver does not enjoy being laughed at.

5 *Kite.* A kind of falcon.

6 *Espalier.* A trellis along which climbing plants might grow.

7 *broke my right Shin.* Broke the skin rather than the bone, no doubt.

8 *ran with him in Triumph to my Nurse.* Gulliver is so eager to perform respectable feats of strength and daring that he runs with his prey to the little girl who guards him, hoping for praise.

9 *the Pleasure of seeing and touching me.* The Brobdingnagian maids of honor are, presumably, curious
about his genitals, and wonder about the effect of
stimulating them.

*Gulliver is undressed and examined by the ladies. Le
Febure, 1797.*

10 *a very offensive Smell came from their Skins.* There
were few even among the upper classes in the England of Swift's time who experienced running water
on their body, except when they were caught in a
downpour or fell into a river. Presumably it was the
same in Brobdingnag, and if the ratio of twelve to
one worked on odors as well, the muskiness of un-
washed skin would have been almost unbearably
strong. Poor Gulliver!

11 *I immediately swooned away.* The usual method of
removing body odor in a bathless society was to
drench one's self in strong, competing odors, if one
were rich enough to afford them. The perfumes, in
the days before modern chemistry, had strength as
their chief virtue and were applied with no stingy
hand. That Gulliver swooned is not remarkable; that
he recovered, is.

next Day for Dinner by the Queen's Command. This Linnet, as
near as I can remember, seemed to be somewhat larger than an
English Swan.

The Maids of Honour often invited *Glumdalclitch* to their Apartments, and desired she would bring me along with her, on Purpose
9 to have the Pleasure of seeing and touching me. They would often
strip me naked from Top to Toe, and lay me at full Length in their
Bosoms; wherewith I was much disgusted; because, to say the
10 Truth, a very offensive Smell came from their Skins; which I do
not mention or intend to the Disadvantage of those excellent
Ladies, for whom I have all Manner of Respect: But, I conceive,
that my Sense was more acute in Proportion to my Littleness; and
that those illustrious Persons were no more disagreeable to their
Lovers, or to each other, than People of the same Quality are with
us in *England*. And, after all, I found their natural Smell was
much more supportable than when they used Perfumes, under
11 which I immediately swooned away. I cannot forget, that an intimate Friend of mine in *Lilliput* took the Freedom in a warm Day,
when I had used a good deal of Exercise, to complain of a strong
Smell about me; although I am as little faulty that way as most of
my Sex: But I suppose, his Faculty of Smelling was as nice with
regard to me, as mine was to that of this People. Upon this Point,
I cannot forbear doing Justice to the Queen my Mistress, and
Glumdalclitch my Nurse; whose Persons were as sweet as those of
any Lady in *England*.

That which gave me most Uneasiness among these Maids of
Honour, when my Nurse carried me to visit them, was to see them
use me without any Manner of Ceremony, like a Creature who
had no Sort of Consequence. For, they would strip themselves to

*Gulliver among the Brobdingnagian ladies.
C. E. Brock, 1894.*

The Brobdingnagian ladies play with Gulliver. Ad. Laluze, 1875.
Suppressed in later editions. Courtesy, Library of Congress.

12 *Toylet.* Toilet. From a French word meaning "a little cloth." A dressing table on which a woman kept her cosmetics, combs, and other paraphernalia would have a little cloth over it, and the whole would be called a "toilet." The act of washing or making up would then be described as "being about one's toilet." The room in which this was done would then also be called the toilet. Since, in the days before internal plumbing, chamber pots were also kept in this room, the toilet came eventually to mean the room in which one relieved one's self, and still later to mean the receptacle into which the waste was deposited and flushed away (a "flush toilet") once internal plumbing was invented. In Swift's time, "toilet" still meant the dressing table, on which Gulliver was placed, by maids of honor who undressed before him either out of indifference to his masculinity (it being so small) or out of mischievous exhibitionism.

13 *two Hogsheads.* A hogshead is a unit of volume. Its exact size varied with the place it was used and with what it was that was being measured. A hogshead of beer in London was 54 gallons, or 432 pints. If the maids of honor discharged more than 864 pints of urine this, being a volume, would have to be divided by 1,728 to bring it down to the European scale. It would be equivalent to half a pint, which is quite reasonable. Of course, if it smelled 12 times as strongly as European urine, poor Gulliver would have had a terrible time of it.

14 *three Tuns.* A tun is equal to 252 gallons, so the chamber pot held about 800 gallons.

"A pleasant frolicksome Girl of sixteen, would sometimes set me astride upon one of her Nipples." Bofa, 1929.

the Skin, and put on their Smocks in my Presence, while I was placed on their Toylet directly before their naked Bodies; which, **12** I am sure, to me was very far from being a tempting Sight, or from giving me any other Motions than those of Horror and Disgust. Their Skins appeared so coarse and uneven, so variously coloured when I saw them near, with a Mole here and there as broad as a Trencher, and Hairs hanging from it thicker than Pack-threads; to say nothing further concerning the rest of their Persons. Neither did they at all scruple while I was by, to discharge what they had drunk, to the Quantity of at least two Hogsheads, in a Vessel that **13** held above three Tuns. The handsomest among these Maids of **14** Honour, a pleasant frolicksome Girl of sixteen, would sometimes set me astride upon one of her Nipples; with many other Tricks, wherein the Reader will excuse me for not being over particular. But, I was so much displeased, that I entreated *Glumdalclitch* to contrive some Excuse for not seeing that young Lady any more.

One Day, a young Gentleman who was Nephew to my Nurse's

15 *an Execution.* Through most of history, down to Swift's time and beyond, executions were public spectacles. People were even given holiday so that they could come and watch. The argument was that it was a good idea for people to see what happened to convicted criminals as a deterrent to further crime. It didn't work, of course. Rather, it encouraged sadism and cruelty. Brobdingnag shared with England this penchant for public executions.

The Idle 'Prentice Executed, engraving by William Hogarth, 1747. Courtesy, Library of Congress.

16 *the great Jet d'Eau.* Versailles, a town ten miles southwest of Paris, was made the seat of government by Louis XIV in 1671. There he began the building of a huge palace that was to symbolize the glory and power of France. Indeed, it was so enormous and extravagant an undertaking that it bankrupted the nation and hastened its decline. Nevertheless, it was an impressive pile and among its various glories was its elaborate system of *jets d'eaux* (jets of water) or fountains.

Nocturnal illuminations at the palace and gardens of Versailles. Engraving by Le Pautre, 1679. Courtesy, Prints Division, The New York Public Library.

17 *Wherry.* A rowboat.

15 Governess, came and pressed them both to see an Execution. It was of a Man who had murdered one of that Gentleman's intimate Acquaintance. *Glumdalclitch* was prevailed on to be of the Company, very much against her Inclination, for she was naturally tender hearted: And, as for my self, although I abhorred such Kind of Spectacles; yet my Curiosity tempted me to see something that I thought must be extraordinary. The Malefactor was fixed in a Chair upon a Scaffold erected for the Purpose; and his Head cut off at one Blow with a Sword of about forty Foot long. The Veins and Arteries spouted up such a prodigious Quantity of Blood, and so high in the Air, that the great *Jet d'Eau* at *Versailles* **16** was not equal for the Time it lasted; and the Head when it fell on the Scaffold Floor, gave such a Bounce, as made me start, although I were at least an *English* Mile distant.

The Queen, who often used to hear me talk of my Sea-Voyages, and took all Occasions to divert me when I was melancholy, asked me whether I understood how to handle a Sail or an Oar; and whether a little Exercise of Rowing might not be convenient for my Health. I answered, that I understood both very well. For although my proper Employment had been to be Surgeon or Doctor to the Ship; yet often upon a Pinch, I was forced to work like a common Mariner. But, I could not see how this could be done in **17** their Country, where the smallest Wherry was equal to a first Rate Man of War among us; and such a Boat as I could manage, would never live in any of their Rivers: Her Majesty said, if I would contrive a Boat, her own Joyner should make it, and she would provide a Place for me to sail in. The Fellow was an ingenious Workman, and by my Instructions in ten Days finished a Pleasure-Boat with all its Tackling, able conveniently to hold eight *Europeans.* When it was finished, the Queen was so delighted, that she ran with it in her Lap to the King, who ordered it to be put in a Cistern full of Water, with me in it, by way of Tryal; where I

"I often used to row for my Diversion." "Alfred Crawquill." 1865.

"The Ladies gave me a Gale with their fans." T. Morten, 1865. Courtesy, Library of Congress.

18 *carried back my Boat into her Closet and hung it on a Nail to dry.* Gulliver's expertise is deliberately made to seem childish and toylike.

19 *officiously.* Now taken to mean "in a meddlesome manner," it is here used in its older meaning of "kindly."

20 *Corking-pin.* An obsolete term for a large pin.

could not manage my two Sculls or little Oars for want of Room. But, the Queen had before contrived another Project. She ordered the Joyner to make a wooden Trough of three Hundred Foot long, fifty broad, and eight deep; which being well pitched to prevent leaking, was placed on the Floor along the Wall in an outer Room of the Palace. It had a Cock near the Bottom, to let out the Water when it began to grow stale; and two Servants could easily fill it in half an Hour. Here I often used to row for my Diversion, as well as that of the Queen and her Ladies, who thought themselves agreeably entertained with my Skill and Agility. Sometimes I would put up my Sail, and then my Business was only to steer, while the Ladies gave me a Gale with their Fans; and when they were weary, some of the Pages would blow my Sail forward with their Breath, while I shewed my Art by steering Starboard or Larboard as I pleased. When I had done, *Glumdalclitch* always carried back my Boat into her Closet, and hung it on a Nail to dry. **18**

In this Exercise I once met an Accident which had like to have cost me my Life. For, one of the Pages having put my Boat into the Trough; the Governess who attended *Glumdalclitch*, very officiously **19** lifted me up to place me in the Boat; but I happened to slip through her Fingers, and should have infallibly fallen down forty Foot upon the Floor, if by the luckiest Chance in the World, I had not been stop'd by a Corking-pin that stuck in the good Gentle- **20**

21 *Stomacher*. A decorative cloth, embroidered or jeweled, worn over the bosom and stomach.

22 *Clerks of the Kitchen*. "Clerk" (a form of "cleric") came to be used for anyone who could read and write, since in medieval times only those trained for the Church could. Someone whose job was keeping accounts was a clerk, and the kitchen clerks were those who kept track of purchases of food and other supplies.

23 *Closet*. A small room. Nowadays it signifies a small windowless room in which clothes and other objects may be stored, but in Swift's time a closet was a room with windows, notable only for being small.

The closet. Painting by Honoré Fragonard, c.1778.

Gulliver encounters a frog. Willy Pogány, 1919.

21 woman's Stomacher; the Head of the Pin passed between my Shirt and the Waistband of my Breeches; and thus I was held by the Middle in the Air, till *Glumdalclitch* ran to my Relief.

Another time, one of the Servants, whose Office it was to fill my Trough every third Day with fresh Water; was so careless to let a huge Frog (not perceiving it) slip out of his Pail. The Frog lay concealed till I was put into my Boat, but then seeing a resting Place, climbed up, and made it lean so much on one Side, that I was forced to balance it with all my Weight on the other, to prevent overturning. When the Frog was got in, it hopped at once half the Length of the Boat, and then over my Head, backwards and forwards, dawbing my Face and Cloaths with its odious Slime. The Largeness of its Features made it appear the most deformed Animal that can be conceived. However, I desired *Glumdalclitch* to let me deal with it alone. I banged it a good while with one of my Sculls, and at last forced it to leap out of the Boat.

But, the greatest Danger I ever underwent in that Kingdom, was
22 from a Monkey, who belonged to one of the Clerks of the Kitchen.
23 *Glumdalclitch* had locked me up in her Closet, while she went somewhere upon Business, or a Visit. The Weather being very warm, the Closet Window was left open, as well as the Windows and the Door of my bigger Box, in which I usually lived, because of its Largeness and Conveniency. As I sat quietly meditating at my Table, I heard something bounce in at the Closet Window, and skip about from one Side to the other; whereat, although I were much alarmed, yet I ventured to look out, but not stirring from my Seat; and then I saw this frolicksome Animal, frisking and leaping up and down, till at last he came to my Box, which he seemed to view with great Pleasure and Curiosity, peeping in at the Door and every Window. I retreated to the farther Corner of my Room, or Box; but the Monkey looking in at every Side, put me into such a Fright, that I wanted Presence of Mind to conceal my self under the Bed, as I might easily have done. After some time spent in peeping, grinning, and chattering, he at last espyed me; and reach-

ing one of his Paws in at the Door, as a Cat does when she plays with a Mouse, although I often shifted Place to avoid him; he at length seized the Lappet of my Coat (which being made of that Country Silk, was very thick and strong) and dragged me out. He took me up in his right Fore-foot, and held me as a Nurse doth a Child she is going to suckle; just as I have seen the same Sort of Creature do with a Kitten in *Europe*: And when I offered to struggle, he squeezed me so hard, that I thought it more prudent to submit. I have good Reason to believe that he took me for a young one of his own Species, by his often stroaking my Face very gently with his other Paw. In these Diversions he was interrupted by a Noise at the Closet Door, as if some Body were opening it; whereupon he suddenly leaped up to the Window at which he had come in, and thence upon the Leads and Gutters, walking upon three Legs, and holding me in the fourth, till he clambered up to a Roof that was next to ours. I heard *Glumdalclitch* give a Shriek at the Moment he was carrying me out. The poor Girl was almost distracted: That Quarter of the Palace was all in an Uproar; the Servants ran for Ladders; the Monkey was seen by Hundreds in the Court, sitting upon the Ridge of a Building, holding me like a Baby in one of his Fore-Paws, and feeding me with the other, by cramming into my Mouth some Victuals he had squeezed out of the Bag on one Side of his Chaps, and patting me when I would not eat; whereat many of the Rabble below could not forbear laughing; neither do I think they justly ought to be blamed; for without Question, the Sight was ridiculous enough to every Body but my self. Some of the People threw up Stones, hoping to drive the Monkey down; but this was strictly forbidden, or else very probably my Brains had been dashed out.

The Ladders were now applied, and mounted by several Men; which the Monkey observing, and finding himself almost encompassed; not being able to make Speed enough with his three Legs, let me drop on a Ridge-Tyle, and made his Escape. Here I sat for some time five Hundred Yards from the Ground, expecting every Moment to be blown down by the Wind, or to fall by my own Giddiness, and come tumbling over and over from the Ridge to the Eves. But an honest Lad, one of my Nurses's Footmen, climbed up, and putting me into his Breeches Pocket, brought me down safe.

I was almost choaked with the filthy Stuff the Monkey had crammed down my Throat; but, my dear little Nurse picked it out of my Mouth with a small Needle; and then I fell a vomiting, which gave me great Relief. Yet I was so weak and bruised in the Sides with the Squeezes given me by this odious Animal, that I was forced to keep my Bed a Fortnight. The King, Queen, and all the Court, sent every Day to enquire after my Health; and her Majesty made me several Visits during my Sickness. The Monkey was killed, and an Order made that no such Animal should be kept about the Palace.

When I attended the King after my Recovery, to return him Thanks for his Favours, he was pleased to railly me a good deal upon this Adventure. He asked me what my Thoughts and Speculations were while I lay in the Monkey's Paw; how I liked the Victuals he gave me, his Manner of Feeding; and whether the fresh Air on the Roof had sharpened my Stomach. He desired to know what I would have done upon such an Occasion in my own

24

Gulliver and the monkey.
Herbert Cole, 1899.

24 *Chaps.* An old term for "jaws," which is still occasionally used. Apparently, the Brobdingnagian monkey had cheek pouches in which it stored food and, mistaking Gulliver for an infant monkey (a new humiliation), was trying to feed him.

25 *all the Mirth, for some Days, was at my Expense.*
Swift has spent five chapters humiliating Gulliver,
finally covering him with cow manure. Even Glumdalclitch, the most lovable of the Brobdingnagians,
does not hesitate to curry favor with the Queen by
telling stories that will humiliate Gulliver.

*Gulliver in the cow dung. J. J. Grandville, 1835.
Courtesy, Library of Congress.*

Country. I told his Majesty, that in *Europe* we had no Monkies,
except such as were brought for Curiosities from other Places, and
so small, that I could deal with a Dozen of them together, if they
presumed to attack me. And as for that monstrous Animal with
whom I was so lately engaged, (it was indeed as large as an
Elephant) if my Fears had suffered me to think so far as to make
Use of my Hanger (looking fiercely, and clapping my Hand upon
the Hilt as I spoke) when he poked his Paw into my Chamber,
perhaps I should have given him such a Wound, as would have
made him glad to withdraw it with more Haste than he put it in.
This I delivered in a firm Tone, like a Person who was jealous lest
his Courage should be called in Question. However, my Speech
produced nothing else besides a loud Laughter; which all the Respect due to his Majesty from those about him, could not make
them contain. This made me reflect, how vain an Attempt it is for
a Man to endeavour doing himself Honour among those who are
out of all Degree of Equality or Comparison with him. And yet I
have seen the Moral of my own Behavior very frequent in *England*
since my Return; where a little contemptible Varlet, without the
least Title to Birth, Person, Wit, or common Sense, shall presume
to look with Importance, and put himself upon a Foot with the
greatest Persons of the Kingdom.

I was every Day furnishing the Court with some ridiculous Story;
and *Glumdalclitch*, although she loved me to Excess, yet was arch
enough to inform the Queen, whenever I committed any Folly
that she thought would be diverting to her Majesty. The Girl who
had been out of Order, was carried by her Governess to take
the Air about an Hour's Distance, or thirty Miles from Town.
They alighted out of the Coach near a small Foot-path in a Field;
and *Glumdalclitch* setting down my travelling Box, I went out of
it to walk. There was a Cow-dung in the Path, and I must needs
try my Activity by attempting to leap over it. I took a Run, but
unfortunately jumped short, and found my self just in the Middle
up to my Knees. I waded through with some Difficulty, and one
of the Footmen wiped me as clean as he could with his Handkerchief;
for I was filthily bemired, and my Nurse confined me to my Box
until we returned home; where the Queen was soon informed of
what had passed, and the Footmen spread it about the Court;
25 so that all the Mirth, for some Days, was at my Expence.

Several contrivances of the Author to please the King and Queen. He shews his skill in Musick. The King enquires into the state of Europe, which the Author relates to him. The King's observations thereon.

I USED to attend the King's Levee¹ once or twice a Week, and had often seen him under the Barber's Hand, which indeed was at first very terrible to behold. For, the Razor was almost as long as an ordinary Scythe. His Majesty, according to the Custom of the Country, was only shaved twice a Week. I once prevailed on the Barber to give me some of the Suds or Lather, out of which I picked Forty or Fifty of the strongest Stumps of Hair, I then took a Piece of fine Wood, and cut it like the Back of a Comb, making several Holes in it at equal Distance, with as small a Needle as I could get from *Glumdalclitch.* I fixed in the Stumps so artificially,² scraping and sloping them with my Knife towards the Points, that I made a very tolerable Comb; which was a seasonable Supply, my own being so much broken in the Teeth, that it was almost useless: Neither did I know any Artist in that Country so nice and exact, as would undertake to make me another.

And this puts me in mind of an Amusement wherein I spent many of my leisure Hours. I desired the Queen's Woman to save for me the Combings of her Majesty's Hair, whereof in time I got a good Quantity; and consulting with my Friend the Cabinet-maker, who had received general Orders to do little Jobs for me; I di-

1 *Levee.* Louis XIV, upon arising in the morning (his *levée*), would often receive visitors. He made a most elaborate ritual out of this, as he did out of everything, however trivial. The term eventually came to be used for any royal audience at whatever time of day. In England, in Swift's time, the term came to be given to an audience held by the king in the early afternoon, with only men invited.

2 *artificially.* Nowadays "artificially" means "unnatural," "affected," "inferior" and is always used pejoratively. Swift uses the older meaning of "artfully" or "with skillful artistry."

"The Noise was so great, that I could hardly distinguish the Tunes." T. Morten, 1865. Courtesy, Library of Congress.

3 *Spinet.* A small harpsichord, which is itself a precursor of the piano. It is a keyed instrument in which the strings are plucked, rather than struck, when a key is depressed. Gulliver is obviously a man of many parts, but Swift never allows the Brobdingnagians to appreciate Gulliver's abilities.

rected him to make two Chair-frames, no larger than those I had in my Box, and then to bore little Holes with a fine Awl round those Parts where I designed the Backs and Seats; through these Holes I wove the strongest Hairs I could pick out, just after the Manner of Cane-chairs in *England*. When they were finished, I made a Present of them to her Majesty, who kept them in her Cabinet, and used to shew them for Curiosities; as indeed they were the Wonder of every one who beheld them. The Queen would have had me sit upon one of these Chairs, but I absolutely refused to obey her; protesting I would rather dye a Thousand Deaths than place a dishonourable Part of my Body on those precious Hairs that once adorned her Majesty's Head. Of these Hairs (as I had always a Mechanical Genius) I likewise made a neat little Purse about five Foot long, with her Majesty's Name decyphered in Gold Letters; which I gave to *Glumdalclitch*, by the Queen's Consent. To say the Truth, it was more for Shew than Use, being not of Strength to bear the Weight of the larger Coins; and therefore she kept nothing in it, but some little Toys that Girls are fond of.

The King, who delighted in Musick, had frequent Consorts at Court, to which I was sometimes carried, and set in my Box on a Table to hear them: But, the Noise was so great, that I could hardly distinguish the Tunes. I am confident, that all the Drums and Trumpets of a Royal Army, beating and sounding together just at your Ears, could not equal it. My Practice was to have my Box removed from the Places where the Performers sat, as far as I could; then to shut the Doors and Windows of it, and draw the Window-Curtains; after which I found their Musick not disagreeable.

3   I had learned in my Youth to play a little upon the Spinet; *Glumdalclitch* kept one in her Chamber, and a Master attended twice a Week to teach her: I call it a Spinet, because it somewhat resembled that Instrument, and was play'd upon in the same Manner. A Fancy came into my Head, that I would entertain the King and Queen with an *English* Tune upon this Instrument. But this appeared extremely difficult: For, the Spinet was near sixty Foot

Gulliver plays the spinet. Herbert Cole, 1899.

Gulliver converses with the king. E. J. Wheeler, 1895.

long, each Key being almost a Foot wide; so that, with my Arms
extended, I could not reach to above five Keys; and to press them
down required a good smart stroak with my Fist, which would be
too great a Labour, and to no purpose. The Method I contrived
was this. I prepared two round Sticks about the Bigness of common Cudgels; they were thicker at one End than the other; and I
covered the thicker End with a Piece of a Mouse's Skin, that by
rapping on them, I might neither Damage the Tops of the Keys,
nor interrupt the Sound. Before the Spinet, a Bench was placed
about four Foot below the Keys, and I was put upon the Bench. I
ran sideling upon it that way and this, as fast as I could, banging
the proper Keys with my two Sticks; and made a shift to play a
Jigg to the great Satisfaction of both their Majesties: But it was
the most violent Exercise I ever underwent, and yet I could not
strike above sixteen Keys, nor, consequently, play the Bass and
Treble together, as other Artists do; which was a great Disadvantage to my Performance.

The King, who as I before observed, was a Prince of excellent
Understanding, would frequently order that I should be brought in
my Box, and set upon the Table in his Closet. He would then command me to bring one of my Chairs out of the Box, and sit down
within three Yards Distance upon the Top of the Cabinet; which
brought me almost to a Level with his Face. In this Manner I had
several Conversations with him. I one Day took the Freedom to tell
his Majesty, that the Contempt he discovered towards *Europe*, and
the rest of the World, did not seem answerable to those excellent
Qualities of Mind, that he was Master of. That, Reason did not

Cicero. Courtesy, Library of Congress.

4 *Demosthenes or Cicero*. Demosthenes (385–322 B.C.) is commonly regarded as the greatest orator of the ancient Greet world, and Marcus Tullius Cicero (106–43 B.C.) the greatest of the ancient Roman world.

5 *two Islands*. I.e., Britain and Ireland, which are together the British Isles and which include a number of smaller islands, the Isle of Man, the Isle of Wight, the Orkneys, Hebrides, Shetland, and so on.

6 *three mighty Kingdoms*. England, Scotland, and Ireland, which were, in 1703, at the time Gulliver landed in Brobdingnag, at least in theory, separate kingdoms with separate governments, united only in the fact that each of the three had the same sovereign who ruled from London and who was king (or queen) of England and of Scotland and of Ireland. In actual fact, of course, Scotland and Ireland were not completely in love with the idea of being ruled from London. Each had risen in the past and would yet again rise and it was the English army that kept the three under a single rule.

7 *one Sovereign*. Anne, who had come to the throne on March 19, 1702, three months before Gulliver left on his second voyage. On May 1, 1707, under Queen Anne, the Act of Union went into effect, whereby England and Scotland were united into a single kingdom with a single Parliament, which was to be called the United Kingdom of Great Britain. It was only after May 1, 1707, that one could speak of the British army, the British navy, the British people, rather than English or Scottish. The United Kingdom existed when *Gulliver's Travels* was published, but not yet when Gulliver was in Brobdingnag.

extend itself with the Bulk of the Body: On the contrary, we observed in our Country, that the tallest Persons were usually least provided with it. That among other Animals, Bees and Ants had the Reputation of more Industry, Art, and Sagacity than many of the larger Kinds. And that, as inconsiderable as he took me to be, I hoped I might live to do his Majesty some signal Service. The King heard me with Attention; and began to conceive a much better Opinion of me than he had ever before. He desired I would give him as exact an Account of the Government of *England* as I possibly could; because, as fond as Princes commonly are of their own Customs (for so he conjectured of other Monarchs by my former Discourses) he should be glad to hear of any thing that might deserve Imitation.

4 Imagine with thy self, courteous Reader, how often I then wished for the Tongue of *Demosthenes* or *Cicero*, that might have enabled me to celebrate the Praises of my own dear native Country in a Style equal to its Merits and Felicity.

5,6 **7,8** I began my Discourse by informing his Majesty, that our Dominions consisted of two Islands, which composed three mighty Kingdoms under one Sovereign, besides our Plantations in *America*. I dwelt long upon the Fertility of our Soil, and the Temperature of our Climate. I then spoke at large upon the Con-

9 stitution of an *English* Parliament, partly made up of an illustrious Body called the House of Peers, Persons of the noblest Blood, and of the most ancient and ample Patrimonies. I described that extraordinary Care always taken of their Education in Arts and Arms, to qualify them for being Counsellors born to the King and Kingdom; to have a Share in the Legislature, to be Members of the highest Court of Judicature from whence there could be no Appeal; and to be Champions always ready for the Defence of their Prince and Country by their Valour, Conduct and Fidelity. That these were the Ornament and Bulwark of the Kingdom; worthy Followers of their most renowned Ancestors, whose Honour had been the Reward of their Virtue; from which their Posterity were never once known to degenerate. To these were joined several holy Persons, as part of that Assembly, under the Title of Bishops; whose peculiar Business it is, to take care of Religion, and of those who instruct the People therein. These were searched and sought out through the whole Nation, by the Prince and wisest Counsellors, among such of the Priesthood, as were most deservedly distinguished by the Sanctity of their Lives, and the Depth of their Erudition; but who were indeed the spiritual Fathers of the Clergy and the People.

That, the other Part of the Parliament consisted of an Assembly called the House of Commons; who were all principal Gentlemen, *freely* picked and culled out by the People themselves, for their great Abilities, and Love of their Country, to represent the Wisdom of the whole Nation. And, these two Bodies make up the most august Assembly in *Europe*; to whom, in Conjunction with the Prince, the whole Legislature is committed.

I then descended to the Courts of Justice, over which the Judges, those venerable Sages and Interpreters of the Law, presided, for determining the disputed Rights and Properties of Men, as well as for the Punishment of Vice, and Protection of Innocence. I mentioned the prudent Management of our Treasury; the Valour and Atchievements of our Forces by Sea and Land. I computed the Number of our People, by reckoning how many Millions there might be of each Religious Sect, or Political Party among us. I did not omit even our Sports and Pastimes, or any other Particular which I thought might redound to the Honour of my Country. And, I finished all with a brief historical Account of Affairs and Events in *England* for about an hundred Years past. **10**

This Conversation was not ended under five Audiences, each of several Hours; and the King heard the whole with great Attention; frequently taking Notes of what I spoke, as well as Memorandums of what Questions he intended to ask me.

When I had put an End to these long Discourses, his Majesty in a sixth Audience consulting his Notes, proposed many Doubts, Queries, and Objections, upon every Article. **11** He asked, what Methods were used to cultivate the Minds and Bodies of our young Nobility; and in what kind of Business they commonly spent the first and teachable Part of their Lives. What Course was taken to supply that Assembly, when any noble Family became extinct. What Qualifications were necessary in those who are to be created new Lords: Whether the Humour of the Prince, a Sum of Money to a Court-Lady, or a Prime Minister; or a Design of strengthening a Party opposite to the publick Interest, ever happened to be Motives in those Advancements. What Share of Knowledge these Lords had in the Laws of their Country, and how they came by it, so as to enable them to decide the Properties of their Fellow-Subjects in the last Resort. Whether they were always so free from Avarice, Partialities, or Want, that a Bribe, or some other sinister View, could have no Place among them. Whether those holy Lords I spoke of, were constantly promoted to that Rank upon Account of their Knowledge in religious Matters, and the Sanctity of their Lives; had never been Compliers with the Times, while they were common Priests; or slavish prostitute Chaplains **12** to some Nobleman, whose Opinions they continued servilely to follow after they were admitted into that Assembly.

He then desired to know, what Arts were practised in electing those whom I called Commoners. Whether, a Stranger with a strong Purse might not influence the vulgar Voters to chuse him before their own Landlords, or the most considerable Gentleman in the

"Canvassing for Votes," engraving by William Hogarth, 1757.
Courtesy, Library of Congress.

8 *Plantations in America.* These included twelve colonies, which later formed part of the United States. (The thirteenth, Georgia, was not established till 1732, six years after *Gulliver's Travels* was published). The plantations also included Nova Scotia, Newfoundland, Bermuda, the Bahamas, and a number of West Indian islands.

9 *English Parliament.* What follows in the next three paragraphs is a lyrical description of the British government as it was in theory, all delivered with a perfectly straight face. It must have been a dull reader indeed who, reading the book at the time of its publication, did not realize that the legislature and the judiciary were nothing at all as described and who was not forced to smile wryly.

Gulliver does not enlarge upon the virtues of the monarch, however. Had he done so, that might have passed for satire, too, and Swift might have been in deep trouble.

10 *an hundred Years past.* That is, from the death of Elizabeth in 1603. The century thereafter is the turbulent history of the Stuart dynasty: James I, Charles I, Charles II, James II, Mary II (and her husband William III), and Anne—a history which includes two rebellions, an eleven year period when England was without a king altogether, and continual party wrangling.

11 *Doubts, Queries, and Objections, upon every Article.* If any of Swift's readers missed the satire in Gulliver's description of England's "ideal" government, the King's questioning that follows would have clued him or her in. It must have been completely obvious to everyone not an utter idiot that every imperfection pointed out by the king was an imperfection that actually existed in Swift's England.

Notice, by the way, that Swift carefully does not allow the Brobdingnagian King to ask specific questions about the English monarch. That, again, would have been going too far.

12 *slavish prostitute Chaplains.* A rather strong phrase, but here Swift was touching on something he felt strongly about, since he himself (he felt) had been denied advancement because of his political views while others who slavishly bent their principles to suit those in authority moved ahead.

13 *Chancery.* One of the three divisions of the English High Court of Justice, presided over by the lord chancellor. It was once known for the length and tediousness of the suits that were handled in that court, suits in which lawyers and judges argued over trivial points of procedure for so long a time that the legal fees would consume any judgment, however large, and all parties in the suit were very likely to be ruined. Charles Dickens, in *Bleak House*, published in 1853, a century and a quarter after *Gulliver's Travels*, satirized Chancery bitterly. It was not till 1875 that the worst abuses were abolished.

Neighbourhood. How it came to pass, that People were so violently bent upon getting into this Assembly, which I allowed to be a great Trouble and Expence, often to the Ruin of their Families, without any Salary or Pension: Because this appeared such an exalted Strain of Virtue and publick Spirit, that his Majesty seemed to doubt it might possibly not be always sincere: And he desired to know, whether such zealous Gentlemen could have any Views of refunding themselves for the Charges and Trouble they were at, by sacrificing the publick Good to the Designs of a weak and vicious Prince, in Conjunction with a corrupted Ministry. He multiplied his Questions, and sifted me thoroughly upon every Part of this Head; proposing numberless Enquiries and Objections, which I think it not prudent or convenient to repeat.

Upon what I said in relation to our Courts of Justice, his Majesty desired to be satisfied in several Points: And, this I was the better able to do, having been formerly almost ruined by a long **13** Suit in Chancery, which was decreed for me with Costs. He asked, what Time was usually spent in determining between Right and Wrong; and what Degree of Expence. Whether Advocates and Orators had Liberty to plead in Causes manifestly known to be unjust, vexatious, or oppressive. Whether Party in Religion or Politicks were observed to be of any Weight in the Scale of Justice. Whether those pleading Orators were Persons educated in the general Knowledge of Equity; or only in provincial, national, and other local Customs. Whether they or their Judges had any Part in penning those Laws, which they assumed the Liberty of interpret-

Court scene. Engraving by Dambrun. Courtesy, Library of Congress.

ing and glossing upon at their Pleasure. Whether they had ever at different Times pleaded for and against the same Cause, and cited Precedents to prove contrary Opinions. Whether they were a rich or a poor Corporation. Whether they received any pecuniary Reward for pleading or delivering their Opinions. And particularly whether they were ever admitted as Members in the lower Senate.

He fell next upon the Management of our Treasury; and said, he thought my Memory had failed me, because I computed our Taxes at about five or six Millions a Year; and when I came to mention the Issues, he found they sometimes amounted to more **14** than double; for, the Notes he had taken were very particular in this Point; because he hoped, as he told me, that the Knowledge of our Conduct might be useful to him; and he could not be deceived in his Calculations. But, if what I told him were true, he was still at a Loss how a Kingdom could run out of its Estate like a private Person. He asked me, who were our Creditors? and, where we found Money to pay them? He wondered to hear me talk of such chargeable and extensive Wars; that, certainly we must be a quarrelsome People, or live among very bad Neighbours; and that our Generals must needs be richer than our Kings. He asked, what **15,16** Business we had out of our own Islands, unless upon the Score of Trade or Treaty, or to defend the Coasts with our Fleet. Above all, he was amazed to hear me talk of a mercenary standing Army in **17** the Midst of Peace, and among a free People. He said, if we were governed by our own Consent in the Persons of our Representatives, he could not imagine of whom we were afraid, or against whom we were to fight; and would hear my Opinion, whether a private Man's House might not better be defended by himself, his Children, and Family; than by half a Dozen Rascals picked up at a Venture in the Streets, for small Wages, who might get an Hundred Times more by cutting their Throats.

He laughed at my odd Kind of Arithmetick (as he was pleased to call it) in reckoning the Numbers of our People by a Computation drawn from the several Sects among us in Religion and Politicks. He said, he knew no Reason, why those who entertain Opinions prejudicial to the Publick, should be obliged to change, or should not be obliged to conceal them. And, as it was Tyranny in any Government to require the first, so it was Weakness not to enforce the second: For, a Man may be allowed to keep Poisons in **18** his Closet, but not to vend them about as Cordials.

He observed, that among the Diversions of our Nobility and Gentry, I had mentioned Gaming. He desired to know at what Age this Entertainment was usually taken up, and when it was laid down. How much of their Time it employed; whether it ever went so high as to affect their Fortunes. Whether mean vicious People, by their Dexterity in that Art, might not arrive at great Riches, and sometimes keep our very Nobles in Dependance, as well as habituate them to vile Companions; wholly take them from the Improvement of their Minds, and force them by the Losses they received, to learn and practice that infamous Dexterity upon others.

He was perfectly astonished with the historical Account I gave him of our Affairs during the last Century; protesting it was only an Heap of Conspiracies, Rebellions, Murders, Massacres, Revolutions, Banishments; the very worst Effects that Avarice, Faction, Hypocrisy, Perfidiousness, Cruelty, Rage, Madness, Hatred, Envy,

14 *they sometimes amounted to more than double.* While Swift is coming down hard on corruption and folly in general, he was a Tory writing during a Whig administration and he is himself moved by those same party considerations he denounces—and consequently has the Brobdingnagian King wonder at those very Whig practices that the Tories protested.

For instance, the Bank of England was founded in 1694 and thereafter the English government discovered that by borrowing money, they could meet the financial requirements of a crisis such as a war without unduly increasing taxation. Then (in theory) the debt could be paid off gradually in peacetime. The War of the Spanish Succession was successfully fought in this way and many governments have since met crises successfully by borrowing. However, experience has shown that the debts are virtually never paid off, and this makes many people nervous.

In general, liberals concentrate on the good that borrowed money can do now, while conservatives concentrate on the troubles that might accrue later as the debts accumulate. In Swift's time, the Whigs seemed content to allow the national debt to rise, while the Tories denounced that practice—and the Brobdingnagian King here follows the Tory party line.

15 *our Generals must needs be richer than our Kings.* This is undoubtedly a blow at Marlborough, who managed to enrich himself in the course of his military career and who was charged by his enemies with avarice, if not corruption. Swift was one of his most biting enemies, and in 1710 he wrote a sarcastic indictment of Marlborough in which he listed all his earnings, one way or another, and had them come to 540,000 pounds (equivalent to tens of millions of dollars in present-day money). Indeed, Swift implied that Marlborough was prolonging the war in order to further enrich himself.

Marlborough had died in 1722, four years before *Gulliver's Travels* was published, but Swift did not easily forgive, and he could not resist this thrust at the dead general.

16 *what Business we had out of our own Islands.* Here, too, the Brobdingnagian King repeats the Tory party line. The Tories, being pro-French, were isolationist and pacifist whenever there was a question of a war against France, and that was their situation, therefore, throughout the War of the Spanish Succession.

The Brobdingnagian King's argument here was much used by American isolationists between the two world wars. It is quite unanswerable as long as *everyone* remains at home. The issue becomes confused when one nation (or group of nations) begins an aggressive career, at which time isolationism becomes slow motion suicide. It becomes still more confused when the aggressor describes itself as enamored of peace but forced, very much against its will, to respond to its victim's aggression—something an aggressor almost always does these days.

17 *a mercenary standing Army.* One more Tory view. The Tories were against a standing army, feeling it was much easier to fight a naval war, and cheaper, too; and if land battles *had* to be fought, they could be fought by the armies of an ally.

18 *a Man may . . . keep Poisons in his Closet, but not to vend them about as Cordials.* Clearly, the Brobdingnagian King (like Swift) comes out four square for freedom of opinion, provided you keep that opinion a secret, unless it fits in with official views. As a battle cry for freedom, this is rather muted.

19 *in its Original might have been tolerable.* Here is a repetition of Swift's feeling that things were better in the past; that good institutions which once existed have been corrupted. We will meet that notion again.

20 *I cannot but conclude the Bulk of your Natives, to be the most . . . odious Vermin that Nature ever suffered to crawl upon the surface of the earth.* This sentence may well be the most quoted passage from *Gulliver's Travels*, and is frequently cited by people who, for one reason or another, are embittered by the state of affairs in the nation or on the planet—and there is always ample reason for such embitterment. And we might as well admit that the Brobdingnagian King and Swift seem to have made a good case.

To suppose from this chapter, however, that the Brobdingnagians themselves are virtuous and with none of the faults of Europeans is incredibly naïve— and yet most commentators seem to have drawn that conclusion.

It does not follow from the fact that we see the faults of others clearly, and disapprove of them, that we ourselves are free of fault—or even free of the very faults we disapprove of. We have no difficulty in seeing the faults of the Lilliputians and in disapproving of them—and yet we possess the very faults of the Lilliputians, as Swift makes every effort to point out in this chapter.

In judging the Brobdingnagians, we can only go by what Swift says. Everyone he has shown us, without exception—the greedy farmer, his miserly neighbor, a heedless boy, a malicious dwarf, the flippant and lascivious maids of honor, the discourteous and condescending monarchs, even the tattletale Glumdalclitch—has the faults of Europeans. As for the nation itself, it has beggars, it has public executions, it has an army—in every respect like England.

To be sure, the King and Queen are kind to Gulliver, but that is nothing. They are amused by him and have nothing to fear of him. Why not be kind under such circumstances? Presumably, even a European would be kind under similar circumstances.

This second voyage is designed to show, more vividly than the first, the faults and shortcomings of England and of Europeans generally; but I do not see that it is intended to be a panegyric for Brobdingnag. At least, not so far. For what I take to be rhetorical reasons, as a means of enhancing the satire, the Brobdingnagians do increase in apparent virtue as this section progresses, and of course the Europeans suffer by comparison.

Lust, Malice, and Ambition could produce.

His Majesty in another Audience, was at the Pains to recapitulate the Sum of all I had spoken; compared the Questions he made, with the Answers I had given; then taking me into his Hands, and stroaking me gently, delivered himself in these Words, which I shall never forget, nor the Manner he spoke them in. My little Friend *Grildrig*; you have made a most admirable Panegyrick upon your Country. You have clearly proved that Ignorance, Idleness, and Vice are the proper Ingredients for qualifying a Legislator. That Laws are best explained, interpreted, and applied by those whose Interest and Abilities lie in perverting, confounding, and eluding them. I observe among you some Lines of an Institution, which in its Original might have been tolerable; but these half erased, and the rest wholly blurred and blotted by Corruptions. It doth not appear from all you have said, how any one Perfection is required towards the Procurement of any one Station among you; much less that Men are ennobled on Account of their Virtue, that Priests are advanced for their Piety or Learning, Soldiers for their Conduct or Valour, Judges for their Integrity, Senators for the Love of their Country, or Counsellors for their Wisdom. As for yourself (continued the King) who have spent the greatest Part of your Life in travelling; I am well disposed to hope you may hitherto have escaped many Vices of your Country. But, by what I have gathered from your own Relation, and the Answers I have with much Pains wringed and extorted from you; I cannot but conclude the Bulk of your Natives, to be the most pernicious Race of little odious Vermin that Nature ever suffered to crawl upon the Surface of the Earth.

19

20

CHAPTER SEVEN

The Author's love of his Country. He makes a Proposal of much advantage to the King; which is rejected. The King's great ignorance in Politicks. The Learning of that Country very imperfect and confined. Their Laws, and Military Affairs, and Parties in the State.

NOTHING but an extreme Love of Truth could have hindered me from concealing this Part of my Story. It was in vain to discover my Resentments, which were always turned into Ridicule: And I was forced to rest with Patience, while my noble and most beloved Country was so injuriously treated. I am heartily sorry as any of my Readers can possibly be, that such an Occasion was given: But this Prince happened to be so curious and inquisitive upon every Particular, that it could not consist either with Gratitude or good Manners to refuse giving him what Satisfaction I was able. Yet thus much I may be allowed to say in my own Vindication; that I artfully eluded many of his Questions; and gave to every Point a more favourable turn by many Degrees than the strictness of Truth would allow. For, I have always born that laudable Partiality to my own Country, which *Dionysius Halicarnassensis* **1** with so much Justice recommends to an Historian. I would hide the Frailties and Deformities of my Political Mother, and place her Virtues and Beauties in the most advantageous Light. This was my sincere Endeavour in those many Discourses I had with that mighty Monarch, although it unfortunately failed of Success.

1 *Dionysius Halicarnassensis.* Halicarnassus was a city on the southwestern shore of what is now Turkey, and Dionysius was a Greek historian who lived there in the first century B.C., dying in 7 B.C.. He settled in Rome about 29 B.C. and wrote a history of Rome in twenty volumes, half of which still exists. It was his avowed purpose to write a panegyric of the Romans in order to reconcile the Greeks to being ruled by them. In other words, Swift is having fun at Gulliver's expense, since Dionysius was not partial to his own country but to the enslavers of his country. Gulliver is no longer the kindly giant he was in Lilliput. His smallness and his frustrations are perverting him.

2 *politer.* The word "polite" is from the same root and has much the same meaning as "polished." Gulliver is speaking of the more cultivated or the more civilized countries of Europe. His sneer at the King is intended as irony since he implies that Brobdingnag is too primitive to have the necessary broadminded understanding of corruption and vice.

3 *Engines.* See Part I, Chapter 1, note 42.

4 *he would rather lose Half his Kingdom than be privy to such a Secret.* Talk is cheap! Brobdingnag is completely isolated from the outside world, has no rivals equivalent to itself, and apparently no internal dissension. I would wait until the King's throne were in jeopardy before I would believe that he would not resort to gunpowder.

But, great Allowances should be given to a King who lives wholly secluded from the rest of the World, and must therefore be altogether unacquainted with the Manners and Customs that most prevail in other Nations: The want of which Knowledge will ever produce many *Prejudices,* and a certain *Narrowness of Thinking;* from which we and the politer Countries of *Europe* are wholly exempted. And it would be hard indeed, if so remote a Prince's Notions of Virtue and Vice were to be offered as a Standard for all Mankind.

To confirm what I have now said, and further to shew the miserable Effects of a *confined Education;* I shall here insert a Passage which will hardly obtain Belief. In hopes to ingratiate my self farther into his Majesty's Favour, I told him of an Invention discovered between three and four hundred Years ago, to make a certain Powder; into an heap of which the smallest Spark of Fire falling, would kindle the whole in a Moment, although it were as big as a Mountain; and make it all fly up in the Air together, with a Noise and Agitation greater than Thunder. That, a proper Quantity of this Powder rammed into an hollow Tube of Brass or Iron, according to its Bigness, would drive a Ball of Iron or Lead with such Violence and Speed, as nothing was able to sustain its Force. That, the largest Balls thus discharged, would not only Destroy whole Ranks of an Army at once; but batter the strongest Walls to the Ground; sink down Ships with a thousand Men in each, to the Bottom of the Sea; and when linked together by a Chain, would cut through Masts and Rigging; divide Hundreds of Bodies in the Middle, and lay all Waste before them. That we often put this Powder into large hollow Balls of Iron, and discharged them by an Engine into some City we were besieging; which would rip up the Pavement, tear the Houses to Pieces, burst and throw Splinters on every Side, dashing out the Brains of all who came near. That I knew the Ingredients very well, which were Cheap, and common; I understood the Manner of compounding them, and could direct his Workmen how to make those Tubes of a Size proportionable to all other Things in his Majesty's Kingdom; and the largest need not be above two hundred Foot long; twenty or thirty of which Tubes, charged with the proper Quantity of Powder and Balls, would batter down the Walls of the strongest Town in his Dominions in a few Hours; or destroy the whole Metropolis, if ever it should pretend to dispute his absolute Commands. This I humbly offered to his Majesty, as a small Tribute of Acknowledgment in return of so many Marks that I had received of his Royal Favour and Protection.

The King was struck with Horror at the Description I had given of those terrible Engines, and the Proposal I had made. He was amazed how so impotent and groveling an Insect as I (these were his Expressions) could entertain such inhuman Ideas, and in so familiar a Manner as to appear wholly unmoved at all the Scenes of Blood and Desolation, which I had painted as the common Effects of those destructive Machines; whereof he said, some evil Genius, Enemy to Mankind, must have been the first Contriver. As for himself, he protested, that although few Things delighted him so much as new Discoveries in Art or in Nature; yet he would rather lose Half his Kingdom than be privy to such a Secret; which he commanded me, as I valued my Life, never to mention any more.

A strange Effect of *narrow Principles* and *short Views!* that a Prince possessed of every Quality which procures Veneration, Love and Esteem; of strong Parts, great Wisdom and profound Learning; endued with admirable Talents for Government, and almost adored by his Subjects; should from a *nice unnecessary Scruple,* whereof in *Europe* we can have no Conception, let slip an Opportunity put into his Hands, that would have made him absolute Master of the Lives, the Liberties, and the Fortunes of his People. Neither do I say this with the least Intention to detract from the many Virtues of that excellent King; whose Character I am sensible will on this Account be very much lessened in the Opinion of an *English* Reader: But, I take this Defect among them to have risen from their Ignorance; by not having hitherto reduced *Politicks* into a *Science,* as the more acute Wits of *Europe* have done. For, I remember very well, in a Discourse one Day with the King; when I happened to say, there were several thousand Books among us written upon the *Art of Government*; it gave him (directly contrary to my Intention) a very mean Opinion of our Understandings. He professed both to abominate and despise all *Mystery, Refinement,* and *Intrigue,* either in a Prince or a Minister. He could not tell what I meant by *Secrets of State,* where an Enemy or some Rival Nation were not in the Case. He confined the Knowledge of governing within very *narrow Bounds*; to common **5** Sense and Reason, to Justice and Lenity, to the Speedy Determination of Civil and criminal Causes; with some other obvious Topicks which are not worth considering. And, he gave it for his Opinion; that whoever could make two Ears of Corn, or two Blades of Grass **6** to grow upon a Spot of Ground where only one grew before; would deserve better of Mankind, and do more essential Service to his Country, than the whole Race of Politicians put together.

The Learning of this People is very defective; consisting only in Morality, History, Poetry and Mathematicks; wherein they must be allowed to excel. But, the last of these is wholly applied to what may be useful in Life; to the Improvements of Agriculture and all mechanical Arts; so that among us it would be little esteemed. And as to Ideas, Entities, Abstractions and Transcendentals, I could never drive the least Conception into their Heads. **7**

No Law of that Country must exceed in Words the Number of Letters in their Alphabet; which consists only of two and twenty. But indeed, few of them extend even to that Length. They are expressed in the most plain and simple Terms, wherein those People are not Mercurial enough to discover above one Interpretation. And, to write a Comment upon any Law, is a capital Crime. As to **8** the Decision of civil Causes, or Proceedings against Criminals, their Precedents are so few, that they have little Reason to boast of any extraordinary Skill in either.

They have had the Art of Printing, as well as the *Chinese,* Time **9** out of Mind. But their Libraries are not very large; for that of the King's, which is reckoned the largest, doth not amount to above a thousand Volumes; placed in a Gallery of twelve hundred Foot long; from whence I had Liberty to borrow what Books I pleased. The Queen's Joyner had contrived in one of *Glumdalclitch's* Rooms a Kind of wooden Machine five and twenty Foot high, formed like a standing Ladder; the Steps were each fifty Foot long: It was indeed a moveable Pair of Stairs, the lowest End placed at ten Foot

5 *common Sense and Reason.* Here again is one of Swift's favorite notions: that anyone can conduct a government since all it takes is common sense and reason. That is a common belief among conservative politicians and theorists. It is also a common belief among liberal politicians and theorists. That is, when they are out of office, and temporarily not responsible for trying to run it.

6 *whoever could make two Ears of Corn . . . grow . . . would . . . do more essential Service to his Country, than the whole Race of Politicians put together.* Next to the remark about the "pernicious Race of little odious Vermin," this is the most quoted passage in *Gulliver's Travels* since it is a humanitarian sentiment and "politicians" are everyone's favorite target (even mine). Nevertheless, the two groups, food increasers and politicians, are not necessarily mutually exclusive. There have indeed been men who have directed national policy who have attempted so to organize that policy as to encourage improvements in the efficiency of agriculture, commerce, industry, together with the arts and sciences, and they have sometimes been successful.

In Swift's younger years, there was such a politician in France—Jean Baptiste Colbert (1619–1683). He contributed a great deal to the enrichment of the nation, but had it all destroyed by Louis XIV's penchant for incredibly expensive palaces and incredibly useless wars. It would be unfair to forget the wisdom of the Colberts in our contempt for the folly of the Louis XIVs.

7 *as to Ideas . . . I could never drive the least Conception into their Heads.* Swift despised learned jargon meant to hide ignorance behind high-sounding words, but it is a mistake to go from that to a quick contempt for anything one doesn't instantly grasp.

It is a common flaw among nonmathematicians to suppose that there are two kinds of mathematics—a simple, honest, decent variety that can be used in everyday life, and a suspect, difficult, crabbed variety that only is used to entertain mathematicians and make them feel a cut above the rest of us.

It was in Swift's time that calculus was developed and it involved a number of concepts that were hard for the uninitiated to grasp: limits, infinitesimals, derivatives, integrals, and so on. And yet so useful is calculus that it is hard to imagine much in the way of material progress past Newton's time without it. As a matter of fact, what seems useless theorizing may very well be the basis for applications that will result in making two blades of grass grow where only one grew before. The fact that Swift doesn't understand this doesn't mean it isn't so.

8 *to write a Comment upon any Law, is a capital Crime.* If one supposes that every simple law can apply with equal justice to all people at all times and under all circumstances, then complications and commentaries are unnecessary. The only people who would suppose this, however, are those who have had no contact with the law. Anyone who has ever been affected adversely by any law naturally believes that his or hers is a "special case."

9 *They have had the Art of Printing, as well as the Chinese.* The Chinese had developed the concept of printing as early as 200, more than twelve centuries before printing was invented in Europe. By 1050, they had invented movable type, and in 1313, a font existed in which 60,000 Chinese characters had been carved into wooden blocks. In Korea, even more elaborate fonts of bronze were prepared.

What allowed Europe to catch up and far surpass China and Korea when it was the latter who had the paper, the ink, the fonts, and all the ideas long before, was that European languages were alphabetical and built up out of two dozen different characters, whereas the Oriental languages needed tens of thousands of elaborate figures. With printing, Europe moved ahead in learning and, in particular, in science and technology, eventually controlling the world for a time. All because of a small matter like the alphabet, which had been invented about 1400 B.C. by some nameless Phoenician.

10 *I first mounted to the upper Step . . . walking to the Right and Left . . . descending gradually till I came to the Bottom.* It's curious that a person as ingenious as Gulliver wouldn't have thought of taking his seat some ten or twenty feet away from the book. From that distance, the print would seem small enough to read easily without his having to walk back and forth, and some servant could have turned the page at a hand signal.

11 *clear, masculine, and smooth, but not Florid.* This describes Swift's style (as Swift well knew) which is why Swift's book has aged well and is still popular.

12 *Nature was degenerated . . . in Comparison of those in ancient Times.* It is one of the most nearly universal assumptions of any people anywhere that there has been a fall-off in all respects from "the good old times." Homer, in his *Iliad*, describing the feats of his heroes, explains more than once that Ajax, for instance, could lift a rock such as two men could not budge in Homer's own degenerate times. Socrates, too, could not help complaining that children of his own time had grown discourteous and no-account in comparison to the wonderful youngsters of the past.

Swift effectively punctures these foolish longings for a golden age that never was by having the monstrous Brobdingnagians moan over their comparative dwarfishness.

And yet Swift himself was a firm and vocal believer in the superiority of the past, a point he makes over and over again in *Gulliver's Travels.* He was surely no more justified in believing so than the Brobdingnagians were.

13 *huge Bones and Skulls.* Fossil remnants of prehistoric animals, some extinct and of considerably larger size than the bodies of related species living today, had on occasion been found during ancient and medieval times, but had merely puzzled those who found them. Some theorized they were practice creations by God before he had gotten around to the real thing; some that they were abortive creations by

Distance from the Wall of the Chamber. The Book I had a Mind
10 to read was put up leaning against the Wall. I first mounted to the
upper Step of the Ladder, and turning my Face towards the Book,
began at the Top of the Page, and so walking to the Right and Left
about eight or ten Paces according to the Length of the Lines, till I
had gotten a little below the Level of my Eyes; and then descending gradually till I came to the Bottom: After which I mounted
again, and began the other Page in the same Manner, and so
turned over the Leaf, which I could easily do with both my Hands,
for it was as thick and stiff as a Paste-board, and in the largest
Folio's not above eighteen or twenty Foot long.

11 Their Stile is clear, masculine, and smooth, but not Florid; for
they avoid nothing more than multiplying unnecessary Words, or
using various Expressions. I have perused many of their Books,
especially those in History and Morality. Among the latter I was
much diverted with a little old Treatise, which always lay in
Glumdalclitch's Bed-chamber, and belonged to her Governess, a
grave elderly Gentlewoman, who dealt in Writings of Morality and
Devotion. The Book treats of the Weakness of Human kind; and
is in little Esteem except among Women and the Vulgar. However, I was curious to see what an Author of that Country could
say upon such a Subject. This Writer went through all the usual
Topicks of *European* Moralists; shewing how diminutive, contemptible, and helpless an Animal was Man in his own Nature;
how unable to defend himself from the Inclemencies of the Air,
or the Fury of wild Beasts: How much he was excelled by one
Creature in Strength, by another in Speed, by a third in Fore-
12 sight, by a fourth in Industry. He added, that Nature was degenerated in these latter declining Ages of the World, and could now
produce only small abortive Births in Comparison of those in
ancient Times. He said, it was very reasonable to think, not only
that the Species of Men were originally much larger, but also that
there must have been Giants in former Ages; which, as it is as-
13 serted by History and Tradition, so it hath been confirmed by huge
Bones and Sculls casually dug up in several Parts of the Kingdom,
far exceeding the common dwindled Race of Man in our Days. He
argued, that the very Laws of Nature absolutely required we
should have been made in the Beginning, of a Size more large and
robust, not so liable to Destruction from every little Accident of a
Tile falling from an House, or a Stone cast from the Hand of a
Boy, or of being drowned in a little Brook. From this Way of
Reasoning the Author drew several moral Applications useful in
the Conduct of Life, but needless here to repeat. For my own Part,
I could not avoid reflecting, how universally this Talent was spread
of drawing Lectures in Morality, or indeed rather Matter of Discontent and repining, from the Quarrels we raise with Nature.
And, I believe upon a strict Enquiry, those Quarrels might be
shewn as ill-grounded among us, as they are among that People.

As to their military Affairs; they boast that the King's Army
consists of an hundred and seventy six thousand Foot, and thirty
two thousand Horse: If that may be called an Army, which is
made up of Tradesmen in the several Cities, and Farmers in the
Country, whose Commanders are only the Nobility and Gentry,
14 without Pay or Reward. They are indeed perfect enough in their
Exercises; and under very good Discipline, wherein I saw no great

Merit: For, how should it be otherwise, where every Farmer is under the Command of his own Landlord, and every Citizen under that of the principal Men in his own City, chosen after the Manner of *Venice* by *Ballot?*   **15**

I have often seen the Militia of *Lorbrulgrud* drawn out to Exercise in a great Field near the City, of twenty Miles Square. They were in all not above twenty five thousand Foot, and six thousand Horse; but it was impossible for me to compute their Number, considering the Space of Ground they took up. A *Cavalier* mounted on a large Steed might be about Ninety Foot high. I have seen this Whole Body of Horse upon the Word of Command draw their Swords at once, and brandish them in the Air. Imagination can Figure nothing so Grand, so surprising and so astonishing. It looked as if ten thousand Flashes of Lightning were darting at the same time from every Quarter of the Sky.

I was curious to know how this Prince, to whose Dominions there is no Access from any other Country, came to think of Armies, or to teach his People the Practice of military Discipline. But I was soon informed, both by Conversation, and Reading their Histories. For, in the Course of many Ages they have been troubled with the same Disease, to which the whole Race of Mankind is Subject; the Nobility often contending for Power, the People for Liberty, and the King for absolute Dominion. All which, however happily tempered by the Laws of that Kingdom, have been sometimes violated by each of the three Parties; and have more than once occasioned Civil Wars, the last whereof was happily   **16** put an End to by this Prince's Grandfather in a general Composition; and the Militia then settled with common Consent hath been ever since kept in the strictest Duty.

the devil, trying to imitate God and failing; some that they were indeed animals who had once lived but who had drowned in the Flood.

(The Danish geologist, Niels Steno [1648–1686] was the first to fail to call upon theology. He said that fossils were the petrified remains of animals who had once lived and who had died in normal manner. Swift's older contemporary, Robert Hooke [1635–1703] agreed with Steno's view.)

Some fossils, which might have been the skulls of elephants or their relatives, or rather large mammals of a few million years ago, were taken to represent the bones of human giants who lived before the Flood, since the Bible clearly states, "There were giants in the earth in those days" (Genesis 6:4).

It was rather a nice touch for Swift to assume that the general expansion of measurements in Brobdingnag extended to the fossils. One shudders to think what Brobdingnagian dinosaurs must have been like a hundred million years ago. A Brobdingnagian diplodocus would have been four and a half city blocks long.

14 *without Pay or Reward.* Swift here describes a voluntary militia, with the local upper classes serving as officers. (The social stratification is as sharp in the Brobdingnagian utopia as in Swift's England.) This is the Tory ideal. To those who believe in the absolute power of an aristocracy against both a central government and the common people such a militia is a good thing—provided, of course, it is never called upon to fight a professional army. There are a few cases in which a militia has done well against a professional army (as at the Battle of Concord in the American Revolutionary war). It is much more common, however, for the militia to run after the first exchange of gunfire.

Notice that there is no mention in the Brobdingnagian utopia of a legislature, of elections, of popular opinion. As in the case of other utopias, imagined in Swift's time and earlier, the government is that of a virtuous upper class, in uncontrolled and absolute power, showering benign blessings upon the people.

15 *chosen after the Manner of Venice by Ballot?* There weren't many European states in Swift's time that weren't hereditary monarchies. Of these, the oldest and most important was Venice. It was governed by an elected "doge" (duke). The first doge, according to tradition, was Paolo Lucio Anafesto, elected in 697. In Swift's time, then, Venice had been a republic for a thousand years and had virtually never been troubled with civil turmoil.

To be sure, Venice was by no means a democracy. Those with any voice at all in the election were from a few leading families, but that was taken for granted in Swift's time.

16 *Civil Wars.* Well, the Brobdingnagians have engaged in civil wars, but without the complications of foreign intervention. Had Gulliver reached Brobdingnag during one of the civil wars one wonders whether the King would have been so entirely nonreceptive to the notion of gunpowder.

1 *Tumbril*. A two-wheeled cart whose function is similar to that of a large wheelbarrow drawn by a horse or other animal. When released, it can be made to tip in such a way (the name is related to "tumble") as to dump its load. Such a cart was often used to carry manure.

Tumbrils became notorious nearly a century after the events in this section are supposed to have taken place when those condemned during the French Revolution were taken to the guillotine in them. Often they were actually manure carts pressed to the new service as one more way of humiliating the condemned.

2 *domestick Pledges*. See Part I, Chapter 8, note 8.

The King and Queen make a progress to the Frontiers. The Author attends them. The manner in which he leaves the Country very particularly related. He returns to England.

HAD always a strong Impulse that I should some time recover my Liberty, although it were impossible to conjecture by what Means, or to form any Project with the least Hope of succeeding. The Ship in which I sailed was the first ever known to be driven within Sight of that Coast; and the King had given strict Orders, that if at any Time another appeared, it should be taken ashore, and with **1** all its Crew and Passengers brought in a Tumbril to *Lorbrulgrud.* He was strongly bent to get me a Woman of my own Size, by whom I might propagate the Breed: But I think I should rather have died than undergone the Disgrace of leaving a Posterity to be kept in Cages like tame Canary Birds; and perhaps in time sold about the Kingdom to Persons of Quality for Curiosities. I was indeed treated with much Kindness; I was the Favourite of a great King and Queen, and the Delight of the whole Court; but it was upon such a Foot as ill became the Dignity of human Kind. I could never **2** forget those domestick Pledges I had left behind me. I wanted to be among People with whom I could converse upon even Terms; and walk about the Streets and Fields without Fear of being trod to Death like a Frog or young Puppy. But, my Deliverance came sooner than I expected, and in a Manner not very common: The whole Story and Circumstances of which I shall faithfully relate.

I had now been two Years in this Country; and, about the Beginning of the third, *Glumdalclitch* and I attended the King and Queen in Progress to the South Coast of the Kingdom. I was carried as usual in my Travelling-Box, which, as I have already described, was a very convenient Closet of twelve Foot wide. I had ordered the Joyner to cut out a Hole of a Foot square to give me Corners at the Top; to break the Jolts, when a Servant carried me before him on Horseback, as I sometimes desired; and would often sleep in my Hammock while we were upon the Road. On the Roof of my Closet, set not directly over the Middle of the Hammock, I ordered the Joyner to cut out a Hole of a Foot square to give me Air in hot Weather as I slept; which Hole I shut at pleasure with a Board that drew backwards and forwards through a Groove.

When we came to our Journey's End, the King thought proper to pass a few Days at a Palace he hath near *Flanflasnic*, a City within eighteen *English* Miles of the Sea-side. *Glumdalclitch* and I were much fatigued: I had gotten a small Cold; but the poor Girl was so ill as to be confined to her Chamber. I longed to see the Ocean, which must be the only Scene of my Escape, if ever it should happen. I pretended to be worse than I really was; and desired leave to take the fresh Air of the Sea, with a Page whom I was very fond of, and who had sometimes been trusted with me. I shall never forget with what Unwillingness *Glumdalclitch* consented; nor the strict Charge she gave the Page to be careful of me; bursting at the same time into a Flood of Tears, as if she had

3 *in Progress.* In the days before photography, newsreels, and television, it was very easy for a monarch to remain in his palace and be utterly unknown to his people. Some actually did this. Philip II of Spain, for instance, remained a recluse in his palace for decades. Where a monarch was not of impressive appearance or was not at ease with people, this might even serve a purpose, rendering him a far-off, awesome, nearly mystic figure.

Other rulers, however, felt it was better to let themselves be seen, and would therefore periodically tour the nation, passing through towns with great pageantry and éclat, and stopping at various estates. Those monarchs who could carry off such tours (called, as here, a "progress") added greatly to their own popularity. It helped the people identify themselves with the sovereign, convince themselves of their sovereign's love, and in this way stabilize the throne generally. Elizabeth I of England had a remarkable ability to elicit her subjects' love in this manner.

4 *Flanflasnic.* In the map that accompanies Part II of *Gulliver's Travels*, Flanflasnic is the only city shown other than Lorbrulgrud, the capital. Flanflasnic is located near the western end of the peninsula.

"I . . . cast many a wistful melancholy Look towards the Sea." Bouchot, 1855. Courtesy, The New York Public Library.

some Foreboding of what was to happen. The Boy took me out in my Box about Half an Hour's Walk from the Palace, towards the Rocks on the Sea-shore. I ordered him to set me down; and lifting up one of my Sashes, cast many a wistful melancholy Look towards the Sea. I found myself not very well; and told the Page that I had a Mind to take a Nap in my Hammock, which I hoped would do me good. I got in, and the Boy shut the Window close down, to keep out the Cold. I soon fell asleep: And all I can conjecture is, that while I slept, the Page, thinking no Danger could happen, went among the Rocks to look for Birds' Eggs; having before observed him from my Window searching about, and picking up one or two in the Clefts. Be that as it will; I found my self suddenly awaked with a violent Pull upon the Ring which was fastned at the Top of my Box for the Conveniency of Carriage. I felt the Box raised very high in the Air, and then born forward with prodigious Speed. The first Jolt had like to have shaken me out of my Hammock; but afterwards the Motion was easy enough. I called out several times as loud as I could raise my Voice, but all to no purpose. I looked towards my Windows, and could see nothing but the Clouds and

Gulliver's box is borne away by an eagle. Willy Pogány, 1919.

Sky. I heard a Noise just over my Head like the Clapping of Wings; and then began to perceive the woful Condition I was in; that some Eagle had got the Ring of my Box in his Beak, with an **5** Intent to let it fall on a Rock, like a Tortoise in a Shell, and then pick out my Body and devour it. For the Sagacity and Smell of this Bird enable him to discover his Quarry at a great Distance, although better concealed than I could be within a two Inch Board.

In a little time I observed the Noise and flutter of Wings to encrease very fast; and my Box was tossed up and down like a Signpost in a windy Day. I heard several Bangs or Buffets, as I thought, given to the Eagle (for such I am certain it must have been that held the Ring of my Box in his Beak) and then all of a sudden felt my self falling perpendicularly down for above a Minute; but with such incredible Swiftness that I almost lost my Breath. My Fall was stopped by a terrible Squash, that sounded louder to my Ears than the Cataract of *Niagara*; after which I was quite in the Dark for another Minute, and then my Box began to rise so high that I could see Light from the Tops of my Windows. I now perceived that I was fallen into the Sea. My Box, by the Weight of my Body, the Goods that were in, and the broad Plates of Iron fixed for Strength at the four Corners of the Top and Bottom, floated about five Foot deep in Water. I did then, and do now suppose, that the Eagle which flew away with my Box was pursued by two or three others, and forced to let me drop while he was defending himself against the Rest, who hoped to share in the Prey. The Plates of Iron fastned at the Bottom of the Box, (for those were the strongest) preserved the Balance while it fell; and hindred it from being broken on the Surface of the Water. Every Joint of it was well grooved, and the Door did not move on Hinges, but up and down like a Sash; which kept my Closet so tight that very little Water came in. I got with much Difficulty out of my Hammock, having first ventured to draw back the Slip board on the Roof already mentioned, contrived on purpose to let in Air; for want of which I found my self almost stifled.

How often did I then wish my self with my dear *Glumdalclitch*, from whom one single Hour had so far divided me! And I may say with Truth, that in the midst of my own Misfortune, I could not forbear lamenting my poor Nurse, the Grief she would suffer for my Loss, the Displeasure of the Queen, and the Ruin of her Fortune. Perhaps many Travellers have been under greater Difficulties and Distress than I was at this Juncture; expecting every Moment to see my Box dashed in Pieces, or at least overset by the first violent Blast, or a rising Wave. A Breach in one single Pane of Glass would have been immediate Death: Nor could any thing have preserved the Windows but the strong Lattice Wires placed on the outside against Accidents in Travelling. I saw the Water ooze in at several Crannies, although the Leaks were not considerable; and I endeavoured to stop them as well as I could. I was not able to lift up the Roof of my Closet, which otherwise I certainly should have done, and sat on the Top of it, where I might at least preserve myself from being shut up, as I may call it, in the Hold. Or, if I escaped these Dangers for a Day or two, what could I expect but a miserable Death of Cold and Hunger! I was four Hours under these Circumstances, expecting and indeed wishing every Moment to be my last.

5 *Eagle*. The largest recorded wingspan of an eagle is eight feet three inches for a female Australian wedge-tailed eagle. The Brobdingnagian eagle might have a wingspan of nearly one hundred feet in that case. Eagles can, in real life, carry weights up to their own, and if a Brobdingnagian eagle weighed 1,728 times an ordinary eagle, then he could certainly carry Gulliver and his cage. However, the support of the wings is only proportional to the square of the linear measurements, while the weight of the eagle is proportional to the cube, and in real life a Brobdingnagian eagle simply couldn't fly, let alone carry weights. (Not that I want to spoil the fun.)

6 *it never came into my Head, that I was now got among People of my own Stature and Strength.* When Gulliver left Lilliput, he had no trouble re-identifying as a European. This time, however, such was the extent of his humiliation in Brobdingnag that he could salvage his self-respect only by identifying with the giants (a respectable and well-attested bit of psychology, these days). He finds he cannot bear to be back in a world of "little people" and has difficulty making the adjustment.

I have already told the Reader, that there were two strong Staples fixed upon the Side of my Box which had no Window, and into which the Servant, who used to carry me on Horseback, would put a Leathern Belt, and buckle it about his Waist. Being in this disconsolate State, I heard, or at least thought I heard some kind of grating Noise on that Side of my Box where the Staples were fixed; and soon after I began to fancy that the Box was pulled, or towed along in the Sea; for I now and then felt a sort of tugging, which made the Waves rise near the Tops of my Windows, leaving me almost in the Dark. This gave me some faint Hopes of Relief, although I were not able to imagine how it could be brought about. I ventured to unscrew one of my Chairs, which were always fastned to the Floor; and having made a hard shift to screw it down again directly under the Slipping-board that I had lately opened; I mounted on the Chair, and putting my Mouth as near as I could to the Hole, I called for Help in a loud Voice, and in all the Languages I understood. I then fastned my Handkerchief to a Stick I usually carried, and thrusting it up the Hole, waved it several times in the Air, that if any Boat or Ship were near, the Seamen might conjecture some unhappy Mortal to be shut up in the Box.

I found no Effect from all I could do, but plainly perceived my Closet to be moved along; and in the Space of an Hour, or better, that Side of the Box where the Staples were, and had no Window, struck against something that was hard. I apprehended it to be a Rock, and found my self tossed more than ever. I plainly heard a Noise upon the Cover of my Closet, like that of a Cable, and the grating of it as it passed through the Ring. I then found my self hoisted up by Degrees at least three Foot higher than I was before. Whereupon, I again thrust up my Stick and Handkerchief, calling for Help till I was almost hoarse. In return to which, I heard a great Shout repeated three times, giving me such Transports of Joy as are not to be conceived but by those who feel them. I now heard a trampling over my Head; and somebody calling through the Hole with a loud Voice in the *English* Tongue: *If there be any Body below, let them speak.* I answered, I was an *Englishman,* drawn by ill Fortune into the greatest Calamity that ever any Creature underwent; and begged, by all that was moving, to be delivered out of the Dungeon I was in. The Voice replied, I was safe, for my Box was fastned to their Ship; and the Carpenter should immediately come, and saw an Hole in the Cover, large

6 enough to pull me out. I answered, that was needless, and would take up too much Time; for there was no more to be done, but let one of the Crew put his Finger into the Ring, and take the Box out of the Sea into the Ship, and so into the Captain's Cabbin. Some of them upon hearing me talk so wildly, thought I was mad; others laughed; for indeed it never came into my Head, that I was now got among People of my own Stature and Strength. The Carpenter came, and in a few Minutes sawed a Passage about four Foot square; then let down a small Ladder, upon which I mounted, and from thence was taken into the Ship in a very weak Condition.

The Sailors were all in Amazement, and asked me a thousand Questions, which I had no Inclination to answer. I was equally confounded at the Sight of so many Pigmies; for such I took them to be, after having so long accustomed my Eyes to the monstrous Objects I had left. But the Captain, Mr. *Thomas Wilcocks,* an honest worthy *Shropshire* Man, observing I was ready to faint, took me into his Cabbin, gave me a Cordial to comfort me, and made me *turn in* upon his own Bed; advising me to take a little Rest, of which I had great need. Before I went to sleep I gave him to understand, that I had some valuable Furniture in my Box too good to be lost; a fine Hammock, an handsome Field-Bed, two Chairs, a Table and a Cabinet: That my Closet was hung on all Sides, or rather quilted with Silk and Cotton: That if he would let one of the Crew bring my Closet into his Cabbin, I would open it before him, and shew him my Goods. The Captain hearing me utter these Absurdities, concluded I was raving: However, (I suppose to pacify me) he promised to give Order as I desired; and going upon Deck, sent some of his Men down into my Closet, from whence (as I afterwards found) they drew up all my Goods, and stripped off the Quilting; but the Chairs, Cabinet and Bed-sted being screwed to the Floor, were much damaged by the Ignorance of the Seamen, who tore them up by Force. Then they knocked off some of the Boards for the Use of the Ship; and when they had got all they had a Mind for, let the Hulk drop into the Sea, which by Reason of many Breaches made in the Bottom and Sides, sunk *to rights*. And indeed I was glad not to have been a Spectator of the Havock they made; because I am confident it would have sensibly touched me, by bringing former Passages into my Mind, which I had rather forget.

I slept some Hours, but perpetually disturbed with Dreams of the Place I had left, and the Dangers I had escaped. However, upon waking I found my self much recovered. It was now about eight a Clock at Night, and the Captain ordered Supper immediately, thinking I had already fasted too long. He entertained me with great Kindness, observing me not to look wildly, or talk inconsistently; and when we were left alone, desired I would give him a Relation of my Travels, and by what Accident I came to be set adrift in that monstrous wooden Chest. He said, that about twelve a Clock at Noon, as he was looking through his Glass, he spied it at a Distance, and thought it was a Sail, which he had a Mind to make; being not much out of his Course, in hopes of buying some Biscuit, his own beginning to fall short. That, upon coming nearer, and finding his Error, he sent out his Long-boat to discover what I was; that his Men came back in a Fright, swearing they had seen a swimming House. That he laughed at their Folly, and went himself in the Boat, ordering his Men to take a strong Cable along with them. That the Weather being calm, he rowed round me

7

8

7 *Shropshire Man.* Shropshire (a shortened version of Shrewsburyshire) is a county in west England on the border of Wales. Shrewsbury is the county seat. In 1974, its name was changed to Salop.

8 *sunk to rights.* Sunk in good order; went straight down. The phrase is usually used constructively as in "put to rights"; it is used here, sardonically, in a destructive sense.

Gulliver is rescued. Rex Whistler. 1930.

9 *three Eagles flying towards the North.* If we were to accept Gulliver's accounts in all seriousness, we would have to suppose that those super-eagles might on some occasion have flown to the North American mainland from Brobdingnag; and that other super-birds might have done so well, with perhaps drastic effects on the native flora and fauna.

10 *great Criminals . . . forced to Sea in a leaky Vessel without Provisions.* Exposure to certain drowning is reminiscent of the Green myth of Danaë, whose father, Acrisius, had learned from an oracle that he would be killed by his grandson. He therefore shut Danaë in a tower to keep men away from her, since she could scarcely bear a son without male help. As it happened, the god Zeus fell in love with her and gladly supplied the necessary help. She bore a son, Perseus.

Acrisius, terrified, dared not kill his grandson for fear of incurring a curse. He therefore locked mother and son into a chest, which he had cast into the sea. His hope was that they would die of exposure, hunger, thirst, or all three, and that the immediate cause of death would be the elements rather than himself so that he would escape the curse. Naturally, mother and son survived and in the end Perseus accidentally killed Acrisius.

In the same way, in William Shakespeare's play *The Tempest*, Sebastian overthrows Prospero, duke of Milan. Sebastian does not quite dare to slay Prospero but, instead, places the overthrown duke with his daughter, Miranda, into the hull of a ship, hoping they will drown. Naturally, Prospero and Miranda survive and have their vengeance at last.

One case in real life occurred sixty-three years after the publication of *Gulliver's Travels*. In 1789, the crew of the *Bounty* mutinied, and took over the ship. They did not kill Captain William Bligh whose se-

Danaë by Arthur Rackham, 1903.

several times, observed my Windows, and the Wire Lattices that defended them. That he discovered two Staples upon one Side, which was all of Boards, without any Passage for Light. He then commanded his Men to row up to that Side; and fastning a Cable to one of the Staples, ordered his Men to tow my Chest (as he called it) towards the Ship. When it was there, he gave Directions to fasten another Cable to the Ring fixed in the Cover, and to raise up my Chest with Pullies, which all the Sailors were not able to do above two or three Foot. He said, they saw my Stick and Handkerchief thrust out of the Hole, and concluded, that some unhappy Man must be shut up in the Cavity. I asked whether he or the Crew had seen any prodigious Birds in the Air about the Time he first discovered me: To which he answered, that discoursing this Matter with the Sailors while I was asleep, one of them said he had **9** *observed* three Eagles flying towards the North; but remarked nothing of their being larger than the usual Size; which I suppose must be imputed to the great Height they were at: And he could not guess the Reason of my Question. I then asked the Captain how far he reckoned we might be from Land; he said, by the best Computation he could make, we were at least an hundred Leagues. I assured him, that he must be mistaken by almost half; for I had not left the Country from whence I came, above two Hours before I dropt into the Sea. Whereupon he began again to think that my Brain was disturbed, of which he gave me a Hint, and advised me to go to Bed in a Cabin he had provided. I assured him I was well refreshed with his good Entertainment and Company, and as much in my Senses as ever I was in my Life. He then grew serious, and desired to ask me freely whether I were not troubled in Mind by the Consciousness of some enormous Crime, for which I was punished at the Command of some Prince, by exposing me in that Chest; as great Criminals in other Countries have been forced to Sea in a leaky Vessel without Provisions: For, although he should be sorry to have taken so ill a Man into his Ship, yet he would engage his Word to set me safe on Shore in the first Port where we arrived. He added, that his Suspicions were much increased by some very absurd Speeches I had delivered at first to the Sailors, and afterwards to himself, in relation to my Closet or Chest, as well as by my odd Looks and Behaviour while I was at Supper.

I begged his Patience to hear me tell my Story; which I faithfully did from the last Time I left *England,* to the Moment he first discovered me. And, as Truth always forceth its Way into rational Minds; so, this honest worthy Gentleman, who had some Tincture of Learning, and very good Sense, was immediately convinced of my Candor and Veracity. But, further to confirm all I had said, I entreated him to give Order that my Cabinet should be brought, of which I kept the Key in my Pocket, (for he had already informed me how the Seamen disposed of my Closet) I opened it in his Presence, and shewed him the small Collection of Rarities I made in the Country from whence I had been so strangely delivered. There was the Comb I had contrived out of the Stumps of the King's Beard; and another of the same Materials, but fixed into a paring of her Majesty's Thumb-nail, which served for the Back. **10** There was a Collection of Needles and Pins from a Foot to half a Yard long. Four Wasp-Stings, like Joyner's Tacks: Some Combings of the Queen's Hair: A Gold Ring which one Day she made

Gulliver shows his collection of rarities. "Alfred Crawquill," 1865.

verity had brought on the mutiny, but placed him and some sailors loyal to him in an open boat with some supplies and abandoned them to the mercy of the sea. But Bligh survived, navigating the open boat for four thousand miles to the Indonesian island of Timor. He lived to see three of the mutineers hanged.

11 *Kentish Pippin.* A pippin is a small apple. Kent is the southeasternmost county of England.

12 *a Footman's Tooth . . . about a Foot long, and four Inches in Diameter.* The captain was right to choose the tooth. A tooth, exactly like that of *Homo sapiens* but of the dimensions given, is as clear an indication of the existence of Brobdingnagians as the giant King and all his court would have been.

me a Present of in a most obliging Manner, taking it from her little Finger, and throwing it over my Head like a Collar. I desired the Captain would please to accept this Ring in Return of his Civilities; which he absolutely refused. I shewed him a Corn that I had cut off with my own Hand from a Maid of Honour's Toe; it was about the Bigness of a *Kentish* Pippin, and grown so hard, that when I **11** returned to *England*, I got it hollowed into a Cup and set in Silver. Lastly, I desired him to see the Breeches I had then on, which were made of a Mouse's Skin.

I could force nothing on him but a Footman's Tooth, which I **12** observed him to examine with great Curiosity, and found he had a Fancy for it. He received it with abundance of Thanks, more than such a Trifle could deserve. It was drawn by an unskilful Surgeon in a Mistake from one of *Glumdalclitch's* Men, who was afflicted with the Toothach; but it was as sound as any in his Head. I got it cleaned, and put it into my Cabinet. It was about a Foot long, and four Inches in Diameter.

The Captain was very well satisfied with this plain Relation I had given him; and said, he hoped when we returned to *England*, I would oblige the World by putting it in Paper, and making it publick. My Answer was, that I thought we were already overstocked with Books of Travels: That nothing could now pass which was not extraordinary; wherein I doubted, some Authors less con-

A footman's tooth. J. J. Grandville, 1835. Courtesy, Library of Congress.

13 *my story could contain little besides common events.* A bit of mock modesty aimed at the travel books of the day. In point of fact, no travel story as "extraordinary" as this one has ever been written as its unbroken popularity for two and a half centuries attests.

14 *admired.* See Part I, Chapter 1, note 26.

15 *winked at my own Littleness.* The present meaning of "wink" is to close one eye in a roguish sort of way. An earlier meaning, here used, is to close one's eyes in order to avoid, deliberately, seeing something one did not want to see.

16 *Phaeton.* In the Greek myths he was a son of Helios, the sun-god. When Phaëthon's descent was doubted, he persuaded his father to let him drive the chariot of the Sun for one day. Phaëthon proved unequal to the task. The horses went wild, the Sun went out of its orbit, and the Earth was in danger of being destroyed. To prevent that, Zeus struck Phaëthon with lightning and his dead body was hurled out of the solar chariot and fell to Earth—like Gulliver in his box.

17 *Conceit.* Nowadays, "conceit" means "vanity" or an overweening opinion of one's own abilities or virtues. An older meaning is "conception" (from the same root as "conceit") or "idea." In particular, it came to be used for witty or fanciful ideas, apt comparisons, and so on. That is the meaning here (used ironically by Gulliver since he did not feel the comparison of himself with Phaëthon to be either amusing or particularly witty). It is because those who are always striving for conceits usually have a higher opinion of their success than do those who listen to them, that the word gained its present meaning.

18 *Tonquin.* Also Tonkin or Tongking, the region we now call North Vietnam.

19 *North Eastward to the Latitude of 44 Degrees, and of Longitude 143.* This would be eleven hundred miles west of the coast of Oregon.

20 *New-Holland.* The name given by the Dutch of the East Indian islands to the coastlines they had discovered south of New Guinea. It was not recognized that these coastlines were part of a huge island (Australia) until Captain Cook's voyage to the area half a century after *Gulliver's Travels* was published.

21 *the Downs.* See Part I, Chapter 8, note 12.

22 *the 3rd Day of June 1706.* This was seventeen days short of four years after Gulliver had left England on his second Voyage. While Gulliver was away, England was winning great victories in the War of the Spanish Succession. Marlborough won his greatest victory at Blenheim on August 13, 1704, and won again at Ramillies on May 23, 1706, just twelve days before Gulliver's return. In addition, the English had taken Gibraltar and Barcelona from Spain.

13 sulted Truth than their own Vanity or Interest, or the Diversion of ignorant Readers. That my Story could contain little besides common Events, without those ornamental Descriptions of strange Plants, Trees, Birds, and other Animals; or the barbarous Customs and Idolatry of savage People, with which most Writers abound. However, I thanked him for his good Opinion, and promised to take the Matter into my Thoughts.

He said, he wondered at one Thing very much; which was, to hear me speak so loud; asking me whether the King or Queen of that Country were thick of Hearing. I told him it was what I had **14** been used to for above two Years past; and that I admired as much at the Voices of him and his Men, who seemed to me only to whisper, and yet I could hear them well enough. But, when I spoke in that Country, it was like a Man talking in the Street to another looking out from the Top of a Steeple, unless when I was placed on a Table, or held in any Person's Hand. I told him, I had likewise observed another Thing; that when I first got into the Ship, and the Sailors stood all about me, I thought they were the most little contemptible Creatures I had ever beheld. For, indeed, while I was in that Prince's Country, I could never endure to look in a Glass after my Eyes had been accustomed to such prodigious Objects; because the Comparison gave me so despicable a Conceit of my self. The Captain said, that while we were at Supper, he observed me to look at every thing with a Sort of Wonder; and that I often seemed hardly able to contain my Laughter; which he knew not well how to take, but imputed it to some Disorder in my Brain. I answered, it was very true; and I wondered how I could forbear, when I saw his Dishes of the Size of a Silver Three-pence, a Leg of Pork hardly a Mouthful, a Cup not so big as a Nutshell: And so I went on, describing the rest of his Household stuff and Provisions after the same Manner. For although the Queen had ordered a little Equipage of all Things necessary for me while I was in her Service; yet my Ideas were wholly taken up with what I saw on every Side of me; and I winked at my own Littleness, as People **15** do at their own Faults. The Captain understood my Raillery very well, and merrily replied with the old *English* Proverb, that he doubted, my Eyes were bigger than my Belly; for he did not observe my Stomach so good, although I had fasted all Day: And continuing in his Mirth, protested he would have gladly given an Hundred Pounds to have seen my Closet in the Eagle's Bill, and afterwards in its Fall from so great an Height into the Sea; which would certainly have been a most astonishing Object, worthy to have the Description of it transmitted to future Ages: And the **16** Comparison of *Phaeton* was so obvious, that he could not forbear **17** applying it, although I did not much admire the Conceit.

The Captain having been at *Tonquin* was in his Return to **18**
19 *England* driven North Eastward to the Latitude of 44 Degrees, and of Longitude 143. But meeting a Trade Wind two Days after I came on board him, we sailed Southward a long Time, and **20** coasting *New-Holland*, kept our Course West-south-west, and then South-south-west till we doubled the *Cape of Good-hope.* Our Voyage was very prosperous, but I shall not trouble the Reader with a Journal of it. The Captain called in at one or two Ports, and sent in his Long-boat for Provisions and fresh Water; but I never went **21** out of the Ship till we came into the *Downs* which was on the 3*d* **22** Day of *June* 1706, about nine Months after my Escape. I offered

to leave my Goods in Security for Payment of my Freight; but the Captain protested he would not receive one Farthing. We took kind Leave of each other; and I made him promise he would come to see me at my House in *Redriff*. I hired a Horse and Guide for five **23** Shillings, which I borrowed of the Captain.

As I was on the Road; observing the Littleness of the Houses, the Trees, the Cattle and the People, I began to think my self in *Lilliput*. I was afraid of trampling on every Traveller I met; and often called aloud to have them stand out of the Way; so that I had like to have gotten one or two broken Heads for my Impertinence.

When I came to my own House, for which I was forced to enquire, one of the Servants opening the Door, I bent down to go in (like a Goose under a Gate) for fear of striking my Head. My Wife ran out to embrace me, but I stooped lower than her Knees, thinking she could otherwise never be able to reach my Mouth. My Daughter kneeled to ask me Blessing, but I could not see her till she arose; having been so long used to stand with my Head and Eyes erect to above Sixty Foot; and then I went to take her up with one Hand, by the Waist. I looked down upon the Servants, and one or two Friends who were in the House, as if they had been Pigmies, and I a Giant. I told my Wife, she had been too thrifty; for I found she had starved herself and her Daughter to nothing. In short, I behaved my self so unaccountably, that they were all of the Captain's Opinion when he first saw me; and concluded I had lost my Wits. This I mention as an Instance of the great Power of Habit and Prejudice.

In a little Time I and my Family and Friends came to a right **24** Understanding: But my Wife protested I should never go to Sea any more; although my evil Destiny so ordered, that she had not Power to hinder me; as the Reader may know hereafter. In the mean Time, I here conclude the second Part of my unfortunate Voyages.

The End of the Second Part.

23 *Redriff*. See Part I, Chapter 8, note 15.

24 *came to a right Understanding*. Gulliver recovers from his near-madness here, but it was originally Swift's plan to follow this second part with the section that now appears as the fourth part, in which Gulliver encounters a still greater disparity than the one between himself and the Brobdingnagians, and comes to feel so greatly inferior that he goes completely mad. It then occurred to Swift, however, to write a satire on contemporary science and he made it the third part in which Gulliver is most nearly a static observer and which breaks the rhythm of what would otherwise have been a tragic progression. And yet, we must not complain. The third part contains some of the most striking passages in the book.

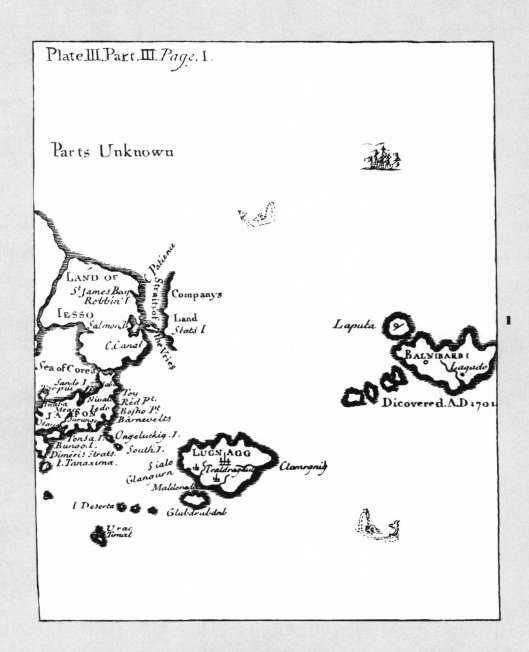

Plate III. Part III. Page. 1.

Parts Unknown

1 *Laputa, Balnibarbi, Luggnagg, Glubbdubdrib, and Japan.* Eight lands are mentioned altogether in the titles of the four parts of *Gulliver's Travels* and of them all, only Japan is real. Japan was, however, so little known to Europeans of Swift's time that it seemed almost as fanciful as the rest. The chief island of Japan, Honshu, is shown in recognizable shape on the map, but the land to the north is an unrecognizable distortion of Siberia and the islands to the east are, of course, imaginary.

PART THREE

A Voyage to Laputa,
Balnibarbi, Luggnagg,
Glubbdubdrib, and Japan

1 *a Cornish Man.* A native of Cornwall, the south-westernmost county of England.

2 *the Levant.* See Part I, Chapter 1, note 10.

The Author sets out on his Third Voyage. Is taken by Pyrates. The malice of a Dutchman. His arrival at an Island. He is received into Laputa.

1

2

HAD not been at home above ten Days, when Captain *William Robinson,* a *Cornish* Man, Commander of the *Hopewell,* a stout Ship of three Hundred Tuns, came to my House. I had formerly been Surgeon of another Ship where he was Master, and a fourth Part Owner, in a Voyage to the *Levant.* He had always treated me more like a Brother than an inferior Officer; and hearing of my Arrival made me a Visit, as I apprehended only out of Friendship, for nothing passed more than what is usual after long Absence. But repeating his Visits often, expressing his Joy to find me in good Health, asking whether I were now settled for Life, adding that he intended a Voyage to the *East Indies,* in two Months, at last he plainly invited me, although with some Apologies, to be Surgeon of the Ship. That I should have another Surgeon under me, besides our two Mates; that my Sallary should be double to the usual Pay; and that having experienced my Knowledge in Sea-Affairs to be at least equal to his, he would enter into any Engagement to follow my Advice, as much as if I had Share in the Command.

He said so many other obliging things, and I knew him to be so honest a Man, that I could not reject his Proposal; the Thirst I had of seeing the World, notwithstanding my past Misfortunes, continuing as violent as ever. The only Difficulty that remained, was to persuade my Wife, whose Consent however I at last obtained, by the Prospect of Advantage she proposed to her Children.

We set out the 5th Day of *August*, 1706, and arrived at Fort St. *George*, the 11th of *April* 1707. We stayed there three Weeks to refresh our Crew, many of whom were sick. From thence we went to *Tonquin*, where the Captain resolved to continue some time; because many of the Goods he intended to buy were not ready, nor could he expect to be dispatched in several Months. Therefore in hopes to defray some of the Charges he must be at, he bought a Sloop, loaded it with several Sorts of Goods, wherewith the *Tonquinese* usually trade to the neighbouring Islands; and putting Fourteen Men on Board, whereof three were of the Country, he appointed me Master of the Sloop, and gave me Power to traffick, while he transacted his Affairs at *Tonquin*.

We had not sailed above three Days, when a great Storm arising, we were driven five Days to the North-North-East, and then to the East; after which we had fair Weather, but still with a pretty strong Gale from the West. Upon the tenth Day we were chased by two Pyrates, who soon overtook us; for my Sloop was so deep loaden, that she sailed very slow; neither were we in a Condition to defend our selves.

We were boarded about the same Time by both the Pyrates, who entered furiously at the Head of their Men; but finding us all pros-

3 *the 5th Day of August, 1706.* Gulliver had remained at home for only two months and two days.

4 *Fort St. George.* This fort had been established on the southeast coast of India. The town of Madras grew up around it.

5 *Tonquin.* See Part II, Chapter 8, note 18.

The battle with the pirate ship.

6 *being Christians and Protestants . . . in strict Alliance.* England and the Netherlands, both Protestant, were allied in the War of the Spanish Succession against the Catholic powers of France and Spain. However, it was a Whig war and a Whig alliance and Swift hated both. In this section of the book, he consistently blackens the Dutch at every opportunity. Tory animus against the Dutch was based on the fact that they continued to be commercial rivals of England. Furthermore, Dutch tolerance of diversity in religion undermined the Tory concept of a national church.

7 *a Japanese Captain.* After 1600, Japan had, as a nation, gone into strict seclusion. By that time, European explorers had reached Japan and missionaries had converted a number of Japanese to Christianity. An anti-Christian campaign was strenuously carried out and by 1640, the Japanese islands were cleansed of the western religion. That is why Swift pictures the Dutchman as informing the Japanese captain that his captives are Christians—appealing to prejudice to insure a death sentence for them.

As part of Japan's self-imposed isolation, all foreigners were expelled, except for some Dutch traders who were allowed to remain on the small island of Deshima (now part of the mainland) in Nagasaki Harbor. This was Japan's sole window to the outside world, and it accounts for the Japanese captain's ability to speak a little Dutch.

Japan, however, as part of its isolation policy, forbade its population to leave the island and put an end to the building of ships large enough to make sea voyages. The very existence of a Japanese captain on the open seas is therefore unrealistic.

The pirate captain.

trate upon our Faces, (for so I gave Order,) they pinioned us with strong Ropes, and setting a Guard upon us, went to search the Sloop.

I observed among them a *Dutchman*, who seemed to be of some Authority, although he were not Commander of either Ship. He knew us by our Countenances to be *Englishmen*, and jabbering to us in his own Language, swore we should be tyed Back to Back, and thrown into the Sea. I spoke *Dutch* tolerably well; I told him **6** who we were, and begged him in Consideration of our being Christians and Protestants, of neighbouring Countries, in strict Alliance, that he would move the Captains to take some Pity on us. This inflamed his Rage; he repeated his Threatnings, and turning to his Companions, spoke with great Vehemence, in the *Japanese* Language, as I suppose; often using the Word *Christianos*.

7 The largest of the two Pyrate Ships was commanded by a *Japanese* Captain, who spoke a little *Dutch*, but very imperfectly. He came up to me, and after several Questions, which I answered in great Humility, he said we should not die. I made the Captain a very low Bow, and then turning to the *Dutchman*, said, I was sorry to find more Mercy in a Heathen, than in a Brother Christian. But I had soon Reason to repent those foolish Words; for that malicious

Reprobate, having often endeavoured in vain to persuade both the Captains that I might be thrown into the Sea, (which they would not yield to after the Promise made me, that I should not die) however prevailed so far as to have a Punishment inflicted on me, worse in all human Appearance than Death it self. My Men were sent by an equal Division into both the Pyrate-Ships, and my Sloop new manned. As to my self, it was determined that I should be set a-drift, in a small Canoe, with Paddles and a Sail, and four Days Provisions; which last the *Japanese* Captain was so kind to double out of his own Stores, and would permit no Man to search me. I got down into the Canoe, while the *Dutchman* standing upon the Deck, loaded me with all the Curses and injurious Terms his Language could afford.

About an Hour before we saw the Pyrates, I had taken an Observation, and found we were in the Latitude of 46 N. and of Longitude 183. When I was at some Distance from the Pyrates, I discovered by my Pocket-Glass several Islands to the South-East. I set up my Sail, the Wind being fair, with a Design to reach the nearest of those Islands, which I made a Shift to do in about three Hours. It was all rocky; however I got many Birds Eggs; and striking Fire, I kindled some Heath and dry Sea Weed, by which I roasted my Eggs. I eat no other Supper, being resolved to spare my Provisions as much as I could. I passed the Night under the Shelter of a Rock, strowing some Heath under me, and slept pretty well.

The next Day I sailed to another Island, and thence to a third and fourth, sometimes using my Sail, and sometimes my Paddles. But not to trouble the Reader with a particular Account of my Distresses; let it suffice, that on the 5th Day, I arrived at the last Island in my Sight, which lay South-South-East to the former.

This Island was at a greater Distance than I expected, and I did not reach it in less than five Hours. I encompassed it almost round before I could find a convenient Place to land in, which was a small Creek, about three Times the Wideness of my Canoe. I found the Island to be all rocky, only a little intermingled with Tufts of Grass, and sweet smelling Herbs. I took out my small Provisions, and after having refreshed my self, I secured the Remainder in a Cave, whereof there were great Numbers. I gathered Plenty of Eggs upon the Rocks, and got a Quantity of dry Seaweed, and parched Grass, which I designed to kindle the next Day, and roast my Eggs as well as I could. (For I had about me my Flint, Steel, Match, and Burning-glass.) I lay all Night in the Cave where I had lodged my Provisions. My Bed was the same dry Grass and Sea-weed which I intended for Fewel. I slept very little; for the Disquiets of my Mind prevailed over my Wearyness, and kept me awake. I considered how impossible it was to preserve my Life, in so desolate a Place; and how miserable my End must be. Yet I found my self so listless and desponding, that I had not the Heart to rise; and before I could get Spirits enough to creep out of my Cave, the Day was far advanced. I walked a while among the Rocks, the Sky was perfectly clear, and the Sun so hot, that I was forced to turn my Face from it: When all on a Sudden it became obscured, as I thought, in a Manner very different from what happens by the Interposition of a Cloud. I turned back, and perceived a vast Opake Body between me and the Sun, moving forwards

8 *the Latitude of 46 N. and of Longitude 183.* Longitude these days is counted both east and west from the observatory at Greenwich. Greenwich is at zero degrees longitude and the continuation of that line on the other side of the world is 180 degrees. The method of counting longitude, however, was not yet fixed in Swift's time and Gulliver is apparently counting eastward from Greenwich and has gone past the 180 degree line. His "Longitude 183" is what we would call 177 degrees west longitude.

If Gulliver were located there and at 46 degrees north, he would be about three hundred miles south of the southernmost Aleutian islands and not very far, I suspect, from the northwestern shore of Brobdingnag. In fact, to reach this point, Gulliver might well have had to go through Brobdingnag, but, of course, he never mentions that kingdom.

9 *Match.* Not the friction match we have today, or the rest of the paraphernalia would not be needed. The friction match was not invented till a century after *Gulliver's Travels* was published.

Gulliver's "match" was a length of cord impregnated with sulfur, which would burn slowly when ignited by sparks from the flint and steel, or by the heat from a burning glass, and would in turn ignite the fuel that would roast the eggs. Such matches were used to ignite gunpowder and set off the firing of a musket (matchlock musket), although flint and steel could also be used directly (flintlock musket).

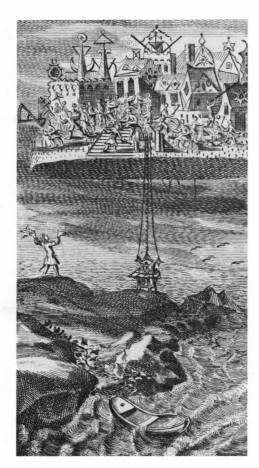

Engraving from the first illustrated edition,
London, 1727. Courtesy, Rare Book Division,
The New York Public Library.

10 *an Island in the Air.* Others had invented fanciful flying cities before this, but Jonathan Swift was the first to attempt an explanation of its workings in line with the findings of contemporary science. This section of the book is therefore true science fiction, perhaps the earliest example we have of it. To include earlier works as science fiction involves broadening the definition of the genre to include works not strictly based on a scientific background, and thus little more than adventure fantasy—like, for instance, the first two parts of *Gulliver's Travels.*

From the satirical standpoint, the city in the sky, which we will later learn is called Laputa, is usually supposed to symbolize the court of Great Britain which, in terms of power and of social position, towered high above the rest of the kingdom.

It also symbolizes the world of science which involves itself in abstract thought high above the conventional interests of ordinary human beings.

11 *philosophise.* In Swift's time this meant to indulge in scientific speculation.

towards the Island: It seemed to be about two Miles high, and hid the Sun six or seven Minutes, but I did not observe the Air to be much colder, or the Sky more darkned, than if I had stood under the Shade of a Mountain. As it approached nearer over the Place where I was, it appeared to be a firm Substance, the Bottom flat, smooth, and shining very bright from the Reflexion of the Sea below. I stood upon a Height about two Hundred Yards from the Shoar, and saw this vast Body descending almost to a Parallel with me, at less than an *English* Mile Distance. I took out my Pocket-Perspective, and could plainly discover Numbers of People moving up and down the Sides of it, which appeared to be sloping, but what those People were doing, I was not able to distinguish.

The natural Love of Life gave me some inward Motions of Joy; and I was ready to entertain a Hope, that this Adventure might some Way or other help to deliver me from the desolate Place and Condition I was in. But, at the same Time, the Reader can hardly **10** conceive my Astonishment, to behold an Island in the Air inhabited by Men, who were able (as it should seem) to raise, or sink, or put it into a progressive Motion, as they pleased. But not **11** being, at that Time, in a Disposition to philosophise upon this Phænomenon, I rather chose to observe what Course the Island would take; because it seemed for a while to stand still. Yet soon after it advanced nearer; and I could see the Sides of it, encompassed with several Gradations of Galleries and Stairs, at certain Intervals, to descend from one to the other. In the lowest Gallery, I beheld some People fishing with long Angling Rods, and others looking on. I waved my Cap, (for my Hat was long since worn out,) and my Handkerchief towards the Island; and upon its nearer Approach, I called and shouted with the utmost Strength of my Voice; and then looking circumspectly, I beheld a Croud gathered to that Side which was most in my View. I found by their pointing towards me and to each other, that they plainly discovered me, although they made no Return to my Shouting: But I could see four or five Men running in great Haste up the Stairs to the Top of the Island, who then disappeared. I happened rightly to conjecture, that these were sent for Orders to some Person in Authority upon this Occasion.

The Number of People increased; and in less than Half an Hour, the Island was moved and raised in such a Manner, that the lowest Gallery appeared in a Parallel of less than an Hundred Yards Distance from the Height where I stood. I then put my self into the most supplicating Postures, and spoke in the humblest Accent, but received no Answer. Those who stood nearest over-against me, seemed to be Persons of Distinction, as I supposed by **12** their Habit. They conferred earnestly with each other, looking often upon me. At length one of them called out in a clear, polite, smooth Dialect, not unlike in Sound to the *Italian;* and therefore I returned an Answer in that Language, hoping at least that the Cadence might be more agreeable to his Ears. Although neither of us understood the other, yet my Meaning was easily known, for the People saw the Distress I was in.

They made Signs for me to come down from the Rock, and go towards the Shoar, which I accordingly did; and the flying Island

"I . . . was drawn up by Pullies." Thomas Stothard, The Novelist's Magazine, *1782. Courtesy, The New York Public Library.*

being raised to a convenient Height, the Verge directly over me, a Chain was let down from the lowest Gallery, with a Seat fastned to the Bottom, to which I fixed my self, and was drawn up by Pullies.

1 *one of their Eyes turned inward, and the other directly up to the Zenith.* At the time *Gulliver's Travels* was published, western Europe was in the Age of Reason, a period in which science was triumphing and Isaac Newton (1642–1727) was the hero of the age. Swift, whose intention it was to castigate all the follies of mankind, did not hesitate to take on Reason—not so much Reason itself as what he considered un-

Isaac Newton, (1642–1727).
Courtesy, Library of Congress.

The Humours and Dispositions of the Laputians described. An Account of their Learning. Of the King and his Court. The Author's reception there. The Inhabitants subject to fears and disquietudes. An Account of the Women.

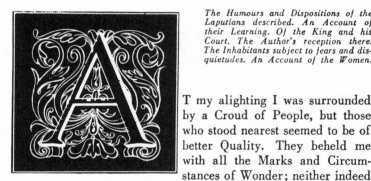

T my alighting I was surrounded by a Croud of People, but those who stood nearest seemed to be of better Quality. They beheld me with all the Marks and Circumstances of Wonder; neither indeed was I much in their Debt; having never till then seen a Race of Mortals so singular in their Shapes, Habits, and Countenances. **1** Their Heads were all reclined to the Right, or the Left; one of their **2** Eyes turned inward, and the other directly up to the Zenith. Their outward Garments were adorned with the Figures of Suns, Moons, and Stars, interwoven with those of Fiddles, Flutes, Harps, Trumpets, Guittars, Harpsicords, and many more Instruments of Musick, unknown to us in *Europe.* I observed here and there many in the Habit of Servants, with a blown Bladder fastned like a Flail to the End of a short Stick, which they carried in their Hands. In each Bladder was a small Quantity of dried Pease, or little Pebbles, (as I was afterwards informed). With these Bladders they now and then flapped the Mouths and Ears of those who stood near them, of which Practice I could not then conceive the Meaning. It seems, the Minds of these People are so taken up with intense Speculations, that they neither can speak, or attend to the Discourses of others, without being rouzed by some external Taction upon the Organs of Speech and Hearing; for which Reason, those Persons who are able to afford it, always keep a *Flapper*, (the Original is *Climenole*) in their Family, as one of their Domesticks; nor ever walk abroad or make Visits without him. And the Business of this Officer is, when two or more Persons are in Company, gently to strike with his Bladder the Mouth of him who is to speak, and the Right Ear of him or them to whom the Speaker addresseth himself. This *Flapper* is likewise employed diligently to attend his Master in his Walks, and upon Occasion to give him a soft Flap on his Eyes; because he is always so wrapped up in Cogitation, that he is in manifest Danger of falling down every Precipice, and bouncing his Head against every Post; and in the Streets, of jostling others, or being jostled himself into the Kennel.

3

4

5

6

It was necessary to give the Reader this Information, without which he would be at the same Loss with me, to understand the

Laputian gentlemen conversing. Ad. Laluze, 1875. Courtesy, Library of Congress.

due faith in it: the making of a religion of Reason to the detriment of a concern for religious faith, morality, and ethics. Laputa is the island of Reason and Swift savagely depicts the follies to which it gives rise.

For instance, he emphasizes that the worshipers of Reason lose contact with the real concerns of life. Thus, the eyes of Laputans do not look forward in order to see the world and their fellow creatures. One eye looks inward to study the workings of the body and the other looks upward at the stars. This may refer to the two great wonder instruments of the age that so greatly extended the sense perception of human beings, the microscope and the telescope, respectively.

2 *Their outward Garments were adorned with . . . Suns, Moons . . . and Instruments of Musick.* The heavenly bodies and the musical instruments represent the abstract studies, since both astronomy and music, pursued in a thoroughly theoretical way, seem to have no application whatever to ordinary human affairs.

Incidentally, it is only fair to state my own prejudices. I am completely out of sympathy with Swift's satire on science. His constantly reiterated belief that abstract studies were useless and that only that which has clear and immediate applications to human life was worth studying is foolish. It is a common mistake of nonscientists and "practical men" to suppose that it is easy to decide whether a scientific investigation is useful or not and that, therefore, if no use is immediately apparent, it should be abandoned. Almost every useful advance in two centuries has had as at least part of its basis some highly theoretical advance Swift would have scorned as foolish.

3 *they neither can speak, nor attend to the Discourses of others, without being rouzed.* It is commonly believed that those who occupy their minds with deep thought have no room in those minds for anything else. Anyone who concentrates on *anything* is likely to forget other things. Someone who plays golf and forgets dinner in the excitement is indulged as a sportsman; someone who is working out an abstruse speculation and forgets dinner is hooted at as an "absentminded professor." Well, the Laputans are absentminded professors to the extreme.

4 *Taction.* Touch.

5 *he is always so wrapped up in Cogitation, that he is in . . . Danger of falling down every Precipice.* Undoubtedly, Swift is thinking of the well-known story of Thales, the philosopher of Miletus, who lived about 600 B.C. Once, when staring at the stars while walking, he failed to see a ditch at his feet, and fell in. A bystander laughed and said, "Here is a man who would understand the motion of the stars, yet who cannot see what lies at his feet." Thales was the prototype of the "absentminded professor."

6 *into the Kennel.* Into the channel, i.e., the trough in which water and sewage flow down the street to join some brook or river eventually. We would say "into the gutter" today.

Proceedings of these People, as they conducted me up the Stairs, to the Top of the Island, and from thence to the Royal Palace. While we were ascending, they forgot several Times what they were about, and left me to my self, till their Memories were again rouzed by their *Flappers;* for they appeared altogether unmoved by the Sight of my foreign Habit and Countenance, and by the Shouts of the Vulgar, whose Thoughts and Minds were more disengaged.

7

At last we entered the Palace, and proceeded into the Chamber of Presence; where I saw the King seated on his Throne, attended on each Side by Persons of prime Quality. Before the Throne, was a large Table filled with Globes and Spheres, and Mathematical Instruments of all Kinds. His Majesty took not the least Notice of us, although our Entrance were not without sufficient Noise, by the Concourse of all Persons belonging to the Court. But, he was then deep in a Problem, and we attended at least an Hour, before he

8

A Laputian gentleman taking a walk. Arthur Rackham, 1900 and 1909.

7 *Vulgar.* See Part I, Chapter 6, note 4.

8 *the King.* The King of Laputa, like the King of Lilliput, is usually taken by the commentators to represent George I. George I patronized scientists and musicians and, while he was still elector of Hanover, was patron of the great scientist Gottfried Wilhelm Leibniz (1646–1716). George I was not particularly learned himself, however, so it was all the more credit to him, then, for appreciating learning in others.

"His Majesty . . . . was then deep in a Problem." T. Morten, 1865. Courtesy, Library of Congress.

could solve it. There stood by him on each Side, a young Page, with Flaps in their Hands; and when they saw he was at Leisure, one of them gently struck his Mouth, and the other his Right Ear; at which he started like one awaked on the sudden, and looking towards me, and the Company I was in, recollected the Occasion of our coming, whereof he had been informed before. He spoke some Words; whereupon immediately a young Man with a Flap came up to my Side, and flapt me gently on the Right Ear; but I made Signs as well as I could, that I had no Occasion for such an Instrument; which as I afterwards found, gave his Majesty and the whole Court a very mean Opinion of my Understanding. The **9** King, as far as I could conjecture, asked me several Questions, and I addressed my self to him in all the Languages I had. When it was found, that I could neither understand nor be understood, I was conducted by his Order to an Apartment in his Palace, (this Prince being distinguished above all his Predecessors for his Hospitality **10** to Strangers,) where two Servants were appointed to attend me. My Dinner was brought, and four Persons of Quality, whom I remembered to have been very near the King's Person, did me the Honour to dine with me. We had two Courses, of three Dishes each. In the first Course, there was a Shoulder of Mutton, cut into an Æquilateral Triangle; a Piece of Beef into a Rhomboides; and a Pudding into a Cycloid. The second Course was two Ducks, trussed up into the Form of Fiddles; Sausages and Puddings resembling Flutes and Haut-boys, and a Breast of Veal in the Shape of a **11** Harp. The Servants cut our Bread into Cones, Cylinders, Parallelograms, and several other Mathematical Figures. While we were at Dinner, I made bold to ask the Names of several Things in their Language; and those noble Persons, by the Assistance of their *Flappers*, delighted to give me Answers, hoping to raise my Admiration of their great Abilities, if I could be brought to converse with them. I was soon able to call for Bread, and Drink, or whatever else I wanted.

After Dinner my Company withdrew, and a Person was sent to me by the King's Order, attended by a *Flapper*. He brought with him Pen, Ink, and Paper, and three or four Books; giving me to understand by Signs, that he was sent to teach me the Language. We sat together four Hours, in which Time I wrote down a great Number of Words in Columns, with the Translations over against them. I likewise made a Shift to learn several short Sentences. For my Tutor would order one of my Servants to fetch something, to turn about, to make a Bow, to sit, or stand, or walk, and the like. Then I took down the Sentence in Writing. He shewed me also in one of his Books, the Figures of the Sun, Moon, and Stars, the Zodiack, the Tropics and Polar Circles, together with the Denominations of many Figures of Planes and Solids. He gave me the Names and Descriptions of all the Musical Instruments, and the general Terms of Art in playing on each of them. After he had left me, I placed all my Words with their Interpretations in alphabetical Order. And thus in a few Days, by the Help of a very faithful Memory, I got some Insight into their Language.

The Word, which I interpret the *Flying* or *Floating Island*, is in the Original *Laputa;* whereof I could never learn the true Etymology. *Lap* in the old obsolete Language signifieth *High*, and *Untuh* a *Governor*; from which they say by Corruption was derived *Laputa* from *Lapuntuh*. But I do not approve of this Derivation,

9 *very mean Opinion of my Understanding.* A very low opinion. The King apparently felt Gulliver must be a very shallow thinker if his attention could so easily be distracted by something as unimportant as having someone speak to him.

10 *distinguished . . . for his Hospitality to Strangers.* This is a clearer stroke at George I. When George I left Hanover to become king of Great Britain on the death of Queen Anne, he brought with him many Hanoverians to whom he gave places about the court. The British naturally resented this, and it is that which occasions Swift's sarcastic comment on the King's hospitality to strangers.

11 *Haut-boys.* Oboes. The whole passage is an indication of the manner in which the Laputans apply their theoretical abstractions to uses that are not natural, and therefore not really useful. In other words, the point Swift makes throughout this section is that scientists are silly.

Gulliver's dinner in Laputa. J. J. Grandville, 1835. Courtesy, Library of Congress.

12 *Lap signifying . . . the dancing of the Sun Beams . . . and outed a Wing.* Gulliver's excursion here into mock etymology is designed by Swift to mock the false learning that so often marked the pseudointellectuals (into which category Swift may, at his bitterest, have lumped scientists generally). It is a plain fact—of which many of his readers would be at once aware—that *la puta* is Spanish for "the whore." That may well have been Swift's bitter opinion of the court of England with a Hanoverian on the throne and Whigs controlling Parliament. Then, too, it may be a reference to reason itself, the deity of the scientists. Martin Luther (1483–1546), exasperated when his opponents used reason to dispute some of the points which he had based on faith, wrathfully cried out against "that Great Whore, Reason."

13 *Quadrant.* An instrument used to measure the heights of those objects whose measurements cannot, for one reason or another, be taken directly with a yardstick or a tape measure. This follows a rather common misconception (believed by many of the ill-educated even today) that scientists deliberately do things in a complicated, "Rube Goldberg" fashion, when actually something very simple and down-to-earth would do just as well.

14 *mistake a Figure in the Calculation.* The very apotheosis of reason was, of course, Isaac Newton, whom Swift did not like. Newton was once embarrassed by a typographical error in a book of his, and this is probably a sly reference to that.

15 *the Musick of the Spheres.* The Greek astronomers had supposed the universe to consist of an elaborate set of concentric transparent spheres, each turning after its own complex fashion and carrying the plan-

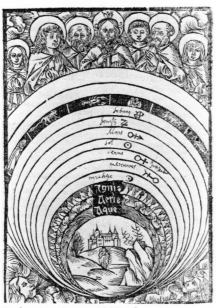

Ptolomeic universe, 1513. Courtesy, Library of Congress.

12 which seems to be a little strained. I ventured to offer to the Learned among them a Conjecture of my own, that *Laputa* was *quasi Lap outed*; *Lap* signifying properly the dancing of the Sun Beams in the Sea; and *outed* a Wing, which however I shall not obtrude, but submit to the judicious Reader.

Those to whom the King had entrusted me, observing how ill I was clad, ordered a Taylor to come next Morning, and take my Measure for a Suit of Cloaths. This Operator did his Office after a different Manner from those of his Trade in *Europe.* He first took **13** my Altitude by a Quadrant, and then with Rule and Compasses, described the Dimensions and Out-Lines of my whole Body; all which he entred upon Paper, and in six Days brought my Cloaths **14** very ill made, and quite out of Shape, by happening to mistake a Figure in the Calculation. But my Comfort was, that I observed such Accidents very frequent, and little regarded.

During my Confinement for want of Cloaths, and by an Indisposition that held me some Days longer, I much enlarged my Dictionary; and when I went next to Court, was able to understand many Things the King spoke, and to return him some Kind of Answers. His Majesty had given Orders, that the Island should move North-East and by East, to the vertical Point over *Lagado,* the Metropolis of the whole Kingdom, below upon the firm Earth. It was about Ninety Leagues distant, and our Voyage lasted four Days and an Half. I was not in the least sensible of the progressive Motion made in the Air by the Island. On the second Morning, about Eleven o'Clock, the King himself in Person, attended by his Nobility, Courtiers, and Officers, having prepared all their Musical Instruments, played on them for three Hours without Intermission; so that I was quite stunned with the Noise; neither could I possibly guess the Meaning, till my Tutor informed me. He said, that the People of their Island had their Ears adapted **15** to hear the Musick of the Spheres, which always played at certain Periods; and the Court was now prepared to bear their Part in whatever Instrument they most excelled.

In our Journey towards *Lagado* the Capital City, his Majesty ordered that the Island should stop over certain Towns and Villages, from whence he might receive the Petitions of his Subjects. And to this Purpose, several Pack-threads were let down with small Weights at the Bottom. On these Pack-threads the People strung their Petitions, which mounted up directly like the Scraps of Paper fastned by School-boys at the End of the String that holds their Kite. Sometimes we received Wine and Victuals from below, which were drawn up by Pullies.

The Knowledge I had in Mathematicks gave me great Assistance in acquiring their Phraseology, which depended much upon that Science and Musick; and in the latter I was not unskilled. Their Ideas are perpetually conversant in Lines and Figures. If they would, for Example, praise the Beauty of a Woman, or any other Animal, they describe it by Rhombs, Circles, Parallelograms, Ellipses, and other Geometrical Terms; or else by Words of Art drawn from Musick, needless here to repeat. I observed in the King's Kitchen all Sorts of Mathematical and Musical Instruments, after the Figures of which they cut up the Joynts that were served to his Majesty's Table.

16 Their Houses are very ill built, the Walls bevil, without one right Angle in any Apartment; and this Defect ariseth from the

Contempt they bear for practical Geometry; which they despise as vulgar and mechanick, those Instructions they give being too refined for the Intellectuals of their Workmen; which occasions perpetual Mistakes. And although they are dextrous enough upon a Piece of Paper, in the Management of the Rule, the Pencil, and the Divider, yet in the common Actions and Behaviour of Life, I have not seen a more clumsy, awkward, and unhandy People, nor so slow and perplexed in their Conceptions upon all other Subjects, except those of Mathematicks and Musick. They are very bad Reasoners, and vehemently given to Opposition, unless when they happen to be of the right Opinion, which is seldom their Case. Imagination, Fancy, and Invention, they are wholly Strangers to, nor have any Words in their Language by which those Ideas can be expressed; the whole Compass of their thoughts and Mind, being shut up within the two forementioned Sciences.

Most of them, and especially those who deal in the Astronomical Part, have great Faith in judicial Astrology, although they are ashamed to own it publickly. But, what I chiefly admired, and thought altogether unaccountable, was the strong Disposition I observed in them towards News and Politicks; perpetually enquiring into publick Affairs, giving their Judgments in Matters of State; and passionately disputing every Inch of a Party Opinion. I have indeed observed the same Disposition among most of the Mathematicians I have known in *Europe*; although I could never discover the least Analogy between the two Sciences; unless those People suppose, that because the smallest Circle hath as many Degrees as the largest, therefore the Regulation and Management of the World require no more Abilities than the handling and turning of a Globe. But, I rather take this Quality to spring from a very common Infirmity of human Nature, inclining us to be more curious and conceited in Matters where we have least Concern, and for which we are least adapted either by Study or Nature.

These People are under continual Disquietudes, never enjoying a Minute's Peace of Mind; and their Disturbances proceed from Causes which very little affect the rest of Mortals. Their Apprehensions arise from several Changes they dread in the Celestial Bodies. For Instance; that the Earth by the continual Approaches of the Sun towards it, must in Course of Time be absorbed or swallowed up. That the Face of the Sun will by Degrees be encrusted with its own Effluvia, and give no more Light to the World. That, the Earth very narrowly escaped a Brush from the Tail of the last Comet, which would have infallibly reduced it to Ashes; and that the next, which they have calculated for One and Thirty Years hence, will probably destroy us. For, if in its Perihelion it should approach within a certain Degree of the Sun, (as by their Calculations they have Reason to dread) it will conceive a Degree of Heat ten Thousand Times more intense than that of red hot glowing Iron; and in its Absence from the Sun, carry a blazing Tail Ten Hundred Thousand and Fourteen Miles long; through which if the Earth should pass at the Distance of one Hundred Thousand Miles from the *Nucleus*, or main Body of the Comet, it must in its Passage be set on Fire, and reduced to Ashes. That the Sun daily spending its Rays without any Nutriment to supply them, will at last be wholly consumed and annihilated; which must be attended with the Destruction of this Earth, and of all the Planets that receive their Light from it.

17
18
19

20

21

22

23

24
25

26

27

28

ets and other heavenly bodies around the Earth. Some mystics supposed that all these turnings produced a kind of celestial music or "Musick of the Spheres," which earthbound mortals could not hear.

Perhaps the last person of note to take the concept of the music of the spheres seriously was the great German astronomer, Johannes Kepler (1571–1630), who, in one of his more mystic moments, tried to work out the notes produced by each planet as it moved about in its elliptical orbit.

For almost a century before Swift's time, therefore, the music of the spheres had been completely discredited.

16 *bevil.* Not at right angles to each other.

17 *practical Geometry.* Here again Swift contrasts the abstract and practical, "pure" versus "applied" science, with all the advantage going to the latter. Actually, the ancient Greek mathematicians did, indeed, despise practical applications of their art and viewed it as, ideally, a feast of pure reason. Yet Swift was an admirer of the ancients and it is rather ironic, and frustrating, that he shifted the vices of the ancient mathematicians, whom he admired, to the shoulders of the modern mathematicians, whom he disliked. The mathematicians of Swift's day were actually using mathematics for practical matters constantly.

18 *judicial Astrology.* "Natural astrology" is the foretelling of future events in the inanimate world from the position of the planets. This, in fact, is a portion of what we would today call astronomy and comparatively few people are interested in that.

"Judicial Astrology," referred to here, involves the prediction of the future of nations and individuals from the position of the planets This is sheer nonsense, of course, and, as a result, is staunchly believed in by many millions of people even today.

Judicial astrology had such a reputation and astrological forecasts were in such demand that some great legitimate astronomers, notably Kepler, cast horoscopes as a way of earning ready cash. Nor did this habit quite die out with Kepler, and it is at this that Swift's shaft is aimed.

19 *admired.* See Part I, Chapter 1, note 26.

20 *the same Disposition among most of the Mathematicians I have known in Europe.* This is probably a dig at Isaac Newton, who served as master of the Mint, from 1696 on. He involved himself completely in coinage reform, moved actively against counterfeiters, and did a good job.

In 1722, Walpole's government had granted a license for the coining of new halfpence and farthings for use in Ireland. The Irish people were not consulted and the conditions were such that everyone involved in England would make a great deal of money.

Swift was living in Dublin at the time, and while he was not a Catholic and while he was of English descent, he came out furiously in favor of the right of the Irish to a voice in matters that so closely affected themselves. He published a series of anonymous essays, purportedly by a man named Drapier, so brilliantly invective that the whole proposal was defeated. What Swift could not forgive was that Newton had lent his prestige to the coinage proposal. To Swift that was an example of a mathematician giving his "Judgments in Matters of State" concerning which he had no expertise.

21 *the Earth . . . must in Course of Time be absorbed or swallowed up.* Here Swift satirizes the "doom-criers" whom, of course, we always have with us. True to the thrust of this section, Swift equates doom-crying with scientists, although the historical fact is that the loudest doom-criers have always been the clergy and others who were convinced that any day God would punish the earth for its sins.

Newton had advanced his system of the universe, based on the laws of motion and the law of universal gravitation, forty years before the publication of *Gulliver's Travels.* In that system, the Earth moves about the Sun because it is attracted to the Sun. It was possible to speculate, therefore, that eventually the attraction would overcome all else and that little by little the Earth would approach the Sun and be swallowed by it. Even if this occurred, though, it was perfectly well understood by astronomers that it could take place only in the extremely and indefinitely remote future (just as many of us now believe that *eventually* any piece of matter, such as the Earth, will be swallowed by a black hole).

How far Swift understood, or permitted himself to understand, the new astronomy, is uncertain. He still could not help but think in Ptolemaic terms, as when he here tells of the continual approach of the Sun toward the Earth, as though he automatically things of the Earth standing still and the Sun moving, or when, as earlier, he speaks of the music of the spheres.

It may be that as a clergyman, he felt mankind was more secure in assuming that God's word kept the Earth and Sun in their respective places. The astronomers, replacing the sure protection of God with the flimsy assurances of mathematical computations, would therefore naturally feel fear.

On the other hand, the Bible clearly states that the Day of Judgment would come in the not-distant future, and religionists have awaited the end of the world through divine fiat far more apprehensively than ever scientists have feared it through the effects of gravity.

22 *the Sun will by Degrees be encrusted with its own Effluvia.* Again, Swift points up the fear that must result in turning from God to mathematics. Once astronomers abandoned the notion of the Sun as a divine and eternal fire and tried to show that the same natural laws ruled both the heavens and the Earth (the core of Newton's system), then the Sun had to be viewed as no more than a very large bonfire. If this were so, would not the accumulating ash and smoke (the "effluvia" Swift talks of) choke the flames eventually and put them out?

The answer, of course, is yes—after a fashion quite different from anything that could have been imagined in Swift's time. There will come a time when enough of the hydrogen fuel of the Sun will be turned into helium "effluvia" to alter the Sun's nature to the point where Earth is longer a livable world, but that time is perhaps 7 billion years in the future.

23 *the Earth very narrowly escaped . . . the last Comet, which would have infallibly reduced it to Ashes.* In ancient and medieval times, comets were thought to be flaming patches of the atmosphere. The superstitious, by which we might as well say everybody, believed them to be signs sent by God betokening misfortune. (Since misfortune always followed the appearance of a comet, this feeling was strengthened. No one seemed to notice that misfortune always followed the nonappearance of a comet, also.)

Beginning with the observations of the Danish astronomer, Tycho Brahe (1546–1601), of a comet in 1577, it began to appear that comets existed far beyond the atmosphere and were members of the solar system, whirling about the Sun as the planets did. It was a natural assumption that they were massive objects, like the planets, especially since they showed visible shapes whereas the ordinary planets were mere dots of light, so that the comets had to be larger in size, it was reasoned.

Comets did not have the regular, nearly circular orbits of the planets, and it was much more likely that a wandering comet might strike the Earth than that a well-regulated planet would, especially if it were not God that ordered the movement of the heavenly bodies, but mathematical formulas.

And would not a collision between a comet and the Earth destroy our planet? Would not even a glancing blow of a comet's tail do so?

We know *now* that comets are small objects and that the insubstantial haze that makes up a comet's extended body and, particularly, its tail, is little more than visible vacuum—but this was not understood in Swift's time.

24 *the next, which they have calculated for One and Thirty Years hence.* Comets came to be understood as well-regulated members of the solar system, obeying the law of gravity as exactly as the planets did. Even if Swift were disposed to accept this new understanding, he would have been tempted to turn away, since this was made final by the calculations of Edmund Halley (1656–1742), a close friend of Swift's enemy, Newton.

In 1705, Halley presented the world with the calculations that led him to identify what had been thought to be a number of comets, which had appeared at intervals of seventy-five or seventy-six years, as a single body (now called "Halley's comet") making regular revolutions about a very elongated elliptical orbit.

Halley predicted that the comet would return in 1758, which was thirty-two years after the publication of *Gulliver's Travels.* Naturally, his prediction didn't carry much conviction among those who preferred to believe in comets as signs from God, sent irregularly to warn sinners. Here Swift satirizes the prediction, sure of getting a laugh.

They are so perpetually alarmed with the Apprehensions of these and the like impending Dangers, that they can neither sleep quietly in their Beds, nor have any Relish for the common Pleasures or Amusements of Life. When they meet an Acquaintance in the Morning, the first Question is about the Sun's Health; how he looked at his Setting and Rising, and what Hopes they have to avoid the Stroak of the approaching Comet. This Conversation they are apt to run into with the same Temper that Boys discover in delighting to hear terrible Stories of Sprites and Hobgoblins, which they greedily listen to, and dare not go to Bed for fear.

The Women of the Island have Abundance of Vivacity; they contemn their Husbands, and are exceedingly fond of Strangers, whereof there is always a considerable Number from the Continent below, attending at Court, either upon Affairs of the several Towns and Corporations, or their own particular Occasions; but are much despised, because they want the same Endowments. Among these the Ladies chuse their Gallants: But the Vexation is, that they act with too much Ease and Security; for the Husband is always so wrapped in Speculation, that the Mistress and Lover may proceed to the greatest Familiarities before his Face, if he be but provided with Paper and Implements, and without his *Flapper* at his Side.

The Wives and Daughters lament their Confinement to the Island, although I think it the most delicious Spot of Ground in the World; and although they live here in the greatest Plenty and Magnificence, and are allowed to do whatever they please: They long to see the World, and take the Diversions of the Metropolis, which they are not allowed to do without a particular Licence from the King; and this is not easy to be obtained, because the People of Quality have found by frequent Experience, how hard it is to persuade their Women to return from below. I was told, that a great Court Lady, who had several Children, is married to the prime Minister, the richest Subject in the Kingdom, a very graceful Person, extremely fond of her, and lives in the finest Palace of the Island; went down to *Lagado,* on the Pretence of Health, there hid her self for several Months, till the King sent a Warrant to search for her; and she was found in an obscure Eating-House all in Rags, having pawned her Cloaths to maintain an old deformed Footman, who beat her every Day, and in whose Company she was taken much against her Will. And although her Husband received her with all possible Kindness, and without the least Reproach; she soon after contrived to steal down again with all her Jewels, to the same Gallant, and hath not been heard of since.

This may perhaps pass with the Reader rather for an *European* or *English* Story, than for one of a Country so remote. But he may please to consider, that the Caprices of Womankind are not limited by any Climate or Nation; and that they are much more uniform than can be easily imagined.

In about a Month's Time I had made a tolerable Proficiency in their Language, and was able to answer most of the King's Questions, when I had the Honour to attend him. His Majesty discovered not the least Curiosity to enquire into the Laws, Government, History, Religion, or Manners of the Countries where I had been; but confined his Questions to the State of Mathematicks, and received the Account I gave him, with great Contempt and Indifference, though often rouzed by his *Flapper* on each Side.

The laugh, however, was on Swift. Halley's comet returned exactly on schedule, though neither Halley nor Swift lived long enough to see it do so.

25 *Perihelion.* Any object orbiting the sun is at its "perihelion" when it is at that point of its orbit closest to the sun.

26 *ten Thousand Times more intense than that of red hot glowing Iron.* In this passage, Swift is satirizing the manner in which astronomers use huge figures and great exactness. The layman's attitude, which Swift is here exploiting, tends to be "How can they know that?" The odd part, though, is that astronomy is a comparatively simple science and astronomers *can* "know that."

A temperature which is "ten Thousand times more intense than that of red hot glowing Iron" would be about 10 million degrees and, of course, any comet raised to that temperature through a close approach to the sun (an impossible temperature rise under the circumstances, by the way) would simply evaporate.

27 *a blazing Tail Ten Hundred Thousand and Fourteen Miles long.* The joke is on Swift. Comet's tails are sometimes far longer than this.

28 *the Sun . . . will at last be wholly consumed and annihilated.* Again Swift is satirizing fears about the end of the sun, this time through the sheer exhaustion of fuel, rather than through accumulations of smoke and ash. Actually, though Swift may not have imagined it, this was an extraordinarily prescient thought. It was not till a century and a quarter after the publication of *Gulliver's Travels* that physicists finally gathered enough data to make the notion of the conservation of energy compelling. It was only in the mid nineteenth century, then, that the first careful scientific consideration was applied to the problem of the energy source of the sun.

29 *contemn.* Despise.

30 *the prime Minister.* In this passage Swift is not only taking another poke at the absentmindedness of scientists, who are so absorbed in their speculations that they are not interested in sex and do not notice their wive's infidelities, but he seems also to be making a specific reference to Walpole. There were stories that Walpole's wife was unfaithful to him and that he was indifferent to the fact and, true or not, Swift was delighted to make use of the story and to imply that a woman would find anyone, even a deformed and sadistic servant, preferable to him.

31 *the Caprices of Womankind.* It has long been an article of faith among men that women are unreasoning beings who act on whim and caprice. Men always seem to be at a loss to explain why women should choose to do something they enjoy instead of something else that pleases their husbands, and put it down to inexplicable fancy.

32 *discovered.* See Part I, Chapter 7, note 15.

1 *I will now give a philosophical Account to the Reader.* The description that follows of the way in which Laputa works is a satirical imitation of papers published in *The Philosophical Transactions of the Royal Society.* Nevertheless, Swift manages to make something quite impossible sound very plausible by using the scientific knowledge and terminology of his day. This particular passage is excellent science fiction in the modern sense.

2 *ten Thousand Acres.* The area of Laputa is about seven-tenths that of the island of Manhattan.

3 *Adamant.* Any of three things:

First, it is an imaginary stone of impenetrable hardness and strength.

Second, it is the hardest substance that actually exists—diamond. In fact, "diamond" is a distorted version of the word "adamant." The hardness of diamond is not to be equated with strength, however. Diamond is brittle and can be made to shatter quite easily, a fact on which the art of diamond cutting depends.

The third meaning arises in a more complicated way. "Adamant" is from Greek words meaning "untameable" while *adamari* is a Latin word meaning "to love." Magnetism was thought to be a phenomenon analogous to love since magnets "attracted" iron. *Adamare* could be used for a magnet and, by confusion, "adamant" came to be used for it.

Swift uses the word in at least two ways. Undoubtedly, the adamant that underlies Laputa is extremely hard, but it also possesses magnetic properties.

A Phoenomenon solved by Modern Philosophy and Astronomy. The Laputians great improvements in the latter. The King's method of suppressing Insurrections.

1 I DESIRED Leave of this Prince to see the Curiosities of the Island; which he was graciously pleased to grant, and ordered my Tutor to attend me. I chiefly wanted to know to what Cause in Art or in Nature, it owed its several Motions; whereof I will now give a philosophical Account to the Reader.

The flying or floating Island is exactly circular; its Diameter 7837 Yards, or about four Miles and an Half, and consequently **2** contains ten Thousand Acres. It is three Hundred Yards thick. The Bottom, or under Surface, which appears to those who view it **3** from below, is one even regular Plate of Adamant, shooting up to the Height of about two Hundred Yards. Above it lye the several Minerals in their usual Order; and over all is a Coat of rich Mould ten or twelve Foot deep. The Declivity of the upper Surface, from the Circumference to the Center, is the natural Cause why all the Dews and Rains which fall upon the Island, are conveyed in small Rivulets towards the Middle, where they are emptied into four large Basons, each of about Half a Mile in Circuit, and two Hundred Yards distant from the Center. From these Basons the Water **4** is continually exhaled by the Sun in the Day-time, which effectually prevents their overflowing. Besides, as it is in the Power of the Monarch to raise the Island above the Region of Clouds and Vapours, he can prevent the falling of Dews and Rains whenever he pleases. For the highest Clouds cannot rise above two Miles, as Naturalists agree, at least they were never known to do so in that Country.

At the Center of the *Island* there is a Chasm about fifty Yards in Diameter, from whence the Astronomers descend into a large Dome, which is therefore called *Flandona Gagnole*, or the *Astronomers Cave*; situated at the Depth of an Hundred Yards beneath the upper Surface of the Adamant. In this Cave are Twenty Lamps continually burning, which from the Reflection of the Adamant cast a strong Light into every Part. The Place is stored with great Variety of Sextants, Quadrants, Telescopes, Astrolabes, and other Astronomical Instruments. But the greatest Curiosity, upon which the Fate of the Island depends, is a Load-stone of a prodigious Size, in Shape resembling a Weaver's Shuttle. It is in Length six Yards, and in the thickest Part at least three Yards over. This Magnet is sustained by a very strong Axle of Adamant, passing through its Middle, upon which it plays, and is poized so exactly that the weakest Hand can turn it. It is hooped round with an hollow Cylinder of Adamant, four Foot deep, as many thick, and twelve Yards in Diameter, placed horizontally, and supported by Eight Adamantine Feet, each Six Yards high. In the Middle of the Concave Side there is a Groove Twelve Inches deep, in which the Extremities of the Axle are lodged, and turned round as there is Occasion.

This Stone cannot be moved from its Place by any Force, be-

5

6

7

8
9
10

4 *exhaled.* Evaporated.

5 *prevents their overflowing.* This is an interesting description of a cycling of resources. Swift is reaching toward a closed ecology for Laputa.

6 *the highest Clouds cannot rise above two Miles.* This is an underestimate. Cirrus clouds will form as high as eight miles. However, if Laputa rises to heights of more than two miles, it would be above the significant clouds and will have little to fear from rainfall.

7 *Astronomers Cave.* There was, apparently, a cave at the Royal Observatory in Paris at this time.

8 *Load-stone.* A mineral with natural magnetic properties called, more properly, "magnetite" or "magnetic oxide of iron," having the formula, Fe_3O_4. It can be used, loosely, for any magnet, even one artificially made of steel or of some metallic alloy, though such a use of the word is not heard in contemporary times.

9 *Weaver's Shuttle.* Shaped like a cylinder which tapers on each end.

10 *three Yards over.* That is, three yards across.

"By Means of this Load-stone, the Island is made to rise and fall." T. Morten, 1865. Courtesy, Library of Congress.

11 *at one of its Sides with an attractive Power, and at the other with a repulsive.* Every magnet has two poles—a north pole and a south pole. Two north poles repel each other, as do two south poles. A north pole will, however, attract a south pole and vice versa. Thus, if you place the north pole of one magnet near the south pole of a second, you will experience an attractive force between them. If you reverse the first magnet and place its south pole near the south pole of the second, you will feel a repulsive force. The first magnet will thus seem to attract with one end and repel with the other.

If, however, a magnet is attracting a piece of unmagnetized iron or steel, either pole will attract equally well. To have Laputa act by magnetic force, as here described, would require the earth below it to be a permanent magnetic north pole (or south pole) and the magnet on Laputa to be of impossible strength.

12 *Upon placing the Magnet erect . . . the Island descends; but when the repelling Extremity points downwards, the Island mounts directly upwards.* Swift is not making this up out of his head. The English physicist, William Gilbert (1540–1603), and also Johannes Kepler after him, speculated that the planetary motions were the result of magnetic forces. Of course, Newton's work had utterly outdated these notions, but Swift would not accept the views of the detested Newton in explaining Laputa. Swift would have performed a remarkable feat of science fictional foresight if he had used the (probably impossible) notion of "antigravity" instead.

13 *the Forces always act in Lines parallel to its Direction.* This is reminiscent of Newton's second law of motion, but Swift is wrong just the same. If the lodestone acted by a straightforward attraction or repulsion of the ground, then if it were positioned obliquely, Laputa would still move up or down, but less rapidly, the speed depending on the cosine of the angle the stone makes to the vertical. If it were positioned horizontally, Laputa wouldn't move at all.

14 *oblique Motion.* Some commentators think this is a reference to the policies of Walpole, which controlled the English government and court (Laputa) and which were cautious, rather than straightforward.

15 *the Manner of its Progress.* Swift explains by a lengthy paragraph and a map, both of which are clearly unnecessary, since they pretend to explain something which does not require a great deal of explanation, and in the end do not succeed in being terribly enlightening. He is here again satirizing the pompous style of many of the papers in the *Transactions.*

16 *Balnibarbi.* The fixed island in the ocean over which Laputa hovers. If the map is to be taken as in scale, then, from the measurements already given for Laputa, Balnibarbi would seem to be thirty-five miles long east and west and twenty miles north and

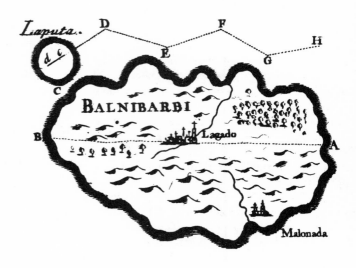

Map from first edition, London, 1726. Courtesy, Rare Book Division, The New York Public Library.

cause the Hoop and its Feet are one continued Piece with that Body of Adamant which constitutes the Bottom of the Island.

By Means of this Load-stone, the Island is made to rise and fall, and move from one Place to another. For, with respect to that Part of the Earth over which the Monarch presides, the Stone is endued **11** at one of its Sides with an attractive Power, and at the other with a **12** repulsive. Upon placing the Magnet erect with its attracting End towards the Earth, the Island descends; but when the repelling Extremity points downwards, the Island mounts directly upwards. When the Position of the Stone is oblique, the Motion of the Island is so too. For in this Magnet the Forces always act in Lines **13** parallel to its Direction.

14 By this oblique Motion the Island is conveyed to different Parts **15** of the Monarch's Dominions. To explain the Manner of its Progress, let *A B* represent a Line drawn cross the Dominions of **16** *Balnibarbi;* let the Line *c d* represent the Load-stone, of which let *d* be the repelling End, and *c* the attracting End, the Island being over *C;* let the Stone be placed in the Position *c d* with its repelling End downwards; then the Island will be driven upwards obliquely towards *D.* When it is arrived at *D,* let the Stone be turned upon its Axle till its attracting End points towards *E,* and then the Island will be carried obliquely towards *E;* where if the Stone be again turned upon its Axle till it stands in the Position *E F,* with its repelling Point downwards, the Island will rise obliquely towards *F,* where by directing the attracting End towards *G,* the Island may be carried to *G,* and from *G* to *H,* by turning the Stone, so as to make its repelling Extremity point directly downwards. And thus by changing the Situation of the Stone as often as there is Occasion, the Island is made to rise and fall by

Turns in an oblique Direction; and by those alternate Risings and Fallings (the Obliquity being not considerable) is conveyed from one Part of the Dominions to the other.

But it must be observed, that this Island cannot move beyond the Extent of the Dominions below; nor can it rise above the Height of four Miles. For which the Astronomers (who have written large Systems concerning the Stone) assign the following Reason: That the Magnetick Virtue does not extend beyond the Distance of four Miles, and that the Mineral which acts upon the Stone in the Bowels of the Earth, and in the Sea about six Leagues distant from the Shoar, is not diffused through the whole Globe, but terminated with the Limits of the King's Dominions: And it was easy from the great Advantage of such a superior Situation, for a Prince to bring under his Obedience whatever Country lay within the Attraction of that Magnet.

When the Stone is put parallel to the Plane of the Horizon, the Island standeth still; for in that Case, the Extremities of it being at equal Distance from the Earth, act with equal Force, the one in drawing downwards, the other in pushing upwards; and consequently no Motion can ensue.

This Load-stone is under the Care of certain Astronomers, who from Time to Time give it such Positions as the Monarch directs. They spend the greatest Part of their Lives in observing the celestial Bodies, which they do by the Assistance of Glasses, far excelling ours in Goodness. For, although their largest Telescopes do not exceed three Feet, they magnify much more than those of a Hundred with us, and shew the Stars with greater Clearness. This Advantage hath enabled them to extend their Discoveries much farther than our Astronomers in *Europe*. They have made a Catalogue of ten Thousand fixed Stars, whereas the largest of ours do not contain above one third Part of that Number. They have likewise discovered two lesser Stars, or *Satellites*, which revolve about *Mars;* whereof the innermost is distant from the Center of the primary Planet exactly three of his Diameters, and the outermost five; the former revolves in the Space of ten Hours, and the latter in Twenty-one and an Half; so that the Squares of their periodical Times, are very near in the same Proportion with the Cubes of their Distance from the Center of *Mars;* which evidently shews them to be governed by the same Law of Gravitation, that influences the other heavenly Bodies.

They have observed Ninety-three different Comets, and settled their Periods with great Exactness. If this be true, (and they affirm it with great Confidence) it is much to be wished that their Observations were made publick; whereby the Theory of Comets, which at present is very lame and defective, might be brought to the same Perfection with other Parts of Astronomy.

The King would be the most absolute Prince in the Universe, if he could but prevail on a Ministry to join with him; but these having their Estates below on the Continent, and considering that the Office of a Favourite hath a very uncertain Tenure, would never consent to the enslaving their Country.

If any Town should engage in Rebellion or Mutiny, fall into violent Factions, or refuse to pay the usual Tribute; the King hath two Methods of reducing them to Obedience. The first and the mildest Course is by keeping the Island hovering over such a

south, for an approximate area of seven hundred square miles. This would make it three-quarters as large as the state of Rhode Island.

Balnibarbi may well represent Ireland over which the British court (Laputa) hovers threateningly.

17 *this Island cannot move beyond the Extent of the Dominions below.* Swift thus explains why Laputa never wanders over known areas of the world. He did not bother to explain why Brobdingnagian life did not spread out over the rest of the world, or why ordinary forms of life did not spread into Lilliput or Blefuscu.

18 *When the Stone is put parallel to the Plane of the Horizon . . . no Motion can ensue.* The argument sounds correct, but the lodestone can only be kept parallel to the plane of the horizon if force is exerted upon it. If it is allowed to swing freely, then the attractive end will swing so as to point downward and the repulsive end will swing so as to point upward. Laputa will then crash. In order to prevent this, enough force must be exerted on the lodestone to bring it parallel, as would be required to maintain the island in mid-air against the downward pull of its weight. Further force would be required to so twist the lodestone as to actually force Laputa upward. If, however, we forget that and follow Swift's earlier statement that the island moved in the direction of the line from one end of the lodestone to the other, then when that line is horizontal, Laputa should move horizontally.

In short, Swift's mechanism to keep Laputa aloft and in motion wouldn't really work, but I suppose that's no surprise to anyone. The explanation sounds scientific and impressive and that's all that counts.

19 *their largest Telescopes do not exceed three Feet.* Swift means three feet in length. In his time, it was difficult to make parabolic lenses, and it was only such lenses that would not distort. Therefore, only the mid-portion of shallow spherical lenses were used, since this mid-portion was close enough to parabolic to minimize the distortion. Those mid-portions, however, had a long focal length so that very long telescopes had to be used. In fact, the greater the magnification of a telescope, the longer it had to be. If good parabolic lenses were made, the full width of which could be used, these would have short focal lengths. That would make possible great magnification in short telescopes. Swift doesn't mention parabolic lenses, but it is possible he had them in mind.

20 *those of a Hundred.* The Dutch astronomer, Christian Huygens (1629–1695), in the 1660s, used a telescope 123 feet long, and in 1673, the German astronomer, Johannes Hevelius (1611–1687) used one that was 150 feet long. In 1722, just four years before *Gulliver's Travels* was published, the English astronomer, James Bradley (1693–1762) used one that was 212 feet long. It was in 1757, thirty-one years after *Gulliver's Travels* was published, that optical advance made achromatic parabolic lenses possible and the long telescopes vanished. Comparatively short

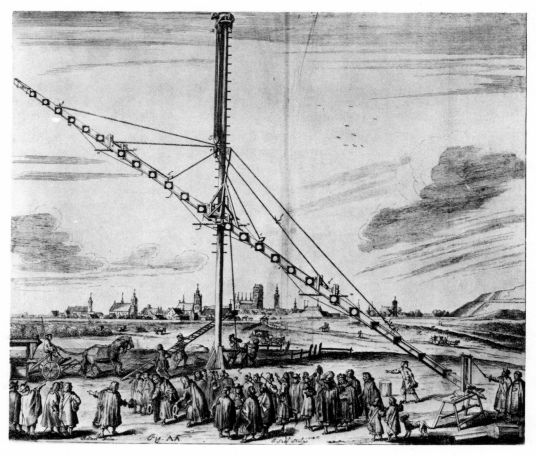

Telescope. Courtesy, Library of Congress.

ones of better magnification, like those of the Laputans, came into existence and, though Swift did not live to see it, he had scored a nice bit of prediction.

21 *two lesser Stars, or Satellites, which revolve about Mars.* This one is a far more interesting prediction and is, in fact, frequently cited as the most remarkable scientific prediction ever made in literature. For, as a matter of fact, although such information was not known in Swift's time, Mars *does* possess two satellites and only two. Those two satellites, however, were not discovered until 1877, 151 years after the publication of *Gulliver's Travels*. Only then did the world catch up to Laputan astronomy.

This has aroused considerable awe and led to speculation about Swift's having arcane knowledge of some sort or other. (I remember at least one tongue-in-cheek article suggesting Swift was a Martian.)

Actually, the prediction is not quite as startling as it sounds. In 1610, Galileo had discovered four satellites revolving about Jupiter. Since Earth had one and Jupiter had four satellites, Kepler, who was fond of number mysticism, at once speculated that Mars, which lay between Earth and Jupiter, ought to have two satellites.

That notion was very much in the air in Swift's time and Swift used it since it worked in convenient-

ly for his purposes. That Mars actually does have two satellites is pure coincidence, for it is now known that Jupiter has many more than four satellites. The present number of known Jovian satellites is thirteen.

22 *the innermost is distant from the Center of the primary Planet exactly three of his Diameters, and the outermost five.* Mars's diameter is 4,220 miles. What Swift is saying is that the inner satellite of Mars is 12,660 miles from the center of Mars and the outer satellite is 21,100.

The actual satellites proved indeed to be very close to Mars and this, too, is considered part of the marvel of Swift's prediction. That, however, is only a matter of common sense on Swift's part. If the satellites were farther removed from Mars they would be easy to discover. It is their closeness to Mars (and their smallness) that obscures them in the brightness of the Martian glow and that prevented their discovery for so long.

If we consider the actual satellites, Phobos (the inner one) is 5,810 miles from the center of Mars, and Deimos (the outer one) is 14,600 miles from the center. The real satellites are even closer to Mars than Swift guessed.

"They have observed ninety-three different Comets." Herbert Cole, 1899.

23 *the former revolves in the Space of ten Hours, and the latter in Twenty-one and an Half.* In actual fact, Phobos revolves about Mars in 7.65 hours and Deimos in 30.3 hours. The correspondence looks close enough to make Swift's guess all the more amazing. Given the distance of a satellite from a planet, however, and guessing at the mass of the planet, you can calculate the orbital periods of the satellite.

24 *the Squares of their periodical Times, are . . . in the same Proportion with the Cubes of their Distance from the Center of Mars.* This is Kepler's third law of planetary motion, which Swift clearly used to work out his periods of revolution.

25 *governed by the same Law of Gravitation.* From Newton's law of gravitation, it is easy to deduce that Kepler's laws of planetary motion must exist. If the Martian satellites obey Kepler's laws, therefore, that is a strong piece of evidence that Newton's gravitational theory is correct. This is one place where Swift brings himself to refer to Newton's work without sneering.

26 *the Theory of Comets, which at present is very lame and defective.* In Europe, only one comet had had its orbit worked out (see Chapter 2 of this part, note 24), and as it had not yet returned, one couldn't be sure whether that one calculation was correct or not.

27 *having their Estates below on the Continent.* Many Englishmen of the upper classes held estates in Ireland and might have been expected, in theory, to find it in their self-interest for the land to prosper. Unfortunately, many absentee English landlords had a tendency to squeeze their Irish tenants to the limit, choosing immediate revenue over a healthy long-term investment. This was made the easier since they did not visit the estates and could not with their own eyes see the misery they caused.

28 *deprive them of the Benefit of Sun and the Rain.* This is usually taken to symbolize the possible interference of the English government with Irish trade, thus reducing Ireland to economic penury.

29 *pelted from above with great Stones.* This may be, perhaps, the first description of aerial bombardment in literature.

Town, and the Lands about it; whereby he can deprive them of **28** the Benefit of the Sun and the Rain, and consequently afflict the Inhabitants with Dearth and Diseases. And if the Crime deserve it, they are at the same time pelted from above with great Stones, **29** against which they have no Defence, but by creeping into Cellars or Caves, while the Roofs of their Houses are beaten to Pieces. But if they still continue obstinate, or offer to raise Insurrections; he proceeds to the last Remedy, by letting the Island drop directly upon their Heads, which makes a universal Destruction both of Houses and Men. However, this is an extremity to which the Prince is seldom driven, neither indeed is he willing to put it in Execution; nor dare his Ministers advise him to an Action, which as it would render them odious to the People, so it would be a great Damage to their own Estates that lie all below; for the Island is the King's Demesn.

But there is still indeed a more weighty Reason, why the Kings of this Country have been always averse from executing so terrible an Action, unless upon the utmost Necessity. For if the Town in-

30 *tall Rocks.* Swift is now talking about the resistance of Ireland to English tyranny, a resistance he supported, thereby becoming a hero to the Irish. To avoid problems, however, he speaks symbolically here. The tall rocks, for instance, are taken to refer to the Irish-based nobility.

31 *high Spires.* The Irish clergy (the Anglicans rather than the submerged Catholics, of course, of whom Swift takes no account).

32 *Pillars of Stone.* The Irish merchants.

33 *crack by too great a Choque.* Read literally, the adamant that undercoats Laputa would seem to be diamond, which is indeed brittle enough to crack under such circumstances (a shock).

Read symbolically, Swift seems to be saying that the English constitution (which is the basis of the English court system) could not withstand acts so unpopular as to give rise to extensive popular resistance. In the century before *Gulliver's Travels* was published, popular resistance resulted in the execution of one king, Charles I, and the exile of another, James II. George I was by no means popular, and waiting in the wings was the Pretender, who called himself James III, and with whom the Tories were in sympathy.

34 *About three years before my arrival among them.* Swift now goes on to talk of the specific case of the attempt to foist upon the Irish a debased coinage without their consent. This was striking pretty near the crown itself, since William Wood, the man who was to produce the coins, had bought the privilege from the duchess of Kendall, who was the king's mistress. To avoid trouble, this last portion of the chapter was omitted when *Gulliver's Travels* was first published and was not included until an edition of 1899. Even the 1735 Faulkner edition which is used in this book as text and which incorporated most of Swift's corrections, omitted this passage—which is here added.

35 *Lindalino.* Generally taken to represent Dublin.

36 *progress.* See Part II, Chapter 8, note 3.

37 *combustible fuel.* Swift probably refers to his own pamphlets, which proved really combustible, firing such a rage in Ireland that the entire coinage proposal was called off.

30 tended to be destroyed should have in it any tall Rocks, as it generally falls out in the larger Cities; a Situation probably chosen at first with a View to prevent such a Catastrophe: Or if it abound in **31,32** high Spires or Pillars of Stone, a sudden Fall might endanger the Bottom or under Surface of the Island, which although it consist as I have said, of one entire Adamant two hundred Yards thick, **33** might happen to crack by too great a Choque, or burst by approaching too near the Fires from the Houses below; as the Backs both of Iron and Stone will often do in our Chimneys. Of all this the People are well apprized, and understand how far to carry their Obstinacy, where their Liberty or Property is concerned. And the King, when he is highest provoked, and most determined to press a City to Rubbish, orders the Island to descend with great Gentleness, out of a Pretence of Tenderness to his People, but indeed for fear of breaking the Adamantine Bottom; in which Case it is the Opinion of all their Philosophers, that the Load-stone could no longer hold it up, and the whole Mass would fall to the Ground.

34 *About three years before my arrival among them, while the King was in his progress over his dominions, there happened an extraordinary accident which had like to have put a period to the fate of that* **35** *monarchy, at least as it is now instituted. Lindalino, the second city* **36** *in the kingdom, was the first his Majesty visited in his progress. Three days after his departure the inhabitants, who had often complained of great oppressions, shut the town gates, seized on the governor, and with incredible speed and labour erected four large towers, one at every corner of the city (which is an exact square), equal in height to a strong pointed rock that stands directly in the centre of the city. Upon the top of each tower, as well as upon the rock, they fixed a great loadstone, and in case their design should fail, they* **37** *had provided a vast quantity of the most combustible fuel, hoping to burst therewith the adamantine bottom of the island, if the loadstone project should miscarry.*

It was eight months before the King had perfect notice that the Lindalinians were in rebellion. He then commanded that the island should be wafted over the city. The people were unanimous, and had laid in store of provisions. The King hovered over them several days to deprive them of the sun and the rain. He ordered many packthreads to be let down, yet not a person offered to send up a petition, but instead thereof, very bold demands, the redress of all their grievances, great immunities, the choice of their own governor, and other the like exorbitances. Upon which his Majesty commanded all the inhabitants of the island to cast great stones from the lower gallery into the town; but the citizens had provided against this mischief by conveying their persons and effects into the four towers, and other strong buildings, and vaults underground.

The King being now determined to reduce this proud people, ordered that the island should descend gently within forty yards of the top of the towers and rock. This was accordingly done; but the officers employed in that work found the descent much speedier than usual, and by turning the loadstone could not without great difficulty keep it in a firm position, but found the island inclining to fall. They sent the King immediate intelligence of this astonishing event, and begged his Majesty's permission to raise the island higher; the King consented, a general council was called, and the officers of the loadstone ordered to attend. One of the oldest and expertest among them obtained leave to try an experiment. He took a strong line of an hundred yards, and the island being raised over the town above the attracting power they had felt, he fastened a piece of adamant to the end of his line, which had in it a mixture of iron mineral, of the same nature with that whereof the bottom or lower surface of the island is composed, and from the lower gallery let it down slowly towards the top of the towers. The adamant was not descended four yards, before the officer felt it drawn so strongly downwards that he could hardly pull it back. He then threw down several small pieces of adamant, and observed that they were all violently attracted by the top of the tower. The same experiment was made on the other three towers, and on the rock with the same effect. **38**

This incident broke entirely the King's measures, and (to dwell no longer on other circumstances) he was forced to give the town their own conditions. **39**

I was assured by a great minister that if the island had descended so near the town as not to be able to raise itself, the citizens were determined to fix it for ever, to kill the King and all his servants, and entirely change the government. **40**

By a fundamental Law of this Realm, neither the King nor either of his two elder Sons, are permitted to leave the Island; nor the Queen till she is past Child-bearing. **41**

38 *iron mineral.* Magnetite (see Chapter 3 of this part, note 8).

39 *forced to give the town their own conditions.* This is a clear reference to the failure of the coinage scheme in August 1725, just a year before *Gulliver's Travels* was published.

40 *kill the King.* Here Swift as much as says that revolution and a royal execution, after the fashion of Charles I, would have followed if the coinage proposal had not been withdrawn. No wonder the printers cautiously refused to print the passage.

41 *neither the King nor either of his two elder Sons, are permitted to leave the Island.* Such a rule did indeed apply to George I, and Swift mentions it to heighten the identification of the King of Laputa with George I. George, however, managed to get the rule modified and visited Hanover periodically, to the indignation of many of his British subjects.

The queen of Laputa. Gavarni, 1850s. Courtesy, Library of Congress.

1 *Women, Tradesmen, Flappers, and Court-Pages.* In other words, Gulliver could find companionship only with nonintellectuals. These included men of the lower classes and all women. As always, it was taken for granted that women, by the mere fact of being women, were not intellectual.

The Author leaves Laputa, is conveyed to Balnibarbi, arrives at the Metropolis. A description of the Metropolis and the Country adjoining. The Author hospitably received by a Great Lord. His Conversation with that Lord.

LTHOUGH I cannot say that I was ill treated in this Island, yet I must confess I thought my self too much neglected, not without some Degree of Contempt. For neither Prince nor People appeared to be curious in any Part of Knowledge, except Mathematicks and Musick, wherein I was far their inferior, and upon that Account very little regarded.

On the other Side, after having seen all the Curiosities of the Island, I was very desirous to leave it, being heartily weary of those People. They were indeed excellent in two Sciences for which I have great Esteem, and wherein I am not unversed; but at the same time so abstracted and involved in Speculation, that I never met with such disagreeable Companions. I conversed only with Women, Tradesmen, *Flappers,* and Court-Pages, during two Months of my Abode there; by which at last I rendered my self extremely contemptible; yet these were the only People from whom I could ever receive a reasonable Answer.

I had obtained by hard Study a good Degree of Knowledge in their Language: I was weary of being confined to an Island where I received so little Countenance; and resolved to leave it with the first Opportunity.

There was a great Lord at Court, nearly related to the King, and for that Reason alone used with Respect. He was universally reckoned the most ignorant and stupid Person among them. He had performed many eminent Services for the Crown, had great natural and acquired Parts, adorned with Integrity and Honour; but so ill an Ear for Musick, that his Detractors reported he had been often known to beat Time in the wrong Place; neither could his Tutors without extreme Difficulty teach him to demonstrate the most easy Proposition in the Mathematicks. He was pleased to shew me many Marks of Favour, often did me the Honour of a Visit, desired to be informed in the Affairs of *Europe*, the Laws and Customs, the Manners and Learning of the several Countries where I had travelled. He listened to me with great Attention, and made very wise Observations on all I spoke. He had two *Flappers* attending him for State, but never made use of them except at Court, and in Visits of Ceremony; and would always command them to withdraw when we were alone together.

I intreated this illustrious Person to intercede in my Behalf with his Majesty for Leave to depart; which he accordingly did, as he was pleased to tell me, with Regret: For, indeed he had made me several Offers very advantageous, which however I refused with Expressions of the highest Acknowledgment.

On the 16*th* Day of *February*, I took Leave of his Majesty and **2** the Court. The King made me a Present to the Value of about two Hundred Pounds *English*; and my Protector his Kinsman as much more, together with a Letter of Recommendation to a Friend of his in *Lagado*, the Metropolis: The Island being then hovering over a Mountain about two Miles from it, I was let down from the lowest Gallery, in the same Manner as I had been taken up.

The Continent, as far as it is subject to the Monarch of the *Flying Island*, passeth under the general Name of *Balnibarbi*; and the Metropolis, as I said before, is called *Lagado*. I felt some little Satisfaction in finding my self on firm Ground. I walked to the City without any Concern, being clad like one of the Natives, and sufficiently instructed to converse with them. I soon found out the Person's House to whom I was recommended; presented my Letter from his Friend the Grandee in the Island, and was received with much Kindness. This great Lord, whose Name was *Munodi*, **3** ordered me an Apartment in his own House, where I continued during my Stay, and was entertained in a most hospitable Manner.

The next Morning after my Arrival he took me in his Chariot to see the Town, which is about half the Bigness of *London*; but the Houses very strangely built, and most of them out of Repair. The People in the Streets walked fast, looked wild, their Eyes fixed, and were generally in Rags. We passed through one of the Town Gates, and went about three Miles into the Country, where I saw many Labourers working with several Sorts of Tools in the Ground but was not able to conjecture what they were about; neither did I observe any Expectation either of Corn or Grass, although the Soil appeared to be excellent. I could not forbear admiring at these **4** odd Appearances both in Town and Country; and I made bold to desire my Conductor, that he would be pleased to explain to me what could be meant by so many busy Heads, Hands and Faces, both in the Streets and the Fields, because I did not discover any good Effects they produced; but on the contrary, I never knew a

2 *the 16th Day of February*. It is now 1708.

3 *Munodi*. There is considerable disagreement as to whom Lord Munodi might represent. The easiest way out is to suggest he is a combination of Oxford and Bolingbroke (see Part I, Chapter 2, note 17), the fallen Tory leaders. Some suggest, though, that he is Viscount Middleton, lord chancellor of Ireland, who, although a Whig, sided with Swift in the matter of the coinage dispute. Others say it was Sir William Temple (1628–1699).

Swift was Temple's secretary in 1689, and again from 1696 to 1699, and Temple wrote an essay, "Of Ancient and Modern Learning," in which he strongly favored what was ancient—as did Swift in his *Battle of the Books*, published in 1704. The identification of Munodi with Temple seems to make sense since, as we shall see, Munodi is a strong advocate of the ancient ways of doing things.

4 *admiring*. See Part I, Chapter 1, note 26.

5 *Cabal.* From the Hebrew word *qabbālāh*, meaning "received information." Since it was usually received by revelation, it was hidden from ordinary people, and thus came to mean secret or occult information. For that reason, the word "cabal" came to be applied to any secret combination of like-minded people aiming at some end they do not wish to make public.

It came to be used in politics particularly, because in 1667 there was a group of ministers who ran the government under Charles II, and whose names were Clifford, Arlington, Buckingham, Ashley, and Lauderdale. The initials spelled CABAL, but that was a coincidence and is unrelated to the derivation of the word.

6 *discharged for Insufficiency.* Discharged for incompetency. This seems to support the view that Oxford and Bolingbroke are the people represented by Munodi. In that case, we might consider Lagado as representing London.

7 *he doubted.* "To doubt" in Swift's time meant "to fear" or "to be apprehensive about."

8 *throw down his Houses . . . destroy all his Plantations, and cast others into such a Form as modern Usage required.* Here Swift satirizes the attempts at improvements in agriculture based on science which were being put into effect in the early eighteenth century, and compares these newfangled methods with the good old ways that worked so well. Swift's apologists tend to explain that Swift was not trying to denounce all change, but was against the tendency to praise the new simply because it was new while abandoning the old simply because it was old. We can't argue with that, except that anyone reading *Gulliver's Travels* is bound to see that Swift falls into the opposite trap—praising the old simply because it was old and denouncing the new for no other reason than that it was new.

Soil so unhappily cultivated, Houses so ill contrived and so ruinous, or a People whose Countenances and Habit expressed so much Misery and Want.

5
6
This Lord *Munodi* was a Person of the first Rank, and had been some Years Governor of *Lagado;* but by a Cabal of Ministers was discharged for Insufficiency. However the King treated him with Tenderness, as a well-meaning Man, but of a low contemptible Understanding.

When I gave that free Censure of the Country and its Inhabitants, he made no further Answer than by telling me, that I had not been long enough among them to form a Judgment; and that the different Nations of the World had different Customs; with other common Topicks to the same Purpose. But when we returned to his Palace, he asked me how I liked the Building, what Absurdities I observed, and what Quarrel I had with the Dress or Looks of his Domesticks. This he might safely do; because every Thing about him was magnificent, regular and polite. I answered, that his Excellency's Prudence, Quality, and Fortune, had exempted him from those Defects which Folly and Beggary had produced in others. He said, if I would go with him to his Country House about Twenty Miles distant, where his Estate lay, there would be more Leisure for this Kind of Conversation. I told his Excellency, that I was entirely at his Disposal; and accordingly we set out next Morning.

During our Journey, he made me observe the several Methods used by Farmers in managing their Lands; which to me were wholly unaccountable: For except in some very few Places, I could not discover one Ear of Corn, or Blade of Grass. But, in three Hours travelling, the Scene was wholly altered; we came into a most beautiful Country; Farmers Houses at small Distances, neatly built, the Fields enclosed, containing Vineyards, Corngrounds and Meadows. Neither do I remember to have seen a more delightful Prospect. His Excellency observed my Countenance to clear up; he told me with a Sigh, that there his Estate began, and would continue the same till we should come to his House. That his Countrymen ridiculed and despised him for managing his Affairs no better, and for setting so ill an Example to the Kingdom; which however was followed by very few, such as were old and wilful, and weak like himself.

We came at length to the House, which was indeed a noble Structure, built according to the best Rules of ancient Architecture. The Fountains, Gardens, Walks, Avenues, and Groves were all disposed with exact Judgment and Taste. I gave due Praises to every Thing I saw, whereof his Excellency took not the least Notice till after Supper; when, there being no third Companion, he
7, 8
told me with a very melancholy Air, that he doubted he must throw down his Houses in Town and Country, to rebuild them after the present Mode; destroy all his Plantations, and cast others into such a Form as modern Usage required; and give the same Directions to all his Tenants, unless he would submit to incur the Censure of Pride, Singularity, Affectation, Ignorance, Caprice; and perhaps encrease his Majesty's Displeasure.

That the Admiration I appeared to be under, would cease or diminish when he had informed me of some Particulars, which probably I never heard of at Court, the People there being too

Illustration by Rex Whistler, 1930.

9 *Academy of Projectors in Lagado.* A satire on the Royal Society of London.

10 *none of these Projects are yet brought to Perfection.* Swift is a little impatient. A half century after his death, the steam engine *was* perfected and *did* do the work of ten, and more.

much taken up in their own Speculations, to have Regard to what passed here below.

The Sum of his Discourse was to this Effect. That about Forty Years ago, certain Persons went up to *Laputa,* either upon Business or Diversion; and after five Months Continuance, came back with a very little Smattering in Mathematicks, but full of Volatile Spirits acquired in that Airy Region. That these Persons upon their Return, began to dislike the Management of every Thing below; and fell into Schemes of putting all Arts, Sciences, Languages, and Mechanics upon a new Foot. To this End they pro-
9 cured a Royal Patent for erecting an Academy of PROJECTORS in *Lagado*: And the Humour prevailed so strongly among the People, that there is not a Town of any Consequence in the Kingdom without such an Academy. In these Colleges, the Professors contrive new Rules and Methods of Agriculture and Building, and new Instruments and Tools for all Trades and Manufacture, whereby, as they undertake, one Man shall do the Work of Ten; a Palace may be built in a Week, of Materials so durable as to last for ever without repairing. All the Fruits of the Earth shall come to Maturity at whatever Season we think fit to chuse, and increase an Hundred Fold more than they do at present; with innumerable
10 other happy Proposals. The only Inconvenience is, that none of

A projector. Herbert Cole. 1899.

these Projects are yet brought to Perfection; and in the mean time, the whole Country lies miserably waste, the Houses in Ruins, and the People without Food or Cloaths. By all which, instead of being discouraged, they are Fifty Times more violently bent upon prosecuting their Schemes, driven equally on by Hope and Despair: That, as for himself, being not of an enterprizing Spirit, he was content to go on in the old Forms; to live in the Houses his Ancestors had built, and act as they did in every Part of Life without Innovation. That, some few other Persons of Quality and Gentry had done the same; but were looked on with an Eye of Contempt and ill Will, as Enemies to Art, ignorant, and ill Commonwealths- **11** men, preferring their own Ease and Sloth before the general Improvement of their Country.

His Lordship added, that he would not by any further Particulars prevent the Pleasure I should certainly take in viewing the grand Academy, whither he was resolved I should go. He only desired me to observe a ruined Building upon the Side of a Mountain about three Miles distant, of which he gave me this Account. That he had a very convenient Mill within Half a Mile of his House, turned by a Current from a large River, and sufficient for his own Family as well as a great Number of his Tenants. That, about seven Years ago, a Club of those Projectors came to him with Proposals to destroy this Mill, and build another on the Side of that Mountain, on the long Ridge whereof a long Canal must be cut for a Repository of Water, to be conveyed up by Pipes and Engines to supply the Mill: Because the Wind and Air upon a Height agitated the Water, and thereby made it fitter for Motion: And because the Water descending down a Declivity would turn the Mill with half the Current of a River whose Course is more upon a Level. He said, that being then not very well with the Court, and pressed by many of his Friends, he complied with the Proposal; and after employing an Hundred Men for two Years, the Work miscarried, the Projectors went off, laying the Blame intirely upon him; railing at him ever since, and putting others upon the same Experiment, with equal Assurance of Success, as well as equal Disappointment.

In a few Days we came back to Town; and his Excellency, considering the bad Character he had in the Academy, would not go with me himself, but recommended me to a Friend of his to bear me Company thither. My Lord was pleased to represent me as a great Admirer of Projects, and a Person of much Curiosity and easy Belief; which indeed was not without Truth; for I had my self been a Sort of Projector in my younger Days. **12**

11 *ill Commonwealths-men.* A commonwealth is a government that, in theory, represents the general welfare (the common weal) of the people as a whole. "Commonwealths-men" are those who concern themselves with the welfare of the people as a whole rather than only for their own private concerns. "Ill commonwealths-men" would be the opposite.

12 *Projector.* A project is some scheme or design of varying degrees of likelihood. If the scheme is a harebrained one or a dishonest one, a projector is a promoter or a con-man. Surely none of these things would describe Gulliver. We could suppose that to Gulliver, the word projector would here be used to describe an honest piece of research (however disappointing its results might be), and a "projector" would then be what we would call today an "inventor" or even a "research scientist."

The projectors described in this chapter, however, are harebrained lunatics who, it seems, would reverse the natural order of things. Apparently, Swift made use of some of the researches actually proposed or in progress at the Royal Society. I can well believe it. It is always possible to go down the list of research projects at any university or institution and come up with a collection of titles that will sound hilarious. By appropriate exaggeration and a careful omission of all the necessary explanations of the purposes and applications of any given project, any sober scientist can easily be made to sound like a crackpot.

1 *Warden*. A word derived from the same source as "guardian." The official referred to would be called "the receptionist" today.

2 *extracting Sun-Beams out of Cucumbers*. This has come to symbolize the epitome of useless projects, thanks to this mention in *Gulliver's Travels*.

Thus, in *Princess Ida*, a century and a half later, when William Schwenck Gilbert (1836–1911) satirized women's education, he can think of nothing better to symbolize the folly of women trying to use their brains. He says: "And weasels at their slumbers/They trepan—they trepan:/To get sunbeams from cucumbers,/They've a plan—they've a plan."

However, for "Sun-Beams" let us think "energy;" for "cucumbers" let us think "plant world." Do we get energy out of the plant world? We've been doing so ever since human beings have been burning wood. Moreover, scientists are concerned these days with the possibility of cultivating fast-growing oily plants that can yield enough fuel to serve as a vital source of energy that, among other things, could be used to run generators that deliver electricity. In that sense we'll be getting the equivalent of sunbeams out of the equivalent of cucumbers—and the last laugh will be on Swift.

3 *intreated me to give him something as an Encouragement to Ingenuity*. Swift has something there. Scientific research is generally starved for funds, even though research in general has returned a millionfold all that has been invested in it.

The Author permitted to see the Grand Academy of Lagado. The Academy largely described. The Arts wherein the Professors employ themselves.

HIS Academy is not an entire single Building, but a Continuation of several Houses on both Sides of a Street; which growing waste, was purchased and applyed to that Use.

1 I was received very kindly by the Warden, and went for many Days to the Academy. Every Room hath in it one or more Projectors; and I believe I could not be in fewer than five Hundred Rooms.

The first Man I saw was of a meagre Aspect, with sooty Hands and Face, his Hair and Beard long, ragged and singed in several Places. His Clothes, Shirt, and Skin were all of the same Colour.

2 He had been Eight Years upon a Project for extracting Sun-Beams out of Cucumbers, which were to be put into Vials hermetically sealed, and let out to warm the Air in raw inclement Summers. He told me, he did not doubt in Eight Years more, that he should be able to supply the Governors Gardens with Sun-shine at a reasonable Rate; but he complained that his Stock was low, and in-

3 treated me to give him something as an Encouragement to Ingenuity, especially since this had been a very dear Season for Cucumbers. I made him a small Present, for my Lord had furnished

Chemistry in the eighteenth century.

4 *to reduce human Excrement to its original Food.* This is not nearly so ridiculous a project as might be thought. It is exactly what has been done as long as life has existed on earth. Through billions of years, living wastes have been recycled through the activities of living cells to materials that serve as food once more. In fact, when human wastes ("night soil") are used as plant fertilizer in China and elsewhere, it is reconverted to food. But when moderns use chemical fertilizers, the Swifts of today, in their longing for the old ways, would have us go back to the use of night soil as "natural fertilizer."

As a matter of fact, if manned space flights of any length are to be undertaken in the future, there will have to be a recycling of food, water, and air, and human excrement will indeed have to be restored to its original food state in one way or another. At that time the poor "projector" of these pages will finally be recognized as an unappreciated pioneer in a vital piece of research.

5 *to calcine Ice into Gunpowder.* The word "calcine" is from the Latin word for "lime." It is used for the process whereby limestone (calcium carbonate) is strongly heated to drive off the volatile carbon dioxide and leave behind lime (calcium oxide). By extension, it is used for any process that will drive off volatile material by heat, leaving a powdery substance behind.

Naturally, if ice is heated, it is melted and vaporized and leaves no solid at all behind, let alone gunpowder. And yet . . .

From water, it is possible to obtain deuterium and of that to make a nuclear fusion bomb which would be many million times as intense an explosive as gunpowder. Could the projector at the Academy of Lagado have had some inkling of this, one wonders?

6 *the Malleability of Fire.* That is malleable which is capable of being beaten into shape. Metals are malleable, but brittle solids such as rocks and glass are not. Liquids are certainly not malleable, gases even less so. Fire, as usually envisaged, is actually a hot and glowing gas mixture, but in ancient times, it was viewed as a separate element on a par with air, water, and earth, and more subtle and shapeless than any gas. Consequently, fire is farthest removed from malleability. And yet . . .

Uranium and plutonium are metals, and malleable, and each is the source of a radiation, a nuclear fire more deadly than anything Swift knew or could imagine. Do not these metals then represent malleable fire?

7 *building Houses, by . . . working downwards to the Foundation.* Once steel-girdered skyscrapers came into being in 1884, it became possible to set up the steel skeleton and then build the superstructure from the top down if that were wanted. Again, when the time comes that we build structures in space, "up" and "down" will lose their meaning and construction will be freed of the constraints of gravity.

8 *to mix Colours . . . by feeling and smelling.* In Swift's time, there was still no hint that there might be such

me with Money on purpose, because he knew their Practice of begging from all who go to see them.

I went into another Chamber, but was ready to hasten back, being almost overcome with a horrible Stink. My Conductor pressed me forward, conjuring me in a Whisper to give no Offence, which would be highly resented; and therefore I durst not so much as stop my Nose. The Projector of this Cell was the most ancient Student of the Academy. His Face and Beard were of a pale Yellow; his Hands and Clothes dawbed over with Filth. When I was presented to him, he gave me a very close Embrace, (a Compliment I could well have excused.) His Employment from his first **4** coming into the Academy, was an Operation to reduce human Excrement to its original Food, by separating the several Parts, removing the Tincture which it receives from the Gall, making the Odour exhale, and scumming off the Saliva. He had a weekly Allowance from the Society, of a Vessel filled with human Ordure, about the Bigness of a *Bristol* Barrel.

5 I saw another at work to calcine Ice into Gunpowder; who like-
6 wise shewed me a Treatise he had written concerning the Malleability of Fire, which he intended to publish.

There was a most ingenious Architect who had contrived a new **7** Method for building Houses, by beginning at the Roof, and working downwards to the Foundations; which he justified to me by the like Practice of those two prudent Insects the Bee and the Spider.

There was a Man born blind, who had several Apprentices in **8** his own Condition: Their Employment was to mix Colours for Painters, which their Master taught them to distinguish by feeling

"I . . . was . . . almost overcome with a horrible Stink." Gavarni. 1850s. Courtesy, Library of Congress.

"The Walls and Ceiling were all hung round with Cobwebs." Herbert Cole. 1899.

a thing as invisible light. It was not till 1800 that the German-British astronomer, Sir William Herschel (1738–1822), discovered infrared light. The next year, the German physicist, Johann Wilhelm Ritter (1776–1810), discovered ultraviolet light. Nowadays, we know of a vast stretch of some sixty octaves of electromagnetic radiation, of which visible light forms only a single octave. And throughout this vast band, scientists can distinguish the wavelengths (which, in visible light define the color) with great precision, though the light is unseen. Even the colors of visible light can be distinguished with greater accuracy by spectroscopy than by the direct use of unaided human sight.

9 *plowing the Ground with Hogs, to save the Charges of Plows, Cattle, and Labour.* To be sure, the use of hogs is clearly not practical, but the notion of labor-saving devices in agriculture was a very fruitful one. In Swift's time, and even today in some regions, ninety-five percent of the population must labor in the fields to feed themselves and the remaining five percent. In contemporary United States, less than five percent of the population are engaged in agriculture and, thanks to the use of labor-saving machinery, they can feed themselves, the remaining ninety-five percent, and many in nations overseas. The advocates of the "old ways" long for a return to labor-intensive agriculture, but I suspect that few of those advocates plan to become farm laborers themselves when the clock is turned back.

10 *Masts.* The nuts of trees, particularly beechnuts.

11 *the fatal Mistake . . . of using Silk-Worms.* The substitution of spider webs for silk is not practical, though it was worth a try, I suppose. After all, silk is not the ultimate. In this century, nylon has virtually replaced it, and other synthetic fibers have become increasingly important. Then, too, if silk had not yet reached Europe, Swift would undoubtedly have waxed very merry over the Laputan projector who tried to make a fine linen from the cocoons of caterpillars.

12 *a vast Number of Flies most beautifully coloured.* There were attempts to extract dyes from colored insects in Swift's time (though not for the purpose of having the dyes fed to other animals in order to color their secretions). It is not, however, a completely, foolish idea. Cochineal is a red dye obtained from female scale insects.

and smelling. It was indeed my Misfortune to find them at that Time not very perfect in their Lessons; and the Professor himself happened to be generally mistaken: This Artist is much encouraged and esteemed by the whole Fraternity.

In another Apartment I was highly pleased with a Projector, who had found a Device of plowing the Ground with Hogs, to save **9** the Charges of Plows, Cattle, and Labour. The Method is this: In an Acre of Ground you bury at six Inches Distance, and eight deep, a Quantity of Acorns, Dates, Chesnuts, and other Masts or Vege- **10** tables whereof these Animals are fondest; then you drive six Hundred or more of them into the Field, where in a few Days they will root up the whole Ground in search of their Food, and make it fit for sowing, at the same time manuring it with their Dung. It is true, upon Experiment they found the Charge and Trouble very great, and they had little or no Crop. However, it is not doubted that this Invention may be capable of great Improvement.

I went into another Room, where the Walls and Ceiling were all hung round with Cobwebs, except a narrow Passage for the Artist to go in and out. At my Entrance he called aloud to me not to disturb his Webs. He lamented the fatal Mistake the World had been **11** so long in of using Silk-Worms, while we had such plenty of domestick Insects, who infinitely excelled the former, because they understood how to weave as well as spin. And he proposed farther, that by employing Spiders, the Charge of dying Silks would be wholly saved; whereof I was fully convinced when he shewed me a vast Number of Flies most beautifully coloured, wherewith he **12**

13 *up the Anus*. In Swift's time, enemas had become a very fashionable treatment for a variety of real or fancied ailments, and this just carries it a satiric step farther.

14 *lank as a dried Bladder*. A bladder is any hollow inflatable sac. Those of living organisms (the urinary bladder, or the gall bladder), if dried, become stiff and inflexible and cannot be inflated.

15 *adventitious Wind*. Something is "adventitious" when it is not there naturally but has been added from the outside.

fed his Spiders; assuring us, that the Webs would take a Tincture from them; and as he had them of all Hues, he hoped to fit every Body's Fancy, as soon as he could find proper Food for the Flies, of certain Gums, Oyls, and other glutinous Matter, to give a Strength and Consistence to the Threads.

There was an Astronomer who had undertaken to place a Sun-Dial upon the great Weather-Cock on the Town-House, by adjusting the annual and diurnal Motions of the Earth and Sun, so as to answer and coincide with all accidental Turnings of the Wind.

I was complaining of a small Fit of the Cholick; upon which my Conductor led me into a Room, where a great Physician resided, who was famous for curing that Disease by contrary Operations from the same Instrument. He had a large Pair of Bellows, with a long slender Muzzle of Ivory. This he conveyed eight Inches **13** up the Anus, and drawing in the Wind, he affirmed he could make **14** the Guts as lank as a dried Bladder. But when the Disease was more stubborn and violent, he let in the Muzzle while the Bellows was full of Wind, which he discharged into the Body of the Patient; then withdrew the Instrument to replenish it, clapping his Thumb strongly against the Orifice of the Fundament; and this **15** being repeated three or four Times, the adventitious Wind would rush out, bringing the noxious along with it (like Water put into a Pump) and the Patient recovers. I saw him try both Experiments upon a Dog, but could not discern any Effect from the former. After the latter, the Animal was ready to burst, and made so violent a Discharge, as was very offensive to me and my Companions. The Dog died on the Spot, and we left the Doctor endeavouring to recover him by the same Operation.

I visited many other Apartments, but shall not trouble my Reader with all the Curiosities I observed, being studious of Brevity.

"I saw him try both Experiments upon a Dog." J. J. Grandville. 1835. Courtesy. Library of Congress.

I had hitherto seen only one Side of the Academy, the other being appropriated to the Advancers of speculative Learning; of whom I shall say something when I have mentioned one illustrious Person more, who is called among them *the universal Artist.* He told us, he had been Thirty Years employing his Thoughts for the Improvement of human Life. He had two large Rooms full of wonderful Curiosities, and Fifty Men at work. Some were condensing Air into a dry tangible Substance, by extracting the Nitre, and letting the aqueous or fluid Particles percolate: Others softening Marble for Pillows and Pin-cushions; others petrifying the Hoofs of a living Horse to preserve them from foundring. The Artist himself was at that Time busy upon two great Designs: The first, to sow Land with Chaff, wherein he affirmed the true seminal Virtue to be contained, as he demonstrated by several Experiments which I was not skilful enough to comprehend. The other was, by a certain Composition of Gums, Minerals, and Vegetables outwardly applied, to prevent the Growth of Wool upon two young Lambs; and he hoped in a reasonable Time to propagate the Breed of naked Sheep all over the Kingdom.

We crossed a Walk to the other Part of the Academy, where, as I have already said, the Projectors in speculative Learning resided.

The first Professor I saw was in a very large Room, with Forty Pupils about him. After Salutation, observing me to look earnestly upon a Frame, which took up the greatest Part of both the Length and Breadth of the Room; he said, perhaps I might wonder to see him employed in a Project for improving speculative Knowledge by practical and mechanical Operations. But the World would soon be sensible of its Usefulness; and he flattered himself, that a more noble exalted Thought never sprang in any other Man's Head. Every one knew how laborious the usual Method is of attaining to Arts and Sciences; whereas by his Contrivance, the most ignorant Person at a reasonable Charge, and with a little bodily Labour, may write Books in Philosophy, Poetry, Politicks, Law, Mathematicks and Theology, without the least Assistance from Genius or Study. He then led me to the Frame, about the Sides whereof all his Pupils stood in Ranks. It was Twenty Foot square, placed in the Middle of the Room. The Superficies was composed of several Bits of Wood, about the Bigness of a Dye, but some larger than others. They were all linked together by slender Wires. These Bits of Wood were covered on every Square with Papers pasted on them; and on these Papers were written all the Words of their Language in their several Moods, Tenses, and Declensions, but without any Order. The Professor then desired me to observe, for he was going to set his Engine at work. The Pupils at his Command took each of them hold of an Iron Handle, whereof there were Forty fixed round the Edges of the Frame; and giving them a sudden Turn, the whole Disposition of the Words was entirely changed. He then commanded Six and Thirty of the Lads to read the several Lines softly as they appeared upon the Frame; and where they found three or four Words together that might make Part of a Sentence, they dictated to the four remaining Boys who were Scribes. This Work was repeated three or four Times, and at every Turn the Engine was so contrived, that the Words shifted into new Places, as the square Bits of Wood moved upside down.

Six Hours a-Day the young Students were employed in this

16

17

18

19

20

16 *condensing Air . . . by extracting the Nitre.* In Swift's time, the chemical nature of air was unknown. Some people supposed it to have a component called nitre or niter, but there was no clear statement of its nature or properties. This sentence is therefore gibberish, more completely so than even Swift intended.

17 *foundring.* To go lame.

18 *Chaff, wherein he affirmed the true seminal Virtue to be contained.* Chaff is the husk or outer covering of kernels of grain. It is dead tissue and cannot possibly have the "true seminal virtue." Swift is deliberately turning common sense on its head to make his satiric point.

19 *naked Sheep.* The notion of modifying the characteristics of domestic animals (or plants, for that matter) is by no means a ridiculous one. Human beings have been doing this since prehistoric times, in fact, by judicious matings and by taking advantage of random mutations. Domestic animals now come in large numbers of varieties, almost all of which are far removed in many respects from the original wild animals from which they are descended.

The satiric point Swift is making is that the projector is trying to foster a characteristic (lack of wool) that is the precise opposite of what is wanted.

Swift does not suggest that this modification is to be achieved through careful mating, however, but through chemical means applied externally. He assumes that a characteristic produced on two lambs by external treatment would then be transmitted to their offspring. The belief that this can be so is called a belief in "the inheritance of acquired characteristics."

Such a belief has always been folk wisdom, but was given formal scientific backing by the French naturalist, Jean Baptiste de Lamarck (1744–1829), in 1809. It was a blind alley, though, and was replaced by Darwin's theory of evolution by natural selection a half century later. Even so, the Swiftian notion has cropped up now and then. In our own time, Trofim Lysenko (1898–1976) adopted the notion in the Soviet Union and thus crippled Soviet genetics for several decades.

20 *Dye.* Die. A small cube. We know it better in its plural form, "dice."

21 *the general Proportion . . . between the Numbers of Particles, Nouns, and Verbs, and other Parts of Speech.* This is one of the best-known bits of scientific satire in this section of the book, and yet Swift, without knowing it, had something there.

As given here it sounds very much like that old bromide that if a thousand monkeys are set to tapping the keys of a typewriter at random, they would, given enough time, turn out all the books in the British Museum (or in the Library of Congress).

The catch is, of course, "given enough time." The entire lifetime of the universe would probably not be enough for a significant chance of turning out a page of significant prose.

However, that bit about making the strictest computation of the various components of the language puts Swift on the right track (and is another example of his astonishing, if accidental, prescience).

We no longer have to have long rows and tiers of blocks to be turned by hand, as shown in the illustration. We have computers now which can work their way through random combinations millions of times faster than human beings can.

Furthermore, if the complete works of certain writers are analyzed, and if, instead of counting the frequency of individual words, we work out the frequency of two word, three word, and four word combinations, a computer could turn out prose which, while still meaningless, begins to sound more and more like Shakespeare, or the Bible, or Dickens, or whatever author is being considered.

While the computerized production of books is not yet on the horizon, it is by no means totally inconceivable.

22 *to steal Inventions from each other.* About fifty years before *Gulliver's Travels* was published, Isaac Newton and Gottfried Leibniz both worked out the principles of the calculus at about the same time, and probably independently. Questions arose about who was first and who deserved to get the credit. The controversy degenerated into rather vicious infighting, and accusations of plagiarism filled the air. Swift may have been alluding to that thunderous controversy in this passage.

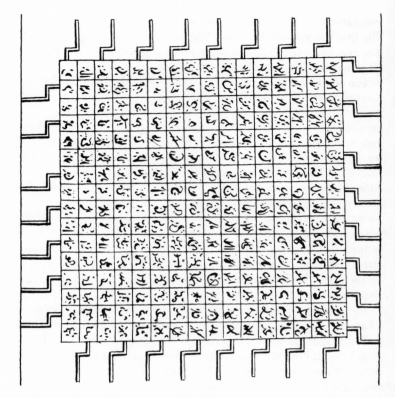

Illustration from the first edition. London, 1726. Courtesy. Rare Book Division. The New York Public Library.

Labour; and the Professor shewed me several Volumes in large Folio already collected, of broken Sentences, which he intended to piece together; and out of those rich Materials to give the World a compleat Body of all Arts and Sciences; which however might be still improved, and much expedited, if the Publick would raise a Fund for making and employing five Hundred such Frames in *Lagado,* and oblige the Managers to contribute in common their several Collections. He assured me, that this Invention had employed all his Thoughts from his Youth; that he had emptied the whole Vocabulary into his Frame, and made the strictest Compu-

21 tation of the general Proportion there is in Books between the Numbers of Particles, Nouns, and Verbs, and other Parts of Speech.

I made my humblest Acknowledgments to this illustrious Person for his great Communicativeness; and promised if ever I had the good Fortune to return to my native Country, that I would do him Justice, as the sole Inventor of this wonderful Machine; the Form and Contrivance of which I desired Leave to delineate upon Paper as in the Figure here annexed. I told him, although it were

22 the Custom of our Learned in *Europe* to steal Inventions from each other, who had thereby at least this Advantage, that it became a Controversy which was the right Owner; yet I would take such Caution, that he should have the Honour entire without a Rival.

We next went to the School of Languages, where three Professors sat in Consultation upon improving that of their own Country. The first Project was to shorten Discourse by cutting Polysyllables into one, and leaving out Verbs and Participles; because in Reality all things imaginable are but Nouns.

The other, was a Scheme for entirely abolishing all Words whatsoever: And this was urged as a great Advantage in Point of Health as well as Brevity. For, it is plain, that every Word we speak is in some Degree a Diminution of our Lungs by Corrosion; and consequently contributes to the shortning of our Lives. An Expedient was therefore offered, that since Words are only Names for *Things*, it would be more convenient for all Men to carry about them, such *Things* as were necessary to express the particular Business they are to discourse on. And this Invention would certainly have taken Place, to the great Ease as well as Health of the Subject, if the Women in Conjunction with the Vulgar and Illiterate had not threatened to raise a Rebellion, unless they might be allowed the Liberty to speak with their Tongues, after the Manner of their Forefathers: Such constant irreconcileable Enemies to Science are the common People. However, many of the most Learned and Wise adhere to the new Scheme of expressing themselves by *Things*; which hath only this Inconvenience attending it; that if a Man's Business be very great, and of various Kinds, he must be obliged in Proportion to carry a greater Bundle of *Things* upon his Back, unless he can afford one or two strong Servants to attend him. I have often beheld two of those Sages almost sinking under the Weight of their Packs, like Pedlars among us; who when they met in the Streets would lay down their Loads, open their Sacks, and hold Conversation for an Hour together; then put up their Implements, help each other to resume their Burthens, and take their Leave.

But, for short Conversations a Man may carry Implements in his Pockets and under his Arms, enough to supply him, and in his House he cannot be at a Loss; therefore the Room where Company meet who practice this Art, is full of all *Things* ready at Hand, requisite to furnish Matter for this Kind of artificial Converse.

Another great Advantage proposed by this Invention, was, that it would serve as an universal Language to be understood in all civilized Nations, whose Goods and Utensils are generally of the same Kind, or nearly resembling, so that their Uses might easily be comprehended. And thus, Embassadors would be qualified to treat with foreign Princes or Ministers of State, to whose Tongues they were utter Strangers.

I was at the Mathematical School, where the Master taught his Pupils after a Method scarce imaginable to us in *Europe*. The Proposition and Demonstration were fairly written on a thin Wafer, with Ink composed of a Cephalick Tincture. This the Student was to swallow upon a fasting Stomach, and for three Days following eat nothing but Bread and Water. As the Wafer digested, the Tincture mounted to his Brain, bearing the Proposition along with it. But the Success hath not hitherto been answerable, partly by some Error in the *Quantum* or Composition, and partly by the Perverseness of Lads; to whom this Bolus is so nauseous, that they generally steal aside, and discharge it upwards before it can operate; neither have they been yet persuaded to use so long an Abstinence as the Prescription requires.

23 **23** *improving that of their own Country.* Next Swift satirizes the desire of some members of the Royal Society to simplify and clarify the language in one way or another. Swift exaggerates, of course, to sharpen the satire.

24 *swallow upon a fasting Stomach.* Some years ago, it was found that if very simple animals called planarians were trained to respond to a flashing light in some way, and if those trained planarians were then cut up and fed to untrained planarians, the untrained planarians could be trained more quickly than otherwise. Apparently, the training had produced a specific type of molecule in the planarians, and when those planarians were eaten, at least some of the molecules would be incorporated whole into the body of the eater, which was then more easily trained.

The results were not beyond dispute, but even if they were accepted, what is true for the simple digestive tracts of planarians is not necessarily true for the much more elaborate digestive tracts of human beings, which are much less likely to allow any molecules to pass through them unchanged for incorporation into the eater's body. Nevertheless, there were tongue-in-cheek suggestions at once that students might learn fastest by eating their professors—perhaps an echo from this passage in *Gulliver's Travels*.

Conversation. C. E. Brock, 1894. Courtesy, Library of Congress.

24

1 *wild impossible Chimaeras*. Swift switches satirical ground here by having the projectors suggest wise remedies and treating them as foolish and unheard of.

Chimaera is a Greek word meaning a "she-goat" and is used in Greek mythology for a particularly deadly variety of goat, one that had a lion's head and a snake for a tail. While this is no more impossible and fanciful than many other creatures in myths, chimaera has come to be applied to any idea that is fanciful and impossible in the extreme.

N the School of political Projectors I was but ill entertained; the Professors appearing in my Judgment wholly out of their Senses; which is a Scene that never fails to make me melancholy. These unhappy People were proposing Schemes for persuading Monarchs to chuse Favourites upon the Score of their Wisdom, Capacity and Virtue; of teaching Ministers to consult the publick Good; of rewarding Merit, great Abilities, and eminent Services; of instructing Princes to know their true Interest, by placing it on the same Foundation with that of their People: Of chusing for Employments Persons qualified to exercise them; with many other

1 wild impossible Chimæras, that never entered before into the Heart of Man to conceive; and confirmed in me the old Observation, that there is nothing so extravagant and irrational which some Philosophers have not maintained for Truth.

But, however I shall so far do Justice to this Part of the Academy, as to acknowledge that all of them were not so visionary. There was a most ingenious Doctor who seemed to be perfectly versed in the whole Nature and System of Government. This illustrious Person had very usefully employed his Studies in finding out effectual Remedies for all Diseases and Corruptions, to which the several Kinds of publick Administration are subject by the Vices or Infirmities of those who govern, as well as by the Licentiousness of those who are to obey. For Instance: Whereas all Writers and Reasoners have agreed, that there is a strict universal Resemblance between the natural and the political Body; can there be any thing more evident, than that the Health of both must be preserved, and the Diseases cured by the same Prescriptions? It is allowed, that Senates and great Councils are often troubled with redundant ebullient, and other peccant Humours; with many Diseases of the **2** Head, and more of the Heart; with strong Convulsions, with grievous Contractions of the Nerves and Sinews in both Hands, but especially the Right: With Spleen, Flatus, Vertigoes and Deliriums; with scrophulous Tumours full of fœtid purulent Matter; with sower frothy Ructations; with Canine Appetites and Crudeness of Digestion; besides many others needless to mention. This Doctor therefore proposed, that upon the meeting of a Senate, certain Physicians should attend at the three first Days of their sitting, and at the Close of each Day's Debate, feel the Pulses of every Senator; after which having maturely considered, and consulted upon the Nature of the several Maladies, and the Methods of Cure; they should on the fourth Day return to the Senate-House, attended by their Apothecaries stored with proper Medicines; and before the Members sat, administer to each of them Lenitives. **3** Aperitives, Abstersives, Corrosives, Restringents, Palliatives, Laxatives, Cephalalgicks, Ictericks, Apophlegmaticks, Acousticks, as their several Cases required; and according as these Medicines should operate, repeat, alter, or omit them at the next Meeting.

This Project could not be of any great Expence to the Publick; and might in my poor Opinion, be of much Use for the Dispatch of Business in those Countries where Senates have any Share in the legislative Power; beget Unanimity, shorten Debates, open a few Mouths which are now closed, and close many more which are now open; curb the Petulancy of the Young, and correct the Positiveness of the Old; rouze the Stupid, and damp the Pert.

Again; Because it is a general Complaint that the Favourites of Princes are troubled with short and weak Memories; the same Doctor proposed, that whoever attended a first Minister, after having

2 *peccant Humours.* The word "humor" is from the Latin word for "fluid," as is the word "humidity." A theory dating back to the Greek Hippocratic school of medicine assumes that the health and temperament of the human body depends upon the proper balance of the various fluids that make it up. Imbalances lead to ailments. Thus Swift lists redundant (overexcessive), ebullient (overexcited), and peccant (faulty) humors.

Harking back to this theory, one can speak of being in a good humor, in a surly humor, and so on. Comedies frequently made use of characters who had some particular temperamental bent that was always on display (like Jack Benny's cheapness) because of a more or less permanent imbalance of their humors. To show a man "in his humor" was sure to get laughs, so that "humorous" came to mean "funny."

Medical theory in Swift's time had not passed much beyond its Greek origins, and humors were still spoken of.

3 *Lenitives . . . Acousticks.* In Swift's time, physicians regularly prescribed any number of substances from the plant and mineral world which were harmless at best and dangerous-to-deadly at worst. They were used to produce certain effects on the body which (it was hoped) would cure the disorder being treated. Since in virtually no case did physicians have the slightest idea as to either the true cause or cure of a disorder, the dosages were chosen for imaginary virtues.

Swift here lists various sorts of effects to be produced, achieving his satire by a dazzling display of mock learning.

A lenitive is supposed to have a soothing effect; an aperitive, an appetite-stimulating one; an abstersive, a cleaning one; a corrosive, a disintegrating one; a restringent, a puckering one; a palliative, a calming one; a laxative, a purgative one; a cephalalgic, a headache-soothing one; an icteric, a jaundice-curing one; an apophlegmatic, an expectorant one; and an acoustic, a hearing-sharpening one.

A minister. Herbert Cole, 1899.

4 *two nice Operators.* The word "nice" in Swift's day carried the connotation of "delicately precise."

5 *Occiputs.* The back of the head. Presumably the internal matter, that is, the back of the brain, is to be cut off with it.

6 *commodious.* From a Latin word meaning "convenient." These days it is used particularly for that kind of convenience that comes with ample space or room for whatever purpose you have in mind, but in Swift's time the more general meaning was common.

told his Business with the utmost Brevity, and in the plainest Words; should at his Departure give the said Minister a Tweak by the Nose, or a Kick in the Belly, or tread on his Corns, or lug him thrice by both Ears, or run a Pin into his Breech, or pinch his Arm black and blue; to prevent Forgetfulness: And at every Levee Day repeat the same Operation, till the Business were done or absolutely refused.

He likewise directed, that every Senator in the great Council of a Nation, after he had delivered his Opinion, and argued in the Defence of it, should be obliged to give his Vote directly contrary; because if that were done, the Result would infallibly terminate in the Good of the Publick.

When Parties in a State are violent, he offered a wonderful Contrivance to reconcile them. The Method is this. You take an Hundred Leaders of each Party; you dispose them into Couples of **4** such whose Heads are nearest of a Size; then let two nice Operators saw off the *Occiput* of each Couple at the same Time, in such a **5** Manner that the Brain may be equally divided. Let the *Occiputs* thus cut off be interchanged, applying each to the Head of his opposite Party-man. It seems indeed to be a Work that requireth some Exactness; but the Professor assured us, that if it were dextrously performed, the Cure would be infallible. For he argued thus; that the two half Brains being left to debate the Matter between themselves within the Space of one Scull, would soon come to a good Understanding, and produce that Moderation as well as Regularity of Thinking, so much to be wished for in the Heads of those, who imagine they came into the World only to watch and govern its Motion: And as to the Difference of Brains in Quantity or Quality, among those who are Directors in Faction; the Doctor assured us from his own Knowledge, that it was a perfect Trifle.

I heard a very warm Debate between two Professors, about the **6** most commodious and effectual Ways and Means of raising Money without grieving the Subject. The first affirmed, the justest Method would be to lay a certain Tax upon Vices and Folly; and the Sum fixed upon every Man, to be rated after the fairest Manner by a Jury of his Neighbours. The second was of an Opinion directly contrary; to tax those Qualities of Body and Mind for which Men chiefly value themselves; the Rate to be more or less according to the Degrees of excelling; the Decision whereof should be left entirely to their own Breast. The highest Tax was upon Men, who are the greatest Favourites of the other Sex; and the Assessments according to the Number and Natures of the Favours they have received; for which they are allowed to be their own Vouchers. Wit, Valour, and Politeness were likewise proposed to be largely taxed, and collected in the same Manner, by every Person giving his own Word for the Quantum of what he possessed. But, as to Honour, Justice, Wisdom and Learning, they should not be taxed at all; because, they are Qualifications of so singular a Kind, that no Man will either allow them in his Neighbour, or value them in himself.

The Women were proposed to be taxed according to their Beauty and Skill in Dressing; wherein they had the same Privilege with the Men, to be determined by their own Judgment. But Constancy, Chasity, good Sense, and good Nature were not rated, because they would not bear the Charge of Collecting.

To keep Senators in the Interest of the Crown, it was proposed that the Members should raffle for Employments; every Man first

7 *Men are never so serious . . . as when they are at Stool.* This is generally assumed to be a sarcastic reference to the trial of Bishop Atterbury (see Part I, Chapter 6, note 31) for his part in a Jacobite conspiracy. Some of the evidence against him was supposed to have been obtained from papers found in his chamber pot.

"It seems indeed to be a Work that requireth some Exactness." T. Morten, 1865. *Courtesy, Library of Congress.*

taking an Oath, and giving Security that he would vote for the Court, whether he won or no; after which the Losers had in their Turn the Liberty of raffling upon the next Vacancy. Thus, Hope and Expectation would be kept alive; none would complain of broken Promises, but impute their Disappointments wholly to Fortune, whose Shoulders are broader and stronger than those of a Ministry.

Another Professor shewed me a large Paper of Instructions for discovering Plots and Conspiracies against the Government. He advised great Statesmen to examine into the Dyet of all suspected Persons; their Times of eating; upon which Side they lay in Bed; with which Hand they wiped their Posteriors; to take a strict View of their Excrements, and from the Colour, the Odour, the Taste, the Consistence, the Crudeness, or Maturity of Digestion, form a Judgment of their Thoughts and Designs: Because Men are never **7** so serious, thoughtful, and intent, as when they are at Stool; which he found by frequent Experiment: For in such Conjunctures, when he used merely as a Trial to consider which was the best Way of

8 *Tribnia.* Clearly an anagram of Britain.

9 *Langden.* Just as clearly an anagram of England.

10 *Close-stool.* A stool or chair with a hole in it, beneath which is placed a chamber pot.

This entire paragraph is a clever bit of double satire. In the first place, it makes fun of the lengths to which the prosecution went in convicting Atterbury. In the absence of real proof they had to pretend that all kinds of innocent references in his letters signified other things (which might have been so, of course, except that the prosecution couldn't prove it).

Secondly, Swift chooses his parallels, pretending that it is ridiculous to derive, in each case, the latter from the former—but, of course, one can see that, if one is suspicious enough, a senate *is* very much like a flock of geese; a standing army *can* be viewed as a plague and so on.

11 *C[our]t.* In some editions this word is simply left out; in others, it is "c - - t." In the Faulkner edition, as you see, the missing letters are supplied and the word is written, ingenuously, as "C[our]t." Clearly, Gulliver would have no reason to refrain from writing "court." Elsewhere he uses it frequently enough, even in insulting ways, even in this very paragraph. Clearly, Swift intends the vulgar term for the female genitalia, "cunt," a term which, until quite recently, couldn't be shown in print.

12 *Anagrammatick Method.* Taking an apparently innocent message and rearranging its letters into a guilty one, as in the example given. Actually, this, too, is ingenuous. Governments and plotters in Swift's time and before used cryptographic systems more advanced and less easily solved than anagrams—although nothing compared to the advanced cryptography used today.

murdering the King, his Ordure would have a Tincture of Green; but quite different when he thought only of raising an Insurrection, or burning the Metropolis.

The whole Discourse was written with great Acuteness, containing many Observations both curious and useful for Politicians, but as I conceived not altogether compleat. This I ventured to tell the Author, and offered if he pleased to supply him with some Additions. He received my Proposition with more Compliance than is usual among Writers, especially those of the Projecting Species; professing he would be glad to receive farther Information.

8
9 I told him, that in the Kingdom of *Tribnia*, by the Natives called *Langden*, where I had long sojourned, the Bulk of the People consisted wholly of Discoverers, Witnesses, Informers, Accusers, Prosecutors, Evidences, Swearers; together with their several subservient and subaltern Instruments; all under the Colours, the Conduct, and pay of Ministers and their Deputies. The Plots in that Kingdom are usually the Workmanship of those Persons who desire to raise their own Characters of profound Politicians; to restore new Vigour to a crazy Administration; to stifle or divert general Discontents; to fill their Coffers with Forfeitures; and raise or sink the Opinion of publick Credit, as either shall best answer their private Advantage. It is first agreed and settled among them, what suspected Persons shall be accused of a Plot: Then, effectual Care is taken to secure all their Letters and other Papers, and put the Owners in Chains. These Papers are delivered to a Set of Artists very dextrous in finding out the mysterious Meanings of Words, Syllables and Letters. For Instance, they can decypher a **10** Close-stool to signify a Privy-Council; a Flock of Geese, a Senate; a lame Dog, an Invader; the Plague, a standing Army; a Buzard, a Minister; the Gout, a High Priest; a Gibbet, a Secretary of State; a Chamber pot, a Committee of Grandees; a Sieve, a Court Lady; a Broom, a Revolution; a Mouse-trap, an Employment; a bottom- **11** less Pit, the Treasury; a Sink, a C[our]t; a Cap and Bells, a Favourite; a broken Reed, a Court of Justice; an empty Tun, a General; a running Sore, the Administration.

When this Method fails, they have two others more effectual; which the Learned among them call Acrosticks, and Anagrams. *First*, they can decypher all initial Letters into political Meanings: Thus, *N*, shall signify a Plot; *B*, a Regiment of Horse; *L*, a Fleet at Sea. Or, *secondly*, by transposing the Letters of the Alphabet, in any suspected Paper, they can lay open the deepest Designs of a discontented Party. So for Example, if I should say in a Letter to a Friend, *Our Brother* Tom *hath just got the Piles*; a Man of Skill in this Art would discover how the same Letters which compose that Sentence, may be analysed into the following Words; *Resist,——* **12** *a Plot is brought home —— The Tour.* And this is the Anagrammatick Method.

The Professor made me great Acknowledgments for communicating these Observations, and promised to make honourable mention of me in his Treatise.

I saw nothing in this Country that could invite me to a longer Continuance; and began to think of returning home to *England*.

The Author leaves Lagado, arrives at Maldonada. No Ship ready. He takes a short Voyage to Glubbdubdrib. His Reception by the Governor.

HE Continent of which this Kingdom is a part, extends itself, as I have Reason to believe, Eastward to that unknown Tract of *America*, Westward of *California*, and North to the Pacifick Ocean, which is not **1** above an hundred and fifty Miles from *Lagado*; where there is a good Port and much Commerce with the great Island of *Luggnagg*; situated to the North-West about 29 Degrees North Latitude, and **2** 140 Longitude. This Island of *Luggnagg* stands South Eastwards of *Japan*, about an hundred Leagues distant. There is a strict Alliance between the *Japanese* Emperor and the King of *Luggnagg*, which affords frequent Opportunities of sailing from one Island to the other. I determined therefore to direct my Course this Way, in order to my Return to *Europe*. I hired two Mules with a Guide to shew me the Way, and carry my small Baggage. I took leave of my noble Protector, who had shewn me much Favour, and made me a generous Present at my Departure.

My Journey was without any Accident or Adventure worth relating. When I arrived at the Port of *Maldonada*, (for so it is called) there was no Ship in the Harbour bound for *Luggnagg*, nor like to be in some Time. The Town is about as large as *Portsmouth*. **3**

1 *Westward of California, and North of the Pacifick Ocean*. This location is not very different from that given for Brobdingnag, which Swift doesn't mention, of course.

2 *about 29 Degrees North Latitude, and 140 Longitude.* Luggnagg, as shown in the map at the beginning of this part, lies to the southwest of Balnibarbi and is of about the same size. If Luggnagg is located at 29 degrees north and 140 degrees (east) longitude, then it is indeed southeastward of Japan. In fact, it is five hundred miles due south of Tokyo and is just about halfway between that city and Iwo Jima. There are islets in the vicinity of Swift's imagined Luggnagg, but nothing of importance.

3 *Portsmouth*. An important seaport and naval base in Hampshire, on the south-central coast of England.

4 *Barque.* More commonly spelled "bark." A small sailing vessel.

5 *the Isle of Wight.* It lies just southwest of Portsmouth and has an area of 147 square miles. Glubbdubdrib, with one-third this area, is about two and a half times the size of the island of Manhattan.

6 *antick.* We are now likely to think of "antic" as signifying grotesque and ludicrous. Conceivably the guards are dressed grotesquely. However, in the light of what is to follow, it is much more likely that "antick" is an alternate and now obsolete variant of the word we now write as "antique." The guards, in other words, were dressed in an antique manner, or, as we would now say, in ancient fashion, which is only to be expected since they were spirits of the dead.

I soon fell into some Acquaintance, and was very hospitably received. A Gentleman of Distinction said to me, that since the Ships bound for *Luggnagg* could not be ready in less than a Month, it might be no disagreeable Amusement for me to take a Trip to the little Island of *Glubbdubdrib,* about five Leagues off to the South-West. He offered himself and a Friend to accompany me, and that **4** I should be provided with a small convenient Barque for the Voyage.

Glubbdubdrib, as nearly as I can interpret the Word, signifies the Island of *Sorcerers* or *Magicians.* It is about one third as large **5** as the Isle of *Wight,* and extreamly fruitful: It is governed by the Head of a certain Tribe, who are all Magicians. This Tribe marries only among each other; and the eldest in Succession is Prince or Governor. He hath a noble Palace, and a Park of about three thousand Acres, surrounded by a Wall of hewn Stone twenty Foot high. In this Park are several small Inclosures for Cattle, Corn and Gardening.

The Governor and his Family are served and attended by Domesticks of a Kind somewhat unusual. By his Skill in Necromancy, he hath Power of calling whom he pleaseth from the Dead, and commanding their Service for twenty four Hours, but no longer; nor can he call the same Persons up again in less than three Months, except upon very extraordinary Occasions.

When we arrived at the Island, which was about Eleven in the Morning, one of the Gentlemen who accompanied me, went to the Governor, and desired Admittance for a Stranger, who came on purpose to have the Honour of attending on his Highness. This was immediately granted, and we all three entered the Gate of the Palace between two Rows of Guards, armed and dressed after a **6** very antick Manner, and something in their Countenances that made my Flesh creep with a Horror I cannot express. We passed through several Apartments between Servants of the same Sort, ranked on each Side as before, till we came to the Chamber of Presence, where after three profound Obeysances, and a few general Questions, we were permitted to sit on three Stools near the lowest Step of his Highness's Throne. He understood the Language of *Balnibarbi,* although it were different from that of his Island. He desired me to give him some Account of my Travels; and to let me see that I should be treated without Ceremony, he dismissed all his Attendants with a Turn of his Finger, at which to my great Astonishment they vanished in an Instant, like Visions in a Dream, when we awake on a sudden. I could not recover myself in some Time, till the Governor assured me that I should receive no Hurt; and observing my two Companions to be under no Concern, who had been often entertained in the same Manner, I began to take Courage; and related to his Highness a short History of my several Adventures, yet not without some Hesitation, and frequently looking behind me to the Place where I had seen those domestick Spectres. I had the Honour to dine with the Governor, where a new Set of Ghosts served up the Meat, and waited at Table. I now observed myself to be less terrified than I had been in the Morning. I stayed till Sun-set, but humbly desired his Highness to excuse me for not accepting his Invitation of lodging in the Palace. My two Friends and I lay at a private House in the Town adjoining, which is the Capital of this little Island; and the next

Sorcery on the island of Glubbdubdrib. Ad. Laluze, 1875. Courtesy,
Library of Congress.

Morning we returned to pay our Duty to the Governor, as he was
pleased to command us.

After this Manner we continued in the Island for ten Days, most
Part of every Day with the Governor, and at Night in our Lodging.
I soon grew so familiarized to the Sight of Spirits, that after the
third or fourth Time they gave me no Emotion at all; or if I had
any Apprehensions left, my Curiosity prevailed over them. For his
Highness the Governor ordered me to call up whatever Persons I
would chuse to name, and in whatever Numbers among all the
Dead from the Beginning of the World to the present Time, and
commanded them to answer any Questions I should think fit to
ask; with this Condition, that my Questions must be confined
within the Compass of the Times they lived in. And one Thing I
might depend upon, that they would certainly tell me Truth; for
Lying was a Talent of no Use in the lower World.

7 *Alexander the Great.* 356–323 B.C.. He was the greatest conqueror of ancient times and, with the exception of Genghis Khan (1162–1227), the greatest of all time.

8 *the Battle of Arbela.* Also called the Battle of Guagamela, fought in Mesopotamia in 331 B.C.. It was Alexander's greatest victory, one in which he defeated the much larger army of Darius III (d. 330 B.C.), the king of Persia. As a result of this battle, Alexander conquered Persia, which was enormous in size compared to his home kingdom of Macedon.

9 *dyed of a Fever by excessive Drinking.* Right up to Swift's time and for a century beyond, it was quite common for people to die suddenly while still young since there were many simple ailments that were not understood and could not be cured by the physicians of the time. In fact, if the physicians were allowed to get at the sick, then their treatment was more likely to kill than to cure. In Swift's own time, not long before *Gulliver's Travels* was published, Louis XIV's sons and grandson were killed by medical treatment rather than by their sicknesses, and his great-grandson, who was to succeed him as Louis XV (1710–1774) in 1715, was only saved by being hidden by his nurse so that the physicians couldn't find him.

Nevertheless, sudden deaths were always greeted with incredulity, and every time someone died, particularly if he was a prominent person, the rumor was that it was by poison. The rumor was generally believed and often found its way into the more scandalous chronicles. To be sure, some people may indeed have been poisoned, but it seems completely out of the question that so many were poisoned as were reported to be.

As for Alexander the Great, he died suddenly at the age of thirty-three, so, of course, poison was suggested. However, Alexander was an alcoholic and died after a three-day banquet during which he drank heavily. Poison was not necessary for the job, unless you want to consider alcohol the poison, in which case it was self-administered.

One of Swift's purposes in this passage is to show that history cannot be believed.

10 *Hannibal.* 247–183 B.C.. Next to Alexander the Great and Genghis Khan, he was the most consummate warrior in history. A Carthaginian, he fought against Rome and defeated it in a series of remarkable battles. He might have won the war if he had been better supported by his pusillanimous home government.

Had Swift been a Whig, rather than a Tory, he might easily have made a very telling comparison between Marlborough and Hannibal to the disadvantage of Britain's Tory government.

11 *not a Drop of Vinegar in his Camp.* Hannibal managed to catch Rome by surprise by invading overland and crossing the Alps in 218 B.C.. It was a most difficult passage, which Hannibal managed with skill. According to some reports, when rocks blocked the way, he managed to split them by applying vinegar

Illustration by Rex Whistler, 1930.

I made my humble Acknowledgments to his Highness for so great a Favour. We were in a Chamber, from whence there was a fair Prospect into the Park. And because my first Inclination was to be entertained with Scenes of Pomp and Magnificence, I desired
7,8 to see *Alexander* the Great, at the Head of his Army just after the Battle of *Arbela;* which upon a Motion of the Governor's Finger immediately appeared in a large Field under the Window, where we stood. *Alexander* was called up into the Room: It was with great Difficulty that I understood his *Greek,* and had but little of my own.
9 He assured me upon his Honour that he was not poisoned, but dyed of a Fever by excessive Drinking.
10,11 Next I saw *Hannibal* passing the *Alps,* who told me he had not a Drop of Vinegar in his Camp.
12 I saw *Cæsar* and *Pompey* at the Head of their Troops just ready
13 to engage. I saw the former in his last great Triumph. I desired that the Senate of *Rome* might appear before me in one large Chamber
14,15 and a modern Representative, in Counterview, in another. The first seemed to be an Assembly of Heroes and Demy-Gods; the other a Knot of Pedlars, Pick-pockets, Highwaymen and Bullies.
The Governor at my Request gave the Sign for *Cæsar* and
16 *Brutus* to advance towards us. I was struck with a profound Ven-

Brutus and Caesar. J. J. Grandville, 1835. Courtesy, Library of Congress.

to the cracks. If the rocks were limestone, carbon dioxide gas would be produced in this way and the rock might split. Swift, however, chooses to suspect these tales are fictional, and he may be right.

12 *Caesar and Pompey . . . just ready to engage.* Gaius Julius Caesar (100–44 B.C.) and Pompey—Gnaeus Pompeius Magnus (106–48 B.C.)—were two generals in the last century of the Roman republic. They were sometimes allies, sometimes rivals.

In 49 B.C., the conservative senate won the assistance of Pompey and moved against Caesar. Caesar, far more capable than any of his opponents, invaded Italy. Pompey and the senate were forced to flee to Greece where, in 48 B.C., they confronted Caesar in the Battle of Pharsalus. Caesar was victorious in this battle (as he was in all his battles) and Pompey fled to Egypt where he was assassinated.

13 *his last great Triumph.* Caesar was granted a number of triumphs in Rome to celebrate his victories. The last one, referred to here, was in September 45 B.C., in which he celebrated his victory in Spain over the last of the adherents of the senatorial cause.

14 *a modern Representative.* This is, of course, the British Parliament.

15 *The first seemed to be . . . Demy-Gods; the other . . . bullies.* Distance lends enchantment. Swift here falls prey to his belief that what is old is good and idealizes the Roman senate. He shouldn't. The Roman senate in the republican days was, by and large, a collection of rapacious oligarchs, without honesty, justice, or pity, and with only a stubborn resolution in the face of looming disaster to recommend it. In fact, the description which Swift intended to apply to the British Parliament might serve just as well for the Roman senate. It is astonishing that Swift, in a section devoted to showing the unreliability of history, should fall such a victim to the lying propaganda of Roman encomiasts. Had he lived in the first century B.C., he would have had a satiric field day at the expense of those "Heroes and Demy-Gods."

16 *Brutus.* Marcus Junius Brutus (85–42 B.C.) was the leader in the conspiracy that succeeded in assassinating Julius Caesar on March 15, 44 B.C.

17 *the most consummate Virtue . . . in every Lineament of his Countenance.* It may be that Swift's extravagant praise of Brutus at the expense of Caesar is but another one of his strokes against Marlborough. He may even see himself as Brutus, bringing about the recall and disgrace of Marlborough with his satiric broadsides.

But then Swift is not alone in deifying Brutus. Roman historians in the second century A.D. indulged in a romantic longing for an idealized republic and they made a hero of Brutus. Brutus did not deserve it. He was, actually, a skinflint oligarch, an oppressor of the provinces he governed, an unskillful politician and general, and, worst of all, an ingrate.

eration at the Sight of *Brutus;* and could easily discover the most **17** consummate Virtue, the greatest Intrepidity, and Firmness of Mind, the truest Love of his Country, and general Benevolence for Mankind in every Lineament of his Countenance. I observed with much Pleasure, that these two Persons were in good Intelligence with each other; and *Cæsar* freely confessed to me, that the **18** greatest Actions of his own Life were not equal by many Degrees to the Glory of taking it away. I had the Honour to have much Conversation with *Brutus;* and was told that his Ancestor *Junius,* **19** *Socrates, Epaminondas, Cato* the Younger, Sir *Thomas More* and himself, were perpetually together: A *Sextumvirate* to which all the Ages of the World cannot add a Seventh. **20**

It would be tedious to trouble the Reader with relating what vast Numbers of illustrious Persons were called up, to gratify that insatiable Desire I had to see the World in every Period of Antiquity placed before me. I chiefly fed my Eyes with beholding the Destroyers of Tyrants and Usurpers, and the Restorers of Liberty to oppressed and injured Nations. But it is impossible to express the Satisfaction I received in my own Mind, after such a Manner as to make it a suitable Entertainment to the Reader.

Brutus had been a supporter of Pompey but had been freely forgiven by Caesar and placed in positions of trust. Brutus then lickspittled his benefactor and conspired against him in secret.

18 *Intelligence.* Information. To be "in good intelligence" is to be in the habit of exchanging information; in other words, to be friendly.

Sir Thomas More. Courtesy, Library of Congress.

19 *Junius . . . Sir Thomas More.* Lucius Junius Brutus, supposedly an ancestor of Marcus Junius Brutus, had helped overthrow the last king of Rome in 509 B.C., and had then served as one of the first two Roman consuls. His exalted reputation rested on his conducting a successful revolution, and on his love of country (or, at any rate, of oligarchy) above family, of which he gave proof when his two sons were con-

victed of conspiring against the new republican government and Brutus ordered them executed.

Socrates (470–399 B.C.) was the most famous of the Greek philosophers, and, largely through the writings of his pupil, Plato, was eventually near-deified as a Christ-like figure without faults. Nevertheless, some of the young aristocrats who absorbed his philosophy proved to be violently antidemocratic. In the aftermath of the Athenian defeat in the Peloponnesian War, one of them, Critias, subjected Athens to a reign of terror. When the democracy was restored, Socrates was convicted of corrupting the Athenian youth (with some reason) and was executed.

Epaminondas (418–362 B.C.) was a Theban general, the first to develop military tactics beyond the collide-and-slash technique. He defeated the Spartans at the Battle of Leuctra in 371 B.C. and ended their long military preeminence in Greece. He defeated them again at the Battle of Mantinea in 362 B.C., but died in action. He was an honest man and, as often happens as a consequence of honesty, he died poor.

Marcus Porcius Cato (95–46 B.C.) was called "Cato the Younger" to distinguish him from his great-grandfather of the same name (234–149 B.C.) who was called "Cato the Elder." Both were incorruptibly honest, but the Elder was a nasty skinflint, and the Younger a self-righteous prig. Cato the Younger fought in Africa against Caesar and committed suicide when the battle was lost.

Sir Thomas More (1478–1535) was the only modern Swift allowed to enter this company of ancients. More held to his principles, refusing to recognize Henry VIII as the head of the English church, for which he was executed.

20 *a Seventh.* If Swift had lived and written a century later, it is conceivable that he might have chosen to add George Washington, not so much for having won the independence of his country, but for not having taken advantage of his deed to make himself king.

AVING a Desire to see those Antients, who were most renowned for Wit and Learning, I set apart one Day on purpose. I proposed that *Homer* and *Aristotle* might **1** appear at the Head of all their Commentators; but these were so numerous, that some Hundreds **2** were forced to attend in the Court and outward Rooms of the Palace. I knew and could distinguish those two Heroes at first Sight, not only from the Croud, but from each other. *Homer* was the taller and comelier Person of the two, walked very erect for one of his Age, and his Eyes were the most quick and piercing I **3** ever beheld. *Aristotle* stooped much, and made use of a Staff. His Visage was meager, his Hair lank and thin, and his Voice hollow. I soon discovered, that both of them were perfect Strangers to the rest of the Company, and had never seen or heard of them before. And I had a Whisper from a Ghost, who shall be nameless, that these Commentators always kept in the most distant Quarters from their Principals in the lower World, through a Consciousness of Shame and Guilt, because they had so horribly misrepresented the Meaning of those Authors to Posterity. I introduced *Didymus* and **4**

1 *Homer and Aristotle*. Homer is supposed to have lived about 850 B.C. and to have been the author of *The Iliad* and *The Odyssey*. These are the oldest known works of Western literature and perhaps the most highly regarded.

Aristotle (384–322 B.C.) was the pupil of Plato, who was the pupil of Socrates. These three were the most influential philosophers who have ever lived.

Aristotle and Homer. J. J. Grandville, 1835. Courtesy, Library of Congress.

Pierre Gassendi. Courtesy, Library of Congress.

René Descartes. Courtesy, Library of Congress.

2 *Commentators.* Throughout ancient times, Homer was considered to embody the quintessence of literature, and Aristotle of science and learning. It seemed that there was nothing left for successors to do but explain and expound on their work, as indeed commentators have continued to do over the centuries, right up to Swift's time and our own.

3 *his Eyes were the most quick and piercing I ever beheld.* Swift is as intent on exposing historians as liars as he was, earlier, on exposing scientists as fools. The one point on which all traditions concerning Homer agreed was that he was blind.

4 *Didymus and Eustathius.* Didymus (80–10 B.C.) was an outstanding commentator who lived in Rome and is supposed to have written 3,500 commentaries on all sorts of authors, including, of course, Homer. His vast output gave him the surname of Chalcenturus ("brazen guts").

Eustathius (?–1194) was an archbishop of Thessalonica, who lived in the medieval Byzantine Empire and was a learned commentator of Homer. He was a religious reformer, highly thought of in his own times, and is considered a saint by the Greek Orthodox church.

5 *Scotus and Ramus.* John Duns Scotus (1265–1308) was born in Duns, Scotland, as his name attests, and was one of the great medieval interpreters of Aristotle's teachings. He and his followers were opponents of the interpretations of Aristotle worked out by Thomas Aquinas and his followers.

Petrus Ramus (1515–1572) is the Latinized form of the French, Pierre de la Ramée. He was a philosopher whose interpretations of Aristotle went very

Eustathius to *Homer,* and prevailed on him to treat them better than perhaps they deserved; for he soon found they wanted a Genius to enter into the Spirit of a Poet. But *Aristotle* was out of all Patience with the Account I gave him of *Scotus* and *Ramus,* as I presented them to him; and he asked them whether the rest of the Tribe were as great Dunces as themselves.

I then desired the Governor to call up *Descartes* and *Gassendi,* with whom I prevailed to explain their Systems to *Aristotle.* This great Philosopher freely acknowledged his own Mistakes in Natural Philosophy, because he proceeded in many things upon Conjecture, as all Men must do; and he found, that *Gassendi,* who had made the Doctrine of *Epicurus* as palatable as he could, and the *Vortices* of *Descartes,* were equally exploded. He predicted the same Fate to *Attraction,* whereof the present Learned are such zealous Asserters. He said, that new Systems of Nature were but new Fashions, which would vary in every Age; and even those who pretend to demonstrate them from Mathematical Principles, would flourish but a short Period of Time, and be out of Vogue when that was determined.

I spent five Days in conversing with many others of the antient Learned. I saw most of the first *Roman* Emperors. I prevailed on the Governor to call up *Eliogabalus's* Cooks to dress us a Dinner; but they could not shew us much of their Skill, for want of Materials. A *Helot* of *Agesilaus* made us a Dish of *Spartan* Broth, but I was not able to get down a second Spoonful.

The two Gentlemen who conducted me to the Island were pressed by their private Affairs to return in three Days, which I employed in seeing some of the modern Dead, who had made the greatest Figure for two or three Hundred Years past in our own and other Countries of *Europe;* and having been always a great Admirer of old illustrious Families, I desired the Governor would call up a Dozen or two of Kings with their Ancestors in order, for eight or much against those of the orthodox establishment. He was converted to Protestantism and was eventually assassinated in the course of the Saint Bartholomew Day's massacres.

6 *Dunces*. The Scotists were worsted by the Thomists, and the word "dunce," which we use today for someone who is ignorant and foolish, is thought to have originated from the derision poked at Duns Scotus' views by the Thomists. Swift plays on the word here.

7 *Descartes and Gassendi*. René Descartes (1596–1650) was a great French scientist and philosopher. He invented analytic geometry, an important branch of mathematics, and discarded the overworn subtleties of medieval philosophy. He worked out the science of thought on a new basis and introduced modern philosophy.
Another French philosopher, Pierre Gassendi (1592–1655), opposed the reasonings of Descartes but united with him in opposing Aristotelianism.

8 *his own Mistakes in Natural Philosophy*. Aristotle's logic, and his writings on literature, politics, and other subjects, could be debated but never proved or disproved. The arguments of the ancients in these subjects are still the arguments of our contemporaries, and will continue to be so indefinitely in all likelihood.
In "natural philosophy" (science), however, it is possible to disprove, and there Aristotle was proven finally and dramatically wrong in key aspects of physics by Galileo about 1600. By Swift's time, the shade of Aristotle would have to own up to "mistakes." Swift, in his idolatry of ancient learning, hates to see him do this and feels it necessary, therefore, to maintain that all the wise-guy scientists who showed Aristotle to be wrong, are themselves wrong, or will later be proven wrong.

9 *Epicurus*. 342–270 B.C. He was an eloquent spokesman for atomism, the notion that all matter is composed of ultra-tiny indivisible particles called "atoms." This had previously been maintained by Democritus (460–370? B.C.).
Aristotle opposed the notion of atomism and won out, for Aristotle's works survived and Epicurus' less-regarded works did not. However, Epicurus' doctrines were supported in the works of the Roman, Titus Lucretius Carus (95–52 B.C.), who wrote a poem describing Epicurean atomism in full. One copy of that poem survived and, once printing was invented, was printed. Gassendi had a copy of the poem and ardently supported atomism.

10 *the Vortices of Descartes, were equally exploded*. In attempting to explain the motions of the heavenly bodies, and to accept Copernican notions while not exactly giving up the notion of a stationary earth, Descartes devised a complex and unconvincing theory in which all space was filled with matter arranged in rotating vortices.
The vortices of Descartes were indeed exploded within half a century by Newton's theory of gravitation. Gassendi's atomism was *not* exploded, however-

er. It was further supported by the British chemist, Robert Boyle (1627–1691), and finally, nearly a century after the publication of *Gulliver's Travels*, the work of the English chemist, John Dalton (1766–1844) established atomism firmly as the basis of chemistry. There is no danger that atomism will ever be overturned (though it has been and will continue to be constantly deepened and made more subtle and sophisticated), whatever the spirit of Aristotle may say.

11 *Attraction*. Swift means what we today call "gravitation." Swift cannot miss the chance to sneer at his enemy, Newton, but Swift is wrong, just the same. Newton's theory went on to triumph over and over for two centuries after it was propounded. Finally, in 1916, Albert Einstein (1879–1955) worked out a more general and useful description of gravitation in his "general theory of relativity." This did not demonstrate Newton to be wrong, however, merely insufficient. General relativity is indistinguishable from Newton's theory at ordinary astronomical speeds and ordinary astronomical distances.

12 *new Systems of Nature . . . would vary in every Age*. This is just a case of Swiftian sour grapes and shows that Swift does not really understand science. To be sure, scientific conclusions vary with time, and are often mistaken, but the general movement is in the direction of the "truth." Theories are not so much replaced as improved on, thanks to the gathering of additional observations and the conducting of more subtle experiments.

13 *determined*. Ended.

14 *Eliogabalus's Cooks*. Heliogabalus (204–222) was Roman emperor from 218 to his death. Though he was only a teen-ager at the time, there were numerous tales about his debauchery and senseless luxury (which may well have been improved in the telling, since chroniclers were no more to be relied on in ancient times than in modern times). He was supposed to dine on rare, imported delicacies such as peacocks' tongues.

15 *A Helot of Agesilaus*. Agesilaus II (440–360 B.C.) was king of Sparta at the height of its power, and was still king when it was felled by Epaminondas (see Chapter 7 of this part, note 19). A helot was, originally, a native of Helos, a city near Sparta, which was captured by the Spartans early in their rise to power. The inhabitants of Helos were reduced to slavery, and eventually all Spartan slaves were called "helots" whatever their origin.

16 *Spartan Broth*. The Spartans in the years of their greatness maintained their military strength by rigorously training their warriors from the age of seven. They lived in military barracks in an ascetic manner that has been much admired through the ages by a variety of writers who have not had to live in that manner.
The Spartans ate at a common table, the chief item of their diet being a very filling, very wholesome,

and very plain soup. When Agesilaus led his army into Asia Minor and defeated the Persians, he made fun of Persian luxury by having the Persian cooks prepare a sumptuous Persian meal and then eating his Spartan broth in the midst of it. That the broth turned the stomach of anyone who was not used to it from childhood is attested by the story of the Athenian, who, having tasted it, said it was no wonder the Spartans were so brave in battle—with food like that to return to, death had no terrors.

17 *Fidlers.* Swindlers.

18 *nice.* See Chapter 6 of this part, note 4.

19 *Polydore Virgil.* 1470–1555. He was an Italian-English historian who wrote a history of England, including, particularly, the reign of Henry VII.

20 *Nec Vir fortis, nec Faemina Casta.* That is, the great house had "not one brave man, not one chaste woman."

21 *Pox.* Any disease that produces pustules, but it was most often understood to be syphilis. Syphilis was not referred to in European history until after Columbus' discovery of America. It is often said that Columbus' sailors picked up syphilis from the Caribbean Indians and brought it back to Europe with them.

On the other hand, there were frequent references to "leprosy" in the Middle Ages, a disease which suddenly fell off in incidence. It may be that the disease was always with Europeans but merely changed its name around 1500. Another possibility is that a mutated strain of the syphilis germ arose about 1500, so that what had been a mild infection became a serious one.

Whatever the explanation, syphilis was clearly associated with sexual intercourse, so that it was viewed as a punishment for sin. Those who suffered the disease were stricken not only with a terrible sickness but with scandal and the scorn of the self-righteous. Hidden under a deadly blanket of shame, the disease ravaged Europe (including many among its victims who were as righteous as any might be expected to be) for four centuries.

22 *an Interruption of Lineages by Pages . . . and Pickpockets.* Apparently, women were generally unfaithful in all the aristocratic houses. Note, however, that Swift automatically accepts the notion that aristocrats are a finer breed of human being than the lower classes, and that if aristocrats are unworthy, it is because of an infusion of lower-class blood into the line.

23 *disgusted with modern History.* Swift goes on to explain why, but he is being prejudiced here. The venality of historians in his time is undoubtedly no greater than in ancient times, and all the marvelous virtue that Swift accepts as characteristic of an older age is undoubtedly the product of just the same sort of self-serving lies.

nine Generations. But my Disappointment was grievous and unexpected. For, instead of a long Train with Royal Diadems, I saw in one Family two Fidlers, three spruce Courtiers, and an *Italian* Prelate. In another, a Barber, an Abbot, and two Cardinals; I have too great a Veneration for crowned Heads to dwell any longer on so nice a Subject: But as to Counts, Marquesses, Dukes, Earls, and the like, I was not so scrupulous. And I confess it was not without some Pleasure that I found my self able to trace the particular Features, by which certain Families are distinguished up to their Originals. I could plainly discover from whence one Family derives a long Chin; why a second hath abounded with Knaves for two Generations, and Fools for two more; why a third happened to be crack-brained, and a fourth to be Sharpers. Whence it came, what *Polydore Virgil* says of a certain great House, *Nec Vir fortis, nec Fœmina Casta.* How Cruelty, Falshood, and Cowardice grew to be Characteristicks by which certain Families are distinguished as much as by their Coat of Arms. Who first brought the Pox into a noble House, which hath lineally descended in scrophulous Tumours to their Posterity. Neither could I wonder at all this, when I saw such an Interruption of Lineages by Pages, Lacqueys, Valets, Coachmen, Gamesters, Fidlers, Players, Captains, and Pickpockets.

I was chiefly disgusted with modern History. For having strictly examined all the Persons of greatest Name in the Courts of Princes for an Hundred Years past, I found how the World had been misled by prostitute Writers, to ascribe the greatest Exploits in War to Cowards, the wisest Counsel to Fools, Sincerity to Flatterers, *Roman* Virtue to Betrayers of their Country, Piety to Atheists, Chastity to Sodomites, Truth to Informers. How many innocent and excellent Persons had been condemned to Death or Banishment, by the practising of great Ministers upon the Corruption of Judges, and the Malice of Factions. How many Villains had been exalted to the highest Places of Trust, Power, Dignity, and Profit: How great a Share in the Motions and Events of Courts, Councils, and Senates might be challenged by Bawds, Whores, Pimps, Parasites, and Buffoons: How low an Opinion I had of human Wisdom and Integrity, when I was truly informed of the Springs and Motives of great Enterprizes and Revolutions in the World, and of the contemptible Accidents to which they owed their Success.

Here I discovered the Roguery and Ignorance of those who pretend to write *Anecdotes,* or secret History; who send so many Kings to their Graves with a Cup of Poison; will repeat the Discourse between a Prince and chief Minister, where no Witness was by; unlock the Thoughts and Cabinets of Embassadors and Secretaries of State; and have the perpetual Misfortune to be mistaken. Here I discovered the true Causes of many great Events that have surprized the World: How a Whore can govern the Backstairs, the Back-stairs a Council, and the Council a Senate. A General confessed in my Presence that he got a Victory purely by the Force of Cowardice and ill Conduct: And an Admiral, that for want of proper Intelligence, he beat the Enemy to whom he intended to betray the Fleet. Three Kings protested to me, that in their whole Reigns they did never once prefer any Person of Merit, unless by Mistake or Treachery of some Minister in whom they confided: Neither would they do it if they were to live again; and they shewed with great Strength of Reason, that the Royal Throne could not be supported without Corruption; because, that positive, confident, restive Temper, which Virtue infused into Man, was a perpetual Clog to publick Business.

I had the Curiosity to enquire in a particular Manner, by what Method great Numbers had procured to themselves high Titles of Honour, and prodigious Estates; and I confined my Enquiry to a very modern Period: However, without grating upon present Times, because I would be sure to give no Offence even to Foreigners (for I hope the Reader need not be told that I do not in the least intend my own Country in what I say upon this Occasion) a great Number of Persons concerned were called up, and upon a very slight Examination, discovered such a Scene of Infamy, that I cannot reflect upon it without some Seriousness. Perjury, Oppression, Subornation, Fraud, Pandarism, and the like *Infirmities* were amongst the most excusable Arts they had to mention; and for these I gave, as it was reasonable, due Allowance. But when some confessed, they owed their Greatness and Wealth to Sodomy or Incest; others to the prostituting of their own Wives and Daughters; others to the betraying their Country or their Prince; some to poisoning, more to the perverting of Justice in order to destroy the Innocent: I hope I may be pardoned if these Discoveries inclined me a little to abate of that profound Veneration which I am naturally apt to pay to Persons of high Rank, who ought to be treated with the utmost Respect due to their sublime Dignity, by us their Inferiors.

I had often read of some great Services done to Princes and States, and desired to see the Persons by whom those Services were performed. Upon Enquiry I was told, that their Names were to be found on no Record, except a few of them whom History hath represented as the vilest Rogues and Traitors. As to the rest, I had never once heard of them. They all appeared with dejected Looks, and in the meanest Habit; most of them telling me they died in Poverty and Disgrace, and the rest on a Scaffold or a Gibbet.

Among others there was one Person whose Case appeared a little singular. He had a Youth about Eighteen Years old standing by his Side. He told me, he had for many Years been Commander of a Ship; and in the Sea Fight at *Actium*, had the good Fortune to break through the Enemy's great Line of Battle, sink three of their Capital Ships, and take a fourth, which was the sole Cause of *Antony's* Flight, and of the Victory that ensued: That the Youth standing by him, his only Son, was killed in the Action. He added, that upon the Confidence of some Merit, the War being at an End, he went to *Rome*, and solicited at the Court of *Augustus* to be preferred to a greater Ship, whose Commander had been killed; but without any regard to his Pretensions, it was given to a Boy who had never seen the Sea, the Son of a *Libertina*, who waited on one of the Emperor's Mistresses. Returning back to his own Vessel, he was charged with Neglect of Duty, and the Ship given to a favourite Page of *Publicola* the Vice-Admiral; whereupon he retired to a poor Farm, at a great Distance from *Rome*, and there ended his Life. I was so curious to know the Truth of this Story, that I desired *Agrippa* might be called, who was Admiral in that Fight. He appeared, and confirmed the whole Account, but with much more Advantage to the Captain, whose Modesty had extenuated or concealed a great Part of his Merit.

I was surprized to find Corruption grown so high and so quick

24 *Sodomites.* Those who practice some form of unorthodox sex. The name is usually applied to male homosexuals specifically, because of the biblical tale of Lot in the city of Sodom (see Genesis 19:4–9).

25 *Anecdotes, or secret History.* "Anecdote" is from the Greek, meaning "unpublished." In earlier times it referred to tales that purported to be revelations of a secret or confidential truth.

Thus, Procopius, a sixth century Byzantine historian, wrote accounts of the wars of his time in which he praised highly the emperor Justinian, the empress Theodora, and the general Belisarius. He is also supposed to be the author of *Anecdota*, an anonymous compilation of scurrilous tales about all three, which are supposed to be the behind-the-scenes "real" truth.

Swift, in his sardonic thrusts, may have been thinking of a contemporary work, *History of My Own Time* by Gilbert Burnet (1643–1715), the first portion of which was published, posthumously, in 1723. Burnet gave a favorable picture of Marlborough, which was enough to damn him in Swift's eyes.

26 *true Causes.* Swift speaks here of precisely the sort of stories "behind-the-scenes" authors are always telling. Whom are we to believe? When we think of all the inside stories told by people with actual roles in World War II incidents, in the Cuban crisis, in Watergate, and realize how mutually exclusive so many of the revelations are, we realize (as a friend of mine once said) that the past is as impenetrable as the future.

27 *Subornation.* Persuading someone, by bribery or otherwise, to commit an illegal act.

28 *Pandarism.* The act of serving as a go-between in love affairs; pimping. Pandarus, the go-between in the love affair of Troilus and Cressida as told by Shakespeare and, before him, by Chaucer, gave his name to the act.

29 *a Scaffold or a Gibbet.* A scaffold is a raised platform on which a criminal is executed. The purpose of raising him is so that more spectators can view the act and be properly impressed with the danger of breaking the law. A gibbet is an upright post with a horizontal extension. From the end of the extension, which allows for better viewing, a criminal can be hanged.

30 *Actium.* This was the greatest of the ancient sea battles. It was fought between Octavian and Mark Antony on September 2, 31 B.C., and was the climax of the civil wars that had racked the Roman republic in its final century.

31 *Antony's Flight.* At the height of the Battle of Actium, Octavian's ships rowed forward against Cleopatra's flagship. (She was Mark Antony's wife and, as queen of Egypt, was fighting with him.) To save the treasury, which she carried with her, she fled the fight, and Antony, besotted with love, fled after her—so the story goes.

27
28

29

30

31

32

33

34
35

36

According to Swift's "true" story, Antony fled because of the brave action of one of Octavian's captains (and for all we know something like that may indeed be the true story).

Either way, as a result of the flight, Octavian won the battle and all the Roman realm.

32 *Augustus.* Once Octavian controlled Rome, he managed to keep the forms of the republic but changed its spirit. He made himself the sole ruler under the name of "Imperator" ("Emperor") meaning "Leader." The Roman republic thus became the Roman Empire, and Octavian its first emperor. Once emperor, he changed his name to "Augustus" (the well-omened).

33 *the Son of a Libertina.* Libertina is not properly a name. The reference is to "the son of a Libertina," that is, the son of a liberated woman slave, a freedwoman. In order to deepen the irony, Swift has the honor go to someone from the lowest social ranks.

34 *Publicola.* This name belongs to no one known in history at this time. Swift probably made it up to give the tale circumstantial verity.

35 *there ended his Life.* The whole story is very unlikely, actually. Augustus was a firm ruler, as decent and virtuous as a ruler can be expected to be, and he surrounded himself with capable men.

It is very likely that Swift was telling the story not because it happened in Rome but because something like it happened in Britain and he expected his readers to see that. One possibility is that the tale is similar to that of Charles Mordaunt, third earl of Peterborough (1658–1735), who was an admiral in the War of the Spanish Succession and who, as a Tory, was treated badly (in Swift's opinion) by the Whig ministry.

36 *Agrippa.* Marcus Vipsanius Agrippa (63–12 B.C.), Octavian's right-hand man, his admiral, and the actual victor at the Battle of Actium.

in that Empire, by the Force of Luxury so lately introduced; which made me less wonder at many parallel Cases in other Countries, where Vices of all Kinds have reigned so much longer, and where the whole Praise as well as Pillage hath been engrossed by the chief Commander, who perhaps had the least Title to either.

As every Person called up made exactly the same Appearance he had done in the World, it gave me melancholy Reflections to observe how much the Race of human Kind was degenerate among us, within these Hundred Years past. How the Pox under all its Consequences and Denominations had altered every Lineament of an *English* Countenance; shortened the Size of Bodies, unbraced the Nerves, relaxed the Sinews and Muscles, introduced a sallow Complexion and rendered the Flesh loose and *rancid.*

I descended so low as to desire that some *English* Yeomen of the old Stamp, might be summoned to appear; once so famous for the Simplicity of their Manners, Dyet and Dress; for Justice in their Dealings; for their true Spirit of Liberty; for their Valour and Love of their Country. Neither could I be wholly unmoved after comparing the Living with the Dead, when I considered how all these pure native Virtues were prostituted for a Piece of Money by their Grand-children; who in selling their Votes, and managing at Elections have acquired every Vice and Corruption that can possibly be learned in a Court.

CHAPTER NINE

The Author's return to Maldonada. Sails to the Kingdom of Luggnagg. The Author confined. He is sent for to Court. The Manner of his admittance. The King's Great Lenity to his Subjects.

HE Day of our Departure being come, I took leave of his Highness the Governor of *Glubbdubdrib*, and returned with my two Companions to *Maldonada*, where after a Fortnight's waiting, a Ship was ready to sail for *Luggnagg*. The two Gentlemen and some others were so generous and kind as to furnish me with Provisions, and see me on Board. I was a Month in this Voyage. We had one violent Storm, and were under a Necessity of steering Westward to get into the Trade-Wind, which holds for above sixty Leagues. On the 21st of *April*, 1708, we sailed in the River of *Clumegnig*, which is a Sea-port Town, at the South-East Point of *Luggnagg*. We cast Anchor within a League of the Town, and made a Signal for a Pilot. Two of them came on Board in less than half an Hour, by whom we were guided between certain Shoals and Rocks, which are very dangerous in the Passage, to a large Basin, where a Fleet may ride in Safety within a Cable's Length of the Town-Wall.

Some of our Sailors, whether out of Treachery or Inadvertence, had informed the Pilots that I was a Stranger and a great Traveller, whereof these gave Notice to a Custom-House Officer, by whom I was examined very strictly upon my landing. This Officer spoke to

1 *the 21st of April, 1708.* It is now two months and five days since Gulliver left Laputa, and a year minus five days since he left Fort St. George.

2 *the Dutch were the only Europeans permitted to enter into that Kingdom.* See Chapter 1 of this part, note 7.

3 *lick the Dust before his Footstool.* In China, it was customary for those who gained audience with the emperor to kneel and knock their heads on the floor. This was the "kowtow" from Chinese words meaning "bump-head." Naturally, Europeans, who considered all Chinese, up to and including the emperor, to be outlandish heathens, resented the practice, but sometimes could not avoid being compelled to perform it. Swift here intensifies the humiliation for satirical purposes.

me in the Language of *Balnibarbi,* which by the Force of much Commerce is generally understood in that Town, especially by Seamen, and those employed in the Customs. I gave him a short Account of some Particulars, and made my Story as plausible and consistent as I could; but I thought it necessary to disguise my country, and call my self a *Hollander;* because my Intentions were **2** for *Japan,* and I knew the *Dutch* were the only *Europeans* permitted to enter into that Kingdom. I therefore told the Officer, that having been shipwrecked on the Coast of *Balnibarbi,* and cast on a Rock, I was received up into *Laputa,* or the flying Island (of which he had heard) and was now endeavouring to get to *Japan,* from whence I might find a Convenience of returning to my own Country. The Officer said, I must be confined till he could receive Orders from Court, for which he would write immediately, and hoped for an Answer in a Fortnight. I was carried to a convenient Lodging, with a Centry placed at the Door; however I had the Liberty of a large Garden, and was treated with Humanity enough, being maintained all the Time at the King's Charge. I was invited by several Persons, chiefly out of Curiosity, because it was reported I came from Countries very remote, of which they had never heard.

I hired a young Man who came in the same Ship to be an Interpreter; he was a Native of *Luggnagg,* but had lived some Years at *Maldonada,* and was a perfect Master of both Languages. By his Assistance I was able to hold a Conversation with those that came to visit me; but this consisted only of their Questions and my Answers.

The Dispatch came from Court about the Time we expected. It contained a Warrant for conducting me and my Retinue to *Traldragdubh* or *Trildrogdrib,* (for it is pronounced both Ways as near as I can remember) by a Party of Ten Horse. All my Retinue was that poor Lad for an Interpreter, whom I persuaded into my Service. At my humble Request we had each of us a Mule to ride on. A Messenger was dispatched half a Day's Journey before us, to give the King Notice of my Approach, and to desire that his Majesty would please to appoint a Day and Hour, when it would **3** be his gracious Pleasure that I might have the Honour to *lick the Dust before his Footstool.* This is the Court Style, and I found it to be more than Matter of Form: For upon my Admittance two Days after my Arrival, I was commanded to crawl upon my Belly, and lick the Floor as I advanced; but on account of my being a Stranger, Care was taken to have it so clean that the Dust was not offensive. However, this was a peculiar Grace, not allowed to any but Persons of the highest Rank, when they desire an Admittance: Nay, sometimes the Floor is strewed with Dust on purpose, when the Person to be admitted happens to have powerful Enemies at Court: And I have seen a great Lord with his Mouth so crammed, that when he had crept to the proper Distance from the Throne, he was not able to speak a Word. Neither is there any Remedy, because it is capital for those who receive an Audience to spit or wipe their Mouths in his Majesty's Presence. There is indeed another Custom, which I cannot altogether approve of. When the King hath a Mind to put any of his Nobles to Death in a gentle indulgent Manner; he commands to have the Floor strewed with a certain brown Powder, of a deadly Composition, which being licked up infallibly kills him in twenty-four Hours. But in Justice to this Prince's great

Licking dust. J. J. Grandville, 1835. Courtesy, Library of Congress.

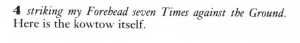

4 *striking my Forehead seven Times against the Ground.* Here is the kowtow itself.

Clemency, and the Care he hath of his Subjects Lives, (wherein it were much to be wished that the Monarchs of *Europe* would imitate him) it must be mentioned for his Honour, that strict Orders are given to have the infected Parts of the Floor well washed after every such Execution; which if his Domesticks neglect, they are in Danger of incurring his Royal Displeasure. I my self heard him give Directions, that one of his Pages should be whipt, whose Turn it was to give Notice about washing the Floor after an Execution, but maliciously had omitted it; by which Neglect a young Lord of great Hopes coming to an Audience, was unfortunately poisoned, although the King at that Time had no Design against his Life. But this good Prince was so gracious, as to forgive the Page his Whipping, upon Promise that he would do so no more, without special Orders.

To return from this Digression; when I had crept within four Yards of the Throne, I raised my self gently upon my Knees, and then striking my Forehead seven Times against the Ground, I pronounced the following Words, as they had been taught me the Night before, *Ickpling Gloffthrobb Squutserumm blhiop Mlashnalt Zwin tnodbalkguffh Slhiophad Gurdlubh Asht.* This is the Compliment established by the Laws of the Land for all Persons admitted to the King's Presence. It may be rendered into *English* thus: *May your cælestial Majesty out-live the Sun, eleven Moons and an half.* To this the King returned some Answer, which although I could not understand, yet I replied as I had been directed; *Fluft drin Yalerick Dwuldum prastrad mirplush,* which properly signifies, *My Tongue is in the Mouth of my Friend;* and by this Expression

4

"I raised my self gently upon my Knees." Le Febure, 1797.

was meant that I desired leave to bring my Interpreter; whereupon the young Man already mentioned was accordingly introduced; by whose Intervention I answered as many Questions as his Majesty could put in above an Hour. I spoke in the *Balnibarbian* Tongue, and my Interpreter delivered my Meaning in that of *Luggnagg*.

The King was much delighted with my Company, and ordered his *Bliffmarklub* or High Chamberlain to appoint a Lodging in the Court for me and my Interpreter, with a daily Allowance for my Table, and a large Purse of Gold for my common Expenses.

I stayed three Months in this Country out of perfect Obedience to his Majesty, who was pleased highly to favour me, and made me very honourable Offers. But I thought it more consistent with Prudence and Justice to pass the Remainder of my Days with my Wife and Family.

CHAPTER TEN

The Luggnuggians Commended. A particular description of the Struldbruggs, with many Conversations between the Author and some Eminent Persons upon that Subject.

HE *Luggnuggians* are a polite and generous People, and although they are not without some Share of that Pride which is peculiar to all *Eastern* Countries, yet they shew themselves courteous to Strangers, especially such who are countenanced by the Court. I had many Acquaintance among Persons of the best Fashion, and being always attended by my Interpreter, the Conversation we had was not disagreeable.

One Day in much good Company, I was asked by a Person of Quality, whether I had seen any of their *Struldbruggs or Immortals*. I said I had not; and desired he would explain to me what he meant by such an Appellation, applyed to a mortal Creature. He told me, that sometimes, although very rarely, a Child happened to be born in a Family with a red circular Spot in the Forehead, directly over the left Eye-brow, which was an infallible Mark that it should never dye. The Spot, as he described it, was about the Compass of a Silver Threepence, but in the Course of Time grew larger, and changed its Colour; for at Twelve Years old it became green, so continued till Five and Twenty, then turned to a deep

1 *Struldbruggs or Immortals.* The concept and consequences of immortality are taken up, now and then, by science fiction writers today. Swift, in the passages that follow, was the first to do so, with any attempt at realism, and he did as well as, if not better than, anyone since.

blue; at Five and Forty it grew coal black, and as large as an *English* Shilling; but never admitted any farther Alteration. He said these Births were so rare, that he did not believe there could be above Eleven Hundred *Struldbruggs* of both Sexes in the whole Kingdom, of which he computed about Fifty in the Metropolis, and among the rest a young Girl born about three Years ago. That, these Productions were not peculiar to any Family, but a meer Effect of Chance; and the Children of the *Struldbruggs* themselves, were equally mortal with the rest of the People.

I freely own myself to have been struck with inexpressible Delight upon hearing this Account: And the Person who gave it me happening to understand the *Balnibarbian* Language, which I spoke very well, I could not forbear breaking out into Expressions perhaps a little too extravagant. I cryed out as in a Rapture; Happy Nation, where every Child hath at least a Chance for being immortal! Happy People who enjoy so many living Examples of antient Virtue, and have Masters ready to instruct them in the Wisdom of all former Ages! But, happiest beyond all Comparison are those excellent *Struldbruggs*, who being born exempt from that universal Calamity of human Nature, have their Minds free and disingaged, without the Weight and Depression of Spirits caused by the continual Apprehension of Death. I discovered my Admiration that I had not observed any of these illustrious Persons at Court; the black Spot on the Fore-head, being so remarkable a Distinction, that I could not have easily overlooked it: And it was impossible that his Majesty, a most judicious Prince, should not provide himself with a good Number of such wise and able Counsellors. Yet perhaps the Virtue of those Reverend Sages was too strict for the corrupt and libertine Manners of a Court. And we often find by Experience, that young Men are too opinionative and volatile to be guided by the sober Dictates of their Seniors. However, since the King was pleased to allow me Access to his Royal Person, I was resolved upon the very first Occasion to deliver my Opinion to him on this Matter freely, and at large by the Help of my Interpreter; and whether he would please to take my Advice or no, yet in one Thing I was determined, that his Majesty having frequently offered me an Establishment in this Country, I would with great Thankfulness accept the Favour, and pass my Life here in the Conversation of those superiour Beings the *Struldbruggs*, if they would please to admit me.

The Gentleman to whom I addressed my Discourse, because (as I have already observed) he spoke the Language of *Balnibarbi*, **said to me with a** Sort of a Smile, which usually ariseth from Pity **to the Ignorant**, that he was glad of any Occasion to keep me among them, and desired my Permission to explain to the Company what I had spoke. He did so; and they talked together for some time in their own Language, whereof I understood not a Syllable, neither could I observe by their Countenances what Impression my Discourse had made on them. After a short Silence, the same Person told me, that his Friends and mine (so he thought fit to express himself) were very much pleased with the judicious Remarks I had made on the great Happiness and Advantages of immortal Life; and they were desirous to know in a particular Manner, what Scheme of Living I should have formed to myself, if it had fallen to my Lot to have been born a *Struldbrugg*.

I answered, it was easy to be eloquent on so copious and delightful a Subject, especially to me·who have been often apt to amuse myself with Visions of what I should do if I were a King, a General, or a great Lòrd: And upon this very Case I had frequently run over the whole System how I should employ myself, and pass the Time if I were sure to live for ever.

That, if it had been my good Fortune to come into the World a *Struldbrugg*; as soon as I could discover my own Happiness by understanding the Difference between Life and Death, I would first resolve by all Arts and Methods whatsoever to procure myself Riches: In the Pursuit of which, by Thrift and Management, I might reasonably expect in about two Hundred Years, to be the wealthiest Man in the Kingdom. In the second Place, I would from my earliest Youth apply myself to the Study of Arts and Sciences, by which I should arrive in time to excel all others in Learning. Lastly, I would carefully record every Action and Event of Consequence that happened in the Publick, impartially draw the Characters of the several Successions of Princes, and great Ministers of State; with my own Observations on every Point. I would exactly set down the several Changes in Customs, Languages, Fashions of Dress, Dyet and Diversions. By all which Acquirements, I should be a living Treasury of Knowledge and Wisdom, and certainly become the Oracle of the Nation.

I would never marry after Threescore, but live in an hospitable Manner, yet still on the saving Side. I would entertain myself in forming and directing the Minds of hopeful young Men, by convincing them from my own Remembrance, Experience and Observation, fortified by numerous Examples, of the Usefulness of Virtue in publick and private Life. But, my choise and constant Companions should be a Sett of my own immortal Brotherhood, among whom I **2** would elect a Dozen from the most ancient down to my own Contemporaries. Where any of these wanted Fortunes, I would provide them with convenient Lodges round my own Estate, and have some of them always at my Table, only mingling a few of the most valuable among you Mortals, whom Length of Time would harden me to lose with little or no Reluctance, and treat your Posterity after the same Manner; just as a Man diverts himself with the annual Succession of Pinks and Tulips in his Garden, without regretting the Loss of those which withered the preceding Year.

These *Struldbruggs* and I would mutually communicate our Observations and Memorials through the Course of Time; remark the several Gradations by which Corruption steals into the World, and oppose it in every Step, by giving perpetual Warning and Instruction to Mankind; which, added to the strong Influence of our own Example, would probably prevent that continual Degeneracy of human Nature, so justly complained of in all Ages.

Add to all this, the Pleasure of seeing the various Revolutions of States and Empires; the Changes in the lower and upper World; **3** antient Cities in Ruins, and obscure Villages become the Seats of Kings. Famous Rivers lessening into shallow Brooks; the Ocean leaving one Coast dry, and overwhelming another: The Discovery of many Countries yet unknown. Barbarity over-running the politest **4** Nations, and the most barbarous becoming civilized. I should then see the Discovery of the *Longitude*, the *perpetual Motion*, the *uni-* **5,6,7** *versal Medicine*, and many other great Inventions brought to the utmost Perfection.

What wonderful Discoveries should we make in Astronomy, by

2 *immortal Brotherhood.* Swift does not seem to notice (nor do any of the commentators as far as I know) that this "immortal Brotherhood" would eventually fill the earth. No matter how rare the incidence of Struldbrugg-ship might be, as long as some are always being born and none die, then the total number will increase steadily until there is no room for any ordinary mortal on earth.

3 *the lower and upper World.* This is sometimes interpreted as referring to Earth and Heaven respectively, but that seems unlikely. What changes in Heaven (or in the secular sky, for that matter) would Gulliver expect to see? It seems much more likely that the reference is to the world of the common man (the lower world) and the world of the ruling classes (the upper world).

4 *the politest Nations.* That is, the most civilized. See Part II, Chapter 7, note 2.

5 *Longitude.* It was impossible to determine the longitude on board ship without an accurate timepiece. The only good timepieces available in Swift's day were pendulum clocks, which were not portable, and could not have kept time on the swaying deck of a ship. The British government had offered up to twenty thousand pounds for the invention of a portable timepiece capable of great accuracy even on board ship.

Actually, Gulliver would not have had to live very long to see this problem solved. One was actually built by an English watchmaker, John Harrison (1692–1776) in 1728. He continually improved his model until finally Parliament accepted it officially and awarded him the prize in 1765. This introduced the modern era of ship navigation.

6 *perpetual Motion.* This was the search for some device that would do work without loss of energy—something that would move forever. In other words, it was a method for creating energy out of nothing, or alternatively, for getting energy by what would be considered in modern terms "a decrease in entropy." The laws of thermodynamics forbid such a thing absolutely, but those laws were not developed for a century and a quarter after the publication of *Gulliver's Travels*. Unlike the case of the longitude, Gulliver might have lived eternally without seeing anyone solve the problem of perpetual motion.

7 *the universal Medicine.* The medieval alchemists sought the missing substance crucial to the conversion of base metals to gold. It was thought to be a dry, solid material and was therefore called "the philosopher's stone" or "elixir" from an Arabic-Greek expression, meaning a "dry substance."

The philosopher's stone, being so magical, was thought to have other wonder properties as well (why not?), such as the property of curing all ailments. It was therefore also called "the elixir of life."

This is the "universal Medicine" Gulliver hoped to live long enough to find. There may be no one universal medicine, but physicians have discovered individual medicines or, at any rate, forms of medical treatment that have cured or ameliorated many diseases, *not one* of which cures was known in Swift's time, though many medicines were used in vain.

The first of the true treatments was discovered by the English physician, Edward Jenner (1749–1823) in 1798, seven decades after the publication of *Gulliver's Travels*. It consisted of an injection of cowpox (since cowpox was "vaccinia" or *vaccinus* (from cows) in Latin, the treatment was called "vaccination"), which did better than cure the dread disease smallpox—it prevented it.

8 *the Progress and Returns of Comets.* Swift has referred to the matter of the return of comets several times in the book. Thanks to Halley's prediction (see Chapter 2 of this part, note 24), this was the hottest aspect of astronomy at the time *Gulliver's Travels* was published.

9 *sublunary Happiness.* In the old Ptolemaic theory, Earth was at the center of the universe and outside it was a series of spheres in which various heavenly bodies were set. The innermost sphere held the Moon. Everything from the Moon outward was perfect and incorruptible and only on Earth, beneath the Moon's sphere ("sublunary"), was there imperfection, corruption, and death. In the heavens, from the Moon outward, there is perfect happiness as a matter of course, but Struldbruggism can offer, at best, sublunary happiness, not heavenly perfection.

10 *a perpetual Life under all the usual Disadvantages which old Age brings along with it.* Certainly, people who think of immortality assume that along with it comes eternal youth or, at least, eternal maturity, since that is always the picture presented in the case of the gods. Nevertheless, there are two famous myths that depict an immortality of ever-increasing age, and Swift's tale of the Struldbruggs may have been inspired by them.

Sibylla, beloved by Apollo, offered to give herself to him in return for the gift of prophecy and for as many years of life as the grains of sand she could hold in her hand (not quite immortality). When Apollo granted the wish and Sibylla reneged on her own promise, the angry god pointed out that the girl had asked for years of life and not for youth and allowed her to grow older and older and older.

A similar case was that of Tithonus, a handsome brother of Priam, king of Troy. The goddess of the dawn, Eos, fell in love with him and managed to obtain the gift of immortality for him from the gods so that she might enjoy him forever. She forgot, however, to specify that eternal youth was to accompany the immortality, so he grew older and older and older. Eos could not bear to listen to his piping voice any longer and finally turned him into a katydid, whose shrill and endless pipings we still listen to.

8 outliving and confirming our own Predictions; by observing the Progress and Returns of Comets, with the Changes of Motion in the Sun, Moon and Stars.

I enlarged upon many other Topicks, which the natural Desire **9** of endless Life and sublunary Happiness could easily furnish me with. When I had ended, and the Sum of my Discourse had been interpreted as before, to the rest of the Company, there was a good Deal of Talk among them in the Language of the Country, not without some Laughter at my Expence. At last the same Gentleman who had been my Interpreter, said, he was desired by the rest to set me right in a few Mistakes, which I had fallen into through the common Imbecility of human Nature, and upon that Allowance was less answerable for them. That, this Breed of *Struldbruggs* was peculiar to their Country, for there were no such People either in *Balnibarbi* or *Japan*, where he had the Honour to be Embassador from his Majesty, and found the Natives in both those Kingdoms very hard to believe that the Fact was possible; and it appeared from my Astonishment when he first mentioned the Matter to me, that I received it as a Thing wholly new, and scarcely to be credited. That in the two Kingdoms above-mentioned, where during his Residence he had conversed very much, he observed long Life to be the universal Desire and Wish of Mankind. That, whoever had one Foot in the Grave, was sure to hold back the other as strongly as he could. That the oldest had still Hopes of living one Day longer, and looked on Death as the greatest Evil, from which Nature always prompted him to retreat; only in this Island of *Luggnagg*, the Appetite for living was not so eager, from the continual Example of the *Struldbruggs* before their Eyes.

That the System of Living contrived by me was unreasonable and unjust, because it supposed a Perpetuity of Youth, Health, and Vigour, which no Man could be so foolish to hope, however **extravagant** he might be in his Wishes. That, the Question therefore was not whether a Man would chuse to be always in the Prime of Youth, **10** attended with Prosperity and Health; but how he would pass a perpetual Life under all the usual Disadvantages which old Age brings along with it. For although few Men will avow their Desires of being immortal upon such hard Conditions, yet in the two Kingdoms beforementioned of *Balnibarbi* and *Japan*, he observed that every Man desired to put off Death for sometime longer, let it approach ever so late; and he rarely heard of any Man who died willingly, except he were incited by the Extremity of Grief or Torture. And he appealed to me whether in those Countries I had travelled as well as my own, I had not observed the same general Disposition.

After this Preface, he gave me a particular Account of the *Struldbruggs* among them. He said they commonly acted like Mortals, till about Thirty Years old, after which by Degrees they grew melancholy and dejected, increasing in both till they came to Fourscore. This he learned from their own Confession; for otherwise there not being above two or three of that Species born in an Age, they were too few to form a general Observation by. When they came to Fourscore Years, which is reckoned the Extremity of living in this Country, they had not only all the Follies and Infirmities of other old Men, but many more which arose from the dreadful Prospect of never dying. They were not only opinionative, peevish, covetous, morose, vain, talkative; but uncapable of Friendship, and dead to all natural Affection, which never descended below their Grand-children. Envy and impotent Desires, are their prevailing Passions. But those Objects against which their Envy seems principally directed, are the Vices of the younger Sort, and the Deaths of the old. By reflecting on the former, they find themselves cut off from all Possibility of Pleasure; and whenever they see a Funeral, they lament and repine that others are gone to an Harbour of Rest, to which they themselves never can hope to arrive. They have no Remembrance of any thing but what they learned and observed in their Youth and middle Age, and even that is very imperfect: And for the Truth or Particulars of any

The Struldbrugs. Arthur Rackham, 1900 and 1909.

11 *their Misery doubled by the Load of a Wife.* If two Struldbruggs marry, one is husband and one is wife. If the former should not have his torture doubled by the load of a wife, does it not follow that the latter should not have her torture doubled by the load of a husband? So casually are the assumptions of male chauvinism accepted, however, that even someone as keenly alive to injustice as Swift would not think of the two-way street.

12 *Meers.* Usually spelled "mere," from the Old English word for "wall" *(maere).* It is therefore synonymous with "bounds." In other words, Struldbruggs can't even be trusted to give evidence in cases involving real estate boundaries.

Fact, it is safer to depend on common Traditions than upon their best Recollections. The least miserable among them, appear to be those who turn to Dotage, and entirely lose their Memories; these meet with more Pity and Assistance, because they want many bad Qualities which abound in others.

If a *Struldbrugg* happen to marry one of his own Kind, the Marriage is dissolved of Course by the Courtesy of the Kingdom, as soon as the younger of the two comes to be Fourscore. For the Law thinks it a reasonable Indulgence, that those who are condemned without any Fault of their own to a perpetual Continuance in the **11** World, should not have their Misery doubled by the Load of a Wife.

As soon as they have compleated the Term of Eighty Years, they are looked on as dead in Law; their Heirs immediately succeed to their Estates, only a small Pittance is reserved for their Support; and the poor ones are maintained at the publick Charge. After that Period they are held incapable of any Employment of Trust or Profit; they cannot purchase Lands, or take Leases, neither are they allowed to be Witnesses in any Cause, either Civil or **12** Criminal, not even for the Decision of Meers and Bounds.

At Ninety they lose their Teeth and Hair; they have at that Age no Distinction of Taste, but eat and drink whatever they can get, without Relish or Appetite. The Diseases they were subject to, still continue without encreasing or diminishing. In talking they forget the common Appellation of Things, and the Names of Persons, even of those who are their nearest Friends and Relations. For the same Reason they never can amuse themselves with reading, because their Memory will not serve to carry them from the Beginning of a Sentence to the End; and by this Defect they are deprived of the only Entertainment whereof they might otherwise be capable.

The Language of this Country being always upon the Flux, the *Struldbruggs* of one Age do not understand those of another; neither are they able after two Hundred Years to hold any Conversation (farther than by a few general Words) with their Neighbours the Mortals; and thus they lye under the Disadvantage of living like Foreigners in their own Country.

This was the Account given me of the *Struldbruggs,* as near as I can remember. I afterwards saw five or six of different Ages, the youngest not above two Hundred Years old, who were brought to me at several Times by some of my Friends; but although they were told that I was a great Traveller, and had seen all the World, they had not the least Curiosity to ask me a Question; only desired I would give them *Slumskudask,* or a Token of Remembrance; which is a modest Way of begging, to avoid the Law that strictly forbids it, because they are provided for by the Publick, although indeed with a very scanty Allowance.

They are despised and hated by all Sorts of People: When one of them is born, it is reckoned ominous, and their Birth is recorded very particularly; so that you may know their Age by consulting the Registry, which however hath not been kept above a Thousand Years past, or at least hath been destroyed by Time or publick Disturbances. But the usual Way of computing how old they are, is, by asking them what Kings or great Persons they can remember, and then consulting History; for infallibly the last Prince in their

The Struldbrugs. Willy Pogány, 1919.

13 *Avarice is the necessary Consequent of old Age.* What makes vices attractive is the pleasure they give the senses. In old age, however, the senses dull and there is nothing left but the joy of material possession. The connection of age and avarice was mentioned as long ago as 160 B.C. by the Roman playwright, Terence (190?–159 B.C.). In *Don Juan*, Lord Byron (1788–1824) said sardonically, "So for a good old-gentlemanly vice / I think I must take up with avarice."

Mind did not begin his Reign after they were Fourscore Years old.

They were the most mortifying Sight I ever beheld; and the Women more horrible than the Men. Besides the usual Deformities in extreme old Age, they acquired an additional Ghastliness in Proportion to their Number of Years, which is not to be described; and among half a Dozen I soon distinguished which was the eldest, although there were not above a Century or two between them.

The Reader will easily believe, that from what I had heard and seen, my keen Appetite for Perpetuity of Life was much abated. I grew heartily ashamed of the pleasing Visions I had formed; and thought no Tyrant could invent a Death into which I would not run with Pleasure from such a Life. The King heard of all that had passed between me and my Friends upon this Occasion, and raillied me very pleasantly; wishing I would send a Couple of *Struldbruggs* to my own Country, to arm our People against the Fear of Death; but this it seems is forbidden by the fundamental Laws of the Kingdom; or else I should have been well content with the Trouble and Expence of transporting them.

I could not but agree, that the Laws of this Kingdom relating to the *Struldbruggs*, were founded upon the strongest Reasons, and such as any other Country would be under the Necessity of enacting in the like Circumstances. Otherwise, as Avarice is the necessary **13** Consequent of old Age, those Immortals would in time become Proprietors of the whole Nation, and engross the Civil Power; which, for want of Abilities to manage, must end in the Ruin of the Publick.

1 *the Dutch . . . will be . . . able enough to supply my Defects.* The Dutch were the only Europeans allowed to remain in Japan, and that under humiliating restrictions (see Chapter 1 of this part, note 7).

The Author leaves Luggnagg and sails to Japan. From thence he returns in a Dutch Ship to Amsterdam, and from Amsterdam to England.

 THOUGHT this Account of the *Struldbruggs* might be some Entertainment to the Reader, because it seems to be a little out of the common Way; at least, I do not remember to have met the like in any Book of Travels that hath come to my Hands: And if I am deceived, my Excuse must be, that it is necessary for Travellers, who describe the same Country, very often to agree in dwelling on the same Particulars, without deserving the Censure of having borrowed or transcribed from those who wrote before them.

There is indeed a perpetual Commerce between this Kingdom and the great Empire of *Japan;* and it is very probable that the *Japanese* Authors may have given some Account of the *Struldbruggs;* but my Stay in *Japan* was so short, and I was so entirely a Stranger to the Language, that I was not qualified to make any **1** Enquiries. But I hope the *Dutch* upon this Notice will be curious and able enough to supply my Defects.

His Majesty having often pressed me to accept some Employment in his Court, and finding me absolutely determined to return to my Native Country; was pleased to give me his Licence to depart; and honoured me with a Letter of Recommendation under his own Hand to the Emperor of *Japan*. He likewise presented me with four Hundred forty-four large Pieces of Gold (this Nation delighting in even Numbers) and a red Diamond which I sold in *England* for Eleven Hundred Pounds.

On the 6*th* Day of *May*, 1709, I took a solemn Leave of his Majesty, and all my Friends. This Prince was so gracious as to order a Guard to conduct me to *Glanguenstald*, which is a Royal Port to the *South West* Part of the Island. In six Days I found a Vessel ready to carry me to *Japan*; and spent fifteen Days in the Voyage. We landed at a small Port-Town called *Xamoschi*, situated on the *South-East* Part of *Japan*. The Town lies on the *Western* Part, where there is a narrow Streight, leading *Northward* into a long Arm of the Sea, upon the *North-West* Part of which *Yedo* the Metropolis stands. At landing I shewed the Custom-House Officers my Letter from the King of *Luggnagg* to his Imperial Majesty: They knew the Seal perfectly well; it was as broad as the Palm of my Hand. The Impression was, *A King lifting up a lame Beggar from the Earth*. The Magistrates of the Town hearing of my Letter, received me as a publick Minister; they provided me with Carriages and Servants, and bore my Charges to *Yedo*, where I was admitted to an Audience, and delivered my Letter; which was opened with great Ceremony, and explained to the Emperor by an Interpreter, who gave me Notice of his Majesty's Order, that I should signify my Request; and whatever it were, it should be granted for the sake of his Royal Brother of *Luggnagg*. This Interpreter was a Person employed to transact Affairs with the *Hollanders*: He soon conjectured by my Countenance that I was an *European*, and therefore repeated his Majesty's Commands in *Low-Dutch*, which he spoke perfectly well. I answered, (as I had before determined) that I was a *Dutch* Merchant, shipwrecked in a very remote Country, from whence I travelled by Sea and Land to *Luggnagg*, and then took Shipping for *Japan*, where I knew my Countrymen often traded, and with some of these I hoped to get an Opportunity of returning into *Europe*: I therefore most humbly entreated his Royal Favour to give Order, that I should be conducted in Safety to *Nangasac*. To this I added another Petition, that for the sake of my Patron the King of *Luggnagg*, his Majesty would condescend to excuse my performing the Ceremony imposed on my Countrymen, of *trampling upon the Crucifix*; because I had been thrown into his Kingdom by my Misfortunes, without any Intention of trading. When this latter Petition was interpreted to the Emperor, he seemed a little surprised; and said, he believed I was the first of my Countrymen who ever made any Scruple in this Point; and that he began to doubt whether I were a real *Hollander* or no; but rather suspected I must be a CHRISTIAN. However, for the Reasons I had offered, but chiefly to gratify the King of *Luggnagg* by an uncommon Mark of his Favour, he would comply with the *singularity* of my Humour; but the Affair must be managed with Dexterity, and his Officers should be commanded to let me pass as it were by Forgetfulness. For he assured me, that if the Secret should be discovered by my Countrymen, the *Dutch*, they would cut my Throat in the Voyage. I returned my Thanks by the Interpreter for so unusual a Favour; and some Troops being at that Time on their March to *Nangasac*, the Commanding Officer

2 *the 6th Day of May, 1709.* Gulliver has been in the imaginary kingdoms of Laputa and its neighboring lands for two years now.

3 *Xamoschi.* Swift apparently had some knowledge of the geography of Japan. After all, unlike the other mysterious lands Gulliver visited, Japan is real enough. As to what town is meant by Xamoschi, it is hard to tell. Swift may have invented it. On the other hand, it may conceivably be Kawasaki, a town lying between Tokyo and Yokohama.

4 *Yedo.* Now known as Tokyo. It really was the Japanese capital in Swift's time, in the sense that Japan was ruled from that city. It was also really on the northwestern shore of an arm of the sea, Tokyo Bay.

It was not the seat of the emperor, though, who lived in the inland town of Kyoto and whose role in Japan was purely ceremonial. The real ruler was the shogun, or prime minister, and he did reside in Yedo. In 1868, after Japan had been forcibly opened to the outside world (1853) by the fleet of the American commodore, Matthew Calbraith Perry, the shogunate was overthrown. The emperor, or mikado, assumed the real power, and moved his seat to Yedo, which was at that time renamed Tokyo.

5 *Emperor.* This, actually, would have to be the shogun, rather than the emperor, but a European would have been hard put to tell the difference.

6 *Nangasac.* Nagasaki. This was the only town through which European imports were allowed to enter. On Deshima, an island in its harbor, a colony of Dutch traders was permitted to reside. From 1641 to 1859, they were the only Europeans allowed to remain on Japanese soil.

7 *trampling upon the Crucifix.* The Japanese, suspicious of the Europeans, tormented them in various humiliating ways, ordering them to step on the crucifix and spit on it at various times, as a condition of being allowed to continue trading with them.

8 *the first of my Countrymen who ever made any Scruple in this Point.* The Dutch, aware of the enormous profits they made in their Japanese trade, and further aware that the anti-Christian games the Japanese forced them to play did them no physical harm, routinely obliged the Japanese and kept the profits. Swift, who is anti-Dutch, remember, is delighted to make a point of this.

9 *the Dutch, they would cut my Throat in the Voyage.* Again Swift points out that the Dutch are less generous and "Christian" than the pagans are.

10 *Amboyna*. Named for one of the smaller Indonesian islands (in the Moluccas) which was located east of Celebes. It is usually written Amboina and is presently called Ambon. In 1623, the English and the Dutch were competing for the control of the trade in valuable spices and other materials produced on this and neighboring islands, and the Dutch killed some dozen Englishmen whom they accused of conspiring against them. This "Amboina massacre" was remembered with indignation by the English for a long time. Swift's deliberate use of this name for the ship is another example of his anti-Dutch feeling.

11 *Leyden*. See Part I, Chapter 1, note 8.

12 *Guelderland*. Or Gelderland, in the east-central part of the Netherlands. Its capital is Arnhem.

13 *Skipper*. The English version of the Dutch *schipper*, meaning a common seaman. Later, it came to be applied to the captain of a small shipping vessel and, eventually, as a slang term to the captain of any vessel. Here it is used in its original meaning, however.

An audience with the emperor. Willy Pogány, 1919.

had Orders to convey me safe thither, with particular Instructions about the Business of the *Crucifix*.

On the 9*th* Day of *June*, 1709, I arrived at *Nangasac*, after a very long and troublesome Journey. I soon fell into Company of **10** some *Dutch* Sailors belonging to the *Amboyna* of *Amsterdam*, a stout Ship of 450 Tuns. I have lived long in *Holland*, pursuing my **11** Studies at *Leyden*, and I spoke *Dutch* well: The Seamen soon knew from whence I came last; they were curious to enquire into my Voyages and Course of Life. I made up a Story as short and probable as I could, but concealed the greatest Part. I knew many Persons in *Holland;* I was able to invent Names for my Parents, whom I pretended to be obscure People in the Province of **12** *Guelderland*. I would have given the Captain (one *Theodorus Vangrult*) what he pleased to ask for my Voyage to *Holland;* but, understanding I was a Surgeon, he was contented to take half the usual Rate, on Condition that I would serve him in the Way of my Calling. Before we took Shipping, I was often asked by some of the Crew, whether I had performed the Ceremony above-mentioned? I evaded the Question by general Answers, that I had satisfied the Emperor and Court in all Particulars. However, a malici- **13** ous Rogue of a Skipper went to an Officer, and pointing to me, told him, I had not yet *trampled on the Crucifix*: But the other, who had received Instructions to let me pass, gave the Rascal twenty Strokes on the Shoulders with a Bamboo; after which I was no more troubled with such Questions.

Nothing happened worth mentioning in this Voyage. We sailed with a fair Wind to the *Cape of Good Hope*, where we staid only to take in fresh Water. On the 16*th* of *April* we arrived safe at *Amsterdam*, having lost only three Men by Sickness in the Voyage, and a fourth who fell from the Fore-mast into the Sea, not far from the Coast of *Guinea*. From *Amsterdam* I soon after set sail for

England in a small Vessel belonging to that City.

On the [2]0*th* of *April,* 1710, we put in at the *Downs.* I landed the next Morning, and saw once more my Native Country after an **14** Absence of five Years and six Months compleat. I went strait to *Redriff,* whither I arrived the same Day at two in the Afternoon, and found my Wife and Family in good Health.

14 *an Absence of five Years and six Months.* Having left on August 5, 1706, Gulliver was actually absent for three years and eight months—a rare stumble for Swift. Following the rule of not allowing reality to obtrude, there is no mention of the changes that had taken place in the course of this third voyage—the conversion of England and Scotland into Great Britain, the fall of a Whig ministry, and the coming into power of the Tories.

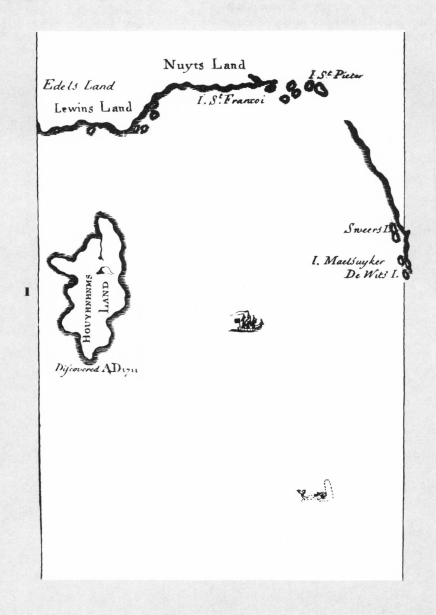

1 *Houyhnhnms Land.* We now begin the fourth, and climactic, voyage of Gulliver. In the first, Swift satirized European politics in the persons of the contemptible Lilliputians; in the second, he satirized European politics by contrasting European statecraft with that of the giant Brobdingnagians. In the third voyage (an apparently hastily put together afterthought), he satirized other aspects of humanity—science, history, the "experience" that comes with age. Now, in the fourth, he is prepared to assemble all the evidence and thereby demolish humanity in all its aspects.

PART FOUR

A Voyage to the Country of the Houyhnhnms

1 *I left my poor Wife big with Child.* For eleven years, except for three brief stays at home, Gulliver has been voyaging. For him to leave again so soon is re-markable considering the difficulties and dangers he has undergone. However, we can't very well expect Swift to spoil his book by overrealism in this respect. Besides, the voyages are making the Gullivers rich. When Gulliver left Luggnagg for Japan, for instance, the King of Luggnagg gave him gold coins and a red diamond, which he sold in England for eleven hundred pounds—a fortune in those days. If he left his wife without a husband, he at least left her with wealth, and that, perhaps, reconciled her to his absences.

2 *the 7th Day of September, 1710.* Gulliver is forty-nine years old now.

3 *Tenariff.* More properly, Tenerife, is the largest of the Canary Islands and about two hundred miles off the coàst of Morocco.

4 *the Boy of Campechy.* Bay of Campeche, the south-ernmost part of the Gulf of Mexico, lying between Yucatan and the rest of Mexico. This is the only oc-casion in the four voyages in which Gulliver pene-trates the Western Hemisphere.

5 *Logwood.* A tree indigenous to Central America and the West Indies. Its heartwood contains the dye, hematoxylin, which is used to color textiles and leather.

The Author sets out as Captain of a Ship. His men conspire against him, confine him a long time to his Cabbin, set him on shore in an unknown Land. He travels up into the Country. The Yahoos, a strange sort of Animal, de-scribed. The Author meets two Houy-hnhnms.

1

CONTINUED at home with my Wife and Children about five Months in a very happy Condition, if I could have learned the Lesson of knowing when I was well. I left my poor Wife big with Child, and accepted an advantageous Offer made me to be Captain of the *Adventure,* a stout Merchant-man of 350 Tuns: For I understood Navigation well, and being grown weary of a Surgeon's Employ-ment at Sea, which however I could exercise upon Occasion, I took a skilful young Man of that Calling, one *Robert Purefoy,* into my

2 Ship. We set sail from *Portsmouth* upon the 7th Day of *September,*
3 1710; on the 14*th* we met with Captain *Pocock* of *Bristol,* at *Tena-*
4,5 *riff,* who was going to the Boy of *Campeachy,* to cut Logwood. On the 16*th* he was parted from us by a Storm: I heard since my Return,
6 that his Ship foundered, and none escaped, but one Cabbin-Boy. He was an honest Man, and a good Sailor, but a little too positive in his own Opinions, which was the Cause of his Destruction, as it hath been of several others. For if he had followed my Advice, he might at this Time have been safe at home with his Family as well as my self.

7 I had several Men died in my Ship of Calentures, so that I was

forced to get Recruits out of *Barbadoes,* and the *Leeward Islands,* **8, 9**
where I touched by the Direction of the Merchants who employed
me; which I had soon too much Cause to repent; for I found afterwards that most of them had been Buccaneers. I had fifty Hands
on Board; and my Orders were, that I should trade with the *Ind-*
ians in the *South-Sea,* and make what Discoveries I could. These **10**
Rogues whom I had picked up, debauched my other Men, and
they all formed a Conspiracy to seize the Ship and secure me;
which they did one Morning, rushing into my Cabbin, and binding
me Hand and Foot, threatening to throw me overboard, if I offered
to stir. I told them, I was their Prisoner, and would submit. This
they made me swear to do, and then unbound me, only fastening
one of my Legs with a Chain near my Bed; and placed a Centry at
my Door with his Piece charged, who was commanded to shoot me
dead if I attempted my Liberty. They sent me down Victuals and
Drink, and took the Government of the Ship to themselves. Their
Design was to turn Pirates, and plunder the Spaniards, which they
could not do, till they got more Men. But first they resolved to sell
the Goods in the Ship, and then go to *Madagascar* for Recruits, **11**
several among them having died since my Confinement. They
sailed many Weeks, and traded with the *Indians;* but I knew not
what Course they took, being kept close Prisoner in my Cabbin,
and expecting nothing less than to be murdered, as they often
threatened me.

Upon the 9*th* Day of *May,* 1711, one *James Welch* came down **12**
to my Cabbin; and said he had Orders from the Captain to set me
ashore. I expostulated with him, but in vain; neither would he so
much as tell me who their new Captain was. They forced me into the
Long-boat, letting me put on my best Suit of Cloaths, which were **13**
as good as new, and a small Bundle of Linnen, but no Arms except
my Hanger; and they were so civil as not to search my Pockets, **14**
into which I conveyed what Money I had, with some other little
Necessaries. They rowed about a League; and then set me down
on a Strand. I desired them to tell me what Country it was: They all
swore, they knew no more than my self, but said, that the Captain **15**
(as they called him) was resolved, after they had sold the Lading, **16**
to get rid of me in the first Place where they discovered Land.
They pushed off immediately, advising me to make haste, for fear
of being overtaken by the Tide; and bade me farewell.

In this desolate Condition I advanced forward, and soon got
upon firm Ground, where I sat down on a Bank to rest my self, and
consider what I had best to do. When I was a little refreshed,
I went up into the Country, resolving to deliver my self to the first
Savages I should meet; and purchase my Life from them by some
Bracelets, Glass Rings, and other Toys, which Sailors usually provide themselves with in those Voyages, and whereof I had some
about me: The Land was divided by long Rows of Trees, not
regularly planted, but naturally growing; there was great Plenty of
Grass, and several Fields of Oats. I walked very circumspectly for
fear of being surprised, or suddenly shot with an Arrow from behind, or on either Side. I fell into a beaten Road, where I saw
many Tracks of human Feet, and some of Cows, but most of Horses.
At last I beheld several Animals in a Field, and one or two of the
same Kind sitting in Trees. Their Shape was very singular, and
deformed, which a little discomposed me, so that I lay down be-

6 *his Ship foundered.* A horse that founders goes lame,
but a ship that founders sinks.

7 *Calentures.* From the Spanish word for "heat," this
represents a tropical fever or a sunstroke, accompanied by delirium.

8 *Barbadoes.* There is a line of small islands running
in a curved arc from Puerto Rico, generally southward, to Venezuela. These are the Lesser Antilles.
Of them, the one farthest to the east (a little more
than halfway down the arc) is Barbadoes, or Barba-
dos. It had been a British possession since 1626.

9 *Leeward Islands.* Of the Lesser Antilles, the southern half are the Windward Islands and the northern
half the Leeward Islands. These are located, respectively, in the direction of the steadily blowing trade
winds and in the direction away from them.

10 *South-Sea.* In this case the South Atlantic Ocean.

11 *Madagascar.* The large island off the southeast
coast of Africa.

12 *the 9th Day of May, 1711.* Gulliver had now been
at sea for eight months.

13 *Long-boat.* The largest boat carried by a sailing
vessel. Interestingly enough, in each voyage, Gulliver's misfortunes are increasingly the result of human malice. He landed at Lilliput as the result of a
storm and in a way that involved no human ill-will at
all. He was left behind in Brobdingnag because his
shipmates deserted him, but in a scarcely blamewor-
thy way, since a human giant was pursuing them.
He began his Laputan adventures when his ship was
captured by pirates. Now, however, in his fourth
adventure, his own crew rebels against him and
leaves him marooned.

14 *Hanger.* See Part II, Chapter 1, note 35.

15 *knew no more than my self.* This is the only voyage
in which Gulliver is apparently unable to give the location of the new land he had discovered. However,
later on Gulliver explains that from some remarks he
had overheard, he believed himself to be about ten
degrees south of the Cape of Good Hope, or at forty-
five degrees south. That area is, in actual fact, unbroken sea. In fact, all the lands discovered by
Gulliver seem to be in areas that are all ocean. None
of them happen, by pure coincidence, to be on the
site of actual land later discovered.

16 *sold the Lading.* That is, the "cargo" with which
the ship is laden.

*Engraving from the first illustrated edition, London, 1727.
Courtesy, Rare Book Division, The New York Public
Library.*

hind a Thicket to observe them better. Some of them coming forward near the Place where I lay, gave me an Opportunity of distinctly marking their Form. Their Heads and Breasts were covered with a thick Hair, some frizzled and others lank; they had Beards like Goats, and a long Ridge of Hair down their Backs, and the fore Parts of their Legs and Feet; but the rest of their Bodies were bare, so that I might see their Skins, which were of a brown Buff Colour. They had no Tails, nor any Hair at all on their Buttocks, except about the *Anus;* which I presume Nature had placed there to defend them as they sat on the Ground; for this Posture they used, as well as lying down, and often stood on their hind Feet. They climbed high Trees, as nimbly as a Squirrel, for they had strong extended Claws before and behind, terminating on sharp Points, hooked. They would often spring, and bound, and leap with prodigious Agility. The Females were not so large as the Males; they had long lank Hair on their Heads, and only a Sort of Down on the rest of their Bodies, except about the *Anus*, and *Pudenda*. Their Dugs hung between their fore Feet, and often reached almost to the Ground as they walked. The Hair of both Sexes was of several Colours, brown, red, black and yellow. Upon the whole, I never beheld in all my Travels so disagreeable an Animal, or one **17** against which I naturally conceived so strong an Antipathy. So that thinking I had seen enough, full of Contempt and Aversion, I got up and pursued the beaten Road, hoping it might direct me to the Cabbin of some *Indian*. I had not gone far when I met one **18** of these Creatures full in my Way, and coming up directly to me. The ugly Monster, when he saw me, distorted several Ways every Feature of his Visage, and stared as at an Object he had never seen before; then approaching nearer, lifted up his fore Paw, whether out of Curiosity or Mischief, I could not tell: But I drew my Hanger, and gave him a good Blow with the flat Side of it; for I durst not strike him with the Edge, fearing the Inhabitants might be provoked against me, if they should come to know, that I had killed or maimed any of their Cattle. When the Beast felt the Smart, he drew back, and roared so loud, that a Herd of at least forty came flocking about me from the next Field, howling and making odious Faces; but I ran to the Body of a Tree, and leaning

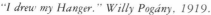

"I drew my Hanger." Willy Pogány, 1919.

Gulliver's reception by the Yahoos. Anonymous illustrator, 1895.

17 *I never beheld . . . so disagreeable an Animal, or one against which I . . . conceived so strong an Antipathy.* With his typical unimaginative accuracy, Gulliver is describing, point by point, a very primitive form of human being.

Where did Swift get the notion of a debased humanlike organism? Throughout ancient and medieval times, Europeans remained unaware of any organisms that resembled human beings. The closest were the monkeys (such as the one that plays a role in Gulliver's trip to Brobdingnag), but these were thought of as, at best, small and amusing caricatures of humanity. There was also the Barbary ape, found in North Africa (hence "Barbary") and at Gibraltar, which differed from other monkeys in being tailless.

In the seventeenth century, however, creatures who were "apes" (since they were tailless) but who were much more humanlike (anthropoid) than any monkeys were discovered by Europeans. In 1641 a description was published of an animal brought from Africa and kept in the Netherlands in a menagerie belonging to the prince of Orange. From the description, it seems to have been a chimpanzee. There were also reports of a large humanlike animal in Borneo, one we now call the orangutan. It may well be that Swift, in describing the creatures on this island, was thinking of the vague descriptions of the orangutan.

Oddly enough, Swift was, in a way, well ahead of his time. There was no hint as yet that in the past humanoid beings had existed that were not quite modern humans but were closer in resemblance to us than to any anthropoid ape. Neanderthal men were not discovered for a century and a quarter after the publication of *Gulliver's Travels*, but the creatures here described by Gulliver might well have been Neanderthals—at least as popular fancy would have had them.

18 *Indian.* Here (despite Gulliver's claim toward the end of the section) he clearly thinks he is somewhere on, or near, the South American coast.

"I saw a Horse walking softly in the Field." Willy Pogány, 1919.

my Back against it, kept them off, by waving my Hanger. Several of this cursed Brood getting hold of the Branches behind, leaped up into the Tree, from whence they began to discharge their Excrements on my Head: However, I escaped pretty well, by sticking close to the Stem of the Tree, but was almost stifled with the Filth, which fell about me on every Side.

In the Midst of this Distress, I observed them all to run away on a sudden as fast as they could; at which I ventured to leave the Tree, and pursue the Road, wondering what it was that could put them into this Fright. But looking on my Left-Hand, I saw a Horse walking softly in the Field; which my Persecutors having sooner discovered, was the Cause of their Flight. The Horse started a little when he came near me, but soon recovering himself, looked full in my Face with manifest Tokens of Wonder: He viewed my Hands and Feet, walking round me several times. I would have pursued my Journey, but he placed himself directly in the Way, yet looking with a very mild Aspect, never offering the least Violence. We stood gazing at each other for some time; at last I took the Boldness, to reach my Hand towards his Neck, with a Design to stroak it; using the common Style and Whistle of Jockies when they are going to handle a strange Horse. But, this Animal seeming to receive my Civilities with Disdain, shook his Head, and bent his Brows, softly raising up his Left Fore-Foot to remove my Hand. Then he neighed three or four times, but in so different a Cadence, that I almost began to think he was speaking to himself in some Language of his own.

While He and I were thus employed, another Horse came up; who applying himself to the first in a very formal Manner, they gently struck each other's Right Hoof before, neighing several times by Turns, and varying the Sound, which seemed to be almost articulate. They went some Paces off, as if it were to confer together, walking Side by Side, backward and forward, like Persons deliberating upon some Affair of Weight; but often turning their Eyes towards me, as it were to watch that I might not escape. I was amazed to see such Actions and Behaviour in Brute Beasts; and concluded with myself, that if the Inhabitants of this Country were endued with a proportionable Degree of Reason, they must needs be the wisest People upon Earth. This Thought gave me so much Comfort, that I resolved to go forward untill I could discover some House or Village, or meet with any of the Natives; leaving the two Horses to discourse together as they pleased. But the first, who was a Dapple-Grey, observing me to steal off, neighed after me in so expressive a Tone, that I fancied myself to understand what he meant; whereupon I turned back, and came near him, to expect his farther Commands; but concealing my Fear as much as I could; for I began to be in some Pain, how this Adventure might terminate; and the Reader will easily believe I did not much like my present Situation. **19 20**

The two Horses came up close to me, looking with great Earnestness upon my Face and Hands. The grey Steed rubbed my Hat all round with his Right Fore-hoof, and discomposed it so much, that I was forced to adjust it better, by taking it off, and settling it again; whereat both he and his Companion (who was a brown Bay) appeared to be much surprized; the latter felt the Lappet of my Coat, and finding it to hang loose about me, they both looked with new Signs of Wonder. He stroked my Right Hand, seeming to admire the Softness, and Colour; but he squeezed it so hard between his Hoof and his Pastern, that I was forced to roar; after which they both touched me with all possible Tenderness. They were under great Perplexity about my Shoes and Stockings, which they felt very often, neighing to each other, and using various Gestures, not **21 22 23**

19 *Dapple-Grey.* In Swift's time, of course, everyone was acquainted with every aspect of the horse, as now everyone is acquainted with the details of an automobile's appearance. For the modern reader, it might be useful to mention that a "Dapple-Grey" is a horse whose general gray color is interrupted by spots or patches of a darker or lighter shade of gray.

20 *expect.* To wait for.

21 *brown Bay.* A horse that has a deep reddish-brown color with a black mane, tail, and points.

22 *Lappet.* The skirt or bottom portion of a coat which hangs free of the body. Clearly, the horses are baffled by the clothing, which they take to be an integral part of Gulliver's body. (The removable hat really astounds them.)

23 *Pastern.* The rear of a horse's foot just above the hoof. These horses have, apparently, a much more maneuverable hoof than ordinary horses do. They can so bend them that they can grip something between the hoof and pastern.

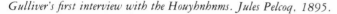

Gulliver's first interview with the Houyhnhnms. Jules Pelcoq, 1895.

24 *orderly and rational.* Gulliver begins to suspect the horses are intelligent and, unable to conceive of intelligent horses, prefers the theory that they are human beings who have taken on the shape of horses through magical arts.

In the end, of course, Gulliver is forced to accept the fact that the horses *are* intelligent, and yet Swift describes them (barring their maneuverable hooves) as precisely like ordinary horses in appearance. A modern writer would have allowed the horses' foreheads to bulge, thus allowing them a larger brain than ordinary horses have since no animal with a brain no larger than a horse's and with a brain/body ratio no larger than a horse's could possibly be intelligent.

However, Swift could not be too seriously blamed for this inaccuracy. Andreas Vesalius (1514–1564), the father of anatomy, had maintained that the brain was the seat of the intelligence, but this remained little more than a suggestion until the work of Franz Joseph Gall (1758–1828) some seven decades after the publication of *Gulliver's Travels*. If Swift ignored the matter of the equine brain in postulating an intelligent horse, his contemporaries would not have seen anything wrong.

unlike those of a Philosopher, when he would attempt to solve some new and difficult Phænomenon.

24

Upon the whole, the Behaviour of these Animals was so orderly and rational, so acute and judicious, that I at last concluded, they must needs be Magicians, who had thus metamorphosed themselves upon some Design; and seeing a Stranger in the Way, were resolved to divert themselves with him; or perhaps were really amazed at the Sight of a Man so very different in Habit, Feature and Complexion from those who might probably live in so remote a Climate. Upon the Strength of this Reasoning, I ventured to address them in the following Manner: Gentlemen, if you be Conjurers, as I have good Cause to believe, you can understand any Language; therefore I make bold to let your Worships know, that I am a poor distressed *Englishman,* driven by his Misfortunes upon

Illustration by Thomas Stothard, The Novelist's Magazine, *1782. Courtesy, The New York Public Library.*

your Coast; and I entreat one of you, to let me ride upon his Back, as if he were a real Horse, to some House or Village, where I can be relieved. In return of which Favour, I will make you a Present of this Knife and Bracelet, (taking them out of my Pocket.) The two creatures stood silent while I spoke, seeming to listen with great Attention; and when I had ended, they neighed frequently towards each other, as if they were engaged in serious Conversation. I plainly observed, that their Language expressed the Passions very well, and the Words might with little Pains be resolved into an Alphabet more easily than the *Chinese.*

I could frequently distinguish the Word *Yahoo,* which was repeated by each of them several times; and although it were impossible for me to conjecture what it meant, yet while the two Horses were busy in Conversation, I endeavoured to practice this Word upon my Tongue; and as soon as they were silent, I boldly pronounced *Yahoo* in a loud Voice, imitating, at the same time, as near as I could, the Neighing of a Horse; at which they were both visibly surprized, and the Grey repeated the same Word twice, as if he meant to teach me the right Accent, wherein I spoke after him as well as I could, and found myself perceivably to improve every time, although very far from any Degree of Perfection. Then the Bay tried me with a second Word, much harder to be pronounced; but reducing it to the *English Orthography,* may be spelt thus, *Houyhnhnm.* I did not succeed in this so well as the former, but after two or three farther Trials, I had better Fortune; and they both appeared amazed at my Capacity.

After some farther Discourse, which I then conjectured might relate to me, the two Friends took their Leaves, with the same Compliment of striking each other's Hoof; and the Grey made me Signs that I should walk before him; wherein I thought it prudent to comply, till I could find a better Director. When I offered to slacken my Pace, he would cry *Hhuun, Hhuun;* I guessed his Meaning, and gave him to understand, as well as I could, that I was weary, and not able to walk faster; upon which, he would stand a while to let me rest.

25 *Yahoo.* As it turns out, "Yahoo" is the name applied to the humanoid creatures Gulliver first saw. There was, apparently, a primitive tribe of Indians known to Europeans as "Yahoos," who lived in the coastal areas of Guiana and northern Brazil, and this may have given Swift the idea for the word. "Yahoo" has now entered the English language to mean any degraded or loutish person.

26 *Houyhnhnm.* This word, which we will see is used by the horses for themselves, seems to represent the sound made by a horse's whinny (a low and gentle neigh). It could be pronounced, most simply, as "WIN-um." All the words of the horses' language seem to be reminiscent of neighing.

1 *wattled.* Covered with reeds, twigs, or flexible rods that are intertwined or interwoven for greater strength.

2 *Nags.* Small horses, or ponies. Used as a derogatory term for any horse of inferior qualities.

3 *Style of Authority.* The horse that originally met Gulliver is of the upper classes and these inside the house are the equivalent of servants and women. Even among the Houyhnhnms, who are treated as superior beings, the social classification is as in England. Swift can't help but assume that.

The Author conducted by a Houyhnhnm to his House. The House described. The Author's reception. The Food of the Houyhnhnms. The Author in distress for want of Meat, is at last relieved. His Manner of Feeding in that Country.

1   AVING travelled about three Miles, we came to a long Kind of Building, made of Timber, stuck in the Ground, and wattled a-cross; the Roof was low, and covered with Straw. I now began to be a little comforted; and took out some Toys, which Travellers usually carry for Presents to the Savage *Indians* of *America* and other Parts, in hopes the People of the House would be thereby encouraged to receive me kindly. The Horse made me a Sign to go in first; it was a large Room with a smooth Clay Floor, and a Rack and Manger extending the whole Length on one Side. There were **2** three Nags, and two Mares, not eating, but some of them sitting down upon their Hams, which I very much wondered at; but wondered more to see the rest employed in domestick Business: The last seemed but ordinary Cattle; however this confirmed my first Opinion, that a People who could so far civilize brute Animals, must needs excel in Wisdom all the Nations of the World. The Grey came in just after, and thereby prevented any ill Treatment, which the others might have given me. He neighed to them several **3** times in a Style of Authority, and received Answers.

Beyond this Room there were three others, reaching the Length

The Houyhnhnms at home. Bofa, 1929.

4 *Vista.* Any long prospect seen through a line of trees (or similar obstruction) on either side. If all three doors were opened, the eye would see an unobstructed view from one end of the house to the other through bounds set by the doorways.

of the House, to which you passed through three Doors, opposite to each other, in the Manner of a Vista: We went through the **4** second Room towards the third; here the Grey walked in first, beckoning me to attend: I waited in the second Room, and got ready my Presents, for the Master and Mistress of the House: They were two Knives, three Bracelets of false Pearl, a small Looking Glass and a Bead Necklace. The Horse neighed three or four Times, and I waited to hear some answers in a human Voice, but I heard no other Returns than in the same Dialect, only one of two a little shriller than his. I began to think that this House must belong to some Person of great Note among them, because there appeared so much Ceremony before I could gain Admittance. But, that a Man of Quality should be served all by Horses, was beyond my Comprehension. I feared my Brain was disturbed by my Sufferings and Misfortunes: I roused my self, and looked about me in the Room where I was left alone; this was furnished as the first, only after a more elegant Manner. I rubbed my Eyes often,

5 *a very comely Mare, together with a Colt and Fole.* The horse-mistress of the house and the children are clearly described here. A colt is a young horse, and frequently specifies a young male horse, whereas a foal (or filly) is a young female horse.

6 *nicely.* Swift means "with close and discriminating attention." See Part III, Chapter 6, note 4.

7 *the Flesh . . . of Asses and Dogs.* Swift degrades the Yahoos in every possible way, even tailoring their diets to fit European aversions.

8 *Wyths.* Thin, flexible twigs or branches.

9 *Sorrel Nag.* A horse of a yellowish-brown color.

10 *the Lineaments of the Countenance are distorted.* Swift naturally assumes that the features of Europeans (particularly Englishmen) are normal, and that if other groups of human beings have other appearances it is only through distortion as a result of their deliberate or careless behavior.

but the same Objects still occurred. I pinched my Arms and Sides, to awake my self, hoping I might be in a Dream. I then absolutely concluded, that all these Appearances could be nothing else but Necromancy and Magick. But I had no Time to pursue these Reflections; for the Grey Horse came to the Door, and made me a **5** Sign to follow him into the third Room; where I saw a very comely Mare, together with a Colt and Fole, sitting on their Haunches, upon Mats of Straw, not unartfully made, and perfectly neat and clean.

The Mare soon after my Entrance, rose from her Mat, and **6** coming up close, after having nicely observed my Hands and Face, gave me a most contemptuous Look; then turning to the Horse, I heard the Word *Yahoo* often repeated betwixt them; the meaning of which Word I could not then comprehend, although it were the first I had learned to pronounce; but I was soon better informed, to my everlasting Mortification: For the Horse beckoning to me with his Head, and repeating the Word *Hhuun, Hhuun,* as he did upon the Road, which I understood was to attend him, led me out into a kind of Court, where was another Building at some Distance from the House. Here we entered, and I saw three of those detestable Creatures, which I first met after my landing, **7** feeding upon Roots, and the Flesh of some Animals, which I afterwards found to be that of Asses and Dogs, and now and then a Cow dead by Accident or Disease. They were all tied by the Neck **8** with strong Wyths, fastened to a Beam; they held their Food between the Claws of their fore Feet, and tore it with their Teeth.

9 The Master Horse ordered a Sorrel Nag, one of his Servants, to untie the largest of these Animals, and take him into a Yard. The Beast and I were brought close together; and our Countenances diligently compared, both by Master and Servant, who thereupon repeated several Times the Word *Yahoo.* My Horror and Astonishment are not to be described, when I observed, in this abominable Animal, a perfect human Figure; the Face of it indeed was flat and broad, the Nose depressed, the Lips large, and the Mouth wide: But these Differences are common to all savage Nations, where **10** the Lineaments of the Countenance are distorted by the Natives suffering their Infants to lie grovelling on the Earth, or by carrying them on their Backs, nuzzling with their Face against the Mother's Shoulders. The Forefeet of the *Yahoo* differed from my Hands in nothing else, but the Length of the Nails, the Coarseness and Brownness of the Palms, and the Hairiness on the Backs. There was the same Resemblance between our Feet, with the same Differences, which I knew very well, although the Horses did not, because of my Shoes and Stockings; the same in every Part of our Bodies, except as to Hairiness and Colour, which I have already described.

The great Difficulty that seemed to stick with the two Horses, was, to see the rest of my Body so very different from that of a *Yahoo,* for which I was obliged to my Cloaths, whereof they had no Conception: The Sorrel Nag offered me a Root, which he held (after their Manner, as we shall describe in its proper Place) between his Hoof and Pastern; I took it in my Hand, and having smelt it, returned it to him again as civilly as I could. He brought out of the *Yahoo's* Kennel a Piece of Ass's Flesh, but it smelt so offensively that I turned from it with loathing; he then threw it to

Gulliver is offered hay and oats. H. K. Browne, 1865.

the *Yahoo,* by whom it was greedily devoured. He afterwards shewed me a Wisp of Hay, and a Fettlock full of Oats; but I shook my Head, to signify that neither of these were Food for me. And indeed, I now apprehended, that I must absolutely starve, if I did not get to some of my own Species: For as to those filthy *Yahoos,* although there were few greater Lovers of Mankind, at that time, than myself; yet I confess I never saw any sensitive Being so detestable on all Accounts; and the more I came near them, the more hateful they grew, while I stayed in that Country. This the Master Horse observed by my Behaviour, and therefore sent the *Yahoo* back to his Kennel. He then put his Forehoof to his Mouth, at which I was much surprized, although he did it with Ease, and with a Motion that appear'd perfectural natural; and made other Signs to know what I would eat; but I could not return him such an Answer as he was able to apprehend; and if he had understood me, I did not see how it was possible to contrive any way for finding myself Nourishment. While we were thus engaged, I

11 *complaisant.* "Complaisant" and "complacent" come from the same Latin word carrying the connotation of pleasing. To be complaisant is to please others, to be obliging. To be complacent is to please one's self, to be self-satisfied. Clearly, only one meaning was likely to survive, the two words being too close in sound and spelling. Complacent survives; complaisant has become obsolete.

12 *common enough in many Parts of Europe.* This may well be a sly dig at Scotland, which has been the butt of English humor since time out of mind. Oatmeal is a perfectly edible food and it is even possible to like it, but it was not a particularly popular food in Swift's England. In Scotland, which was a much poorer land, oatmeal was an important staple. So, with an audible sigh, Gulliver the Englishman, is forced to content himself with the food of a Scotsman.

In 1755, a quarter century after the publication of *Gulliver's Travels,* Samuel Johnson (1709–1784) defined "oats," in his famous dictionary, as a grain which, in England, was fed to horses and, in Scotland, was fed to men. Whether Johnson was inspired by this passage from Swift in his oats definition is impossible to say, but he had certainly read *Gulliver's Travels* for he made the remarkably ungracious (and foolish) observation that there was nothing much to it, in that once Swift had thought of little men and big men, all the rest followed naturally.

observed a Cow passing by; whereupon I pointed to her, and expressed a Desire to let me go and milk her. This had its Effect; for he led me back into the House, and ordered a Mare-servant to open a Room, where a good Store of Milk lay in Earthen and Wooden Vessels, after a very orderly and cleanly Manner. She gave me a large Bowl full, of which I drank very heartily, and found myself well refreshed.

About Noon I saw coming towards the House a Kind of Vehicle, drawn like a Sledge by four *Yahoos.* There was in it an old Steed, who seemed to be of Quality; he alighted with his Hind-feet forward, having by Accident got a Hurt in his Left Fore-foot. He came to dine with our Horse, who received him with great Civility. They dined in the best Room, and had Oats boiled in Milk for the second Course, which the old Horse eat warm, but the rest cold. Their Mangers were placed circular in the Middle of the Room, and divided into several Partitions, round which they sat on their Haunches upon Bosses of Straw. In the Middle was a large Rack with Angles answering to every Partition of the Manger. So that each Horse and Mare eat their own Hay, and their own Mash of Oats and Milk, with much Decency and Regularity. The Behaviour of the young Colt and Fole appeared very modest; and that of the **11** Master and Mistress extremely chearful and complaisant to their Guest. The Grey ordered me to stand by him; and much Discourse passed between him and his Friend concerning me, as I found by the Stranger's often looking on me, and the frequent Repetition of the Word *Yahoo.*

I happened to wear my Gloves; which the Master Grey observing, seemed perplexed; discovering Signs of Wonder what I had done to my Fore-feet; he put his Hoof three or four times to them, as if he would signify, that I should reduce them to their former Shape, which I presently did, pulling off both my Gloves, and putting them into my Pocket. This occasioned farther Talk, and I saw the Company was pleased with my Behaviour, whereof I soon found the good Effects. I was ordered to speak the few Words I understood; and while they were at Dinner, the Master taught me the Names for Oats, Milk, Fire, Water, and some others; which I could readily pronounce after him; having from my Youth a great Facility in learning Languages.

When Dinner was done, the Master Horse took me aside, and by Signs and Words made me understand the Concern he was in, that I had nothing to eat. Oats in their Tongue are called *Hlunnh.* This Word I pronounced two or three times; for although I had refused them at first, yet upon second Thoughts, I considered that I could contrive to make a Kind of Bread, which might be sufficient with Milk to keep me alive, till I could make my Escape to some other Country, and to Creatures of my own Species. The Horse immediately ordered a white Mare-servant of his Family to bring me a good Quantity of Oats in a Sort of wooden Tray. These I heated before the Fire as well as I could, and rubbed them till the Husks came off, which I made a shift to winnow from the Grain; I ground and beat them between two Stones, then took Water, and made them into a Paste or Cake, which I toasted at the Fire, and eat **12** warm with Milk. It was at first a very insipid Diet, although common enough in many Parts of *Europe,* but grew tolerable by Time; and having been often reduced to hard Fare in my Life, this was

Illustration by Rex Whistler, 1930.

13 *Springes made of Yahoos Hairs*. Gulliver is portrayed as becoming more and more repelled by the Yahoos and attracted to the Houyhnhnms, so that he increasingly renounces his own humanity in favor of the unemotional rationality of the horses. His refusal to accept himself for what he is, and to acknowledge his kinship with the Yahoos, leads him to make use of the varying parts of the Yahoo body as though the Yahoos were purely animal, with no relationship to himself at all.

14 *no Animal to be fond of it but Man*. Gulliver is quite wrong here. Human beings may indeed overdo the use of salt, but it is essential, in reasonable quantities, to life for all animals. Carnivorous animals get it in their diet in ample quantity, but the diet of herbivorous animals is generally salt deficient so that they must seek out salt licks, which are natural deposits of salt-containing minerals. As a matter of fact, it would be the Houyhnhnms who would require salt and go to all lengths to get it, while the carnivorous Yahoos would be able to do without.

15 *Six Yards from the House, and separated from the Stable of the Yahoos*. The Houyhnhnms are puzzled by Gulliver. In some respects, he resembles the Yahoos; in other respects (thanks to his clothes) he does not, and he can clearly reason, which the Yahoos cannot. Because of his mixture of qualities, he is given a place to live that is between that of the Yahoos and the Houyhnhnms. Symbolically, Gulliver (man) is halfway between the Houyhnhnms (innocence) and the Yahoos (depravity) and partakes of the qualities of both. The Houyhnhnms are portrayed throughout as we might imagine Adam and Eve to have been before the Fall. The Yahoos are as they might have been had they Fallen beyond redemption.

It is Gulliver's tragedy that he cannot accept his midway status, or understand that to be a Houyhnhnm is as unsatisfying as to be a Yahoo, because to lack passion is as great a loss as to lack reason.

not the first Experiment I had made how easily Nature is satisfied. And I cannot but observe, that I never had one Hour's Sickness, while I staid in this Island. It is true, I sometimes made a shift to **13** catch a Rabbet, or Bird, by Springes made of *Yahoos* Hairs; and I often gathered wholesome Herbs, which I boiled, or eat as Salades with my Bread; and now and then, for a Rarity, I made a little Butter, and drank the Whey. I was at first at a great Loss for Salt; but Custom soon reconciled the Want of it; and I am confident that the frequent Use of Salt among us is an Effect of Luxury, and was first introduced only as a Provocative to Drink; except where it is necessary for preserving of Flesh in long Voyages, or **14** in Places remote from great Markets. For we observe no Animal to be fond of it but Man: And as to myself, when I left this Country, it was a great while before I could endure the Taste of it in any thing that I eat.

This is enough to say upon the Subject of my Dyet, wherewith other Travellers fill their Books, as if the Readers were personally concerned, whether we fare well or ill. However, it was necessary to mention this Matter, lest the World should think it impossible that I could find Sustenance for three Years in such a Country, and among such Inhabitants.

When it grew towards Evening, the Master Horse ordered a **15** Place for me to lodge in; it was but Six Yards from the House, and separated from the Stable of the *Yahoos*. Here I got some Straw, and covering myself with my own Cloaths, slept very sound. But I was in a short time better accommodated, as the Reader shall know hereafter, when I come to treat more particularly about my Way of living.

CHAPTER THREE

The Author studious to learn the Language, the Houyhnhnm his Master assists in teaching him. The Language described. Several Houyhnhnms of Quality come out of Curiosity to see the Author. He gives his Master a short Account of his Voyage.

MY principal Endeavour was to learn the Language, which my Master (for so I shall henceforth call him) and his Children, and every Servant of his House were desirous to teach me. For they looked upon it as a Prodigy, that a brute Animal should discover such Marks of a rational Creature. I pointed to every thing, and enquired the Name of it, which I wrote down in my *Journal Book* when I was alone, and corrected my bad Accent, by desiring those of the Family to pronounce it often. In this Employment, a Sorrel Nag, one of the under Servants, was very ready to assist me.

In speaking, they pronounce through the Nose and Throat, and their Language approaches nearest to the *High Dutch* or *German*, of any I know in *Europe;* but is much more graceful and significant. The Emperor *Charles* V. made almost the same Observation, when he said, That if he were to speak to his Horse, it should be in *High Dutch*. **1**

2

The Curiosity and Impatience of my Master were so great, that he spent many Hours of his Leisure to instruct me. He was convinced (as he afterwards told me) that I must be a *Yahoo*, but my Teachableness, Civility and Cleanliness astonished him; which

1 *the Emperor Charles V*. Charles V (1500–1558) was Holy Roman Emperor, king of Spain, ruler over parts of Italy and the Netherlands, over much of North and South America, and over various islands in the far-flung ocean.

2 *High Dutch*. Charles V, in discussing the chief languages of his dominions, is supposed to have said that he would "speak Spanish to God, Italian to women, French to men, and German to my horse." This was, of course, an expression of his contempt for German (which he didn't speak well).

Emperor Charles V. Courtesy, Library of Congress.

3 *I . . . got them on before they waked in the Morning.* It is clear that Gulliver is deliberately trying to fool the Houyhnhnms (and himself) by masking, as far as he can, the similarity between himself and the Yahoos.

4 *the Inhabitants have not the least Idea of Books on Literature.* Many critics have been deeply angered by this fourth section of the book, thinking that Swift went entirely too far in his condemnation of humanity. It seems to me, however, that Swift is not describing the Houyhnhnms as ideal in all respects. Can we seriously believe Swift would approve of a way of life in which there was no idea of books and literature?

5 *He was sure no Houyhnhnm alive could make such a Vessel, or would trust Yahoos to manage it.* The inability of the Houyhnhnms to conceive of lying seems an expression of their virtue, but their inability to accept what they do not already know indicates their profound lack of imagination. Surely, we would refuse reason if it meant the loss of culture; and we would accept lies, if that were the penalty of imagination, rather than buy truth with utter dullness.

is Gulliver more intelligent
us 1) He can read & write
2) He can conceive of lying.
H's don't seem
h've developed

3 were Qualities altogether so opposite to those Animals. He was most perplexed about my Cloaths, reasoning sometimes with himself, whether they were a Part of my Body; for I never pulled them off till the Family were asleep, and got them on before they waked in the Morning. My Master was eager to learn from whence I came; how I acquired those Appearances of Reason, which I discovered in all my Actions; and to know my Story from my own Mouth, which he hoped he should soon do by the great Proficiency I made in learning and pronouncing their Words and Sentences. To help my Memory, I formed all I learned into the *English* Alphabet, and writ the Words down with the Translations. This last, after some time, I ventured to do in my Master's Presence. It **4** cost me much Trouble to explain to him what I was doing; for the Inhabitants have not the least Idea of Books or Literature.

In about ten Weeks time I was able to understand most of his Questions; and in three Months could give him some tolerable Answers. He was extremely curious to know from what Part of the Country I came, and how I was taught to imitate a rational Creature; because the *Yahoos*, (whom he saw I exactly resembled in my Head, Hands and Face, that were only visible,) with some Appearance of Cunning, and the strongest Disposition to Mischief, were observed to be the most unteachable of all Brutes. I answered; that I came over the Sea, from a far Place, with many others of my own Kind, in a great hollow Vessel made of the Bodies of Trees: That, my Companions forced me to land on this Coast, and then left me to shift for myself. It was with some Difficulty, and by the Help of many Signs, that I brought him to understand me. He replied, That I must needs be mistaken, or that I *said the thing which was not.* (For they have no Word in their Language to express Lying or Falshood.) He knew it was impossible that there could be a Country beyond the Sea, or that a Parcel of Brutes could move a wooden Vessel whither they pleased upon Water. **5** He was sure no *Houyhnhnm* alive could make such a Vessel, or would trust *Yahoos* to manage it.

The Word *Houyhnhnm,* in their Tongue, signifies a *Horse;* and in its Etymology, *the Perfection of Nature.* I told my Master, that I was at a Loss for Expression, but would improve as fast as I could; and hoped in a short time I should be able to tell him Wonders: He was pleased to direct his own Mare, his Colt and Fole, and the Servants of the Family to take all Opportunities of instructing me; and every Day for two or three Hours, he was at the same Pains himself: Several Horses and Mares of Quality in the Neighbourhood came often to our House, upon the Report spread of a wonderful *Yahoo,* that could speak like a *Houyhnhnm,* and seemed in his Words and Actions to discover some Glimmerings of Reason. These delighted to converse with me; they put many Questions, and received such Answers, as I was able to return. By all which Advantages, I made so great a Progress, that in five Months from my Arrival, I understood whatever was spoke, and could express myself tolerably well.

The *Houyhnhnms* who came to visit my Master, out of a Design of seeing and talking with me, could hardly believe me to be a right *Yahoo,* because my Body had a different Covering from others of my Kind. They were astonished to observe me without the usual Hair or Skin, except on my Head, Face and Hands: but

I discovered that Secret to my Master, upon an Accident which happened about a Fortnight before.

I have already told the Reader, that every Night when the Family were gone to Bed, it was my Custom to strip and cover myself with my Cloaths: It happened one Morning early, that my Master sent for me, by the Sorrel Nag, who was his Valet; when he came, I was fast asleep, my Cloaths fallen off on one Side, and my Shirt above my Waste. I awaked at the the Noise he made, and observed him to deliver his Message in some Disorder; after which he went to my Master, and in a great Fright gave him a very confused Account of what he had seen: This I presently discovered; for going as soon as I was dressed, to pay my Attendance upon his Honour, he asked me the Meaning of what his Servant had reported; that I was not the same Thing when I slept as I appeared to be at other times; that his Valet assured him, some Part of me was white, some yellow, at least not so white, and some brown.

I had hitherto concealed the Secret of my Dress, in order to distinguish myself as much as possible, from that cursed Race of

Illustration from French edition, 1795. Courtesy, Library of Congress.

6 *to conceal what Nature had given.* This is another example of the manner in which the Houyhnhnms represent un-Fallen humanity. In the garden of Eden, Adam and Eve were naked "and were not ashamed." Shame came at the instant of the Fall.

7 *Whiteness.* Notice that a white skin is enough in itself to decrease the resemblance to the Yahoo. Swift seems to take it for granted, as Europeans generally did, that the darker the skin the closer to the beast.

8 *shuddering with Cold.* This makes sense. If the land of the Houyhnhnms is at forty-five degrees south, it is not as far from the equator as Paris is, but in the Southern Hemisphere it would be exposed to the wintry blasts from the enormous Antarctica ice cap, so that it would be distinctly colder than Paris.

Yahoos; but now I found it in vain to do so any longer. Besides, I considered that my Cloaths and Shoes would soon wear out, which already were in a declining Condition, and must be supplied by some Contrivance from the Hides of *Yahoos,* or other Brutes; whereby the whole Secret would be known. I therefore told my Master, that in the Country from whence I came, those of my Kind always covered their Bodies with the Hairs of certain Animals prepared by Art, as well for Decency, as to avoid Inclemencies of Air both hot and cold; of which, as to my own Person I would give him immediate Conviction, if he pleased to command me; only desiring his Excuse, if I did not expose those Parts that Nature taught us to conceal. He said, my Discourse was all very strange, but especially the last Part; for he could not understand why

6 Nature should teach us to conceal what Nature had given. That neither himself nor Family were ashamed of any Parts of their Bodies; but however I might do as I pleased. Whereupon, I first unbuttoned my Coat, and pulled it off. I did the same with my Waste-coat; I drew off my Shoes, Stockings and Breeches. I let my Shirt down to my Waste, and drew up the Bottom, fastening it like a Girdle about my Middle to hide my Nakedness.

My Master observed the whole Performance with great Signs of Curiosity and Admiration. He took up all my Cloaths in his Pastern, one Piece after another, and examined them diligently; he then stroaked my Body very gently, and looked round me several Times; after which he said, it was plain I must be a perfect *Yahoo;* but that I differed very much from the rest of my Species, in the

7 Whiteness, and Smoothness of my Skin, my want of Hair in several Parts of my Body, the Shape and Shortness of my Claws behind and before, and my Affectation of walking continually on my two hinder Feet. He desired to see no more; and gave me leave to put

8 on my Cloaths again, for I was shuddering with Cold.

I expressed my Uneasiness at his giving me so often the Appelation of *Yahoo,* an odious Animal, for which I had so utter an Hatred and Contempt. I begged he would forbear applying that Word to me, and take the same Order in his Family, and among his Friends whom he suffered to see me. I requested likewise, that the Secret of my having a false Covering to my Body might be known to none but himself, at least as long as my present Cloath-

Gulliver's clothes are examined by his Master. Willy Pogány. 1919.

ing should last: For as to what the Sorrel Nag his Valet had observed, his Honour might command him to conceal it.

All this my Master very graciously consented to; and thus the Secret was kept till my Cloaths began to wear out, which I was forced to supply by several Contrivances, that shall hereafter be mentioned. In the mean Time, he desired I would go on with my utmost Diligence to learn their Language, because he was more astonished at my Capacity for Speech and Reason, than at the Figure of my Body, whether it were covered or no; adding, that he waited with some Impatience to hear the Wonders which I promised to tell him.

From thenceforward he doubled the Pains he had been at to instruct me; he brought me into all Company, and made them treat me with Civility, because, as he told them privately, this would put me into good Humour, and make me more diverting.

Every Day when I waited on him, beside the Trouble he was at in teaching, he would ask me several Questions concerning my self, which I answered as well as I could; and by those Means he had already received some general Ideas, although very imperfect. It would be tedious to relate the several Steps, by which I advancd to a more regular Conversation: But the first Account I gave of my self in any Order and Length, was to this Purpose:

That, I came from a very far Country, as I already had attempted to tell him, with about fifty more of my own Species; that we travelled upon the Seas, in a great hollow Vessel made of Wood, and larger than his Honour's House. I described the Ship to him in the best Terms I could; and explained by the Help of my Handkerchief displayed, how it was driven forward by the Wind. That, upon a Quarrel among us, I was set on Shoar on this Coast, where I walked forward without knowing whither, till he delivered me from the Persecution of those execrable *Yahoos*. He asked me, Who made the Ship, and how it was possible that the *Houyhnhnms* of my Country would leave it to the Management of Brutes? My Answer was, that I durst proceed no farther in my Relation, unless he would give me his Word and Honour that he would not be offended; and then I would tell him the Wonders I had so often promised. He agreed; and I went on by assuring him, that the Ship was made by Creatures like myself, who in all the Countries I had travelled, as well as in my own, were the only governing, rational Animals; and that upon my Arrival hither, I was as much astonished to see the *Houyhnhnms* act like rational Beings, as he or his Friends could be in finding some Marks of Reason in a Creature he was pleased to call a *Yahoo*; to which I owned my Resemblance in every Part, but could not account for their degenerate and brutal Nature. I said farther, That if good Fortune ever restored me to my native Country, to relate my Travels hither, as I resolved to do; every Body would believe that I *said the Thing which was not*; that I invented the Story out of my own Head: And with all possible Respect to Himself, his Family, and Friends, and under his Promise of not being offended, our Countrymen would hardly think it probable, that a *Houyhnhnm* should be the presiding Creature of a Nation, and a *Yahoo* the Brute.

CHAPTER FOUR

1 *Manhood.* We are accustomed to using "manhood" in the sense of "admirable masculine qualities," but here it is being used in the more general sense of "humanity."

The Houyhnhnms notion of Truth and Falshood. The Author's Discourse disapproved by his Master. The Author gives a more particular Account of himself, and the Accidents of his Voyage.

Y Master heard me with great Appearances of Uneasiness in his Countenance; because *Doubting* or *not believing,* are so little known in this Country, that the Inhabitants cannot tell how to behave themselves under such Circumstances. And I remember in frequent

1 Discourses with my Master concerning the Nature of Manhood, in other Parts of the World; having Occasion to talk of *Lying,* and *false Representation,* it was with much Difficulty that he comprehended what I meant; although he had otherwise a most acute Judgment. For he argued thus; That the Use of Spech was to make us understand one another, and to receive Information of Facts; now if any one *said the Thing which was not,* these Ends were defeated; because I cannot properly be said to understand him; and I am so far from receiving Information, that he leaves me worse than in Ignorance; for I am led to believe a Thing *Black* when it is *White,* and *Short* when it is *Long.* And these were all the Notions he had concerning that Faculty of *Lying,* so perfectly well understood, and so universally practised among human Creatures.

To return from this Digression; when I asserted that the *Yahoos* were the only governing Animals in my Country, which my Master said was altogether past his Conception, he desired to know, whether we had *Houyhnhnms* among us, and what was their Employment: I told him, we had great Numbers; that in Summer they grazed in the Fields, and in Winter were kept in Houses, with Hay and Oats, where *Yahoo* Servants were employed to rub their Skins smooth, comb their Manes, pick their Feet, serve them with Food, and make their Beds. I understand you well, said my Master; it is now very plain from all you have spoken, that whatever Share of Reason the *Yahoos* pretend to, the *Houyhnhnms* are your Masters; I heartily wish our *Yahoos* would be so tractable. I begged his Honour would please to excuse me from proceeding any farther, because I was very certain that the Account he expected from me would be highly displeasing. But he insisted in commanding me to let him know the best and the worst: I told him he should be obeyed. I owned, that the *Houyhnhnms* among us, whom we called *Horses,* were the most generous and comely Animal we had; that they excelled in Strength and Swiftness; and when they belonged to Persons of Quality, employed in Travelling, Racing, and drawing Chariots, they were treated with much Kindness and Care, till they fell into Diseases, or became foundered in the Feet; but then they were sold, and used to all kind of Drudgery till they died; after which their Skins were stripped and sold for

Horse being currycombed. Engraving by Jost Amman, 1599.

"Second Stage of Cruelty," engraving by William Hogarth, 1751. Courtesy, Library of Congress.

2 *mean People*. Lower classes. See Part 1, Chapter 6, note 21.

what they were worth, and their Bodies left to be devoured by Dogs and Birds of Prey. But the common Race of Horses had not so good **2** Fortune, being kept by Farmers and Carriers, and other mean People, who put them to greater Labour, and feed them worse. I described as well as I could, our way of Riding; the Shape and Use of a Bridle, a Saddle, a Spur, and a Whip; of Harness and Wheels. I added, that we fastened Plates of a certain hard Substance called *Iron* at the Bottom of their Feet, to preserve their Hoofs from being broken by the Stony Ways on which we often travelled.

My Master, after some Expressions of great Indignation, wondered how we dared to venture upon a *Houyhnhnm's* Back; for he was sure, that the weakest Servant in his House would be able to shake off the strongest *Yahoo*; or by lying down, and rouling upon his Back, squeeze the Brute to Death. I answered, That our Horses were trained up from three or four Years old to the several Uses we intended them for; That if any of them proved intolerably vicious, they were employed for Carriages; that they were severely beaten while they were young for any mischievous Tricks: That the Males, designed for the common Use of Riding or Draught, were generally *castrated* about two Years after their Birth, to take down their Spirits, and make them more tame and

"The Sad History of the Horse," wood engraving by Fritz Eichenberg from *Heritage Club edition, 1940. Courtesy of the artist.*

gentle: That they were indeed sensible of Rewards and Punishments; but his Honour would please to consider, that they had not the least Tincture of Reason any more than the *Yahoos* in this Country.

It put me to the Pains of many Circumlocutions to give my Master a right Idea of what I spoke; for their Language doth not **3** abound in Variety of Words, because their Wants and Passions are fewer than among us. But it is impossible to express his noble Resentment at our savage Treatment of the *Houyhnhnm* Race; particularly after I had explained the Manner and Use of *Castrating* Horses among us, to hinder them from propagating their Kind, and to render them more servile. He said, if it were possible there could be any Country where *Yahoos* alone were endued with Reason, they certainly must be the governing Animal, because Reason will in Time always prevail against Brutal Strength. But, considering the Frame of our Bodies, and especially of mine, he thought no Creature of equal Bulk was so ill-contrived, for employing that Reason in the common Offices of Life; whereupon he desired to know whether those among whom I lived, resembled me or the *Yahoos* of his Country. I assured him, that I was as well shaped as most of my Age; but the younger and the Females were much more soft and tender, and the Skins of the latter generally as white as Milk. He said, I differed indeed from other *Yahoos,* being much more cleanly, and not altogether so deformed; but in point of real Advantage, he thought I differed for the worse. That my Nails were of no Use either to my fore or hinder Feet: As to my fore Feet, he could not properly call them by that Name, for he never observed me to walk upon them; that they were too soft to bear the Ground; that I generally went with them uncovered, neither was the Covering I sometimes wore on them, of the same Shape, or so strong as that on my Feet behind. That I could not walk with any Security; for if either of my hinder Feet slipped, I must inevitably fall. He then began to find fault with other Parts of my Body; the Flatness of my Face, the Prominence of my Nose, my Eyes placed directly in Front, so that I could not look on either Side without turning my Head: That I was not able to feed my self, without lifting one of my fore Feet to my Mouth: And therefore Nature had placed those Joints to answer that Necessity. He knew not what could be the Use of those several Clefts and Divisions in my Feet behind; that these were too soft to bear the Hardness and Sharpness of Stones without a Covering made from the Skin of some other Brute; that my whole Body wanted a Fence against Heat and Cold, which I was forced to put on and off every Day with Tediousness and Trouble. And lastly, that he observed every Animal in this Country naturally to abhor the *Yahoos,* whom the Weaker avoided, and the Stronger drove from them. So that supposing us to have the Gift of Reason, he could not see how it were possible to cure that natural Antipathy which every Creature discovered against us; nor consequently, how we could tame and render them serviceable. However, he would (as he said) debate the Matter no farther, because he was more desirous to know my own Story, the Country, where I was born, and the several Actions and Events of my Life before I came hither.

I assured him, how extreamly desirous I was that he should be satisfied in every Point; but I doubted much, whether it would be possible for me to explain my self on several Subjects whereof his

3 *their Language doth not abound in Variety of Words.* This is another example of cultural limitation for which the Houyhnhnm-like utopia might not console us.

4 *Queen*. Queen Anne was still on the throne at the time Gulliver left on his fourth voyage. She died on August 1, 1714.

5 *Yahoos*. Gulliver has taken to calling men Yahoos, as he identifies more and more with the Houyhnhnms, and tries more and more desperately to be a non-Yahoo. However, he describes the Queen as a "female man." To have called her a "female Yahoo" would have gotten him in trouble, if, indeed, it would have passed the printer.

Honour could have no Conception, because I saw nothing in his Country to which I could resemble them. That however, I would do my best, and strive to express my self by Similitudes, humbly desiring his Assistance when I wanted proper Words; which he was pleased to promise me.

I said, my Birth was of honest Parents, in an Island called *England*, which was remote from this Country, as many Days Journey as the strongest of his Honour's Servants could travel in the Annual Course of the Sun. That I was bred a Surgeon, whose Trade it is to cure Wounds and Hurts in the Body, got by Accident or Violence. That my Country was governed by a Female Man, **4** whom we called a *Queen*. That I left it to get Riches, whereby I might maintain my self and Family when I should return. That in my last Voyage, I was Commander of the Ship and had about fifty **5** *Yahoos* under me, many of which died at Sea, and I was forced to supply them by others picked out from several Nations. That our Ship was twice in Danger of being sunk; the first Time by a great Storm, and the second, by striking against a Rock. Here my Master interposed, by asking me, How I could persuade Strangers out of different countries to venture with me, after the Losses I had sustained, and the Hazards I had run. I said, they were Fellows of desperate Fortunes, forced to fly from the Places of their Birth, on Account of their Poverty or their Crimes. Some were undone by Law-suits; others spent all they had in Drinking, Whoring and Gaming; others fled for Treason; many for Murder, Theft, Poysoning, Robbery, Perjury, Forgery, Coining false Money; for committing Rapes or Sodomy; for flying from their Colours, or deserting to the enemy; and most of them had broken Prison. None of these durst return to their native Countries for fear of being hanged, or of starving in a Jail; and therefore were under a Necessity of seeking a Livelihood in other Places.

During this Discourse, my Master was pleased often to interrupt me. I had made Use of many Circumlocutions in describing to him the Nature of the several crimes, for which most of our Crew had been forced to fly their Country. This Labour took up several Days Conversation before he was able to comprehend me. He was wholly at a Loss to know what could be the Use or Necessity of practising those Vices. To clear up which I endeavoured to give him some Ideas of the Desire of Power and Riches; of the terrible Effects of Lust, Intemperance, Malice, and Envy. All this I was forced to define and describe by putting of Cases, and making Suppositions. After which, like one whose Imagination was struck with something never seen or heard of before, he would lift up his Eyes with Amazement and Indignation. Power, Government, War, Law, Punishment, and a Thousand other Things had no Terms, wherein that Language could express them; which made the Difficulty almost insuperable to give my Master any Conception of what I meant: But being of an excellent Understanding, much improved by Contemplation and Converse, he at last arrived at a competent Knowledge of what human Nature in our Parts of the World is capable to perform; and desired I would give him some particular Account of that Land, which we call *Europe*, especially, of my own Country.

CHAPTER FIVE

The Author at his Master's Commands informs him of the State of England. The Causes of War among the Princes of Europe. The Author begins to explain the English Constitution.

HE Reader may please to observe, that the following Extract of many Conversations I had with my Master, contains a Summary of the most material Points, which were discoursed at several times for above two Years; his Honour often desiring fuller Satisfaction as I farther improved in the *Houyhnhnm* Tongue. I laid before him, as well as I could, the whole State of *Europe*; I discoursed of Trade and Manufactures, of Arts and Sciences; and the Answers I gave to all the Questions he made, as they arose upon several Subjects, were a Fund of Conversation not to be exhausted. But I shall here only set down the Substance of what passed between us concerning my own Country, reducing it into Order as well as I can, without any Regard to Time or other Circumstances, while I strictly adhere to Truth. My only Concern is, that I shall hardly be able to do Justice to my Master's Arguments and Expressions; which must needs suffer by my Want of Capacity, as well as by a Translation into our barbarous *English*.

In Obedience therefore to his Honour's Commands, I related to him the *Revolution* under the *Prince of Orange*; the long War

1 *our barbarous English.* Gulliver is pictured as becoming thoroughly unreasonable in his pro-Houyhnhnm prejudices. In comparing the limited vocabulary of the Houyhnhnms with the language of Shakespeare, it is simply mad to call English "barbarous" and, in fact, Gulliver is on his way to madness.

2 *the Prince of Orange.* James II of England, who had come to the throne in 1685, was a Catholic, while most of the nation was Protestant. He was a poor politician and increasingly offended the leaders of the nation. When he married again and had a son in 1688, a plan was hatched whereby he was to be removed from the throne in favor of his older daughter, Mary, by a previous marriage, a woman who had been raised as a Protestant. She was married to her first cousin, William of Orange, stadtholder of the Netherlands, and also a Protestant.

The plot was successful. James II was forced to flee and was succeeded by his nephew and his daughter, who ruled jointly as William III and Mary II. The changeover was virtually bloodless and was therefore called "the Glorious Revolution." It was accompanied by the acceptance by William and Mary of "the Declaration of Rights" on February 13, 1689. This made Parliament supreme in the nation.

1

2

3 *said Prince.* James II fled to Catholic France. The French king, Louis XIV, supported James' government in exile and supplied him with the wherewithal to invade Ireland. William III was an inveterate enemy of Louis XIV from 1672, when Louis had sent his armies to invade the Netherlands. William III had no trouble, then, in going to war with Louis XIV in 1689 in response to the latter's support of James. James was defeated in Ireland by William in 1690 and the war with France continued until 1697 (it is called "the War of the Grand Alliance") and ended with the Treaty of Ryswick.

4 *Queen.* Mary II died on December 28, 1694, while the War of the League of Augsburg was still proceeding. William III continued as sole king and survived that war, but died on March 19, 1702. He was succeeded by his sister-in-law, Anne, who was the younger daughter of James II. Six weeks after her accession, Great Britain declared war on France and the War of the Spanish Succession began.

5 *the greatest Powers of Christendom were engaged.* Allied with Great Britain in the War of the Spanish Succession were the Netherlands, Austria, Prussia, Portugal, and various minor German states. Allied with France were Spain, Bavaria, and various minor German states.

6 *whether Flesh be Bread . . . whether . . . be Blood or Wine.* As he has done in other places in the book, Swift accentuates human folly by deliberately trivializing causes for dispute. There were strong doctrinal disputes between Catholics and Protestants on whether the unleavened bread in the Mass did or did not turn into the flesh of Christ, and on whether the wine in the Mass ("the Juice of a certain Berry") was or was not turned into the blood of Christ—that is, on whether Jesus' words were to be taken literally or metaphorically.

7 *Whether Whistling be a Vice or a Virtue.* A reference to disputes over church music.

8 *to kiss a Post, or throw it into the Fire.* The post referred to is, of course, the crucifix—whether it was to be venerated or considered an idolatrous abomination.

9 *What is the best Colour for a Coat.* A reference to disputes over vestments.

10 *hire out their Troops to richer Nations.* This is a thrust at George I who, when he was elector of Hanover, sold his subjects for soldiers. Other German princelings did the same. In fact, when George I's great-grandson, George III, was on the throne, fifty years after *Gulliver's Travels* was published, he bought soldiers from the German state of Hesse-Cassel and sent these "Hessians" to fight against the American colonists who were then in rebellion.

3
4,5 with *France* entered into by the said Prince, and renewed by his Successor the present Queen; wherein the greatest Powers of *Christendom* were engaged, and which still continued: I computed at his Request, that about a Million of *Yahoos* might have been killed in the whole Progress of it; and perhaps a Hundred or more Cities taken, and five times as many Ships burnt or sunk.

He asked me what were the usual Causes or Motives that made one Country go to War with another. I answered, they were innumerable; but I should only mention a few of the chief. Sometimes the Ambition of Princes, who never think they have Land or People enough to govern: Sometimes the Corruption of Ministers, who engage their Master in a War in order to stifle or divert the Clamour of the Subjects against their evil Administration. Difference in Opinions hath cost many Millions of Lives: For Instance, **6** whether *Flesh* be *Bread,* or *Bread* be *Flesh:* Whether the Juice of **7** a certain *Berry* be *Blood* or *Wine:* Whether *Whistling* be a Vice or **8** a Virtue: Whether it be better to *kiss* a *Post,* or throw it into the **9** Fire: What is the best Colour for a *Coat,* whether *Black, White, Red* or *Grey;* and whether it should be *long* or *short, narrow* or *wide, dirty* or *clean;* with many more. Neither are any Wars so furious and bloody, or of so long Continuance, as those occasioned by Difference in Opinion, especially if it be in things indifferent.

Sometimes the Quarrel between two Princes is to decide which of them shall dispossess a Third of his Dominions, where neither of them pretend to any Right. Sometimes one Prince quarrelleth with another, for fear the other should quarrel with him. Sometimes a War is entered upon, because the Enemy is too *strong,* and sometimes because he is too *weak.* Sometimes our *Neighbours* want the *Things* which we *have,* or *have* the Things which we want; and we both fight, till they take ours or give us theirs. It is a very justifiable Cause of War to invade a Country after the People have been wasted by Famine, destroyed by Pestilence, or embroiled by Factions amongst themselves. It is justifiable to enter into a War against our nearest Ally, when one of his Towns lies convenient for us, or a Territory of Land, that would render our Dominions round and compact. If a Prince send Forces into a Nation, where the People are poor and ignorant, he may lawfully put half of them to Death, and make Slaves of the rest, in order to civilize and reduce them from their barbarous Way of Living. It is a very kingly, honourable, and frequent Practice, when one Prince desires the Assistance of another to secure him against an Invasion, that the Assistant, when he hath driven out the Invader, should seize on the Dominions himself, and kill, imprison or banish the Prince he came to relieve. Allyance by Blood or Marriage, is a sufficient Cause of War between Princes; and the nearer the Kindred is, the greater is their Disposition to quarrel: *Poor* Nations are *hungry,* and *rich* Nations are *proud;* and Pride and Hunger will ever be at Variance. For these Reasons, the Trade of a *Soldier* is held the most honourable of all others: Because a *Soldier* is a *Yahoo* hired to kill in cold Blood as many of his own Species, who have never offended him, as possibly he can.

10 There is likewise a Kind of beggarly Princes in *Europe* not able to make War by themselves, who hire out their Troops to richer Nations for so much a Day to each Man; of which they keep three

Fourths to themselves, and it is the best Part of their Maintenance; such are those in many *Northern* Parts of *Europe*.

What you have told me, (said my Master) upon the Subject of War, doth indeed discover most admirably the Effects of that Reason you pretend to: However, it is happy that the *Shame* is greater than the *Danger*; and that Nature hath left you utterly uncapable of doing much Mischief: For your Mouths lying flat with your Faces, you can hardly bite each other to any Purpose, unless by Consent. Then, as to the Claws upon your Feet before and behind, they are so short and tender, that one of our *Yahoos* would drive a Dozen of yours before him. And therefore in recounting the Numbers of those who have been killed in Battle, I cannot but think that you have *said the Thing which is not.*

I could not forbear shaking my Head and smiling a little at his Ignorance. And, being no Stranger to the Art of War, I gave him a Description of Cannons, Culverins, Muskets, Carabines, Pistols, Bullets, Powder, Swords, Bayonets, Battles, Sieges, Retreats, Attacks, Undermines, Countermines, Bombardments, Sea-fights; Ships sunk with a Thousand Men; twenty Thousand killed on each Side; dying Groans, Limbs flying in the Air: Smoak, Noise, Confusion, trampling to Death under Horses Feet: Flight, Pursuit, Victory; Fields strewed with Carcases left for Food to Dogs, and Wolves, and Birds of Prey; Plundering, Stripping, Ravishing, Burning and Destroying. And, to set forth the Valour of my own dear Countrymen, I assured him, that I had seen them blow up a Hundred Enemies at once in a Siege, and as many in a Ship; and beheld the dead Bodies drop down in Pieces from the Clouds, to the great Diversion of all the Spectators.

I was going on to more Particulars, when my Master commanded me Silence. He said, whoever understood the Nature of *Yahoos* might easily believe it possible for so vile an Animal, to be capable of every Action I had named, if their Strength and Cunning equalled their Malice. But, as my Discourse had increased his Abhorrence of the whole Species, so he found it gave him a Disturbance in his Mind, to which he was wholly a Stranger before. He thought his Ears being used to such abominable Words, might **11** by Degrees admit them with less Detestation. That, although he hated the *Yahoos* of this Country, yet he no more blamed them for their odious Qualities, than he did a *Gnnauyh* (a Bird of Prey) for its Cruelty, or a sharp Stone for cutting his Hoof. But, when a Creature pretending to Reason, could be capable of such Enormities, he dreaded lest the Corruption of that Faculty might be worse than Brutality itself. He seemed therefore confident, that instead of Reason, we were only possessed of some Quality fitted to increase our natural Vices; as the Reflection from a troubled Stream returns the Image of an ill-shapen Body, not only *larger*, but more *distorted*.

He added, That he had heard too much upon the Subject of War, both in this, and some former Discourses. There was another Point which a little perplexed him at present. I had said, that some of our Crew left their Country on Account of being ruined by *Law*: That I had already explained the Meaning of the Word; but he was at a Loss how it should come to pass, that the *Law* which was intended for *every* Man's Preservation, should be any Man's Ruin. Therefore he desired to be farther satisfied what I meant by *Law*,

11 *his Ears being used to such abominable words, might by Degrees admit them with less Detestation.* Seven years after *Gulliver's Travels* was published, Swift's friend, Alexander Pope (1688–1744), wrote in *An Essay on Man:*

> Vice is a monster of so frightful mien
> As to be hated needs but to be seen;
> Yet seen too oft, familiar with her face,
> We first endure, then pity, then embrace.

Pope's views were often Swiftian and we might wonder whether the idea of the quatrain came from the Houyhnhnm's remark here.

12 *Faculty*. Swift, who hated lawyers, is at his brilliant best in this passage. "Faculty" here means "profession."

and the Dispensers thereof, according to the present Practice in my own Country: Because he thought, Nature and Reason were sufficient Guides for a reasonable Animal, as we pretended to be, in shewing us what we ought to do, and what to avoid.

I assured his Honour, that *Law* was a Science wherein I had not much conversed, further than by employing Advocates, in vain, upon some Injustices that had been done me. However, I would give him all the Satisfaction I was able.

I said there was a Society of Men among us, bred up from their Youth in the Art of proving by Words multiplied for the Purpose, that *White* is *Black*, and *Black* is *White*, according as they are paid. To this Society all the rest of the People are Slaves.

For Example. If my Neighbour hath a mind to my *Cow*, he hires a Lawyer to prove that he ought to have my *Cow* from me. I must then hire another to defend my Right; it being against all Rules of *Law* that any Man should be allowed to speak for himself. Now in this Case, I who am the true Owner lie under two great Disadvantages. First, my Lawyer being practiced almost from his Cradle in defending Falshood; is quite out of his Element when he would be an Advocate for Justice, which as an Office unnatural, he always attempts with great Awkwardness, if not with Ill-will. The second Disadvantage is, that my Lawyer must proceed with great Caution: Or else he will be reprimanded by the Judges, and abhorred by his Brethren, as one who would lessen the Practice of the Law. And therefore I have but two Methods to preserve my *Cow*. The first is, to gain over my Adversary's Lawyer with a double Fee; who will then betray his Client, by insinuating that he hath Justice on his Side. The second Way is for my Lawyer to make my Cause appear as unjust as he can; by allowing the *Cow* to belong to my Adversary; and this if it be skilfully done, will certainly bespeak the Favour of the Bench.

Now, your Honour is to know, that these Judges are Persons appointed to decide all Controversies of Property, as well as for the Tryal of Criminals; and picked out from the most dextrous Lawyers who are grown old or lazy: And having been byassed all their Lives against Truth and Equity, lie under such a fatal Necessity of favouring Fraud, Perjury and Oppression; that I have known some of them to have refused a large Bribe from the Side **12** where Justice lay, rather than injure the *Faculty*, by doing any thing unbecoming their Nature or their Office.

It is a Maxim among these Lawyers, that whatever hath been done before, may legally be done again: And therefore they take special Care to record all the Decisions formerly made against common Justice and the general Reason of Mankind. These, under the Name of *Precedents*, they produce as Authorities to justify the most iniquitous Opinions; and the Judges never fail of directing accordingly.

In pleading, they studiously avoid entering into the *Merits* of the Cause; but are loud, violent and tedious in dwelling upon all *Circumstances* which are not to the Purpose. For Instance, in the Case already mentioned: They never desire to know what Claim or Title my Adversary hath to my *Cow*; but whether the said *Cow* were Red or Black; her Horns long or short; whether the Field I graze her in be round or square; whether she were milked at home or abroad; what Diseases she is subject to, and the like. After which they consult *Precedents*, adjourn the Cause, from Time to Time, and in Ten, Twenty, or Thirty Years come to an Issue.

It is likewise to be observed, that this Society hath a peculiar Cant and Jargon of their own, that no other Mortal can understand, and wherein all their Laws are written, which they take special Care to multiply; whereby they have wholly confounded the very Essence of Truth and Falshood, of Right and Wrong; so that it will take Thirty Years to decide whether the Field, left me by my Ancestors for six Generations, belong to me, or to a Stranger three Hundred Miles off.

In the Tryal of Persons accused for Crimes against the State, the Method is much more short and commendable: The Judge first sends to sound the Disposition of those in Power; after which he can easily hang or save the Criminal, strictly preserving all the Forms of Law.

Here my Master interposing, said it was a Pity, that Creatures endowed with such prodigious Abilities of Mind as these Lawyers, by the Description I gave of them must certainly be, were not rather encouraged to be Instructors of others in Wisdom and Knowledge. In Answer to which, I assured his Honour, that in all Points out of their own Trade, they were usually the most ignorant and stupid Generation among us, the most despicable in common Conversation, avowed Enemies to all Knowledge and Learning; and equally disposed to pervert the general Reason of Mankind, in every other Subject of Discourse, as in that of their own Profession.

CHAPTER SIX

A continuation of the state of England, under Queen Anne. The Character of a First Minister in the Courts of Europe.

Y Master was yet wholly at a Loss to understand what Motives could incite this Race of Lawyers to perplex, disquiet, and weary themselves by engaging in a Confederacy of Injustice, merely for the Sake of injuring their Fellow-Animals; neither could he comprehend what I meant in saying they did it for *Hire*. Whereupon I was at much Pains to describe to him the Use of *Money*, the Materials it was made of, and the Value of the Metals: That when a *Yahoo* had got a great Store of this precious Substance, he was able to purchase whatever he had a mind to; the finest Cloathing, the noblest Houses, great Tracts of Land, the most costly Meats and Drinks; and have his Choice of the most beautiful Females. Therefore since *Money* alone, was able to perform all these Feats, our *Yahoos* thought, they could never have enough of it to spend or to save, as they found themselves inclined from their natural Bent either to Profusion or Avarice. That, the rich Man enjoyed the Fruit of the poor Man's Labour, and the latter were a Thousand to One in Proportion to the former. That the Bulk of our People was forced to live miserably, by labouring every Day for small Wages to make a few live plentifully. I enlarged myself much on these and many other Particulars to the same Purpose: But his Honour was still to seek: For he went upon a Supposition that all Animals had a Title to their Share in the Productions of the Earth; and especially those who presided over the rest. Therefore he desired I would let him know, what these costly Meats were, and how any of us happened to want them. Whereupon I enumerated as many Sorts as came into my Head, with the various Methods of dressing them, which could not be done without sending Vessels by Sea to every Part of the World, as well for Liquors to drink, as for Sauces, and innumerable other Conveniencies. I assured him, that this whole Globe of Earth must be at least three Times gone round, before one of our better Female *Yahoos* could get her Breakfast, or a Cup to put it in. He said, That must needs be a miserable Country which cannot furnish Food for its own Inhabitants. But what he chiefly wondered at, was how such vast Tracts of Ground as I described, should be wholly without *Fresh-water*, and the People put to the Necessity of sending over the Sea for Drink. I replied, that *England* (the dear Place of my Nativity) was computed to produce three Times the Quantity of Food, more than its Inhabitants are able to consume, as well as Liquors extracted from Grain, or pressed out of the Fruit of certain Tress, which made excellent Drink; and the same Proportion in every other Convenience of Life. But, in order to feed the Luxury and Intemperance of the Males, and the Vanity of the Females, we sent away the greatest Part of our necessary Things to other Countries, from whence in Return we brought the Materials of Diseases, Folly, and Vice, to spend among ourselves. Hence it follows of Necessity, that vast Numbers of our People are compelled to seek their Livelihood by Begging, Robbing, Stealing, Cheating, Pimping, Forswearing, Flattering, Suborning, Forging, Gaming, Lying, Fawning, Hectoring, Voting, Scribling, Stargazing, Poysoning, Whoring, Canting, Libelling, Free-thinking, and the like Occupations: Every one of which Terms, I was at much Pains to make him understand. **1**

That, *Wine* was not imported among us from foreign Countries to supply the Want of Water or other Drinks, but because it was a Sort of Liquid which made us merry, by putting us out of our Senses; diverted all melancholy Thoughts, begat wild extravagant Imaginations in the Brain, raised our Hopes, and banished our Fears; suspended every Office of Reason for a Time, and deprived us of the Use of our Limbs, untill we fell into a profound Sleep; although it must be confessed, that we always awaked sick and dispirited; and that the Use of this Liquor filled us with Diseases, which made our Lives uncomfortable and short.

But beside all this, the Bulk of our People supported themselves by furnishing the Necessities or Conveniencies of Life to the Rich, and to each other. For Instance, when I am at home and dressed as I ought to be, I carry on my Body the Workmanship of an Hundred Tradesmen; the Building and Furniture of my House employ as many more; and Five Times the Number to adorn my Wife.

I was going on to tell him of another Sort of People, who get their Livelihood by attending the Sick; having upon some Occasions informed his Honour that many of my Crew had died of Diseases. But here it was with the utmost Difficulty, that I brought him to apprehend what I meant. He could easily conceive, that a *Houyhnhnm* grew weak and heavy a few Days before his Death; or

1 *seek their Livelihood by Begging . . . Free-thinking.* Swift rattles off many activities, some criminal, some merely unpleasant, which can be used for gain. Voting, for instance, is of course not a vice, except when votes are exchanged for money. And scribbling (a slang term for writing), is Swift's own profession, but of course in this context Swift means writing lies for money. However, I wish Swift would describe how one makes money out of free-thinking. Granted that it is a vice in a religious society, yet how does one get anything out of it but blows, disabilities, and imprisonment?

2 *we fed on a Thousand Things which operated contrary to each other.* The fact that infectious disease is caused by microorganisms was, of course, not yet known in Swift's time. Therefore, a great deal of the blame for disease was placed on the diet. To be sure, improper diet is the cause of many diseases, but in Swift's day, the lack of knowledge concerning the chemistry of food was so abysmal that many of the notions about diet were completely wrong.

3 *a certain Malady.* Syphilis, of course, which, as always, is associated with women—although if the prostitutes had it, they certainly acquired it from men.

4 *the whole Mystery and Method by which they proceed.* Swift's satire on medicine, almost as bitter as his satire on law, finds an easy—and justified—target, for physicians in his time did indeed operate entirely through ignorance. In addition to the laxatives and emetics which Swift derides, there was the practice of bleeding (which he doesn't mention), which deprived the body of the very substance that was most useful in combating many diseases naturally.

5 *many that are only imaginary . . . with these our Female Yahoos are always infested.* Men have always been most impatient with the ailments of women, since it has always been considered the proper duty of the woman to wait upon the ailing man. For a woman herself to be ailing and, worse still, to need care, seems unbearably annoying, and the easiest way out is to insist that the woman's ailment is only imaginary. There was considerable feeling in Swift's time, therefore, as well as in the ages before and in the ages since (including our own) that women are much more prone to hypochondria than men.

by some Accident might hurt a Limb. But that Nature, who worketh all things to Perfection, should suffer any Pains to breed in our Bodies, he thought impossible; and desired to know the Reason of **2** so unaccountable an Evil. I told him, we fed on a Thousand Things which operated contrary to each other; that we eat when we were not hungry, and drank without the Provocation of Thirst: That we sat whole Nights drinking strong Liquors without eating a Bit; which disposed us to Sloth, enflamed our Bodies, and precipitated or prevented Digestion. That, prostitute Female *Yahoos* acquired **3** a certain Malady, which bred Rottenness in the Bones of those, who fell into their Embraces: That this and many other Diseases, were propagated from Father to Son; so that great Numbers come into the World with complicated Maladies upon them: That, it would be endless to give him a Catalogue of all Diseases incident to human Bodies; for they could not be fewer than five or six Hundred, spread over every Limb, and Joynt: In short, every Part, external and intestine, raving Diseases appropriated to each. To remedy which, there was a Sort of People bred up among us, in the Profession or Pretence of curing the Sick. And because I had some Skill in the Faculty, I would in Gratitude to his Honour, let **4** him know the whole Mystery and Method by which they proceed.

Their Fundamental is, that all Diseases arise from *Repletion;* from whence they conclude, that a great *Evacuation* of the Body is necessary, either through the natural Passage, or upwards at the Mouth. Their next Business is, from Herbs, Minerals, Gums, Oyls, Shells, Salts, Juices, Seaweed, Excrements, Barks of Trees, Serpents, Toads, Frogs, Spiders, dead Men's Flesh and Bones, Birds, Beasts and Fishes, to form a Composition for Smell and Taste the most abominable, nauseous and detestable, that they can possibly contrive, which the Stomach immediately rejects with Loathing: And this they call a *Vomit.* Or else from the same Store-house, with some other poysonous Additions, they command us to take in at the Orifice *above* or *below,* (just as the Physician then happens to be disposed) a Medicine equally annoying and disgustful to the Bowels; which relaxing the Belly, drives down all before it: And this they call a *Purge,* or a *Clyster.* For Nature (as the Physicians alledge) having intended the superior anterior Orifice only for the *Intromission* of Solids and Liquids, and the inferior Posterior for Ejection; these Artists ingeniously considering that in all Diseases Nature is forced out of her Seat; therefore to replace her in it, the Body must be treated in a Manner directly contrary, by interchanging the Use of each Orifice; forcing Solids and Liquids in at the *Anus,* and making Evacuations at the Mouth.

5 But, besides real Diseases, we are subject to many that are only imaginary, for which the Physicians have invented imaginary Cures; these have their several Names, and so have the Drugs that are proper for them; and with these our Female *Yahoos* are always infested.

One great Excellency in this Tribe is their Skill at *Prognosticks,* wherein they seldom fail; their Predictions in real Diseases, when they rise to any Degree of Malignity, generally portending *Death,* which is always in their Power, when Recovery is not: And therefore, upon any unexpected Signs of Amendment, after they have pronounced their Sentence, rather than be accused as false Prophets, they know how to approve their Sagacity to the World by a seasonable Dose.

They are likewise of special Use to Husbands and Wives, who are grown weary of their Mates; to eldest Sons, to great Ministers of State, and often to Princes.

I had formerly upon Occasion discoursed with my Master upon the Nature of *Government* in general, and particularly of our own *excellent Constitution,* deservedly the Wonder and Envy of the whole World. But having here accidentally mentioned a *Minister of State;* he commanded me some Time after to inform him, what Species of *Yahoo* I particularly meant by that Appellation.

I told him, that a *First* or *Chief Minister of State,* whom I intended to describe, was a Creature wholly exempt from Joy and Grief, Love and Hatred, Pity and Anger; at least makes use of no other Passions but a violent Desire of Wealth, Power, and Titles: That he applies his Words to all Uses, except to the Indication of his Mind; That he never tells a *Truth,* but with an Intent that you should take it for a *Lye;* nor a *Lye,* but with a Design that you should take it for a *Truth;* That those he speaks worst of behind their Backs, are in the surest way to Preferment; and whenever he begins to praise you to others or to your self, you are from that Day forlorn. The worst Mark you can receive is a *Promise,* especially when it is confirmed with an Oath; after which every wise Man retires, and gives over all Hopes.

There are three Methods by which a Man may rise to be Chief Minister: The first is, by knowing how with Prudence to dispose of a Wife, a Daughter, or a Sister: The second, by betraying or undermining his Predecessor: And the third is, by a *furious Zeal* in publick Assemblies against the Corruptions of the Court. But a wise Prince would rather chuse to employ those who practise the last of these Methods; because such Zealots prove always the most obsequious and subservient to the Will and Passions of their Master. That, these *Ministers* having all Employments at their Disposal, preserve themselves in Power by bribing the Majority of a Senate or great Council; and at last by an Expedient called an *Act of Indemnity* (whereof I described the Nature to him) they secure themselves from After-reckonings, and retire from the Publick, laden with the Spoils of the Nation.

The Palace of a *Chief Minister,* is a Seminary to breed up others in his own Trade: The Pages, Lacquies, and Porter, by imitating their Master, become *Ministers of State* in their several Districts, and learn to excel in the three principal *Ingredients,* of *Insolence, Lying,* and *Bribery.* Accordingly, they have a *Subaltern* Court paid to them by Persons of the best Rank; and sometimes by the Force of Dexterity and Impudence, arrive through several Gradations to be Successors to their Lord.

He is usually governed by a decayed Wench, or favourite Foot man, who are the Tunnels through which all Graces are conveyed, and may properly be called, *in the last Resort,* the Governors of the Kingdom.

One Day, my Master, having heard me mention the *Nobility* of my Country, was pleased to make me a Compliment which I could not pretend to deserve: That, he was sure, I must have been born of some Noble Family, because I far exceeded in Shape, Colour, and Cleanliness, all the *Yahoos* of his Nation, although I seemed to fail in Strength, and Agility, which must be imputed to my different Way of Living from those other Brutes; and besides, I was not only endowed with the Faculty of Speech, but likewise

6 *a First or Chief Minister of State . . . makes use of no other Passions but a violent Desire of Wealth, Power, and Titles.* Here, once again, Swift is satirizing Walpole (see Part I, Chapter 3, note 2).

7 *forlorn.* The word "forlorn" is most frequently used today to mean "miserable," "wretched," "pitifully sorrowful." It is actually homologous to the German word *verloren,* meaning "lost" or "abandoned," and that is the meaning here.

8 *Act of Indemnity.* This would be a special law that would exempt some official of state from penalties for illegal acts, or that would reimburse him for losses he suffered in carrying out his official duties, or both. It is rather analogous to the pardoning of Richard M. Nixon, which not only made it unnecessary for him to suffer punishment for any of the illegal acts he committed, though all his underlings were punished for obeying him, but also qualified him to continue to receive a vast pension as a reward for breaking the law.

9 *Subaltern.* Subordinate.

10 *continued always in the Condition of Servants.* The Houyhnhnms apparently have a thoroughly racist society in which the horses know their place in society by the color of their hair (though, interestingly enough, the black Houyhnhnms are superior to the white). So ingrained is inequality in Swift's time, that it exists, without question, even in a utopia of perfect reason.

11 *our young Noblemen . . . marry some Woman of mean Birth . . . whom they hate and despise.* In the third part, Gulliver blames the decay of noble families on the infidelities of wives with members of the lower classes (see Chapter 8, note 22). Here the opposite is suggested. It is the privilege of satirists to get you coming and going, if they can. Swift always can.

12 *Spleen.* A brownish-red organ lying on the left side of the body just behind the stomach. Its spongy structure serves as a blood reservoir. Because it is an organ rich in blood, it was viewed in earlier times as having a profound effect on the emotions—like the heart and liver, which are also blood-suffused. To have an overactive spleen resulted in (depending on who it was who was guessing) ill-temper or melancholy or hypochondria.

with some Rudiments of Reason, to a Degree, that with all his Acquaintance I passed for a Prodigy.

He made me observe, that among the *Houyhnhnms,* the *White,* the *Sorrel,* and the *Iron-grey,* were not so exactly shaped as the *Bay,* the *Dapple-grey,* and the *Black;* nor born with equal Talents of Mind, or a Capacity to improve them; and therefore continued **10** always in the Condition of Servants, without ever aspiring to match out of their own Race, which in that Country would be reckoned monstrous and unnatural.

I made his Honour my most humble Acknowledgements for the good Opinion he was pleased to conceive of me; but assured him at the same Time, that my Birth was of the lower Sort, having been born of plain, honest Parents, who were just able to give me a tolerable Education: That, *Nobility* among us was altogether a different Thing from the Idea he had of it; That, our young *Noble-* **11** *men* are bred from their Childhood in Idleness and Luxury; that, as soon as Years will permit, they consume their Vigour, and contract odious Diseases among lewd Females; and when their Fortunes are almost ruined, they marry some Woman of mean Birth, disagreeable Person, and unsound Constitution, merely for the sake of Money, whom they hate and despise. That, the Productions of such Marriages are generally, scrophulous, rickety or deformed Children; by which Means the Family seldom continues above three Generations, unless the Wife take Care to provide a healthy Father among her Neighbours, or Domesticks, in order to improve and continue the Breed. That, a weak diseased Body, a meager Countenace, and sallow Complexion, are the true Marks of *noble Blood;* and a healthy robust Appearance is so disgraceful in a Man of Quality, that the World concludes his real Father to have been a Groom or a Coachman. The Imperfections of his Mind run parallel with **12** those of his Body; being a Composition of Spleen, Dulness, Ignorance, Caprice, Sensuality and Pride.

Without the Consent of this illustrious Body, no Law can be enacted, repealed, or altered: And these Nobles have likewise the Decision of all our Possessions without Appeal.

CHAPTER SEVEN

The Author's great Love of his Native Country. His Master's Observations upon the Constitution and Administration of England, as described by the Author, with parallel cases and comparisons. His Master's Observations upon Human Nature.

1 *managing*. That is, treating with care, or consideration.

HE Reader may be disposed to wonder how I could prevail on my self to give so free a Representation of my own Species, among a Race of Mortals who were already too apt to conceive the vilest Opinion of Human Kind, from that entire Congruity betwixt me and their *Yahoos*. But I must freely confess, that the many Virtues of those excellent *Quadrupeds* placed in opposite View to human Corruptions, had so far opened my Eyes, and enlarged my Understanding, that I began to view the Actions and Passions of Man in a very different Light; and to think the Honour of my own Kind not worth managing; which, besides, it was impossible for me to **1** do before a Person of so acute a Judgment as my Master, who daily convinced me of a thousand Faults in my self, whereof I had not the least Perception before, and which with us would never be numbered even among human Infirmities. I had likewise learned from his Example an utter Detestation of all Falshood or Disguise; and *Truth* appeared so amiable to me, that I determined upon sacrificing every thing to it.

Let me deal so candidly with the Reader, as to confess, that there was yet a much stronger Motive for the Freedom I took in

2 *gave as favourable a Turn as the Matter would bear.* This is the final thrust. After having read and winced through Gulliver's scathing catalogue of the iniquities of mankind, we end by being told that he has bent over backwards to make us seem better than we are.

3 *a Contrivance to make my Claws of no Use or Defence, and to remove the Hair from my Chin.* In other words, man's technology serves but to emphasize his weakness, as we cut our nails with scissors and our beards with razors.

my Representation of Things. I had not been a Year in this Country, before I contracted such a Love and Veneration for the Inhabitants, that I entered on a firm Resolution never to return to human Kind, but to pass the rest of my Life among these admirable *Houyhnhnms* in the Contemplation and Practice of every Virtue; where I could have no Example or Incitement to Vice. But it was decreed by Fortune, my perpetual Enemy, that so great a Felicity should not fall to my Share. However, it is now some Comfort to reflect, that in what I said of my Countrymen, I *extenuated* their Faults as much as I durst before so strict an Examiner; and **2** upon every Article, gave as *favourable* a Turn as the Matter would bear. For, indeed, who is there alive that will not be swayed by his Byass and Partiality to the Place of his Birth?

I have related the Substance of several Conversations I had with my Master, during the greatest Part of the Time I had the Honour to be in his Service; but have indeed for Brevity sake omitted much more than is here set down.

When I had answered all his Questions, and his Curiosity seemed to be fully satisfied; he sent for me one Morning early, and commanding me to sit down at some Distance, (an Honour which he had never before conferred upon me) He said, he had been very seriously considering my whole Story, as far as it related both to my self and my Country: That, he looked upon us as a Sort of Animals to whose Share, by what Accident he could not conjecture, some small Pittance of *Reason* had fallen, whereof we made no other Use than by its Assistance to aggravate our *natural* Corruptions, and to acquire new ones which Nature had not given us. That, we disarmed our selves of the few Abilities she had bestowed; had been very successful in multiplying our original Wants, and seemed to spend our whole Lives in vain Endeavours to supply them by our own Inventions. That, as to my self, it was manifest I had neither the Strength or Agility of a common *Yahoo;* **3** that I walked infirmly on my hinder Feet; had found out a Contrivance to make my Claws of no Use or Defence, and to remove the Hair from my Chin, which was intended as a Shelter from the Sun and the Weather. Lastly, That I could neither run with Speed, nor climb Trees like my *Brethren* (as he called them) the *Yahoos* in this Country.

That, our Institutions of *Government* and *Law* were plainly owing to our gross Defects in *Reason,* and by consequence, in *Virtue;* because *Reason* alone is sufficient to govern a *Rational* Creature; which was therefore a Character we had no Pretence to challenge, even from the Account I had given of my own People; although he manifestly perceived, that in order to favour them, I had concealed many Particulars, and often *said the Thing which was not.*

He was the more confirmed in this Opinion, because he observed, that as I agreed in every Feature of my Body with other *Yahoos,* except where it was to my real Disadvantage in point of Strength, Speed and Activity, the Shortness of my Claws, and some other Particulars where Nature had no Part; so, from the Representation I had given him of our Lives, our Manners, and our Actions, he found as near a Resemblance in the Disposition of our Minds. He said, the *Yahoos* were known to hate one another more than they did any different Species of Animals; and the Reason usually assigned, was, the Odiousness of their own Shapes, which all could see in the rest, but not in themselves. He had therefore begun to think it not unwise in us to *cover* our Bodies, and by that Invention, conceal many of our Deformities from each other, which would else be hardly supportable. But, he now found he had been mistaken; and that the Dissentions of those Brutes in his Country were owing to the same Cause with ours, as I had described them. For, if (said he) you throw among five *Yahoos* as much Food as would be sufficient for fifty, they will, instead of eating peaceably, fall together by the Ears, each single one impatient to *have all to it self;* and therefore a Servant was usually employed to stand by while they were feeding abroad, and those kept at home were tied at a Distance from each other. That, if a Cow died of Age or Accident before a *Houyhnhnm* could secure it for his own *Yahoos,* those in the Neighbourhood would come in Herds to seize it, and then would ensue such a Battle as I had described, with terrible Wounds made by their Claws on both Sides, although they seldom were able to kill one another, for want of such convenient Instruments of Death as we had invented. At other Times the like Battles have been fought between the *Yahoos* of several Neighbourhoods without any visible Cause: Those of one District watching all Opportunities to surprise the next before they are prepared. But if they find their Project hath miscarried, they return home, and for want of Enemies, engage in what I call a *Civil War* among themselves.

That, in some Fields of his Country, there are certain *shining* **4** *Stones* of several Colours, whereof the *Yahoos* are violently fond; and when Part of these *Stones* are fixed in the Earth, as it sometimes happeneth, they will dig with their Claws for whole Days to get them out, and carry them away, and hide them by Heaps in their Kennels; but still looking round with great Caution, for fear their Comrades should find out their Treasure. My Master said, he could never discover the Reason of this unnatural Appetite, or how these *Stones* could be of any Use to a *Yahoo;* but now he believed it might proceed from the same Principle of *Avarice,* which I had ascribed to Mankind. That he had once, by way of Experiment, privately removed a Heap of these *Stones* from the Place where one of his Yahoos had buried it: Whereupon, the sordid Animal missing his Treasure, by his loud lamenting brought the whole Herd to the Place, there miserably howled, then fell to biting and tearing the rest; began to pine away, would neither eat nor sleep, nor work, till he ordered a Servant privately to convey the *Stones* into the same Hole, and hide them as before; which when his *Yahoo* had found, he presently recovered his Spirits and good Humour; but took Care to remove them to a better hiding Place; and hath ever since been a very serviceable Brute.

My Master farther assured me, which I also observed my self; That in the Fields where these *shining Stones* abound, the fiercest and most frequent Battles are fought, occasioned by perpetual Inroads of the neighbouring *Yahoos.*

He said, it was common when two *Yahoos* discovered such a *Stone* in a Field, and were contending which of them should be the Proprietor, a third would take the Advantage, and carry it away from them both; which my Master would needs contend to have some Resemblance with our *Suits at Law;* wherein I thought it for our Credit not to undeceive him; since the Decision he mentioned

4 *shining Stones of several Colours.* Presumably this is a reference to gold, silver, and copper.

5 *undistinguished*. We would say "undiscriminating." Human beings are essentially omnivorous, as are bears, pigs, and rats. The ability to live on a varied diet is an important characteristic from the standpoint of survival. Omnivorous species are few, but successful, and while Swift makes much of the connection of disease with what he considers a departure from simple, wholesome food, the fact remains (just to keep our perspectives in order) that healthy, well-cared-for human beings have life spans three times that of healthy, well-cared-for horses—even though horses are larger than human beings and, in general, larger mammals live longer than smaller ones.

Illustration by Willy Pogány, 1919.

was much more equitable than many Decrees among us: Because the Plaintiff and Defendant there lost nothing beside the *Stone* they contended for; whereas our *Courts of Equity*, would never have dismissed the Cause while either of them had any thing left.

My Master continuing his Discourse, said, There was nothing **5** that rendered the *Yahoos* more odious, than their undistinguished Appetite to devour every thing that came in their Way, whether Herbs, Roots, Berries, corrupted Flesh of Animals, or all mingled together: And it was peculiar in their Temper, that they were fonder of what they could get by Rapine or Stealth at a greater Distance, than much better Food provided for them at home. If their Prey held out, they would eat till they were ready to burst, after which Nature had pointed out to them a certain *Root* that gave them a general Evacuation.

There was also another kind of *Root* very *juicy*, but something
rare and difficult to be found, which the *Yahoos* fought for with
much Eagerness, and would suck it with great Delight: It produced
the same Effects that Wine hath upon us. It would make them
sometimes hug, and sometimes tear one another; they would howl
and grin, and chatter, and roul, and tumble, and then fall asleep
in the Mud.

I did indeed observe, that the *Yahoos* were the only Animals in
this Country subject to any Diseases; which however, were much
fewer than Horses have among us, and contracted not by any ill
Treatment they meet with, but by the Nastiness and Greediness
of that sordid Brute. Neither has their Language any more than
a general Appellation for those Maladies; which is borrowed from
the Name of the Beast, and called *Hnea Yahoo*, or the *Yahoo's*-

6 *the She-Yahoo would admit the Male, while she was pregnant*. Swift comments obliquely on some of what he considers humanity's most repellent traits by attributing them to the Yahoos, and making his point even stronger by including such qualities—particularly sexuality—among those which Gulliver failed, out of his previously mentioned *partiality* to his kind, to describe to his master. It does seem that human beings are exceptional in that the females of the species do not have specific times when they are in heat and when they are interested in sex. Contrary to Swift's view that this is evidence of humanity's corruption, however, the fact that human beings are interested in sex at times when fertilization is unlikely or impossible (or has already occurred) would seem to indicate that among human beings sex has a social function as well as a reproductive one. Sex heightens the continuing interest between men and women and leads to stronger and longer-lasting family ties, which are essential in view of the long period of helplessness of the human infant. Those who think sex is only justified for the sake of reproduction view it as an animal, rather than as a human, act, and would deprive the mutual love of husband and wife of its strongest support and most affectionate demonstration.

Evil; and the Cure prescribed is a Mixture of *their own Dung* and *Urine*, forcibly put down the *Yahoo's* Throat. This I have since often known to have been taken with Success: And do here freely recommend it to my Countrymen, for the publick Good, as an admirable Specifick against all Diseases produced by Repletion.

As to Learning, Government, Arts, Manufactures, and the like; my Master confessed he could find little or no Resemblance between the *Yahoos* of that Country and those in ours. For, he only meant to observe what Parity there was in our Natures. He had heard indeed some curious *Houyhnhnms* observe, that in most Herds there was a Sort of ruling *Yahoo,* (as among us there is generally some leading or principal Stag in a Park) who was always more *deformed* in Body, and *mischievous in Disposition,* than any of the rest. That, this *Leader* had usually a Favourite as *like himself* as he could get, whose Employment was to *lick his Master's Feet and Posteriors, and drive the Female* Yahoos *to his Kennel;* for which he was now and then rewarded with a Piece of Ass's Flesh. This *Favourite* is hated by the whole Herd; and therefore to protect himself, keeps always *near the Person of his Leader.* He usually continues in Office till a worse can be found; but the very Moment he is discarded, his Successor, at the Head of all the *Yahoos* in that District, Young and Old, Male and Female, come in a Body, and discharge their Excrements upon him from Head to Foot. But how far this might be applicable to our *Courts* and *Favourites*, and *Ministers of State*, my Master said I could best determine.

I durst make no Return to this malicious Insinuation, which debased human Understanding below the Sagacity of a common *Hound,* who hath Judgment enough to distinguish and follow the Cry of the *ablest Dog in the Pack,* without being ever mistaken.

My Master told me, there were some Qualities remarkable in the *Yahoos,* which he had not observed me to mention, or at least very slightly, in the Accounts I had given him of human Kind. He said, those Animals, like other Brutes, had their Females in common; but in this they differed, that the She-*Yahoo* would admit the Male, while she was pregnant; and that the Hees would quarrel and fight with the Female as fiercely as with each other. Both which Practices were such Degrees of infamous Brutality, that no other sensitive Creature ever arrived at.

Another Thing he wondered at in the *Yahoos,* was their strange Disposition to Nastiness and Dirt; whereas there appears to be a natural Love of Cleanliness in all other Animals. As to the two former Accusations, I was glad to let them pass without any Reply, because I had not a Word to offer upon them in Defence of my Species, which otherwise I certainly had done from my own Inclinations. But I could have easily vindicated human Kind from the Imputation of Singularity upon the last Article, if there had been any *Swine* in that Country, (as unluckily for me there were not) which although it may be a *sweeter Quadruped* than a *Yahoo,* cannot I humbly conceive in Justice pretend to more Cleanliness; and so his Honour himself must have owned, if he had seen their filthy Way of feeding, and their Custom of wallowing and sleeping in the Mud.

My Master likewise mentioned another Quality, which his Servants had discovered in several *Yahoos,* and to him was wholly unaccountable. He said, a Fancy would sometimes take a *Yahoo*, to retire into a Corner, to lie down and howl, and groan, and spurn away all that came near him, although he were young and fat, and wanted neither Food nor Water; nor did the Servants imagine what could possibly ail him. And the only Remedy they found was to set him to hard Work, after which he would infallibly come to himself. To this I was silent out of Partiality to my own Kind; yet here I could plainly discover the true Seeds of *Spleen*, which only seizeth on the *Lazy*, the *Luxurious*, and the *Rich*; who, if they were forced to undergo the *same Regimen*, I would undertake for the Cure.

His Honour had farther observed, that a Female-*Yahoo* would often stand behind a Bank or a Bush, to gaze on the young Males passing by, and then appear, and hide, using many antick Gestures and Grimaces; at which time it was observed, that she had a most *offensive Smell*; and when any of the Males advanced, would slowly retire, looking often back, and with a counterfeit Shew of Fear, run off into some convenient Place where she knew the Male would follow her.

At other times, if a Female Stranger came among them, three or four of her own Sex would get about her, and stare and chatter, and grin, and smell her all over; and then turn off with Gestures that seemed to express Contempt and Disdain.

Perhaps my Master might refine a little in these Speculations, which he had drawn from what he observed himself, or had been told by others; However, I could not reflect without some Amazement, and much Sorrow, that the Rudiments of *Lewdness, Coquetry, Censure*, and *Scandal*, should have Place by Instinct in Womankind.

I expected every Moment, that my Master would accuse the *Yahoos* of those unnatural Appetites in both Sexes, so common among us. But Nature it seems hath not been so expert a Schoolmistress; and these politer Pleasures are entirely the Productions of Art and Reason, on our Side of the Globe.

7 *Spleen*. See Chapter 6 of this part, note 12. Here it would most likely refer to a fashionable languor, or a hypochondriacal helplessness.

8 *unnatural Appetites*. One presumes that Swift alludes to masturbation, homosexuality, oral-genital contacts. He goes on to remark sardonically that in this matter even the Yahoos cannot compete with Europeans. This example of reverse pride is inaccurate, however. Without benefit of "Art and Reason," animals will engage in every sexual act that they are physically capable of performing.

CHAPTER EIGHT

The Author relateth several particulars of the Yahoos. The great Virtues of the Houyhnhnms. The Education and Exercise of their Youth. Their General Assembly.

S I ought to have understood human Nature much better than I supposed it possible for my Master to do, so it was easy to apply the Character he gave of the *Yahoos* to myself and my Countrymen; and I believed I could yet make farther Discoveries from my own Observation. I therefore often begged his Honour to let me go among the Herds of *Yahoos* in the Neighbourhood; to which he always very graciously consented, being perfectly convinced that the Hatred I bore those Brutes would never suffer me to be corrupted by them; and his Honour ordered one of his Servants, a strong Sorrel Nag, very honest and good-natured, to be my Guard; without whose Protection I durst not undertake such Adventures. For I have already told the Reader how much I was pestered by those odious Animals upon my first Arrival. I afterwards failed very narrowly three or four times of falling into their Clutches, when I happened to stray at any Distance without my Hanger. And I have Reason to believe, they had some Imagination that I was of their own Species, which I often assisted myself, by stripping up my Sleeves, and shewing my naked Arms and Breast in their Sight, when my protector was with me: At which times they would approach as near as they durst, and imitate my Actions after the Manner of Monkeys, but ever with great Signs of Hatred; as a tame *Jack Daw* with Cap and Stockings, is always persecuted by the wild ones, when he happens to be got among them.

They are prodigously nimble from their Infancy; however, I once caught a young Male of three Years old, and endeavoured by all Marks of Tenderness to make it quiet; but the little Imp fell a squalling and scratching, and biting with such Violence, that I was forced to let it go; and it was high time, for a whole Troop of old ones came about us at the Noise; but finding the Cub was safe, (for away it ran) and my Sorrel Nag being by, they durst not venture near us. I observed the young Animal's Flesh to smell very rank, and the Stink was somewhat between a *Weasel* and a *Fox,* but much more disagreeable. I forgot another Circumstance, (and perhaps I might have the Reader's Pardon, if it were wholly omitted) that while I held the odious Vermin in my Hands, it voided its filthy Excrements of a yellow liquid Substance, all over my Cloaths; but by good Fortune there was a small Brook hard by, where I washed myself as clean as I could; although I durst not come into my Master's Presence, until I were sufficiently aired.

By what I could discover, the *Yahoos* appear to be the most unteachable of all Animals, their Capacities never reaching higher than to draw or carry Burthens. Yet I am of Opinion, this Defect ariseth chiefly from a perverse, restive Disposition. For they are cunning, malicious, treacherous and revengeful. They are strong and hardy, but of a cowardly Spirit, and by Consequence insolent, abject, and cruel. It is observed, that the *Red-haired* of both Sexes **1** are more libidinous and mischievous than the rest, whom yet they much exceed in Strength and Activity.

The *Houyhnhnms* keep the *Yahoos* for present Use in Huts not far from the House; but the rest are sent abroad to certain Fields,

1 *the Red-haired . . . are more libidinous and mischievous than the rest.* We still have the stereotype of the redhead as more passionate and short-tempered than blonds or brunettes, perhaps from the association of red with the color of blood.

Gulliver and the Yahoo cub. J. J. Grandville, 1835. Courtesy, Library of Congress.

Gulliver pursued by a female Yahoo. Ad. Laluze, 1875. Suppressed in later editions. Courtesy, Library of Congress.

where they dig up Roots, eat several Kinds of Herbs, and search about for Carrion, or sometimes catch *Weasels* and *Luhimuhs* (a Sort of *wild Rat*) which they greedily devour. Nature hath taught them to dig deep Holes with their Nails on the Side of a rising Ground, wherein they lie by themselves; only the Kennels of the Females are larger, sufficient to hold two or three Cubs.

They swim from their Infancy like Frogs, and are able to continue long under Water, where they often take Fish, which the Females carry home to their Young. And upon this Occasion, I hope the Reader will pardon my relating an odd Adventure.

Being one Day abroad with my Protector the Sorrel Nag, and the Weather exceeding hot, I entreated him to let me bathe in a River that was near. He consented, and I immediately stripped myself stark naked, and went down softly into the Stream. It happened that a young Female *Yahoo* standing behind a Bank, saw the whole Proceeding; and inflamed by Desire, as the Nag and I conjectured, came running with all Speed, and leaped into the Water within five Yards of the Place where I bathed. I was never in my Life so terribly frighted; the Nag was grazing at some Distance, not suspecting any Harm: She embraced me after a most fulsome Manner; I roared as loud as I could, and the Nag came galloping towards me, whereupon she quitted her Grasp, with the utmost Reluctancy, and leaped upon the opposite Bank, where she stood gazing and howling all the time I was putting on my Cloaths.

This was Matter of Diversion to my Master and his Family, as well as of Mortification to my self. For now I could no longer deny, that I was a real *Yahoo,* in every Limb and Feature, since the Females had a natural Propensity to me as one of their own Species: Neither was the Hair of this Brute of a Red Colour, (which might have been some Excuse for an Appetite a little irregular) but black as a Sloe, and her Countenance did not make an Appearance altogether so hideous as the rest of the Kind; for, I think, she could not be above Eleven Years old. **2**

Having already lived three Years in this Country, the Reader I suppose will expect, that I should, like other Travellers, give him some Account of the Manners and Customs of its Inhabitants, which it was indeed my principal Study to learn.

As these noble *Houyhnhnms* are endowed by Nature with a general Disposition to all Virtues, and have no Conceptions or Ideas of what is evil in a rational Creature; so their grand Maxim is, to cultivate *Reason,* and to be wholly governed by it. Neither is *Reason* among them a Point problematical as with us, where Men can argue with Plausibility on both Sides of a Question; but strikes you with immediate Conviction; as it must needs do where it is not mingled, obscured, or discoloured by Passion and Interest. I remember it was with extreme Difficulty that I could bring my Master to understand the Meaning of the Word *Opinion,* or how a Point could be disputable; because *Reason* taught us to affirm or deny only where we are certain; and beyond our Knowledge we cannot do either. So that Controversies, Wranglings, Disputes, and Positiveness in false or dubious Propositions, are Evils unknown among the *Houyhnhnms.* In the like Manner when I used to explain to him our several Systems of *Natural Philosophy,* he would laugh that a Creature pretending to *Reason,* should value itself upon the Knowledge of other Peoples Conjectures, and in Things, where that Knowledge, if it were certain, could be of no Use. Wherein he agreed entirely with the Sentiments of *Socrates,* as *Plato* de-

2 *her Countenance did not make an Appearance altogether so hideous as the rest of the Kind.* Gulliver is apparently sufficiently flattered by the attention to find this particular Yahoo a shade more palatable than the rest. Incidentally, in the lands of the Lilliputians, the Brobdingnagians, and the Houyhnhnms, Gulliver, over a period of some years in each case, has no opportunity for normal sex, yet he never gives any indication of missing it, or of any discomfort as a result.

3 *reflected what Destruction . . . would make . . . in the Learned World.* Under the rule of pure reason, there is no disagreement, for to every question there is always one immediately apparent answer and only one. It is easy to see that human beings cannot possibly attain this degree of "pure reason," nor should they aspire to it.

It seems clear to me that if Swift is loudly and strenuously denouncing human passion and all its viler emotions, he is also subtly satirizing the life of pure reason. In fact, like Socrates, he seems to be intent on stripping away *all* our careless assumptions and leaving us with nothing at all; so that, left with nothing, we can begin from scratch and see, if we can, how to build a better world.

4 *Fondness.* The word "fond" has weakened and we now think of it as meaning "mildly affectionate," but in Swift's time it meant "affectionate to a foolish extreme." What Swift is saying is that the Houyhnhnms didn't dote on their children, didn't love them excessively so as to be blind to their faults, or to prefer them to other children who might be equally virtuous.

5 *to prevent the Country from being overburthened with Numbers.* The only method of birth control Swift could conceive of as rational was abstinence.

livers them; which I mention as the highest Honour I can do that **3** Prince of Philosophers. I have often since reflected what Destruction such a Doctrine would make in the Libraries of *Europe;* and how many Paths to Fame would be then shut up in the Learned World.

Friendship and *Benevolence* are the two principal Virtues among the *Houyhnhnms;* and these not confined to particular Objects, but universal to the whole Race. For, a Stranger from the remotest Part, is equally treated with the nearest Neighbour, and where-ever he goes, looks upon himself as at Home. They preserve *Decency* and *Civility* in the highest Degrees, but are altogether ignorant of **4** *Ceremony.* They have no Fondness for their Colts or Foles; but the Care in educating them proceedeth entirely from the Dictates of *Reason.* And, I observed my Master to shew the same Affection to his Neighbour's Issue that he had for his own. They will have it that *Nature* teaches them to love the whole Species, and it is *Reason* only that maketh a Distinction of Persons, where there is a superior Degree of Virtue.

When the Matron *Houyhnhnms* have produced one of each Sex, they no longer accompany with their Consorts, except they lose one of their Issue by some Casualty, which very seldom happens: But in such a Case they meet again; or when the like Accident befalls a Person, whose Wife is past bearing, some other Couple bestows on him one of their own Colts, and then go together a second **5** Time, until the Mother be pregnant. This Caution is necessary to prevent the Country from being overburthened with Numbers. But the Race of inferior *Houyhnhnms* bred up to be Servants is not so strictly limited upon this Article; these are allowed to produce three of each Sex, to be Domesticks in the Noble Families.

In their Marriages they are exactly careful to chuse such Colours as will not make any disagreeable Mixture in the Breed. *Strength* is chiefly valued in the Male, and *Comeliness* in the Female; not upon the Account of *Love,* but to preserve the Race from degenerating: For, where a Female happens to excel in *Strength,* a Consort is chosen with regard to *Comeliness.* Courtship, Love, Presents, Joyntures, Settlements, have no Place in their Thoughts; or Terms whereby to express them in their Language. The young Couple meet and are joined, merely because it is the Determination of their Parents and Friends: It is what they see done every Day; and they look upon it as one of the necessary Actions in a reasonable Being. But the Violation of Marriage, or any other Unchastity, was never heard of: And the married Pair pass their Lives with the same Friendship, and mutual Benevolence that they bear to all others of the same Species, who come in their Way; without Jealousy, Fondness, Quarrelling, or Discontent.

In educating the Youth of both Sexes, their Method is admirable, and highly deserveth our Imitation. These are not suffered to taste a Grain of *Oats,* except upon certain Days, till Eighteen Years old; nor *Milk,* but very rarely; and in Summer they graze two Hours in the Morning, and as many in the Evening, which their Parents likewise observe; but the Servants are not allowed above half that Time; and a great Part of the Grass is brought home, which they eat at the most convenient Hours, when they can be best spared from Work.

Temperance, *Industry, Exercise* and *Cleanliness* are the Lessons equally enjoyned to the young ones of both Sexes: And my Master thought it monstrous in us to give the Females a different Kind of Education from the Males, except in some Articles of Domestick **6** Management; whereby, as he truly observed, one Half of our Natives were good for nothing but bringing Children into the World: And to trust the Care of their Children to such useless Animals, he said was yet a greater Instance of Brutality.

But the *Houyhnhnms* train up their Youth to Strength, Speed, and Hardiness, by exercising them in running Races up and down steep Hills, or over hard stony Grounds; and when they are all in a Sweat, they are ordered to leap over Head and Ears into a Pond or a River. Four times a Year the Youth of certain Districts meet to shew their Proficiency in Running, and Leaping, and other Feats of Strength or Agility; where the Victor is rewarded with a Song made in his or her Praise. On this Festival the Servants drive a Herd of *Yahoos* into the Field, laden with Hay, and Oats, and Milk for a Repast to the *Houyhnhnms*; after which, these Brutes are immediately driven back again, for fear of being noisome to **7** the Assembly.

Every fourth Year, at the *Vernal Equinox*, there is a Representative Council of the whole Nation, which meets in a Plain about twenty Miles from our House, and continueth about five or six Days. Here they inquire into the State and Condition of the several Districts; whether they abound or be deficient in Hay or Oats, or

6 *except in some Articles of Domestick Management.* Swift's feminism always stops short of completion. That the sexes may share domestic management seems unthinkable to him.

7 *noisome.* Obnoxious or disgusting to the senses, particularly that of smell.

Representative council of the Houyhnhnms. Jules Pelcoq, 1895.

Cows or *Yahoos?* And where-ever there is any Want (which is but seldom) it is immediately supplied by unanimous Consent and Contribution. Here likewise the Regulation of Children is settled: As for instance, if a *Houyhnhnm* hath two Males, he changeth one of them with another who hath two Females: And when a Child hath been lost by any Casualty; where the Mother is past Breeding, it is determined what Family in the District shall breed another to supply the Loss.

A Grand Debate at the General Assembly of the Houyhnhnms; and how it was determined. The Learning of the Houyhnhnms. Their Buildings. Their Manner of Burials. The Defectiveness of their Language.

1 *indocible.* Incapable of being taught.

2 *produced by the Heat of the Sun . . . or from the Ooze and Froth of the Sea.* In the Greek myths, the great serpent Python was produced by the heat of the sun upon the mud and slime left over by the Flood. Aphrodite, according to some myths, was born of the froth of the sea.

NE of these Grand Assemblies was held in my time, about three Months before my Departure, whither my Master went as the Representative of our District. In this Council was resumed their old Debate, and indeed, the only Debate that ever happened in their Country; whereof my Master after his Return gave me a very particular Account.

The Question to be debated, was, Whether the *Yahoos* should be exterminated from the Face of the Earth. One of the *Members* for the Affirmative offered several Arguments of great Strength and Weight; alledging, That, as the *Yahoos* were the most filthy, noisome, and deformed Animal which Nature ever produced, so they were the most restive and indocible, mischievous and malicious: They would privately suck the Teats of the *Houyhnhnms* Cows; kill and devour their Cats, trample down their Oats and Grass, if they were not continually watched; and commit a Thousand other Extravagancies. He took Notice of a general Tradition, that *Yahoos* had not been always in their Country: But, that many Ages ago, two of these Brutes appeared together upon a Mountain; whether produced by the Heat of the Sun upon corrupted Mud

3 *Aborigines.* This piece of Swiftian natural history is purely imaginary.

and Slime, or from the Ooze and Froth of the Sea, was never known. That these *Yahoos* engendered, and their Brood in a short time grew so numerous as to over-run and infest the whole Nation. That the *Houyhnhnms* to get rid of this Evil, made a general Hunting, and at last inclosed the whole Herd; and destroying the Older, every *Houyhnhnm* kept two young Ones in a Kennel, and brought them to such a Degree of Tameness, as an Animal so savage by Nature can be capable of acquiring; using them for Draught and Carriage. That, there seemed to be much Truth in this Tradition, and that those Creatures could not be *Ylnhniamshy* (or *Aborigines* of the Land) because of the violent Hatred the *Houyhnhnms* as well as all other Animals, bore them; which although their evil Disposition sufficiently deserved, could never have arrived at so **3** high a Degree, if they had been *Aborigines,* or else they would have long since been rooted out. That, the Inhabitants taking a Fancy to use the Service of the *Yahoos*, had very imprudently neglected to cultivate the Breed of *Asses*, which were a comely Animal, easily kept, more tame and orderly, without any offensive Smell, strong enough for Labour, although they yield to the other

Illustration by Bofa, 1929.

YAHOUS DOMESTIQUES

in Agility of Body; and if their Braying be no agreeable Sound, it is far preferable to the horrible Howlings of the *Yahoos*.

Several others declared their Sentiments to the same Purpose; when my Master proposed an Expedient to the Assembly, whereof he had indeed borrowed the Hint from me. He approved of the Tradition, mentioned by the *Honourable Member*, who spoke before; and affirmed, that the two *Yahoos* said to be first seen among them, had been driven thither over the Sea; that coming to Land, and being forsaken by their Companions, they retired to the Mountains, and degenerating by Degrees, became in Process of Time, much more savage than those of their own Species in the Country from whence these two Originals came. The Reason of his Assertion was, that he had now in his Possession, a certain wonderful *Yahoo*, (meaning myself) which most of them had heard of, and many of them had seen. He then related to them, how he first found me; that, my Body was all covered with an artificial Composure of the Skins and Hairs of other Animals: That, I spoke in a Language of my own; and had thoroughly learned theirs: That, I had related to him the Accidents which brought me thither: That, when he saw me without my Covering, I was an exact *Yahoo* in every Part, only of a whiter Colour, less hairy, and with shorter Claws. He added, how I had endeavoured to persuade him, that in my own and other Countries the *Yahoos* acted as the governing, rational Animal, and held the *Houyhnhnms* in Servitude: That, he observed in me all the Qualities of a *Yahoo*, only a little more civilized by some Tincture of Reason; which however was in a Degree as far inferior to the *Houyhnhnm* Race, as the *Yahoos* of their Country were to me: That, among other things, I mentioned a Custom we had of *castrating Houyhnhnms* when they were young, in order to render them tame; that the Operation was easy and safe; that it was no Shame to learn Wisdom from Brutes, as Industry is taught by the Ant, and Building by the Swallow. (For so I translate the Word *Lyhannh*, although it be a much larger Fowl.) That, this Invention might be practiced upon the younger *Yahoos* here, which, besides rendering them tractable and fitter for Use, would in an Age put an End to the whole Species without destroying Life. That, in the mean time the *Houyhnhnms* should be *exhorted* to cultivate the Breed of Asses, which, as they are in all respects more valuable Brutes; so they have this Advantage, to be fit for Service at five Years old, which the others are not till Twelve.

This was all my Master thought fit to tell me at that Time, of what passed in the Grand Council. But he was pleased to conceal one Particular, which related personally to myself, whereof I soon felt the unhappy Effect, as the Reader will know in its proper Place, and from whence I date all the succeeding Misfortunes of my Life.

The *Houyhnhnms* have no Letters, and consequently, their Knowledge is all traditional. But there happening few Events of any Moment among a People so well united, naturally disposed to every Virtue, wholly governed by Reason, and cut off from all Commerce with other Nations; the historical Part is easily preserved without burthening their Memories. I have already observed, that they are subject to no Diseases, and therefore can have no Need of Physicians. However, they have excellent Medicines composed of Herbs, to cure accidental Bruises and Cuts in the

4 *degenerating by Degrees, became . . . much more savage than those of their own Species.* This doctrine of evolution by degeneration is a bit of interesting foresight on the part of Swift. Comte Georges de Buffon (1707–1788), some decades after *Gulliver's Travels* was published, suggested this in detail. He pointed out that an ape was a degenerated man, a donkey a degenerated horse, and so on. We might wonder if the idea came to him from this passage.

5 *there happening few Events of any Moment.* Over a century later, the English writer, Thomas Carlyle (1795–1881), said in his *Life of Frederick the Great:* "Happy the people whose annals are blank in history books." He attributed the thought to the French lawyer, Charles de Montesquieu (1689–1755). The English historian, Edward Gibbon (1737–1794), said, "History . . . is indeed little more than the register of the crimes, follies, and misfortunes of mankind." Still no one has ever tried living in a time without crime, folly, or misfortune, so we don't really know how happy it would be. Such a time might, like Milton's Paradise, be so boring that even its happiness would be insupportable.

Pastern or Frog of the Foot by sharp Stones, as well as other Maims and Hurts in the several Parts of the Body.

They calculate the Year by the Revolution of the Sun and the Moon, but use no Subdivisions into Weeks. They are well enough acquainted with the Motions of those two Luminaries, and understand the Nature of *Eclipses;* and this is the utmost Progress of their *Astronomy.*

In *Poetry* they must be allowed to excel all other Mortals; wherein the Justness of their Similes, and the Minuteness, as well as Exactness of their Descriptions, are indeed inimitable. Their Verses abound very much in both of these; and usually contain either some exalted Notions of Friendship and Benevolence, or the Praises of those who were Victors in Races, and other bodily Exercises. Their Buildings, although very rude and simple, are not inconvenient, but well contrived to defend them from all Injuries of Cold and Heat. They have a Kind of Tree, which at Forty Years old loosens in the Root, and falls with the first Storm; it grows very strait, and being pointed like Stakes with a sharp Stone, (for the *Houyhnhnms* know not the Use of Iron) they stick them erect in the Ground about ten Inches asunder, and then weave

"They have a Kind of Tree." J. J. Grandville, 1835. Courtesy, Library of Congress.

"They milk their Cows." C. E. Brock, 1894. Courtesy, Library of Congress.

6 *hard Flints, which . . . they form into Instruments.* This is a rather interestingly accurate description of the Stone Age (a phrase invented by the Danish paleontologist, Christian J. Thomsen [1788–1865] in 1834, a century after *Gulliver's Travels* was published).

7 *discover.* That is, "display." And at that, why should he? The Houyhnhnm life, like the Spartan broth (see Part III, Chapter 8, note 16) sounds like a good thing to give up.

in Oat-straw, or sometimes Wattles betwixt them. The Roof is made after the same Manner, and so are the Doors.

The *Houyhnhnms* use the hollow Part between the Pastern and the Hoof of their Fore-feet, as we do our Hands, and this with greater Dexterity, than I could at first imagine. I have seen a white Mare of our Family thread a Needle (which I lent her on Purpose) with that Joynt. They milk their Cows, reap their Oats, and do all the Work which requires Hands, in the same Manner. They have a Kind of hard Flints, which by grinding against other **6** Stones, they form into Instruments, that serve instead of Wedges, Axes, and Hammers. With Tools made of these Flints, they likewise cut their Hay, and reap their Oats, which there groweth naturally in several Fields: The *Yahoos* draw home the Sheaves in Carriages, and the Servants tread them in certain covered Hutts, to get out the Grain, which is kept in Stores. They make a rude Kind of earthen and wooden Vessels, and bake the former in the Sun.

If they can avoid Casualties, they die only of old Age, and are buried in the obscurest Places that can be found, their Friends and Relations expressing neither Joy nor Grief at their Departure; nor does the dying Person discover the least Regret that he is leav- **7** ing the World, any more than if he were upon returning home from a Visit to one of his Neighbours: I remember, my Master having once made an Appointment with a Friend and his Family to come to his House upon some Affair of Importance; on the Day fixed, the Mistress and her two Children came very late; she made two

Excuses, first for her Husband, who, as she said, happened that very Morning to *Lhnuwnh*. The Word is strongly expressive in their Language, but not easily rendered into *English*; it signifies, *to retire to his first Mother*. Her Excuse for not coming sooner, was, that her Husband dying late in the Morning, she was a good while consulting her Servants about a convenient Place where his Body should be laid; and I observed she behaved herself at our House, as chearfully as the rest: She died about three Months after.

They live generally to Seventy or Seventy-five Years, very seldom to Fourscore: Some Weeks before their Death they feel a gradual Decay, but without Pain. During this time they are much visited by their Friends, because they cannot go abroad with their usual Ease and Satisfaction. However, about ten Days before their Death, which they seldom fail in computing, they return the Visits that have been made by those who are nearest in the Neighbourhood, being carried in a convenient Sledge drawn by *Yahoos;* which Vehicle they use, not only upon this Occasion, but when they grow old, upon long Journeys, or when they are lamed by any Accident. And therefore when the dying *Houyhnhnms* return those Visits, they take a solemn Leave of their Friends, as if they were going to some remote Part of the Country, where they designed to pass the rest of their Lives.

I know not whether it may be worth observing, that the *Houyhnhnms* have no Word in their Language to express any thing that is *evil*, except what they borrow from the Deformities or ill Qualities of the *Yahoos*. Thus they denote the Folly of a Servant, an Omission of a Child, a Stone that cuts their Feet, a Continuance of foul or unseasonable Weather, and the like, by adding to each the Epithet of *Yahoo*. For Instance, *Hhnm Yahoo, Whnaholm Yahoo, Ynlhmndwihlma Yahoo,* and an ill contrived House, *Ynholmhnmrohlnw Yahoo.*

I could with great Pleasure enlarge farther upon the Manners and Virtues of this excellent People; but intending in a short time to publish a Volume by itself expressly upon that Subject, I refer the Reader thither. And in the mean time, proceed to relate my own sad Catastrophe.

CHAPTER TEN

The Author's Oeconomy and Happy Life among the Houyhnhnms. His great improvement in Virtue, by conversing with them. Their Conversations. The Author hath Notice given him by his Master that he must depart from the Country. He falls into a Swoon for Grief, but submits. He contrives and finishes a Canoo, by the help of a fellow-servant, and puts to Sea at a Venture.

 HAD settled my little Oeconomy to my own Heart's Content. My Master had ordered a Room to be made for me after their Manner, about six Yards from the House; the Sides and Floors of which I plaistered with Clay, and covered with Rush-mats of my own contriving: I had beaten Hemp, which there grows wild, and made of it a Sort of Ticking: This I filled with the Feathers of several Birds I had taken with Springs made of *Yahoos* Hairs; and were excellent Food. I had worked two Chairs with my Knife, the Sorrel Nag helping me in the grosser and more laborious Part. When my Cloaths were worn to Rags, I made my self others with the Skins of Rabbets, and of a certain beautiful Animal about the same Size, called Nnuhnoh, the Skin of which is covered with a fine Down. Of these I likewise made very tolerable Stockings. I soaled my Shoes with Wood which I cut from a Tree, and fitted to the upper Leather, and when this was worn out, I supplied it with the Skins **1** of *Yahoos*, dried in the Sun. I often got Honey out of hollow Trees, which I mingled with Water, or eat it with my Bread. No Man could more verify the Truth of these two Maxims, *That, Nature is very easily satisfied*; and, *That, Necessity is the Mother of Inven-*

1 *Skins of Yahoos.* Gulliver's total alienation from himself (and the Yahoos are after all a reflection of the worst of humanity and therefore of Gulliver) is indicated by the ease with which he wears Yahoo skins. Although Gulliver doesn't say so, it seems to me that the noble Houyhnhnms would find this a very Yahoo-like thing for Gulliver to do and would despise him for it.

2 *Minion.* From the French word *mignonne*, which is roughly equivalent to our "darling" and which came to be used for a king's mistress. It was broadened and applied, usually in a derogatory manner, to the king's favorite, or the favorite of any person in power, particularly a favorite who keeps his place by toadying and fawning.

3 *Spleneticks.* Those suffering from spleen (see Chapter 6 of this part, note 12).

4 *Controvertists.* Controversialists; those delighting in argument and disputation for their own sake.

5 *Virtuoso's.* May refer to the type of natural philosophers or "projectors" which Swift pilloried so mercilessly in the third part of the book.

6 *Fidlers.* Swindlers.

7 *Dancing-Masters.* Probably those who can dance nimbly to either side of a question in such a way as to make sure of pleasing their superiors, without regard to principle.

8 *discant.* Originally a musical term, it was used, among other things, for devising changes upon a theme. Its meaning came to be broadened to describe the kind of discourse that goes into every aspect of a subject, bringing changes on *that* theme.

tion. I enjoyed perfect Health of Body, and Tranquillity of Mind; I did not feel the Treachery or Inconstancy of a Friend, nor the Injuries of a secret or open Enemy. I had no Occasion of bribing, flattering or pimping, to procure the Favour of any great Man, or of **2** his Minion. I wanted no Fence against Fraud or **Oppression: Here** was neither Physician to destroy my Body, nor Lawyer to ruin my Fortune: No Informer to watch my Words and Actions, or forge Accusations against me for Hire: Here were no Gibers, Censurers, **3** Backbiters, Pick-pockets, Highwaymen, House-breakers, Attorneys, Bawds, Buffoons, Gamesters, Politicians, Wits, Spleneticks, tedious **4,5** Talkers, Controvertists, Ravishers, Murderers, Robbers, Virtuoso's; no Leaders or Followers of Party and Faction; no Encouragers to Vice, by Seducement or Examples: No Dungeon, Axes, Gibbets, Whipping posts, or Pillories; No cheating Shop-keepers or Mechanicks: No Pride, Vanity or Affectation: No Fops, Bullies, Drunkards, strolling Whores, or Poxes: No ranting, lewd, expensive Wives: No stupid, proud Pedants: No importunate, overbearing, quarrelsome, noisy, roaring, empty, conceited, swearing Companions: No Scoundrels raised from the Dust upon the Merit of their Vices; or Nobility thrown into it on account of their **6,7** Virtues: No Lords, Fidlers, Judges or Dancing-Masters.

I had the Favour of being admitted to several *Houyhnhnms*, who came to visit or dine with my Master; where his Honour graciously suffered me to wait in the Room, and listen to their Discourse. Both he and his Company would often descend to ask me Questions, and to receive my Answers. I had also sometimes the Honour of attending my Master in his Visits to others. I never presumed to speak, except in answer to a Question; and then I did it with inward Regret, because it was a Loss of so much Time for improving my self: But I was infinitely delighted with the Station of an humble Auditor in such Conversations, where nothing passed but what was useful, expressed in the fewest and most significant Words: Where (as I have already said) the greatest *Decency* was observed, without the least Degree of Ceremony; where no Person spoke without being pleased himself, and pleasing his Companions: Where there was no Interruption, Tediousness, Heat, or Difference of Sentiments. They have a Notion, That when People are met together, a short Silence doth much improve Conversation: This I found to be true; for during those little Intermissions of Talk, new Ideas would arise in their Minds, which very much enlivened the Discourse. Their Subjects are generally on Friendship and Benevolence; on Order and Oeconomy; sometimes upon the visible Operations of Nature, or ancient Traditions; upon the Bounds and Limits of Virtue; upon the unerring Rules of Reason; or upon some Determinations, to be taken at the next great Assembly; and often upon the various Excellencies of *Poetry.* I may add, without Vanity, that my Presence often gave them sufficient Matter for Discourse, because it afforded my Master an Occasion of letting his Friends into the History of me and my Country, upon which they were all pleased to discant in a Manner not very advantageous **8** to human Kind and for that Reason I shall not repeat what they said: Only I may be allowed to observe, That his Honour, to my great Admiration, appeared to understand the Nature of *Yahoos* much better than my self. He went through all our Vices and Follies, and discovered many which I had never mentioned to him; by

Gulliver has the honor of being questioned by his Master's guests. Arthur Rackham. 1900.

only supposing what Qualities a *Yahoo* of their Country, with a small Proportion of Reason, might be capable of exerting: And concluded, with too much Probability, how vile as well as miserable such a Creature must be.

I freely confess, that all the little Knowledge I have of any Value, was acquired by the Lectures I received from my Master, and from hearing the Discourses of him and his Friends; to which I should be prouder to listen, than to dictate to the greatest and wisest Assembly in *Europe*. I admired the Strength, Comeliness and Speed of the Inhabitants; and such a Constellation of Virtues in such amiable Persons produced in me the highest Veneration. At first, indeed, I did not feel that natural Awe which the *Yahoos*

9 *I am apt to fall into the Voice and manner of the Houyhnhnms.* When Gulliver returned from the lands where he felt himself to be superior to the inhabitants (Lilliput or Laputa), he readjusted himself to English life at once. But when he returned from lands where he felt inferior to the inhabitants, he identified with them, and had trouble becoming an ordinary Englishman again. This happened after his return from Brobdingnag, and will happen again upon his expulsion from the land of Houyhnhnms. His detestation of himself and his effort to become a Houyhnhnm were so intense and continued for so long, even after his return, that we can only assume, in human terms, that he had gone mad with frustration over his inability to transform himself into a completely rational horse.

10 *either to employ me . . . or command me . . . back to the Place from whence I came.* Here the innocence of the Houyhnhnms comes into play. It did not occur to them that if the civilized Yahoos to whom Gulliver belonged were even worse than the savage Yahoos of the island and possessed of such warlike powers as Gulliver had described, that the last thing the Houyhnhnms should want would be to let Gulliver go and have him reveal to the world the existence of the Island of the Houyhnhnms. Do they want a massive and dreadful invasion of civilized Yahoos? (And it would certainly have happened if the Island of the Houyhnhnms had not been imaginary.) Perhaps Swift meant this as an indication that even supreme reason is no defense against folly—or perhaps he didn't think of it.

11 *Pravity.* That is, depravity.

and all other Animals bear towards them; but it grew upon me by Degrees, much sooner than I imagined, and was mingled with a respectful Love and Gratitude, that they would condescend to distinguish me from the rest of my Species.

When I thought of my Family, my Friends, my Countrymen, or human Race in general, I considered them as they really were, *Yahoos* in Shape and Disposition, perhaps a little more civilized, and qualified with the Gift of Speech; but making no other Use of Reason, than to improve and multiply those Vices, whereof their Brethren in this Country had only the Share that Nature allotted them. When I happened to behold the Reflection of my own Form in a Lake or Fountain, I turned away my Face in Horror and detestation of my self; and could better endure the Sight of a common *Yahoo*, than of my own Person. By conversing with the *Houyhnhnms*, and looking upon them with Delight, I fell to imitate their Gait and Gesture, which is now grown into a Habit; and my Friends often tell me in a blunt Way, that *I trot like a Horse*; which, however, I take for a great Compliment: Neither shall I **9** disown, that in speaking I am apt to fall into the Voice and manner of the *Houyhnhnms*, and hear my self ridiculed on that Account without the least Mortification.

In the Midst of this Happiness, when I looked upon my self to be fully settled for Life, my Master sent for me one Morning a little earlier than his usual Hour. I observed by his Countenance that he was in some Perplexity, and at a Loss how to begin what he had to speak. After a short Silence, he told me, he did not know how I would take what he was going to say: That, in the last general Assembly, when the Affair of the *Yahoos* was entered upon, the Representatives had taken Offence at his keeping a *Yahoo* (meaning my self) in his Family more like a *Houyhnhnm* than a Brute Animal. That, he was known frequently to converse with me, as if he could receive some Advantage or Pleasure in my Company: That, such a Practice was not agreeable to Reason or Nature, or a thing ever heard of before among them. The Assembly did there- **10** fore *exhort* him, either to employ me like the rest of my Species, or command me to swim back to the Place from whence I came. That, the first of these Expedients was utterly rejected by all the *Houyhnhnms*, who had ever seen me at his House or their own: For, they alledged, That because I had some Rudiments of Reason, added **11** to the natural Pravity of those Animals, it was to be feared, I might be able to seduce them into the woody and mountainous Parts of the Country, and bring them in Troops by Night to destroy the *Houyhnhnms* Cattle, as being naturally of the ravenous Kind, and averse from Labour.

My Master added, That he was daily pressed by the *Houyhnhnms* of the Neighbourhood to have the Assembly's *Exhortation* executed, which he could not put off much longer. He doubted, it would be impossible for me to swim to another Country; and therefore wished I would contrive some Sort of Vehicle resembling those I had described to him, that might carry me on the Sea; in which Work I should have the Assistance of his own Servants, as well as those of his Neighbours. He concluded, that for his own Part he could have been content to keep me in his Service as long as I lived; because he found I had cured myself of some bad Habits and Dispositions, by endeavouring, as far as my inferior Nature was capable, to imitate the *Houyhnhnms*.

I should here observe to the Reader, that a Decree of the general Assembly in this Country, is expressed by the Word *Hnhloayn*, which signifies an *Exhortation*; as near as I can render it: For they have no Conception how a rational Creature can be *compelled*, but only advised, or *exhorted*; because no Person can disobey Reason, without giving up his Claim to be a rational Creature. **12**

I was struck with the utmost Grief and Despair at my Master's *Discourse*; and being unable to support the Agonies I was under, I fell into a Swoon at his Feet: When I came to myself, he told me, that he concluded I had been dead. (For these People are subject to no such Imbecillities of Nature.) I answered, in a faint Voice, that Death would have been too great an Happiness; that although I could not blame the Assembly's *Exhortation*, or the Urgency of his Friends; yet in my weak and corrupt Judgment, I thought it might consist with Reason to have been less rigorous. That, I could not swim a League, and probably the nearest Land to theirs might be distant above an Hundred: That, many Materials, necessary for making a small Vessel to carry me off, were wholly wanting in this Country, which however, I would attempt in Obedience and Gratitude to his Honour, although I concluded the thing to be impossible, and therefore looked on myself as already devoted to Destruction. That, the certain Prospect of an unnatural Death, was the least of my Evils: For, supposing I should escape with Life by some strange Adventure, how could I think with Temper, of passing **13** my Days among *Yahoos*, and relapsing into my old Corruptions, for want of Examples to lead and keep me within the Paths of Virtue. That, I knew too well upon what solid Reasons all the Determinations of the wise *Houyhnhnms* were founded, not to be **14** shaken by Arguments of mine, a miserable *Yahoo*; and therefore after presenting him with my humble Thanks for the Offer of his Servants Assistance in making a Vessel, and desiring a reasonable Time for so difficult a Work, I told him, I would endeavour to preserve a wretched Being; and, if ever I returned to *England*, was not without Hopes of being useful to my own Species, by celebrating the Praises of the renowned *Houyhnhnms*, and proposing their Virtues to the Imitation of Mankind.

My Master in a few Words made me a very gracious Reply, allowed me the Space of two *Months* to finish my Boat; and ordered the Sorrel Nag, my Fellow-Servant, (for so at this Distance I may presume to call him) to follow my Instructions, because I told my Master, that his Help would be sufficient, and I knew he had a Tenderness for me.

In his Company my first Business was to go to that Part of the Coast, where my rebellious Crew had ordered me to be set on Shore. I got upon a Height, and looking on every Side into the Sea, fancied I saw a small Island, towards the *North-East*: I took out my Pocket-glass, and could then clearly distinguish it about five Leagues off, as I computed; but it appeared to the Sorrel Nag to be only a blue Cloud: For, as he had no Conception of any Country beside his own, so he could not be as expert in distinguishing remote Objects at Sea, as we who so much converse in that Element.

After I had discovered this Island, I considered no farther; but resolved, it should, if possible, be the first Place of my Banishment, leaving the Consequence to Fortune.

I returned home, and consulting with the Sorrel Nag, we went into a Copse at some Distance, where I with my Knife, and he

12 *no Person can disobey Reason, without giving up his Claim to be a rational Creature.* What's the difference? If a person is "exhorted" but if the penalty of refusing to obey the exhortation is the loss of a claim to rationality in a society where rationality is the supreme virtue, then the exhortation has the force of a compulsion. Something which is truly an exhortation and no more is something that carries with it no penalty if it is disobeyed.

13 *with Temper.* That is, temperately, or dispassionately.

14 *not to be shaken by Arguments of mine.* Clearly, another quality lacking in the utterly rational Houyhnhnms is compassion or empathy.

15 *artificially*. That is, "artfully" or "adroitly."

16 *the youngest I could get*. How did Gulliver get young Yahoo skins? Having but a limited time to complete his task, he could scarcely count on finding dead Yahoo infants. Certainly he would say so, if he did. The conclusion is that he must have killed them for the purpose or had them killed. Surely self-loathing, and loathing of the species to which he is so closely kin, could go no further.

15 with a sharp Flint fastened very artificially, after their Manner, to a wooden Handle, cut down several Oak Wattles about the Thickness of a Walking-staff, and some larger Pieces. But I shall not trouble the Reader with a particular Description of my own Mechanicks: Let it suffice to say, that in six Weeks time, with the Help of the Sorrel Nag, who performed the Parts that required most Labour, I finished a Sort of *Indian* Canoo; but much larger, covering it with the Skins of *Yahoos*, well stitched together, with hempen Threads of my own making. My Sail was likewise composed of the Skins of the same Animal; but I made use of the **16** youngest I could get; the older being too tough and thick; and I likewise provided myself with four Paddles. I laid in a Stock of boiled Flesh, of Rabbets and Fowls; and took with me two Vessels, one filled with Milk, and the other with Water.

I tried my Canoo in a large Pond near my Master's House, and then corrected in it what was amiss; stopping all the Chinks with *Yahoos* Tallow, till I found it stanch, and able to bear me, and my Freight. And when it was as compleat as I could possibly make it, I had it drawn on a Carriage very gently by *Yahoos*, to the Seaside, under the Conduct of the Sorrel Nag, and another Servant.

When all was ready, and the Day came for my Departure, I took Leave of my Master and Lady, and the whole Family, my Eyes flowing with Tears, and my Heart quite sunk with Grief. But his Honour, out of Curiosity, and perhaps (if I may speak it without Vanity) partly out of Kindness, was determined to **see me** in my Canoo; and got several of his neighbouring Friends to accompany him. I was forced to wait above an Hour for the Tide, and then observing the Wind very fortunately bearing towards the Island, to which I intended to steer my Course, I took a second Leave of my Master: But as I was going to prostrate myself to kiss his Hoof, he did me the Honour to raise it gently to my Mouth. I am not ignorant how much I have been censured for mentioning this last Particular. Detractors are pleased to think it improbable, that so illustrious a Person should descend to give so great a Mark of Distinction to a Creature so inferior as I. Neither have I forgot, how apt some Travellers are to boast of extraordinary Favours they have received. But, if these Censurers were better acquainted with

The sorrel nag helps Gulliver build a canoe. Willy Pogány. 1919.

Gulliver takes leave of the Houyhnhnms. Le Febure. 1797.

the noble and courteous Disposition of the *Houyhnhnms*, they would soon change their Opinion.

I paid my Respects to the rest of the *Houyhnhnms* in his Honour's Company; then getting into my Canoo, I pushed off from Shore.

1 *February 15, 1714–15.* In Swift's time, the British year began on March 25. Between January 1 and March 24 inclusive it would have been 1714 in Great Britain and 1715 in the rest of Europe. The British calendar was not made uniform with the rest of Europe till 1752. On February 15, 1715, it was four years and five months since Gulliver had left Great Britain on this fourth and final voyage.

2 *Take Care of thy self, gentle Yahoo.* The sorrel nag, being of the lower orders, has the human qualities of affection and can feel love. (May he live long and prosper.)

3 *politest.* See Part II, Chapter 7, note 2.

The Author's dangerous Voyage. He arrives at New-Holland, hoping to settle there. Is wounded with an Arrow by one of the Natives. Is seized and carried by force into a Portugueze Ship. The Great Civilities of the Captain. The Author arrives at England.

1 I BEGAN this desperate Voyage on *February* 15, 1714-15, at 9 o'Clock in the Morning. The Wind was very favourable; however, I made use at first only of my Paddles; but considering I should soon be weary, and that the Wind might probably chop about, I ventured to set up my little Sail; and thus, with the Help of the Tide, I went at the Rate of a League and a Half an Hour, as near as I could guess. My Master and his Friends continued on the Shoar, till I was almost out of Sight; and I often heard the Sorrel Nag (who **2** always loved me) crying out, *Hnuy illa nyha maiah Yahoo*, Take Care of they self, gentle *Yahoo.*

My Design was, if possible, to discover some small Island uninhabited, yet sufficient by my Labour to furnish me with Necessaries of Life, which I would have thought a greater Happiness **3** than to be first Minister in the politest Court of *Europe;* so horrible was the Idea I conceived of returning to live in the Society and under the Government of *Yahoos.* For in such a Solitude as I desired, I could at least enjoy my own Thoughts, and reflect with Delight on the Virtues of those inimitable *Houyhnhnms,* without

4 *New-Holland.* See Part II, Chapter 8, note 20. Considering that New Holland were those coasts of Australia already sighted, Gulliver gets there from his island south of the Cape of Good Hope with impossible celerity and ease.

Gulliver embarks. Richard Corbould. 1816. Courtesy. The New York Public Library.

any Opportunity of degenerating into the Vices and Corruptions of my own Species.

The Reader may remember what I related when my Crew conspired against me, and confined me to my Cabin. How I continued there several Weeks, without knowing what Course we took; and when I was put ashore in the Long-boat, how the Sailors told me with Oaths, whether true or false, that they knew not in what Part of the World we were. However, I did then believe us to be about ten Degrees *Southward* of the *Cape of Good Hope,* or about 45 Degrees *Southern* Latitude, as I gathered from some general Words I overheard among them, being I supposed to the *South-East* in their intended Voyage to *Madagascar.* And although this were but little better than Conjecture, yet I resolved to steer my Course *Eastward,* hoping to reach the *South-West* Coast of *New-Holland,* and perhaps some such Island as I desired, lying *Westward* of it. The Wind was full West, and by six in the Evening I computed I had gone *Eastward* at least eighteen Leagues; when I spied a very small Island about half a League off, which I soon

5 *Mr. Herman Moll.* A Dutch map maker and geographer who settled in London about 1698.

6 *stark naked, Men, Women and Children.* These are, we might suppose, Australian aborigines.

7 *suck the Wound.* If the wound was on the inside of his left knee, he would be supple indeed if he could suck it. If he succeeded, his spinal column bends through a considerable greater arc than mine does.

8 *admiration.* See Part I, Chapter 1, note 26.

reached. It was nothing but a Rock with one Creek, naturally arched by the Force of the Tempests. Here I put in my Canoo, and climbing a Part of the Rock, I could plainly discover Land to the *East,* extending from *South* to *North.* I lay all Night in my Canoo; and repeating my Voyage early in the Morning, I arrived in seven Hours to the *South-East* Point of *New Holland.* This confirmed me in the Opinion I have long entertained, that the *Maps* and *Charts* place this Country at least three Degrees more to the *East* than it really is; which Thought I communicated many Years ago to my **5** worthy Friend Mr. *Herman Moll,* and gave him my Reasons for it, although he hath rather chosen to follow other Authors.

I saw no Inhabitants in the Place where I landed; and being unarmed, I was afraid of venturing far into the Country, I found some Shell-Fish on the Shore, and eat them raw, not daring to kindle a Fire, for fear of being discovered by the Natives. I continued three Days feeding on Oysters and Limpits, to save my own Provisions; and I fortunately found a Brook of excellent Water, which gave me great Relief.

On the fourth Day, venturing out early a little too far, I saw twenty or thirty Natives upon a Height, not above five hundred **6** Yards from me. They were stark naked, Men, Women and Children round a Fire, as I could discover by the Smoke. One of them spied me, and gave Notice to the rest; five of them advanced towards me, leaving the Women and Children at the Fire. I made what haste I could to the Shore, and getting into my Canoo, shoved off: The Savages observing me retreat, ran after me; and before I could get far enough into the Sea, discharged an Arrow, which wounded me deeply on the Inside of my left Knee (I shall carry the Mark to my Grave.) I apprehended the Arrow might be poisoned; and paddling out of the Reach of their Darts (being a calm **7** Day) I made a shift to suck the Wound, and dress it as well as I could.

I was at a Loss what to do, for I durst not return to the same Landing-place, but stood to the *North,* and was forced to paddle; for the Wind, although very gentle, was against me, blowing *North-West.* As I was looking about for a secure Landing-place, I saw a Sail to the *North North-East,* which appearing every Minute more visible, I was in some Doubt, whether I should wait for them or no; but at last my Detestation of the *Yahoo* Race prevailed; and turning my Canoo, I sailed and paddled together to the *South,* and got into the same Creek from whence I set out in the Morning; choosing rather to trust my self among these *Barbarians* than live with *European Yahoos.* I drew up my Canoo as close as I could to the Shore, and hid my self behind a Stone by the little Brook, which, as I have already said, was excellent Water.

The Ship came within half a League of this Creek, and sent out her Long-Boat with Vessels to take in fresh Water (for the Place it seems was very well known) but I did not observe it until the Boat was almost on Shore; and it was too late to seek another Hiding-Place. The Seamen at their landing observed my Canoo, and rummaging it all over, easily conjectured that the Owner could not be far off. Four of them well armed searched every Cranny and Lurking-hole, till at last they found me flat on my Face behind **8** the Stone. They gazed a while in Admiration at my strange uncouth Dress; my Coat made of Skins, my wooden-soaled Shoes, and my furred Stockings; from whence, however, they concluded I

"One of the Seamen in Portugueze bid me rise, and asked who I was." T.
Morten, 1865. Courtesy, Library of Congress.

was not a Native of the Place, who all go naked. One of the Seamen in *Portugueze* bid me rise, and asked who I was. I understood
that Language very well, and getting upon my Feet, said, I was a
poor *Yahoo*, banished from the *Houyhnhnms*, and desired they
would please to let me depart. They admired to hear me answer
them in their own Tongue, and saw by my Complection I must be
an *European*; but were at a Loss to know what I meant by *Yahoos*
and *Houyhnhnms*, and at the same Time fell a laughing at my
strange Tone in speaking, which resembled the Neighing of a
Horse. I trembled all the while betwixt Fear and Hatred: I again
desired Leave to depart, and was gently moving to my Canoo; but
they laid hold on me, desiring to know what Country I was of?
whence I came? with many other Questions. I told them, I was
born in *England*, from whence I came about five Years ago, and
then their Country and ours was at Peace. I therefore hoped they
would not treat me as an Enemy, since I meant them no Harm, but

9 *Lisbon.* The capital of Portugal.

10 *I wondered to find such Civilities from a Yahoo.* Pedro de Mendez is portrayed as an utterly decent and humane human being who treats Gulliver with every consideration, yet all Gulliver can see is a Yahoo. His alienation and his madness are complete.

was a poor *Yahoo*, seeking some desolate Place where to pass the Remainder of his unfortunate Life.

When they began to talk I thought I never heard or saw any thing so unnatural; for it appeared to me as monstrous as if a Dog or a Cow should speak in *England*, or a *Yahoo* in *Houyhnhnm-Land*. The honest *Portugueze* were equally amazed at my strange Dress, and the odd Manner of delivering my Words, which however they understood very well. They spoke to me with great Humanity, and **9** said they were sure their Captain would carry me *gratis* to *Lisbon*, from whence I might return to my own Country; that two of the Seamen would go back to the Ship, to inform the Captain of what they had seen and receive his Orders; in the mean Time, unless I would give my solemn Oath not to fly, they would secure me by Force. I thought it best to comply with their Proposal. They were very curious to know my Story, but I gave them very little Satisfaction; and they all conjectured, that my Misfortunes had impaired my Reason. In two Hours the Boat, which went loaden with Vessels of Water, returned with the Captain's Commands to fetch me on Board. I fell on my Knees to preserve my Liberty; but all was in vain, and the Men having tied me with Cords, heaved me into the Boat, from whence I was taken into the Ship, and from thence into the Captain's Cabbin.

His Name was *Pedro de Mendez*; he was a very courteous and generous Person; he entreated me to give some Account of my self, and desired to know what I would eat or drink; said, I should be **10** used as well as himself, and spoke so many obliging Things, that I wondered to find such Civilities from a *Yahoo*. However, I remained silent and sullen; I was ready to faint at the very Smell of him and his Men. At last I desired something to eat out of my own *Canoo*; but he ordered me a Chicken and some excellent Wine, and then directed that I should be put to Bed in a very clean Cabbin. I would not undress my self, but lay on the Bed-cloaths; and in half an Hour stole out, when I thought the Crew was at Dinner; and getting to the Side of the Ship, was going to leap into the Sea, and swim for my Life, rather than continue among *Yahoos*. But one of the Seamen prevented me, and having informed the Captain, I was chained to my Cabbin.

After Dinner *Don Pedro* came to me, and desired to know my Reason for so desperate an Attempt; assured me he only meant to do me all the Service he was able; and spoke so very movingly, that at last I descended to treat him like an Animal which had some little Portion of Reason. I gave him a very short Relation of my Voyage; of the Conspiracy against me by my own Men; of the Country where they set me on Shore, and of my five Years Residence there. All which he looked upon as if it were a Dream or a Vision; whereat I took great Offence: For I had quite forgot the Faculty of Lying, so peculiar to *Yahoos* in all Countries where they preside, and consequently the Disposition of suspecting Truth in others of their own Species. I asked him, Whether it were the Custom of his Country to *say the Thing that was not?* I assured him I had almost forgot what he meant by Falshood; and if I had lived a thousand Years in *Houyhnhnm-land*, I should never have heard a Lie from the meanest Servant. That I was altogether indifferent whether he believed me or no; but however, in return for his Favours, I would give so much Allowance to the Corruption of his

Nature, as to answer any Objection he would please to make; and he might easily discover the Truth.

The Captain, a wise Man, after many Endeavours to catch me tripping in some Part of my Story, at last began to have a better Opinion of my Veracity. But he added, that since I professed so inviolable an Attachment to Truth, I must give him my Word of Honour to bear him Company in this Voyage without attempting any thing against my Life; or else he would continue me a Prisoner till we arrived at *Lisbon*. I gave him the Promise he required; but at the same time protested that I would suffer the greatest Hardships rather than return to live among *Yahoos*.

Our Voyage passed without any considerable Accident. In Gratitude to the Captain I sometimes sate with him at his earnest Request, and strove to conceal my Antipathy against human Kind, although it often broke out; which he suffered to pass without Observation. But the greatest Part of the Day, I confined myself to my Cabbin, to avoid seeing any of the Crew. The Captain had often intreated me to strip myself of my savage Dress, and offered to lend me the best Suit of Cloaths he had. This I would not be prevailed on to accept, abhorring to cover myself with any thing that had been on the Back of a *Yahoo*. I only desired he would lend me two clean Shirts, which having been washed since he wore them, I believed would not so much defile me. These I changed every second Day, and washed them myself.

We arrived at *Lisbon, Nov.* 5, 1715. At our landing, the Captain forced me to cover myself with his Cloak, to prevent the Rabble from crouding about me. I was conveyed to his own House; and at my earnest Request, he led me up to the highest Room backwards. **11** I conjured him to conceal from all Persons what I had told him of the *Houyhnhnms*; because the least Hint of such a Story would not only draw Numbers of People to see me, but probably put me in Danger of being imprisoned, or burnt by the *Inquisition*. **12** The Captain persuaded me to accept a Suit of Cloaths newly made; but I would not suffer the Taylor to take my Measure; however, Don *Pedro* being almost of my Size, they fitted me well enough. He accoutred me with other Necessaries all new, which I aired for Twenty-four Hours before I would use them. The Captain had no Wife, nor above three Servants, none of which were suffered to attend at Meals; and his whole Deportment was so obliging, added to very good *human* Understanding, that I really began to tolerate his Company. He gained so far upon me, that I ventured to look out of the back Window. By Degrees I was brought into another Room, from whence I peeped into the Street, but drew my Head back in a Fright. In a Week's Time he seduced me down to the Door. I found my Terror gradually lessened, but my Hatred and Contempt seemed to increase. I was at last bold enough to walk Street in his Company, but kept my Nose well stopped with Rue, **13** or sometimes with Tobacco.

In ten days, Don *Pedro*, to whom I had given some Account of my domestick Affairs, put it upon me as a Point of Honour and Conscience, that I ought to return to my native Country, and live at home with my Wife and Children. He told me, there was an *English* Ship in the Port just ready to sail, and he would furnish me with all things necessary. It would be tedious to repeat his Arguments, and my Contradictions. He said, it was altogether im-

11 *backwards.* To the rear.

12 *in Danger of being imprisoned, or burnt by the Inquisition.* The suggestion that there were rational beings who were not human and were, indeed, superior to human beings, not having fallen from the state of grace, would certainly be heretical. Gulliver's fears were not without reason.

13 *Rue.* A strong-scented herb.

14 *the Fifth of December, 1715.* Gulliver has been away from home for five and a quarter years. In his absence, the War of the Spanish Succession has come to an end, Queen Anne has died, George I has succeeded, and the Whigs have taken over the government. Gulliver is fifty-four years old on his last return, his four voyages having taken up sixteen years.

possible to find such a solitary Island as I had desired to live in; but I might command in my own House, and pass my time in a Manner as recluse as I pleased.

I complied at last, finding I could not do better. I left *Lisbon* the 24*th* Day of *November,* in an *English* Merchantman, but who was the Master I never inquired. Don *Pedro* accompanied me to the Ship, and lent me Twenty Pounds. He took kind Leave of me, and embraced me at parting; which I bore as well as I could. During this last Voyage I had no Commerce with the Master, or any of his Men; but pretending I was sick kept close in my Cabbin. **14** On the Fifth of *December,* 1715, we cast Anchor in the *Downs* about Nine in the Morning, and at Three in the Afternoon I got safe to my House at *Redriff.*

My Wife and Family received me with great Surprize and Joy, because they concluded me certainly dead; but I must freely confess, the Sight of them filled me only with Hatred, Disgust and Contempt; and the more, by reflecting on the near Alliance I had to them. For, although since my unfortunate Exile from the *Houyhnhnm* Country, I had compelled myself to tolerate the Sight of

Illustration by Bofa, 1929.

"I converse with them at least four Hours every Day." Rex Whistler. 1930.

15 *five Years since my last Return to England.* The end of 1720 or the beginning of 1721. He is writing this at the age of fifty-nine.

16 *Stone-Horses.* Stallions; their "stones" (testicles) have not been removed.

17 *I converse with them at least four Hours every Day.* Here Gulliver's madness is clear, for he imagines he is talking to his horses.

Yahoos, and to converse with Don *Pedro de Mendez;* yet my Memory and Imaginations were perpetually filled with the Virtues and Ideas of those exalted *Houyhnhnms.* And when I began to consider, that by copulating with one of the *Yahoo*-Species, I had become a Parent of more; it struck me with the utmost Shame, Confusion and Horror.

As soon as I entered the House, my Wife took me in her Arms, and kissed me; at which, having not been used to the Touch of that odious Animal for so many Years, I fell in a Swoon for almost an Hour. At the Time I am writing, it is five Years since my last Re- **15** turn to *England*: During the first Year I could not endure my Wife or Children in my Presence, the very Smell of them was intolerable; much less could I suffer them to eat in the same Room. To this Hour they dare not presume to touch my Bread, or drink out of the same Cup; neither was I ever able to let one of them take me by the Hand. The first Money I laid out was to buy two young Stone-Horses, which I keep in a good Stable, and next to **16** them the Groom is my greatest Favourite; for I feel my Spirits revived by the Smell he contracts in the Stable. My Horses understand me tolerably well; I converse with them at least four Hours **17** every Day. They are Strangers to Bridle or Saddle; they live in great Amity with me, and Friendship to each other.

CHAPTER TWELVE

The Author's Veracity. His Design in publishing this Work. His censure of those Travellers who swerve from the Truth. The Author clears himself from any Sinister ends in writing. An Objection answered. The Method of Planting Colonies. His Native Country commended. The Right of the Crown to those Countries described by the Author, is justified. The Difficulty of conquering them. The Author takes his last leave of the Reader; proposeth his Manner of Living for the Future; gives good Advice, and Concludeth.

HUS, gentle Reader, I have given thee a faithful History of my Travels for Sixteen Years, and above Seven Months; wherein I have not been so studious of Ornament as of Truth. I could perhaps like others have astonished thee with strange improbable Tales; but I rather chose to relate plain Matter of Fact in the simplest Manner and Style; because my principal Design was to inform, and not to amuse thee.

It is easy for us who travel into remote Countries, which are seldom visited by *Englishmen* or other *Europeans*, to form Descriptions of wonderful Animals both at Sea and Land. Whereas, a Traveller's chief Aim should be to make Men wiser and better, and to improve their Minds by the bad, as well as good Example of what they deliver concerning foreign Places.

I could heartily wish a Law were enacted, that every Traveller, before he were permitted to publish his Voyages, should be obliged to make Oath before the *Lord High Chancellor*, that all he intended to print was absolutely true to the best of his Knowledge; for then

Gulliver ends his story. Willy Pogány. 1919.

1 *Nec . . . finget.* The Latin, translated, reads "Though Fortune has made Sinon wretched, she has not made him untrue and a liar." It is from Vergil's *Aeneid.* The incident takes place at the end of the Trojan War when the Greeks have built a large horse and filled it with warriors. Sinon lets himself be taken prisoner and tells a sad, false tale of having been mistreated by the Greeks, and states that the wooden horse is an offering to Athena and will forever protect Troy if it is brought within the city. The Trojans bring it in, the warriors emerge at night, and Troy falls. Sinon is thus the archetypical traitor and he *is* "untrue and a liar." Swift knows that and it may well be his way of satirizing the truth of travel tales, even Gulliver's.

the World would no longer be deceived as it usually is, while some Writers, to make their Works pass the better upon the Publick, impose the grossest Falsities on the unwary Reader. I have perused several Books of Travels with great Delight in my younger Days; but, having since gone over most Parts of the Globe, and been able to contradict many fabulous Accounts from my own Observation; it hath given me a great Disgust against this Part of Reading, and some Indignation to see the Credulity of Mankind so impudently abused. Therefore, since my Acquaintance were pleased to think my poor Endeavours might not be unacceptable to my Country; I imposed on myself as a Maxim, never to be swerved from, that I would *strictly adhere to Truth*; neither indeed can I be ever under the least Temptation to vary from it, while I retain in my Mind the Lectures and Example of my noble Master, and the other illustrious *Houyhnhnms,* of whom I had so long the Honour to be an humble Hearer.

    ——*Nec si miserum Fortuna Sinonem*   **1**
    Finxit, vanum etiam, mendacemque improba finget.

    I know very well, how little Reputation is to be got by Writings which require neither Genius nor Learning, nor indeed any other Talent, except a good Memory, or an exact *Journal.* I know likewise, that Writers of Travels, like *Dictionary*-Makers, are sunk into Oblivion by the Weight and Bulk of those who come last, and therefore lie uppermost. And it is highly probable, that such Travellers who shall hereafter visit the Countries described in this Work of mine, may be detecting my Errors, (if there be any) and adding many new Discoveries of their own, jostle me out of Vogue, and stand in my Place; making the World forget that ever I was an Author. This indeed would be too great a Mortification if I wrote for Fame: But, as my sole Intention was the PUBLICK GOOD, I cannot be altogether disappointed. For, who can read the Virtues I have mentioned in the glorious *Houyhnhnms,* without being ashamed of his own Vices, when he considers himself as the reasoning, governing Animal of his Country? I shall say nothing of those remote Nations where *Yahoos* preside; amongst which the least corrupted are the *Brobdingnagians,* whose wise Maxims in Morality and Government, it would be our Happiness to observe. But I

2 *descanting.* See Chapter 10 of this part, note 8.

3 *meddle not the least with any Party.* All of Gulliver's protestations here, however gravely and seriously stated, derive their satiric humor from being manifestly false. Swift certainly used the book to serve party passion, for long passages of it are diatribes against Whig principles and against Walpole in particular.

4 *naked Americans.* The Aztecs of Mexico whom Cortez conquered were not literally naked. They were a civilized people. However, they lacked horses and gunpowder, and a small band of Europeans with both could conquer them. It was that lack that rendered them "naked" of any means of defense.

5 *battering the Warrior's Faces into Mummy, by terrible Yerks from their hinder Hoofs.* Gulliver's madness shows here, too, as he seems to relish the picture of his beloved Houyhnhnms reducing Yahoo faces to pulp (mummy) by kicks (yerks) with their hind legs. Clearly, the Houyhnhnms would be as helpless before artillery as the Aztecs were and their very fearlessness (which might lead them to charge rather than to take evasive action) would accelerate their downfall.

Indeed, if we consider the advances in military power since Swift's time on the part of the Europeans, they have long ago reached the stage of being quite able to handle the Brobdingnagians, too, if the latter have retained their aversion to gunpowder.

2 forbear descanting further, and rather leave the judicious Reader to his own Remarks and Applications.

I am not a little pleased that this Work of mine can possibly meet with no Censurers: For what Objections can be made against a Writer who relates only plain Facts that happened in such distant Countries, where we have not the least Interest with respect either to Trade or Negotiations? I have carefully avoided every Fault with which common Writers of Travels are often too justly charged.

3 Besides, I meddle not the least with any *Party,* but write without Passion, Prejudice, or Ill-will against any Man or Number of Men whatsoever. I write for the noblest End, to inform and instruct Mankind, over whom I may, without Breach of Modesty, pretend to some Superiority, from the Advantages I received by conversing so long among the most accomplished *Houyhnhnms.* I write without any View towards Profit or Praise. I never suffer a Word to pass that may look like a Reflection, or possibly give the least Offence even to those who are most ready to take it. So that, I hope, I may with Justice pronounce myself an Author perfectly blameless; against whom the Tribes of Answers, Considers, Observers, Reflecters, Detecters, Remarkers, will never be able to find Matter for exercising their Talents.

I confess, it was whispered to me, that I was bound in Duty as a Subject of *England,* to have given in a Memorial to a Secretary of State, at my first coming over; because, whatever Lands are discovered by a Subject, belong to the Crown. But I doubt, whether our Conquests in the Countries I treat of, would be as easy as

4 those of *Ferdinando Cortez* over the naked *Americans.* The *Lilliputians* I think, are hardly worth the Charge of a Fleet and Army to reduce them; and I question whether it might be prudent or safe to attempt the *Brobdingnagians:* Or, whether an *English* Army would be much at their Ease with the Flying Island over their Heads. The *Houyhnhnms,* indeed, appear not to be so well prepared for War, a Science to which they are perfect Strangers, and especially against missive Weapons. However, supposing myself to be a Minister of State, I could never give my Advice for invading them. Their Prudence, Unanimity, Unacquaintedness with Fear, and their Love of their Country would amply supply all Defects in the military Art. Imagine twenty Thousand of them breaking into the Midst of an *European* Army, confounding the

5 Ranks, overturning the Carriages, battering the Warriors Faces into Mummy, by terrible Yerks from their hinder Hoofs: For they

6 would well deserve the Character given to *Augustus; Recalcitrat undique tutus.* But instead of Proposals for conquering that magnanimous Nation, I rather wish they were in a Capacity or Disposition to send a sufficient Number of their Inhabitants for civilizing *Europe;* by teaching us the first Principles of Honour, Justice, Truth, Temperance, publick Spirit, Fortitude, Chastity, Friendship, Benevolence, and Fidelity. The *Names* of all which Virtues are still retained among us in most Languages, and are to be met with in modern as well as ancient Authors; which I am able to assert from my own small Reading.

But, I had another Reason which made me less forward to enlarge his Majesty's Dominions by my Discoveries: To say the Truth, I had conceived a few Scruples with relation to the distributive Justice of Princes upon those Occasions. For Instance, A Crew of Pyrates are driven by a Storm they know not whither;

at length a Boy discovers Land from the Top-mast; they go on Shore to rob and plunder; they see an harmless People, are entertained with Kindness, they give the Country a new Name, they take formal Possession of it for the King, they set up a rotten Plank or a Stone for a Memorial, they murder two or three Dozen of the Natives, bring away a Couple more by Force for a Sample, return home, and get their Pardon. Here commences a new Dominion acquired with a Title by *Divine Right*. Ships are sent with the first Opportunity; the Natives driven out or destroyed, their Princes tortured to discover their Gold; a free Licence given to all Acts of Inhumanity and Lust; the Earth reeking with the Blood of its Inhabitants: And this execrable Crew of Butchers employed in so **7** pious an Expedition, is a *modern Colony* sent to convert and civilize an idolatrous and barbarous People.

But this Description, I confess, doth by no means affect the **8** *British* Nation, who may be an Example to the whole World for their Wisdom, Care, and Justice in planting Colonies; the liberal Endowments for the Advancement of Religion and Learning; their Choice of devout and able Pastors to propagate *Christianity*; their Caution in stocking their Provinces with People of sober Lives and Conversations from this the Mother Kingdom; their strict Regard to the Distribution of Justice, in supplying the Civil Administration through all their Colonies with Officers of the greatest Abilities, utter Strangers to Corruption: And to crown all, by sending the most vigilant and virtuous Governors, who have no other Views than the Happiness of the People over whom they preside, and the Honour of the King their Master.

But, as those Countries which I have described do not appear to have a Desire of being conquered, and enslaved, murdered or driven out by Colonies; nor abound either in Gold, Silver, Sugar or Tobacco; I did humbly conceive they were by no Means proper Objects of our Zeal, our Valour, or our Interest. However, if those whom it may concern, think fit to be of another Opinion, I am ready to depose, when I shall be lawfully called, That no *European* did ever visit these Countries before me. I mean, if the Inhabitants ought to be believed; *unless a dispute may arise about the two Yahoos, said to have been seen many ages ago in a mountain in Houyhnhnm-land, from whence the opinion is, that the race of* **9** *those brutes hath descended; and these, for anything I know, may have been English, which indeed I was apt to suspect from the lineaments of their posterity's countenances, although very much defaced. But, how far that will go to make out a title, I leave to the learned in colony-law.*

But, as to the Formality of taking Possession in my Sovereign's Name, it never came once into my Thoughts; and if it had, yet as my Affairs then stood, I should perhaps in point of Prudence and Self-Preservation, have put it off to a better Opportunity.

Having thus answered the *only* Objection that can be raised against me as a Traveller; I here take a final Leave of my Courteous Readers, and return to enjoy my own Speculations in my little Garden at *Redriff*; to apply those excellent Lessons of **10** Virtue which I learned among the *Houyhnhnms*; to instruct the *Yahoos* of my own Family as far as I shall find them docible **11** Animals; to behold my Figure often in a Glass, and thus if possible habituate my self by Time to tolerate the Sight of a human Creature: To lament the Brutality of *Houyhnhnms* in my own **12**

6 *Recalcitrat undique tutus.* "He kicks backward, protected on each side." This sardonic tribute to Augustus' cautious advance from teen-age great-nephew of the assassinated Julius Caesar to undisputed absolute ruler of the Roman Empire is from one of the satires of Horace (65–8 B.C.).

7 *Crew of Butchers . . . is a modern Colony sent to convert and civilize an idolatrous and barbarous People.* This scarcely requires satire. In this paragraph Swift gives an exact description of the discovery of the American continent by Columbus, and the subsequent establishment of Spanish colonies, particularly in Mexico and Peru.

8 *the British Nation . . . have no other Views than the Happiness of the People over whom they preside.* It may well be argued that the British were indeed more efficient colonizers than other European nations were; certainly more successful ones. The British colonists, however, were far more systematic than were those of other nations in wiping out the native population where that was possible, and this passage is heavy with Swiftian irony.

9 *the race of those brutes hath descended; and these, for anything I know, may have been English.* This sentence, with its direct and deliberate insult to Swift's fellow countrymen has been omitted from many editions of *Gulliver's Travels*, including the Faulkner edition we are using as the text.

10 *Redriff.* See Part I, Chapter 8, note 15.

11 *docible.* See Chapter 9 of this part, note 1.

12 *Brutality.* The "brutalization" of the horses in Great Britain; their treatment as animals.

13 *Intellectuals*. That is, their intellectuality, their faculties of intelligence. Swift doesn't say "brains" because it wasn't clear in his time that the brain was the seat of intelligence.

Illustration by Herbert Cole, 1899.

Country, but always treat their Persons with Respect, for the Sake of my noble Master, his Family, his Friends, and the whole *Houyhnhnm* Race, whom these of ours have the Honour to resemble in **13** all their Lineaments, however their Intellectuals came to degenerate.

I began last Week to permit my Wife to sit at Dinner with me, at the farthest End of a long Table; and to answer (but with the utmost Brevity) the few Questions I asked her. Yet the Smell of a *Yahoo* continuing very offensive, I always keep my Nose well stopt with Rue, Lavender, or Tobacco-Leaves. And although it be hard for a Man late in Life to remove old Habits; I am not altogether out of Hopes in some Time to suffer a Neighbour *Yahoo* in my Company, without the Apprehensions I am yet under of his Teeth or his Claws.

My Reconcilement to the *Yahoo-kind* in general might not be so difficult, if they would be content with those Vices and Follies only which Nature hath entitled them to. I am not in the least provoked at the Sight of a Lawyer, a Pick-pocket, a Colonel, a Fool, a Lord, a Gamster, a Politician, a Whoremunger, a Physician, an Evidence, a Suborner, an Attorney, a Traytor, or the like: This is all according to the due Course of Things: But, when I behold a Lump of Deformity, and Diseases both in Body and Mind, smitten with *Pride,* it immediately breaks all the Measures of my Patience; neither shall I be ever able to comprehend how such an Animal and such a Vice could tally together. The wise and virtuous *Houyhnhnms,* who abound in all Excellencies that can adorn a rational Creature, have no Name for this Vice in their Language, which hath no Terms to express any thing that is evil, except those whereby they describe the detestable Qualities of their *Yahoos;* among which they were not able to distinguish this of Pride, for want of thoroughly understanding Human Nature, as it sheweth it self in other Countries, where that Animal presides. But I, who had more Experience, could plainly observe some Rudiments of it among the wild *Yahoos.*

But the *Houyhnhnms,* who live under the Government of Reason, are no more proud of the good Qualities they possess, than I should be for not wanting a Leg or an Arm, which no Man in his Wits would boast of, although he must be miserable without them. I dwell the longer upon this Subject from the Desire I have to make the Society of an *English Yahoo* by any Means not insupportable; and therefore I here intreat those who have any Tincture of this absurd Vice, that they will not presume to appear in my Sight.

14

15

FINIS

14 *an Evidence.* Presumably, a giver of false evidence.

15 *Pride.* This is bitter satire, for, of course, the source of Gulliver's madness rests in his pride, which causes him to reject his own Yahoo-hood, and pretend to an emulation of the Houyhnhnms it is impossible for him to maintain.

A Letter

from Capt. Gulliver, to his Cousin Sympson **1**

I HOPE you will be ready to own publickly, whenever you shall
be called to it, that by your great and frequent Urgency you
prevailed on me to publish a very loose and uncorrect Account
of my Travels; with Direction to hire some young Gentlemen of
either University to put them in Order, and correct the Style, as
my Cousin *Dampier* did by my Advice, in his Book called, *A*   **2**
Voyage round the World. But I do not remember I gave you
Power to consent, that any thing should be omitted, and much less
that any thing should be inserted: Therefore, as to the latter, I
do here renounce every thing of that Kind; particularly a Para-   **3**
graph about her Majesty the late Queen *Anne*, of most pious and
glorious Memory; although I did reverence and esteem her more
than any of human Species. But you, or your Interpolator, ought
to have considered, that as it was not my Inclination, so was it not
decent to praise any Animal of our Composition before my Master
Houyhnhnm: And besides, the Fact was altogether false; for to
my Knowledge, being in *England* during some Part of her Majesty's
Reign, she did govern by a chief Minister; nay, even by two successively; the first whereof was the Lord of *Godolphin,* and the   **4**
second the Lord of *Oxford*; so that you have made me *say the thing*   **5**
that was not. Likewise, in the Account of the Academy of Projectors, and several Passages of my Discourse to my Master
Houyhnhnm, you have either omitted some material Circumstances,
or minced or changed them in such a Manner, that I do hardly   **6**
know mine own Work. When I formerly hinted to you something
of this in a Letter, you were pleased to answer, that you were afraid
of giving Offence; that People in Power were very watchful over

1 *Cousin Sympson*. This letter did not appear in the
first edition of the book at all but appeared first in
the Faulkner edition, printed in 1734, eight years
after the first edition had appeared. It is even dated
after the appearance of the first edition.

As for "Cousin Sympson," that is a fictitious name.
The manuscript was originally brought to the printers anonymously through the agency of "Richard
Sympson," who, of course, did not really exist. The
name may have been suggested by one William
Symson who, in 1715, had published his account of
a voyage to the Indonesian islands.

2 *Cousin Dampier*. William Dampier (1652–1715)
was a buccaneer and explorer. He circumnavigated
the world twice and in 1709 rescued Alexander Selkirk from the island on which he was marooned. Alexander Selkirk was the inspiration for *Robinson
Crusoe*, written by Daniel Defoe (1660–1731) and
published in 1719, the only book of the time to rival
the enduring popularity of *Gulliver's Travels*. The
book *A New Voyage Around the World* was published
in 1697.

3 *a Paragraph about her Majesty the late Queen Anne*.
Though expressed through the mouth of Gulliver,
Swift had real grievances against Benjamin Motte,
the original publisher of *Gulliver's Travels*, who freely
censored the book. Thus, in the sixth chapter of the
fourth part where Swift engaged in a bitter satire on
Walpole (see Part 1, Chapter 3, Note 2), Motte in-

serted a few lines of panegyric to Queen Anne, which Swift saw to it were removed in later editions.

4 *Lord of Godolphin.* Sidney, earl of Godolphin (1645–1712) was Lord High Treasurer of England under Anne. He was an ally of John Churchill, duke of Marlborough, and was dismissed by Anne in 1710, when the Tories took over.

5 *Lord of Oxford.* Robert Harley, earl of Oxford (1661–1724), Tory secretary of state for the north under Anne, who was forced out of office by John Churchill, and recalled to power in 1710.

6 *I do hardly know mine own Work.* The printer omitted or softened many passages where he felt the satire was pointed enough to cause trouble. Most of these were reinserted in later editions.

7 *Yahoos, who now are said to govern the Herd.* The satire continues, for even as Swift has Gulliver wonder how he can possibly be considered to be insulting or giving offense, he is doing so.

8 *one single Effect according to mine Intentions.* In the fourth part of the book, Gulliver goes mad, and it is clear that Gulliver is still mad. Although he constantly states there that Yahoos are "indocible," he is still embittered by the fact that after six months he has not yet accomplished anything. It's the equivalent of Swift complaining that his satire, *Gulliver's Travels*, is producing no effect on the faults, sins, and crimes being satirized. (We can be sure Swift did not seriously expect it to.)

9 *Smithfield.* Smithfield was an area of England in the sixteenth century where, at a time when England was repeatedly shifting back and forth from Catholicism to Protestantism, those who happened to be too firmly on the "wrong" side at any given moment, were burned as heretics. The suggestion is, therefore, that the law books be set burning as heretics to the law of reason.

"The Punishment Inflicted on Lemuel Gulliver," by William Hogarth. Courtesy, Library of Congress.

the Press; and apt not only to interpret, but to punish every thing which looked like an *Inuendo* (as I think you called it.) But pray, how could that which I spoke so many Years ago, and at above five Thousand Leagues distance, in another Reign, he applyed to **7** any of the *Yahoos*, who now are said to govern the Herd; especially, at a time when I little thought on or feared the Unhappiness of living under them. Have not I the most Reason to complain, when I see these very *Yahoos* carried by *Houyhnhnms* in a Vehicle, as if these were Brutes, and those the rational Creatures? And, indeed, to avoid so monstrous and detestable a Sight, was one principal Motive of my Retirement hither.

Thus much I thought proper to tell you in Relation to your self, and to the Trust I reposed in you.

I do in the next Place complain of my own great Want of Judgment, in being prevailed upon by the Intreaties and false Reasonings of you and some others, very much against mine own Opinion, to suffer my Travels to be published. Pray bring to your Mind how often I desired you to consider, when you insisted on the Motive of *publick Good;* that the *Yahoos* were a Species of Animals utterly incapable of Amendment by Precepts or Examples: And so it hath proved; for instead of seeing a full Stop put to all Abuses and Corruptions, at least in this little Island, as I had Reason to expect: Behold, after above six Months Warning, I cannot learn **8** that my Book hath produced one single Effect according to mine Intentions: I desired you would let me know by a Letter, when Party and Faction were extinguished; Judges learned and upright; Pleaders honest and modest, with some Tincture of common **9** Sense; and *Smithfield* blazing with Pyramids of Law-Books; the young Nobility's Education entirely changed; the Physicians banished; the Female *Yahoos* abounding in Virtue, Honour, Truth and good Sense: Courts and Levees of great Ministers thoroughly weeded and swept; Wit, Merit and Learning rewarded; all Disgracers of the Press in Prose and Verse, condemned to eat nothing but their own Cotten, and quench their Thirst with their own Ink. **10** These, and a Thousand other Reformations, I firmly counted upon by your Encouragement; as indeed they were plainly deducible from the Precepts delivered in my Book. And, it must be owned that seven Months were a sufficient Time to correct every Vice and Folly to which *Yahoos* are subject; if their Natures had been capable of the least Disposition to Virtue or Wisdom: Yet so far have you been from answering mine Expectation in any of your Letters; that on the contrary, you are loading our Carrier every Week with Libels, and Keys, and Reflections, and Memoirs, and Second Parts; **11** wherein I see myself accused of reflecting upon great States-Folk; of degrading Human Nature, (for so they have still the Confidence to stile it) and of abusing the Female Sex. I find likewise, that the Writers of those Bundles are not agreed among themselves; for some of them will not allow me to be Author of mine own Travels; and others make me Author of Books to which I am wholly **12** a Stranger.

I find likewise, that your Printer hath been so careless as to confound the Times, and mistake the Dates of my several Voyages and Returns; neither assigning the true Year, or the true Month, or Day of the Month: And I hear the original Manuscript is all destroyed, since the Publication of my Book. Neither have I any Copy left; however, I have sent you some Corrections, which you may insert, if ever there should be a second Edition: And yet I cannot stand to them, but shall leave that Matter to my judicious and candid Readers, to adjust it as they please.

I hear some of our Sea-*Yahoos* find Fault with my Sea-Language, as not proper in many Parts, nor now in Use. I cannot help it. In my first Voyages, while I was young, I was instructed by the oldest Mariners, and learned to speak as they did. But I have since found that the Sea-*Yahoos* are apt, like the Land ones, to become new fangled in their Words; which the latter change every Year; insomuch, as I remember upon each Return to mine own Country, their old Dialect was so altered, that I could hardly understand the new. And I observe, when any *Yahoo* comes from *London* out of Curiosity to visit me at mine own House, we neither of us are able to deliver our Conceptions in a Manner intelligible to the other.

If the Censure of *Yahoos* could any Way affect me, I should have great Reason to complain, that some of them are so bold as to think my Book of Travels a meer Fiction out of mine own Brain; and have gone so far as to drop Hints, that the *Houyhnhnms*, and *Yahoos* have no more Existence than the Inhabitants of *Utopia*.

Indeed I must confess, that as the People of *Lilliput, Brobdingrag* (for so the Word should have been spelt, and not erroneously *Brobdingnag*), and *Laputa;* I have never yet heard of any *Yahoo* so presumptuous as to dispute their Being, or the Facts I have related concerning them; because the Truth immediately strikes every Reader with Conviction. And, is there less Probability in my Account of the *Houyhnhnms* or *Yahoos,* when it is manifest as to the latter, there are so many Thousands even in this City, who only differ from their Brother Brutes in *Houyhnhnmland,* because they use a Sort of a *Jabber,* and do not go naked. I wrote for their Amendment, and not their Approbation. The united Praise of the whole Race would be of less Consequence to me, than the

10 *Cotten.* The cotton swabs used by printers to wipe excess ink from the type.

11 *Keys.* Commentaries (keys) on *Gulliver's Travels,* explaining the nature of the satire and the identity of the targeted people, began to appear in the very year of its publication. This present annotated edition is only the latest of a long line.

12 *Author of Books to which I am wholly a Stranger.* Unscrupulous authors in those days often produced sequels to popular books, purportedly by the original author. *Don Quixote* was one notorious sufferer in this respect.

13 *April 2, 1727.* Gulliver is sixty-six years old now, and although it is twelve years since he left the Houyhnhnms, he still has not recovered.

neighing of those two degenerate *Houyhnhnms* I keep in my Stable; because, from these, degenerate as they are, I still improve in some Virtues, without any Mixture of Vice.

Do these miserable Animals presume to think that I am so far degenerated as to defend my Veracity; *Yahoo* as I am, it is well known through all *Houyhnhnmland,* that by the Instructions and Example of my illustrious Master, I was able in the Compass of two Years (although I confess with the utmost Difficulty) to remove that infernal Habit of Lying, Shuffling, Deceiving, and Equivocating, so deeply rooted in the very Souls of all my Species; especially the Europeans.

I have other Complaints to make upon this vexatious Occasion; but I forbear troubling myself or you any further. I must freely confess, that since my last Return, some Corruptions of my *Yahoo* Nature have revived in me by conversing with a few of your Species, and particularly those of mine own Family, by an unavoidable Necessity; else I should never have attempted so absurd a Project as that of reforming the *Yahoo* Race in this Kingdom; but, I have now done with all such visionary Schemes for ever.

13   *April 2, 1727.*

The Publisher to the Reader

THE Author of these Travels, Mr. *Lemuel Gulliver,* is my antient and intimate Friend; there is likewise some Relation between us by the Mother's Side. About three Years ago Mr. *Gulliver* growing weary of the Concourse of curious People coming to him at his House in *Redriff,* made a small Purchase of Land, with a convenient House, near *Newark,* in *Nottinghamshire,* his native Country; where he now lives retired, yet in good Esteem among his Neighbours. **1**

Although Mr. *Gulliver* were born in *Nottinghamshire,* where his Father dwelt, yet I have heard him say, his Family came from *Oxfordshire;* to confirm which, I have observed in the Church-Yard at *Banbury,* in that County, several Tombs and Monuments of the *Gullivers.* **2** **3**

Before he quitted *Redriff* he left the Custody of the following Papers in my Hands, with the Liberty to dispose of them as I should think fit. I have carefully perused them three Times; The Style is very plain and simple; and the only Fault I find is, that the Author, after the Manner of Travellers, is a little too circumstantial. There is an Air of Truth apparent through the whole; and indeed the Author was so distinguished for his veracity, that it became a Sort of Proverb among his Neighbours at *Redriff,* when any one affirmed a Thing, to say, it was as true as if Mr. **4** *Gulliver* had spoke it.

By the Advice of several worthy Persons, to whom, with the Author's Permission, I communicated these Papers, I now venture to send them into the World; hoping they may be, at least for some time, a better Entertainment to our young Noblemen, than the common Scribbles of Politicks and Party.

This Volume would have been at least twice as large, if I had not made bold to strike out innumerable Passages relating to the Winds and Tides, as well as to the Variations and Bearings in the

1 *Newark.* Newark is about twenty miles northeast of Nottingham. One of the early settlers of a town in New Jersey, founded in 1666, was from Newark in Nottinghamshire (the county), and the New Jersey town was also named Newark in consequence.

2 *Oxfordshire.* About eighty miles south of Nottingham and about fifty miles northwest of London.

3 *Banbury.* About sixty-two miles south of Nottingham.

4 *as true as if Mr. Gulliver had spoke it.* One of the running gags in *Gulliver's Travels* is Gulliver's repeated protestations of his honesty, his contempt for the exaggerations of other writers, his fears that his own telling of a simple, unadorned story will not be able to compete with the floridness of others—when it is all the time obvious that Gulliver is telling the most successfully circumstantial and interesting lies in the world.

Here for the first time someone else is telling us how honest Gulliver is in his account. But of course, Gulliver and Sympson are both, and alike, Swift.

Dr. Swift. Courtesy. Library of Congress.

several Voyages; together with the minute Descriptions of the Management of the Ship in Storms, in the Style of Sailors: Likewise the Account of the Longitudes and Latitudes; wherein I have Reason to apprehend that Mr. *Gulliver* may be a little dissatisfied: But I was resolved to fit the Work as much as possible to the general Capacity of Readers. However, if my own Ignorance in Sea-Affairs shall have led me to commit some Mistakes, I alone am answerable for them: And if any Traveller hath a Curiosity to see the whole Work at large, as it came from the Hand of the Author, I will be ready to gratify him.

As for any further Particulars relating to the Author, the Reader will receive Satisfaction from the first Pages of the Book.

Richard Sympson

BIBLIOGRAPHY

GENERAL REFERENCES

Barroll, J. Leeds. "Gulliver and the Struldbruggs." *PMLA*, March 1928, pp. 43–50.

Brady, Frank, ed. *Twentieth Century Interpretations of Gulliver's Travels.* Englewood Cliffs, N.J.: Prentice-Hall, 1968.

Carnochan, W. B. *Lemuel Gulliver's Mirror for Man.* Berkeley and Los Angeles: University of California Press, 1968.

Case, Arthur Ellicott. *Four Essays on Gulliver's Travels.* Gloucester, Mass.: Peter Smith, 1958.

Davis, Herbert. *Satire of Jonathan Swift.* New York: Macmillan, 1947.

Eddy, William Alfred. *Gulliver's Travels: a Critical Study.* New York: Russell & Russell, 1963.

Ehrenpreis, Irvin. *The Personality of Jonathan Swift.* London: Methuen, 1958.

———. *Swift: The Man, His Work, and the Age.* London: Methuen, 1962.

Ewald, W. B., Jr. *The Masks of Jonathan Swift.* Cambridge, Mass.: Harvard University Press, 1954.

Ferguson, Oliver. *Jonathan Swift and Ireland.* Urbana: University of Illinois Press, 1962.

Forster, John. *The Life of Jonathan Swift.* London: J. Murray, 1875.

Greenacre, Phyllis. *Swift and Carroll: A Psychoanalytic Study of Two Lives.* New York: International Universities Press, 1955.

Harth, John Philip. *Swift and Anglican Rationalism.* Chicago: University of Chicago, 1961.

Hubbard, Elbert. "The Haunts of Jonathan Swift." *Little Journeys,* vol. 1, no. 6. New York: G. P. Putnam's Sons, 1895.

Jackson, Robert Wise. *Jonathan Swift, Dean and Pastor.* London: Society for Promoting Christian Knowledge, 1939.

———. *Swift and His Circle.* Dublin: Talbot Press, 1945.

Kallich, Martin. *The Other End of the Egg: Religious Satire in Gulliver's Travels.* Bridgeport, Conn.: University of Bridgeport, 1970.

Kelling, Harold D. "Gulliver's Travels: A Comedy of Humours." *University of Toronto Quarterly,* 1952, pp. 362–375.

Landa, Louis A. *Swift and the Church of Ireland.* Oxford: Clarendon Press, 1954.

Leslie, Shane. *The Skull of Swift.* Indianapolis, Ind: Bobbs-Merrill, Co., 1928.

McManmon, John H. "The Problem of a Religious Interpretation of Gulliver's Fourth Voyage." *JHI,* 1966, pp. 59–72.

Moriarity, G. P. *Dean Swift and his Writings.* New York: Charles Scribner's Sons, 1893.

Murry, John Middleton. *Jonathan Swift: A Critical Biography.* London: Jonathan Cape, 1954.

Nicolson, Marjorie and Nora Mohler. "The Scientific Background of Swift's 'Voyage of Laputa.'" *Annals of Science,* 1937, pp. 299–334.

Poll, Max. "The Source of Gulliver's Travels." *Cincinnati University Bulletin,* vol. 3 (1902), no. 24.

Quintana, Ricardo. *The Mind and Art of Jonathan Swift.* Gloucester, Mass.: Peter Smith, 1965.

———. *Swift: An Introduction.* London: Oxford University Press, 1955.

Rosenheim, Edward R. *Swift and the Satirist's Art.* Chicago: University of Chicago, 1963.

Scott, Sir Walter. *Life of Swift.* Edinburgh: Cadell and Co., 1827.

Sheridan, Thomas. *The Life of the Rev. Dr. Jonathan Swift.* London: J. F. & C. Rivington, 1787.

Stephen, Leslie. *Swift.* London: Macmillan, 1882.

Thackeray, William Makepeace. "Swift." *The English Humourists of the Eighteenth Century.* London: Smith, Elder & Co., 1853.

Vickers, Brian, ed. *The World of Jonathan Swift.* Oxford: B. Blackwell, 1968.

Williams, Kathleen. *Jonathan Swift and the Age of Compromise.* Lawrence: University of Kansas Press, 1958.

Williams, Kathleen, ed. *Swift, The Critical Heritage.* London: Routledge & Kegan Paul, 1970.

Notable Editions Of *Gulliver's Travels*

Travels into several Remote Nations of the World. By Lemuel Gulliver. London: Benjamin Motte, 1726.

Travels into several Remote Nations of the World. Dublin: J. Hyde, 1726.

Travels into several Remote Nations of the World. London: Benjamin Motte, 1727. The first illustrated edition.

Travels into several Remote Nations of the World. By Captain L. G. London, 1727. "Faithfully abridged."

The Travels and Adventures of Captain L. G. London, circa 1750. Chapbook abridgment.

"Travels into several Remote Nations of the World." *The Novelist's Magazine.* Illustrated by Thomas Stothard. London, 1782.

The Adventures of Captain Gulliver: Abridged from the works of the celebrated Dean Swift. London: E. Newbery, circa 1789.

Gulliver's Travels. London: Tabart & Co., 1805.

Travels into several Remote Nations of the World. Illustrated by Richard Corbould. London: C. Cooke, 1816.

Travels into several Remote Nations of the World. Illustrated by A. Bowen. Boston: James Loring, 1820.

Travels into several Remote Nations of the World. With notes by Sir Walter Scott. Edinburgh: A. Constable, 1824.

Travels into several Remote Nations of the World. Illustrated by Grandville. With notes, a life of the author, and an essay on satirical fiction by W. C. Taylor. London: Hayward & Moore, 1840.

Gulliver's Travels. Illustrated by H. K. Browne. London: J. Burns, 1847.

Gulliver's Travels. Illustrated by J. G. Thomson. London: Frederick Warne, 1864.

Gulliver's Travels into several Remote Nations of the World. With explanatory notes and a life of the author by John Frances Waller. Illustrated by T. Morten. London: Cassell, Peter & Galpin, 1865. This became the standard illustrated English edition during the nineteenth century, and Morten's designs were reprinted in several translations.

Gulliver's Travels. Illustrated by E. Forest and J. Pelocq. London: Routledge, 1882.

Gulliver's Travels. Illustrated by Gordon Browne. London: Blackie & Son, 1885.

Travels into several Remote Nations of the World. Preface by Henry Craik. Illustrated by Charles E. Brock. London: Macmillan, 1894.

Gulliver's Travels. Illustrated by Arthur Rackham. London: J. M. Dent, 1900. An expanded edition, with many of the illustrations colored and a few new illustrations, was issued in 1909.

Gulliver's Travels. Illustrated by Herbert Cole. London: John Lane, 1900.

Travels into several Remote Nations of the World. Illustrated by Stephen Baghot De La Bere. London: A. & C. Black, 1904.

Gulliver's Travels. Retold by Agnes G. Herbertson. Illustrated by John Hassall. London: Blackie & Son, 1908.

Gulliver's Travels. Illustrated by Milo Winter. Chicago: Rand McNally & Co., 1912.

Gulliver's Travels. Introduction by William Dean Howells. Illustrated by Louis Rhead. New York: Harper & Bros., 1913.

Gulliver's Travels. Edited by Padraic Colum. Illustrated by Willy Pogany. New York: Macmillan, 1917.

Gulliver's Travels. Illustrated by Jean deBosshere. London: Wm. Heinemann, 1920.

Gulliver's Travels. Introduction by H. L. Mencken. New York: Alfred A. Knopf, 1925.

Travels into several Remote Nations of the World. Illustrated by David Jones. Waltham St. Lawrence, Eng.: Golden Cockerell Press, 1925.

Gulliver's Travels. Edited by Harold Williams. London: First Edition Club, 1926.

Travels into several Remote Nations of the World. Edited by F. J. Harvey Darton. Illustrated by René Bull. New York: F. A. Stokes, 1928.

The Travels of Lemuel Gulliver. Introduction by Shane Leslie. Illustrated by Alexander King. New York: Limited Editions Club, 1929.

Gulliver's Travels. Illustrated by Rex Whistler. London: Crescent Press, 1930.

Gulliver's Travels. Introduction by Carl Van Doren. New York: Modern Library, 1931.

Gulliver's Travels. Illustrated by Fritz Eichenberg. New York: Heritage Press, 1940.

Gulliver's Travels. Introduction by Jacques Barzun. Illustrated by Louis Quintanilla. New York: Crown Publishers, 1947.

Gulliver's Travels. Illustrated by Aldren Watson. New York: Grosset & Dunlap, 1947.

Travels into several Remote Nations of the World. Illustrations and decorations by W. A. Dwiggins. Mount Vernon, N.Y.: Peter Pauper Press, 1948.

The Voyages of Lemuel Gulliver. Illustrated by Edward Bawden. London: Folio Society, 1948.

A Voyage to Brobdingnag. New York: Limited Editions Club, 1950. This oversized volume is a companion to the following, undersized editiion.

A Voyage to Lilliput. New York: Limited Editions Club, 1950.

Gulliver's Travels. Illustrated by Leonard Weisgard. Garden City, N.Y.: Junior Deluxe Editions, 1954.

Gulliver's Travels. Edited by John Hayward. Illustrated by Robin Jacques. London: Oxford University Press, 1955.

Gulliver's Travels. Edited by James Reeves. London: Wm. Heinemann, 1964.

Representative Translations of *Gulliver's Travels*

Reisbeschryving na verscheyde afgelegene nation in de Wereld. Translated into Dutch. Gravenhage, 1727.

Voyages de Gulliver. Translated into French. Paris, 1727.

Voyages du capitaine Lemuel Gulliver, en divers pays éloigné. Translated into French. La Haye, 1727.

Des Capitains Gulliver Reisen. Translated into German. Hamburg, 1727–1728.

Reisbeschryving na verscheyde afgelegene natien in de Wereld. Translated into Dutch. Gravenhage, 1727–1728.

Viaggi del Capitano Lemuel Gulliver in diversi paesi lontani. Translated into Italian. Venice, 1729.

Voyages du capitaine Gulliver en divers pays éloignés. Translated into French. La Haye, 1765.

Kapitain Lemuel Gullivers reise til Lilliput eller til de smaae folk. Translated into Danish. Copenhagen, 1768.

Kapitana Samuily Brunta pueshestvie v kaklogaliniyu. Translated into Russian. Saint Petersburg, 1770.

Capitain Lemuel Gullivers Resor. Translated into Swedish. Waesteras, 1772.

Capitain Lemuel Gullivers reise til Brobdingnag eller de store folk. Translated into Danish. Copenhagen, 1775.

Relacao deas viagens do Capitao Gulliver por varios paizes remotos. Translated into Portuguese. Coimbra, 1789.

L. Gulliver's reize. Translated into Dutch. Amsterdam, 1791.

Gulliver's reizen. Translated into Dutch. Amsterdam, 1792.

Voyages de Gulliver. Illustrated by Lefebvre. Translated into French. Paris, 1797.

Viages del capitan Lemuel Gulliver. Translated into Spanish. Madrid, 1793–1800.

Gulliverovy puteshestviya. Translated into Russian. Moscow, 1820.

Voyages de Gulliver. Illustrated by Grandville. Translated into French. Paris, 1838. These illustrations have appeared also in English, German, Polish, Swedish, Italian, and Hebrew editions.

Gulliver's Reisen. Illustrated by Grandville. Translated into German. Stuttgart, 1839.

Gulliwers Resor. Translated into Swedish. Linköping, 1840–1841.

Lotgevallen van kapitein Gulliver. Translated into Dutch. Gravenhage, 1841.

Viages del capitan Lemuel Gulliver. Translated into Spanish. Mexico, 1849.

Voyages de Gulliver. Illustrated by Gavarni. Translated into French. Paris, 1850s.

Podróze Gulliwera. Illustrated by Grandville. Translated into Polish. Lipetsk, 1851.

Voyages de Gulliver. Illustrated by Bouchot. Translated into French. Paris, 1855.

Reizen van Lemuel Gulliver. Translated into Dutch. Haarlem, 1862.

Gullivers reizen naar Lilliput en andere vreemde landen. Translated into Dutch. Leiden, 1872.

Gullivers Resor. Translated into Swedish. Stockholm, 1872.

Viajes del Capitain Lemuel Gulliver. Translated into Spanish. Madrid, 1873.

Les quatre voyages du capitaine Lemuel Gulliver. Illustrated by Ad. Lalauze. Translated into French. Paris, 1875. A selection of these illustrations appeared in a British edition of 1882.

Gullivers rejser til Lilleput og Brobdingnag. Illustrated by T. Morten. Translated into Norwegian. Kristiana, 1878.

Gullivers reisen in fremde weltteile. Illustrated by Heinrich Leautemann. Translated into German. Leipzig, 1884.

Viajes de Gulliver. Illustrated by F. Gomes Soler. Translated into Spanish. Barcelona, 1884.

Voyages de Gulliver. Translated into French. Paris, 1885.

Gulliver's Reizen. Translated into Dutch. Rotterdam, 1887.

As viagens de Gulliver. Translated into Portuguese. Rio de Janeiro, 1888.

Gullivers Rejse til Lilliput. Translated into Danish. Copenhagen, 1888.

Voyages de Gulliver. Illustrated by F. Lix. Translated into French. Paris, 1888.

Gullivers Reiser. Translated into Norwegian. Kristiana, 1889.

Puteshestviya Gullivera. Translated into Russian. Moscow, 1889.

Gullivers reizen naar Lilliput en andere vreemde landen. Illustrated by Wm. Steelink. Translated into Dutch. Amsterdam, 1890s.

Gullivers Reisen in unbekannte Laender. Illustrated by C. Offterdinger and A. Wald. Translated into German. Stuttgart, 1896.

Gullivers reisen. Illustrated by Max Wulff. Translated into German. Berlin, 1906.

Gullivers reisen. Illustrated by W. Zweigle, Hans W. Schmidt, and E. Zimmer. Translated into German. Leipzig, 1906.

Gullivero kelionés in nézinomas šalis. Translated into Lithuanian. Chicago, 1907.

Gullivers reizen. Translated into Dutch. Amsterdam, 1907.

Potovanje v Liliput. Translated into Slovenian. Ljubljana, 1907.

Podróze Gulliwera w ukladzie dla mlodziezy. Translated into Polish, 1911.

Puteshestviya doktora Gullivera. Translated into Russian. St. Petersburg, 1911.

Foer Gúllívers til Putalands. Translated into Icelandic. Reykjavik, 1913.

Viatges de Gulliver. Translated into Catalon. Barcelona, 1913.

Gullivers Resor. Translated into Swedish. Stockholm, 1917.

Des Capitain Lemuel Gulliver Reise in das Land derer Houyhnhmns. Illustrated by Richard Janthur. Translated into German. Berlin, 1919.

Podróze Gulliwera. Translated into Polish. Warsaw, 1920.

Gullivers reisen. Illustrated by Rolf Winkler. Translated into German. Stuttgart, 1921.

Lelakoné Gulliver. Translated into Javanese. Weltevreden, 1921.

Voyages de Gulliver a Lilliput et a Brobdingnag. Illustrated by R. G. Mossa. Translated into French. Paris, 1921. British and American editions were issued in 1923 and 1924.

Ferd Gullivers til Pinkulinganna. Translated into Faeroese. Tofshavn, 1922.

Gullivers reisen. Illustrated by Lovis Corinth. Translated into German. Berlin, 1922.

Mas'e Guliver. Translated into Hebrew. Jerusalem, 1922–1923.

Mas'e Guliver. Translated into Hebrew. Warsaw, 1923.

Viaggi di Gulliver. Translated into Italian. Milan, 1923.

Gullivers rejse til Lilliputernes land. Translated into Danish. Copenhagen, 1924.

Di kleyne menshelekh. Translated into Yiddish. New York, 1925.

Gulliverovi putovi k raznim dalekim narodima na svijetu. Translated into Croatian. Zagreb, 1925.

Gullivers reisen. Illustrated by Erik Richter. Translated into German. Berlin, 1926.

Gulliversin retket. Translated into Finnish. Helsinki, 1926.

Cesty k rozlicnym vzdalenym narodum sveta ve otyrech dile.n od Lemuela Gulivera druhdy Lekare. Translated into Czechoslovakian. Prague, 1929.

Voyages de Gulliver. Illustrated by Gus Bofa. Translated into French. Brussels, 1929.

I viaggi di Gulliver. Illustrated by Enrico Sacchetti. Translated into Italian. Rome, 1930.

Uit Gulliver se reise. Translated into Afrikaans. Pretoria, 1930.

Gulliverovy cesty. Translated into Czechoslovakian. Prague, 1931.

Safari za Gulliver. Translated into Swahili. London, 1932.

Guliverove cesty. Translated into Slovak. Prague, 1934.

Gulliver se reise. Translated into Afrikaans. London, 1936.

Mandry Gullivera. Translated into Ukranian. Odessa, 1938.

Viajes de Gulliver. Translated into Spanish. Buenos Aires, 1940.

Gulliver'in seyahatleri. Translated into Turkish. Ankara, 1943–1944.

Mas'e Guliver. Translated into Hebrew. Jerusalem, 1944.

Gulliver's seyahatleri. Translated into Turkish. Istanbul, 1945.

Gulliver se reise. Translated into Afrikaans. Pretoria, 1945.

I viaggi di Gulliver. Translated into Italian. Torino, 1945.

Putshestviya v nekotoriie ot galennye strany sveta. Translated into Russian. Moscow, 1947.

Puteshestviya Gullivera. Translated into Russian. Moscow, 1949.

Gulliver utazasai. Translated into Hungarian. Noviszad, 1950.

Gulliverjeva potovanja. Translated into Slovenian. Ljubljana, 1951.

Podróze Gulliwera. Translated into Polish. Warsaw, 1951.

Gulivera celojumi. Translated into Latvian. Stockholm, 1952.

Gulliverova putovanja. Translated into Croatian. Zagreb, 1955.

Puteshestviya Gullivera. Translated into Russian. Moscow, 1955.

Resor, til flera avlaegset belaegra laender i vaerlden. Illustrated by Mark Sylwan. Translated into Swedish. Stockholm, 1955.

Gullivers Reisen. Retold by Erich Kastner, illustrated by Horst Lemke. Translated into German. Vienna, 1961.

INDEX

Page numbers in italics indicate illustrations.

Acrisius, 134
Actium, battle of, 191, 192
Act of Union, 118
Adamant, 154
Age of Reason, 146
Agesilaus II, 189, 190
Agincourt, battle of, 97
Agrippa, Marcus Vipsanius, 192
Ajax, 126
Alexander the Great, 184
Amboina, 206
American colonies, 119
A Modest Proposal, xvii
Anafesto, Paolo Lucio, 127
Anne, Queen, xiv, xv, xvi, 49,
  49, 68, 118, 119, 149, 234, 236,
  278, 288
Antarctica, 9
Antony, Mark, 191, 192
Apes, 213
Aphrodite, 259
Apollo, 200
Aquinas, Thomas, 188
Arbela, battle of, 184
Arbuthnot, John, xv
Arctic Ocean, 74
Aristotle, 187, 187, 188, 189
Astrology, 151
A Tale of a Tub, xii, xiv, xv, 49
Atoms, 189
Atterbury, Bishop Francis, 56,
  179
Augustus, 192, 283
Australia, 7, 136, 273
Aztecs, 282

Balboz, Vasco Nunez, 7
Banbury, 291
Bank of England, 121
Barbadoes, 211
Barbary ape, 213
Barcelona, 136
Bath, Order of the, 30
Battle of the Books, The, xiii, xiv,
  163
Beachy Head, battle of, 41
Belisarius, 191
Bering, Vitus Jonassen, 74
Bering Strait, 74
Berkeley, Earl of, xiv
Berkeley, George, 76
Blenheim, battle of, 45, 136
Bligh, William, 134, 135
Bolingbroke, Viscount, 22, 22,
  28, 46, 51, 59, 60, 61, 63, 66,
  163, 164

Borneo, 73
Boyle, Robert, 189
Bradley, James, 157
Brahe, Tycho, 152
Bristol, 7
British Isles, 118
Brutus, Lucius Junius, 186
Brutus, Marcus Junius, 185, 185,
  186
Buffon, Georges de, 261
Burgundy, 12
Burnet, Gilbert, 191
Byron, Lord, 203

Cabal, 164
Caesar, Julius, 185, 185, 283
Calculus, 123, 174
Cambridge University, 5
Campeche, bay of, 210
Canary Islands, 210
Cape of Good Hope, 72
Carlyle, Thomas, 261
Caroline of Anspach, 37
Catholics, 40
Cato, Marcus Porcius, 186
Celebes, 73
Chancery, 120
Chares, 31
Charles I, xii, 16, 39, 119, 160,
  161
Charles II, xii, 5, 6, 32, 46, 62,
  69, 119, 164
Charles II (Spain), 19
Charles V, 225, 225
Chaucer, Geoffrey, 191
Chelsea, 81
Chemistry, in 18th century, 169
Chimaera, 176
Chimpanzee, 213
China, 123
Churchill, John, 45, 45
Churchill, Sara, xv
Cicero, Marcus Tullius, 118, 118
Cleopatra, 191
Closet, 112, 112
Clouds, 155
Colbert, Jean Baptiste, 41, 123
Colossus of Rhodes, 31, 32
Columbus, Christopher, 7, 66,
  190, 283
Comets, 152, 153, 159, 200
Computers, 174
Concord, battle of, 127
Cook, Captain James, 7, 74, 100,
  136
Cortez, Hernando, 282
Crecy, battle of, 97
Critias, 186
Cromwell, Oliver, 5

Dalton, John, 189
Dampier, William, 287
Danae, 134, 134
Darius III, 184
Darwin, Charles, 173
Day of Judgement, 152
Declaration of Rights, The, 235
Defoe, Daniel, xxi, 287
Deimos, 158, 159
Democritus, 189
Demosthenes, 118
Descartes, René, 188, 188, 189
Deshima, 142
Diamond, 154
Dickens, Charles, xi, 120
Didymus, 188
Dingley, Rebecca, xiv
Dionysius Halicarnassensis, 125
Dissenters, 40
Downs, The, 68
Drake, Francis, 74
Drapier's Letters, xvi, xvii
Dublin, 160
Duns Scotus, John, 188, 189
Dunstable, 99
Dutch, 20
Dwarfs, 94, 94

Eagles, 131
East Indies, 7
Edward I, 6
Edward III, 30
Edward IV, 41
Einstein, Albert, 189
Eisenhower, Dwight, 52
Elizabeth I, 128
Enemas, 172
England, 118
English Channel, 42
Eos, 200
Epaminondas, 186, 189
Epicurus, 189
Epping, 69
Eustathius, 188
Everest, Mount, 100
Evolution, 173, 261
Executions, 110, 110

Flinders Island, 68
Fort St. George, 141
Fossils, 126
Furneaux, Tobias, 68
Furneaux Islands, 68

Galileo, 158, 189
Gall, Franz Joseph, 216
Garter, Order of the, 30

Gassendi, Pierre, 188, 188, 189
Gaugamela, battle of, 184
Gay, John, xv, xvi
Gelderland, 206
Genghiz Khan, 184
George I, xvi, 18, 18, 28, 36, 38,
  39, 46, 47, 56, 62, 86, 148, 149,
  160, 161, 236, 278
George III, 236
Georgia, 119
Gibbon, Edward, 261
Gibraltar, 45, 47, 136
Gilbert, William, 156
Gilbert, William Schwenk, 168
Godolphin, Earl of, 288
Grand Alliance, War of the, 7,
  38, 40, 236
Granville, Earl, 30, 58
Gravitation, law of, 159, 189
Great Britain, 33, 118
Greenwich, 69, 143
Gresham College, 99
Gulliver, Lemuel, xxii, 4, 5, 73
Gulliver's Travels, cartoon versions,
  xx; films, xviii, xix; public reac-
  tion to, xxi, xxii; original intent,
  xviii, xix

Halicarnassus, 125
Halley, Edmund, 152, 153
Halley's Comet, 152, 153
Halmahera, 73
Hannibal, 184
Hanover, 18
Hapsburg family, 19; lip, 19
Harley, Robert, xv, 22, 23
Harrison, John, 199
Heliogabalus, 189
Helios, 31
Helots, 189
Henrietta Maria, Queen, 94
Henry IV, 30
Henry V, 46
Henry VI, 41
Henry VIII, 38, 38, 39, 186
Hercules, 60, 60
Herschel, William, 171
Hevelius, Johannes, 157
Hogsheads, 12, 109
Homer, 126, 187, 187, 188, 189
Homosexuals, 191
Honshu, 138
Hooke, Robert, 126
Horace, 283
Hudson, Jeffrey, 94
Hudson, Bay, 47
Humors, 177
Huygens, Christian, 157
Hypochondria, 242

India, 69
Indies, 7
Infrared light, 171
Ireland, 118, 157, 159, 160

Jackson, Andrew, 52
James I, xvi, 119
James II, xii, xiv, 6, 7, 18, 30, 39,
    39, 40, 45, 46, 47, 56, 62, 119,
    160, 235, 236
Japan, 138, 142, 205, 206
Java, 9
Jeffreys, George, 62
Jenner, Edward, 200
Jews, 6
Johnson, Esther, xiii, xiv, xiv
Johnson, Samuel, 222
Jupiter, 158
Justinian, 191

Kendall, Duchess of, 30, 160
Kepler, Johannes, 151, 156, 158,
    159
Koran, 40
Korea, 123
Kowtow, 194
Kyoto, 205

La Hogue, battle of, 41, 41
Lamarck, Jean Baptiste de, 173
League of Augsburg, War of the,
    41
Leeward Islands, 211
Leibniz, Gottfried Wilhelm, 148,
    174
Leprosy, 190
Leuctra, battle of, 186
Levant, 6
Levee, 115
Leyden, 5
Liberty, Statue of, 103
Lingua franca, 20
Loadstone, 155
Logwood, 210
London Bridge, 81
London, in the 18th century, 6
Longitude, 143, 199
Louis XIV, xiv, xv, 39, 40, 41,
    45, 46, 47, 99, 99, 110, 115,
    123, 184, 236
Louis XV, 184
Lucretius Carus, Titus, 189
Lunar calendar, 24
Luther, Martin, 150
Lysenko, Trofim, 173

McCarthy, Joseph R., 51
Madagascar, 72
Madhouse, 85, 85
Madras, 141
Magellan, Ferdinand, 7
Magnetism, 154, 155, 156
Malayan peninsula, 9
Malplaquet, battle of, 45
Mantinea, battle of, 186
Maria, Henrietta, Queen, 94
Marlborough, Duke of, xiv, xv,
    45, 46, 72, 74, 121, 136, 185,
    191, 288

Mars, 158, 159
Marshall Islands. 74
Martian satellites, 158, 159
Martinus Scriblerus Club, xv,
    xviii, xix
Mary II, xii, xiv, 7, 39, 119, 235,
    236
Masham, Abigail Hill, xv
Matches, 143
Middle East, 6
Middleton, Viscount, 163
Moll, Herman, 274
Moluccas, 73
Monarchy, 12
Mongols, 74
Monsoon, 72
Monterey, 74
Montesquieu, Charles de, 261
More, Thomas, 186, 186
Motte, Benjamin, 287
Moydore, 92
Mozambique Channel, 72
Music of the Spheres, 150, 151

Nagasaki, 142, 206
Navigation, 5
Neanderthal men, 213
Near East, 6
Nessus, 60
Netherlands, 142
New Albion, 74
Newark, 291
Newfoundland, 47
New Holland, 136, 273
Newton, Isaac, xvii, xix, 5, 6,
    123, 146, 146, 150, 151, 152,
    156, 174, 189
Nixon, Richard M., 243
Nottingham, 4
Nottingham, Earl of, 32
Nova Scotia, 47

Oates, Titus, 62
Oatmeal, 222
Octavian, 191, 192
Old Pretender, xiv, 61, 66, 160
Orange, Prince of, 235
Orange, William of, 235
Orangutan, 213
Oudenarde, battle of, 45
Oxford, Earl of, 22, 22, 28, 32,
    46, 51, 59, 60, 61, 63, 163, 164,
    288
Oxfordshire, 291
Oxford University, 5

Pacific Ocean, 7, 68, 74
Panama, 7
Pandarus, 191
Parliament, 119
Parnell, Thomas, xv
Partridge, John, xiv
Perihelion, 153
Perpetual motion, 199
Perry, Matthew Calbraith, 205
Perseus, 134
Peterborough, Earl of, 192
Phaethon, 136
Pharsalus, battle of, 185
Philip II, 19, 128
Philip V, 47
Philosopher's Stone, 199

Phobos, 158, 159
Phoenix, 92, 92
Pike, 15
Planaria, 175
Plato, 53, 186, 187
Poitiers, battle of, 97
Polo, Marco, 35
Polydore Vergil, 190
Pompey, 185
Pope, Alexander, xv, xv, xvi, 39,
    237
Portsmouth, 181
Priam, 200
Printing, 123
Procopius, 191
Ptolomeic universe, 15, 15
Python, 259

Quadrant, 33, 150

Ramillies, battle of, 45, 136
Ramus, Petrus, 188
Rhodes, 31
Richard II, 41
Richard III, 41
Ritter, Johann Wilhelm, 171
Robin Hood, 4
Rotherhithe, 69
Royal Observatory, 69
Royal Society of London, 166
Ryswick, Treaty of, 7, 236

St. Albans, 86
St. Bartholomew's Day Massacre,
    189
St. John, Henry, 22, 22
St. Patrick's Cathedral, xv, xvii
St. Paul's Cathedral, 103, 103
St. Peter's Cathedral, 103
Salisbury Cathedral, 103, 103
Salt, 224
San Francisco, 74
Sanson, Nicolas, 90
Science fiction, 13, 144, 197
Scotland, 118, 222
Sears Tower, 103
Selkirk, Alexander, 287
Seychelles Islands, 72, 73
Shakespeare, William, 134, 191
Shaw, George Bernard, 6
Shogun, 205
Shorter, Catherine, 57
Shrewsbury, 132
Shropshire, 133
Siberia, 74, 138
Sibylla, 200
Silk, 171
Sinon, 281
Skyscrapers, 170
Smithfield, 288
Socrates, 126, 186, 187, 255
South Seas, 7
Spanish Succession, War of the,
    xiv, 38, 40, 45, 46, 66, 68, 121,
    136, 142, 192, 236, 278
Spartans, 189, 190
Spice Islands, 73
Spinet, 116
Spleen, 244
Stanhope, Earl of, 30
Steam engine, 166
"Stella," xiv, xiv

Steno, Niels, 126
Stevenson, Adlai, 52
Stone Age, 263
Suez Canal, 72
Sumatra, 9, 73
Sun, 152, 153
Sunda Strait, 9
Surat, 69
Swift, Godwin, xii
Swift, Jonathan, death of, xxi;
    family background, xii; house
    of, xii; political affiliations of,
    xi–xv; writings by, xiii–xviii;
    portraits of, x, xv, xvi, xvii, 292
Swift, Jonathan (senior), xii
Swift, Thomas, xii
Sympson, William, 287
Syphilis, 190, 242

Tartary, 74
Tasman, Abel Janszoon, 7
Tasmania, 7, 9, 68
Telescopes, 157, 158
Temple, Sir William, xii, xiii, xiv,
    163
Tenerife, 210
Thales, 147
Theodora, 191
Thistle, Order of the, 30
Thomsen, Christian J., 263
Tithonus, 200
Toilet, 109
Tokyo, 181, 205
Tonkin, 136
Tories, 18, 36
Townshend, Viscount, 28, 30
Triangular trade, 7
Trinity College, 5
Tumbril, 128
Tun, 109
Twain, Mark, xi

Ultraviolet light, 171
United Kingdom, 118
Utrecht, Treaty of, 32, 47, 49, 59

Vaccination, 200
Van Diemen's Land, 7, 9, 68
"Vanessa," xiv
Vanhomrigh, Esther, xiv, xiv
Venice, 127
Versailles, 110, 110
Vesalius, Andreas, 216
Voltaire, xi

Wales, Prince of, 37
Walpole, Robert, xvi, 28, 30, 31,
    31, 57, 151, 153, 156, 243, 287
Watt, James, 5
Wellington, Duke of, 46
Westminster Hall, 16, 16, 102
Whales, Greenland, 101, 101
Whigs, 18, 36
Wight, Isle of, 182
William I, 33
William III, xii, xiv, 7, 39, 45,
    68, 119, 235, 236
Windward Islands, 211
Wood, William, 160
Wottom, William, xiii

Zeus, 134, 136